FORGOTTEN C

Michael Reid is Latin American co.
The Economist. Previously based in Brazil, Mexico and Peru, he has travelled throughout Latin America and reported for the BBC, the *Guardian* and *The Economist*, where he was Americas Editor from 1999 to 2013.

Further praise for *Forgotten Continent*:

'Reid's cogent and sweeping treatment of Latin America's place in the world is a must-read.'
Ted Piccone, *Democracy Journal*

'Formidably well informed and written with exceptional clarity ... It combines all the strengths of journalistic experience with an explanatory energy rarely found in scholarly volumes.'
James Dunkerley, Institute for the Study of the Americas, University of London

'The incoming administration's Latin American decision-makers have Michael Reid's excellent work on their must-read list.'
Colonel John C. McKay, *Proceedings* (U.S. Naval Institute)

'Will captivate experts and amateurs alike. No one who seriously aspires to discuss Latin American politics, economics and culture should go without reading *Forgotten Continent*.'
Jorge Castañeda and Patricio Navia, *National Interest*

'Offers something valuable to both specialists and the general reading public ... Reid writes of Latin America with great empathy, intelligence, and insight.'
James Brennan, *Hispanic American Historical Review*

MICHAEL REID

FORGOTTEN CONTINENT

A HISTORY OF THE NEW LATIN AMERICA

YALE UNIVERSITY PRESS
NEW HAVEN AND LONDON

For information about this and other Yale University Press publications, please contact:

US Office: sales.press@yale.edu   yalebooks.com

Europe Office: sales@yaleup.co.uk   yalebooks.co.uk

Set in Minion Pro by IDSUK (DataConnection) Ltd

Printed in the United States of America

Library of Congress Control Number: 2017910087

ISBN978- 0-300-22465-8

A catalogue record for this book is available from the British Library.

10 9 8 7 6 5 4

For Maximilian, in the hope that it will help him understand
part of his heritage

First, we must cure ourselves of the intoxication of simplistic and simplifying ideologies.
OCTAVIO PAZ

The democratic will is vulgar; its laws, imperfect. I admit all this. But if it is true that soon there will be no middle way between the empire of democracy and the yoke of one man, ought we not try rather for the former than submit voluntarily to the latter?
ALEXIS DE TOCQUEVILLE

It is not by chance that reforms are so difficult.
FERNANDO HENRIQUE CARDOSO

Contents

Illustrations

Charts and Tables

Charts

Tables

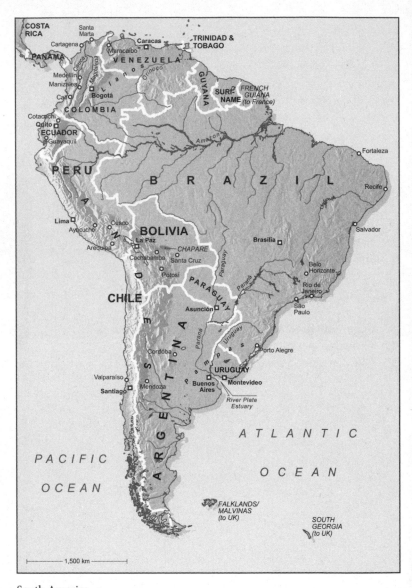

South America

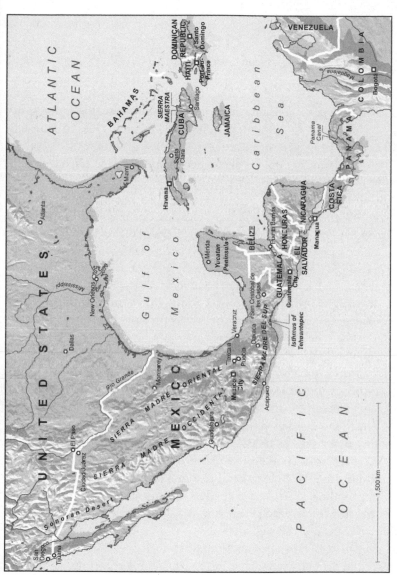

Mexico, Central America and the Caribbean

Preface

Much has happened in Latin America and the world since the first edition of this book went to press in early 2007. The financial crisis of 2007–08 ushered in a new and more uncertain period in world history. In its wake, populism, a familiar political phenomenon in Latin America, has arisen in the United States and in Europe. China has consolidated its position as a global economic power. In Latin America, the commodity boom has come and gone, and the political landscape has changed. Both Hugo Chávez and Fidel Castro are dead. Luiz Inácio Lula da Silva is fighting multiple charges of corruption in Brazil's courts. Latin American societies have changed significantly in the past ten years. So it seemed opportune to revise the book to take account of all these developments, and more.

The original book was inspired by my conviction, contrary to the prevailing pessimism at the turn of this century, that Latin America was undergoing a deep-rooted process of economic reform, democratisation and progressive social change. The outlook for the region is more difficult now. If I have tempered, but not abandoned, that underlying conviction, it is chiefly because of the rise of a politically engaged civil society in much of Latin America.

What follows is based on my own observation and experience of a region I first visited in 1980. I have been fortunate to have been able to view Latin America both from within (having lived in Peru, Mexico and Brazil for a total of 16 years) and as a frequent visitor from a distance. During all these years, I have enjoyed the journalist's enormous privilege of being able to watch history unfold at close quarters and ask questions of many of its protagonists.

Forgotten Continent is an attempt to make sense of what I have learned in a more systematic way, drawing on my reporting, especially for *The Economist* (and sometimes on that of colleagues at the newspaper). It was my original intention that the book's narrative would begin around 1980, but it quickly became apparent to me that I would have to start much further back. That decision was in the spirit of the conversations I had each time I ventured into a country new to me in Latin America. A seemingly simple question about some aspect of contemporary politics would lead within a few minutes to an exposition of the peculiarities of that country's nineteenth-century history. Since history and historical figures are daily invoked by Latin American politicians, I make no apology for having decided to begin the story around 1810, when most Latin American countries began their struggle for independence.

Readers of the first edition will find much that is familiar but much that has changed. In revising the book, my vantage point was Latin America today and the dilemmas the region faces in the post-boom, post-Chávez era. Between 2014 and 2016, I lived once again in Lima, and have included much fresh reporting gathered in that period.

A new introductory chapter sets out what is at stake in the region and why it matters to the world. I have revised Chapter 2, which discusses prevailing explanations for Latin America's relative difficulty in establishing prosperous democracies, to take account of recent additions to the literature. The three historical chapters that follow are largely unchanged. The rest of the book is radically revised and updated. The next chapter looks at the region's economic record since the 1980s. There follow chapters on the Venezuelan disaster and the varied stumbles of reformists in Chile, Brazil and Mexico. Later chapters include much new material on the changes in Latin American societies, and the struggles of governments and state institutions to respond to more educated, demanding and connected citizens, as well as to new challenges, such as climate change and conflicts over extractive industries. While Venezuela and Nicaragua have slipped into dictatorship, elsewhere democracy has held up in the region, but it is marred by corruption and ossified political structures – the subject of Chapter 11. The penultimate chapter looks at what opportunities Latin America might have in the world of Donald Trump, a powerful China and an introverted Europe. The book concludes by assessing what the region needs to do to escape the 'middle-income trap' and achieve the goals of economic development, stable democracy and more inclusive and less unequal societies that have so long eluded it.

Over the decades, I have benefited from the time, opinions and wisdom of many hundreds of Latin Americans, ranging from presidents to peasant farmers, as well as of professional observers of the region. Unfortunately, it is impossible to name them individually here, and invidious to single out a few. Many of them crop up in the text or in the references. Thanks to all of you.

I am grateful to *The Economist* and its recent editors, Bill Emmott, John Micklethwait and now Zanny Minton Beddoes, for having indulged my interest in Latin America, their generosity in granting me leave in which to write and the freedom to express my own views, and for having allowed me to live where I have wanted to. No journalist could ask for more. Thanks, too, to *The Economist*'s correspondents and stringers in Latin America for their unfailing help; to Phil Gunson for comments on Chapter 7; to Arthur Goodhart, my agent; to Celina Dunlop for once again helping me to obtain photographs; to Adam Meara and Christopher Wilson for the charts; to Robert Baldock and his team at Yale for their customary efficiency; and to Clive Liddiard for his copy-edit, which caught many small errors.

As always, my greatest debt is to my family. Roxani and Torsten Wilberg were exceptionally understanding of my recent unavailability. Maximilian Wilberg, to whom this edition is dedicated, showed a precocious respect for the closed door of his grandpa's study. Finally, this book would have been impossible without the constant love and support of Emma Raffo. Her ideas and criticisms influenced it throughout.

Madrid, May 2017

CHAPTER ONE

The Forgotten Continent

The future of the world, we are told with increasing insistence, lies in Asia and particularly in China and India. The terrorist attacks of 11 September 2001 and those that followed, the disastrous aftermath of the invasion of Iraq, the bitter failure of the Arab Spring and the emergence of the chiliastic and brutal Islamic State group have all meant that the Middle East and the broader Islamic world are of unavoidable strategic interest to the United States and Europe. Despite some recent progress, Africa's wars and dictators, its epidemics and poverty, still tug at the consciences of the rich world.

What of Latin America, the other great region of the developing world? 'Latin America doesn't matter ... People don't give one damn about Latin America now', Richard Nixon told a young Donald Rumsfeld in 1971, when advising the future American defence secretary which part of the world to avoid if he wanted a brilliant career.[1] With the exception of the violent overthrow of Salvador Allende in Chile in 1973, which Nixon's administration encouraged, and the debt crisis and the Central American wars of the 1980s, his judgement largely held true in the following decades. To be sure, the sickening collapse of Argentina's economy in 2001–02 attracted horrified glances. Colombia's drug lords and guerrilla violence sometimes made headlines. Fidel Castro remained a curiosity, stubbornly ensconced in his communist island well into old age. But this only served to underline Latin America's status as a largely forgotten continent. It was neither poor enough to attract pity and aid, nor dangerous enough to excite strategic calculation, nor was it growing fast enough economically to quicken board-room pulses.

Then, suddenly, the veil of oblivion thrown over Latin America by much of the media in Europe and the United States parted. Presidential elections in the region brought to power a cohort of left-wing leaders of various kinds in a 'pink tide', inspiring the notion that Latin America was moving out from under the thumb of the United States, where it was asserted to have forever languished. Much of the interest was catalysed by Hugo Chávez, Venezuela's voluble populist president who aroused fears in some quarters and hopes in others that he was another Castro – but one armed with oil. Seemingly in his wake stood Evo Morales, a coca growers' leader and socialist, who became the first Bolivian of Andean Indian descent to be elected to his country's presidency, and Ecuador's Rafael Correa, a self-described 'Christian leftist'. In Brazil, the election in 2002 of Luiz Inácio Lula da Silva, a former trade-union leader born in poverty, brought to power the Partido dos Trabalhadores (PT, or Workers' Party), Latin America's largest left-wing party. Néstor Kirchner, a previously obscure provincial governor from Patagonia, and his feisty wife, Cristina Fernández, took charge in Argentina, declaring war on the International Monetary Fund (IMF), foreign-owned utilities and holders of the country's bonds. In Chile, Michelle Bachelet, a socialist whose father died after being tortured by General Pinochet's secret police and who was herself briefly a political prisoner, became the first woman to be elected president in Latin America who did not owe this distinction to marriage to a famous husband (she was a separated mother of three children). José Mujica, who as a captured Tupamaro guerrilla had spent ten years in solitary confinement, two of them at the bottom of a well with only ants and rats for company, was elected president of Uruguay in 2009 for the left-wing Frente Amplio (Broad Front). In office, he continued to live austerely in his three-room farmhouse, drove an ancient VW Beetle and lunched in the nondescript cafeterias of Montevideo's Avenida 18 de Julio, its main commercial street. He attracted worldwide attention not just for his modest lifestyle, but also for successfully promoting the legalisation of marijuana in Uruguay.[2]

By 2008, eight of the ten republics of South America (excluding the Guyanas) were governed by the left, broadly defined. Something, it seemed, was stirring in the region. This led Eric Hobsbawm, a British historian and unrepentant communist, to declare: 'today, ideologically, I feel most at home in Latin America, because it remains the one part of the world where people still talk and conduct their politics in the old language, in the nineteenth- and twentieth-century language of socialism, communism and Marxism'.[3] Others despaired that in the twenty-first century, Latin America remained seemingly locked in what they saw as archaic ideological battles. But in a region long notorious for its extreme inequalities of income and wealth, in part racially based, many saw the new left-wing governments as an overdue response to the lingering legacy of Iberian colonialism.

Soon Latin America began to attract notice for a second reason. China's breakneck industrialisation and its entry into the global economy unleashed unprecedented demand for the metals, fuels and foodstuffs that the region (and especially South America) produces in abundance. Helped by the sharp and sustained rise in world commodity prices, much of Latin America joined the emerging-market boom. At its height, from 2004 to 2008, the region's economy, taken as a whole, grew at an annual average rate of 5.5 per cent, while inflation remained low and foreign investment poured in. This was Latin America's best economic performance since the 1960s. The region seemed to sail through the 2008–09 world financial crisis, suffering only a brief slowdown; thanks to its new economic robustness, governments were able to respond not with austerity, but rather with 'counter-cyclical' (i.e. expansionary) fiscal and monetary policies, without triggering inflation. The economic boom went hand in hand with extraordinarily swift social progress. In 2002, 44 per cent of Latin Americans lived below the poverty line; by 2012 that figure had fallen to 28 per cent, meaning that some 60 million Latin Americans escaped from poverty.[4] Even the region's income distribution became somewhat less unequal. The middle class expanded, and on some definitions began to outnumber the poor. All in all, the years from 2003 to 2012 were a golden decade for Latin America.

Because of its size, Brazil attracted particular attention among foreign investors. In 2003, Goldman Sachs, an investment bank, published a report in which it highlighted the growing importance for the world economy of the 'BRICs', a new acronym in which Brazil took its place alongside Russia, India and China. Brazil is the world's fifth-largest country in area and population, and its fourth-largest democracy. By 2012 it had become the world's seventh-biggest economy, neck-and-neck with Britain. It began to be seen as a country of global significance in other respects, such as in world trade and environmental negotiations. It had aspirations to become a permanent member of the United Nations Security Council. Lula's expansive diplomacy landed the 2014 World Cup for Brazil and the 2016 Olympics for Rio de Janeiro. The award of the latter meant that Brazil was at last recognised as a 'first class country', he declared.

Latin America's left-wing leaders proclaimed a new era of 'South–South' ties and regional solidarity, in more or less explicit rejection of the United States and what they claimed was its hegemony over the region. They were pushing at an open door: the Iraq debacle and the financial crisis damaged the self-confidence of the United States and its claims to world leadership. The long-drawn-out agony of the Euro zone and the challenges of enlargement and mass migration plunged the European Union into introspection and tension, culminating in Brexit (Britain's vote to leave the EU in a referendum in June 2016). Meanwhile, China became the largest trading partner of several Latin American countries, including Brazil, and a growing source of investment and of loans to governments.

From triumphalism to stagnation

By the time the Rio Olympics took place, the triumphalism had congealed and the mood in Brazil and across Latin America was much more sombre. The slowing and maturing of China's economy prompted commodity prices to fall from 2011 onwards. By 2016, Latin America's economies, taken as a whole, were suffering their sixth consecutive year of deceleration. According to the IMF, the region's GDP stagnated in 2015 and contracted by 1 per cent in 2016.[5] The average hid dramatic variations. While the commodity boom saw uniform growth across South America, the bust exposed the recklessness and mistakes of some of the left-wing governments. By 2016, Venezuela was suffering the world's highest inflation rate and its economy was in free fall. Brazil was mired in its deepest slump since records began; Argentina was locked in stagflation; and Ecuador sank into recession. In the region as a whole, poverty began to edge up again. By contrast, growth continued, albeit at a slower rate, in Chile, Colombia, Mexico and Peru, as well as in Bolivia.

Not surprisingly, the political cycle began to turn against the left. In a presidential election in Argentina in November 2015, Mauricio Macri, a former businessman of the centre-right, inflicted a narrow defeat on Fernández's candidate. Chávez died of cancer in 2013, just when Venezuela was paying the socio-economic price of his 'twenty-first-century socialism'. His successor, Nicolás Maduro, lacked his mentor's political skills. In a parliamentary contest in December, the regime suffered its first clear electoral defeat at the hands of the variegated opposition. In February 2016, Morales, who had held Bolivia's presidency for a decade, lost a referendum that would potentially have allowed him to remain in power until 2025 (though he later indicated that he would try to overturn this vote). In Brazil, Dilma Rousseff, Lula's handpicked successor, was impeached for fiscal misdemeanours; behind her ouster, which she called a 'coup' but which followed constitutional procedures, lay a collapse of governability brought about by her deep unpopularity and lack of elementary political skill, the recession and a massive corruption scandal involving Petrobras, the state oil company (in which the PT was deeply implicated, though there was no evidence that she was personally involved). In Chile, Michelle Bachelet, elected by a landslide for a second term in 2013 after a centre-right interlude, lost popularity and was obliged to scale back an ambitious but technically flawed programme of social-democratic reform. In Peru, a centre-left president, Ollanta Humala, was followed by Pedro-Pablo Kuczynski, a former investment banker, who narrowly defeated another candidate of the centre-right, Keiko Fujimori. Only Ecuador bucked the trend – just. Correa opted not to run for a fourth term, but his candidate, Lenín Moreno, narrowly defeated Guillermo Lasso, a conservative banker.

Behind this ebbing of the 'pink tide' lay a combination of voter anger over harder economic times, rage against corruption and frustration over the failure of governments of all political persuasions to provide the better public services that Latin America's societies, less poor and more middle class than in the past, were demanding. Empowered by the spread of smartphones and social media in the region, Latin Americans took to the streets to vent their anger. In Brazil in 2013, small protests over an increase in bus fares in São Paulo mushroomed into a nationwide outpouring of anger against the graft of self-serving politicians, symbolised in the unnecessarily expensive stadiums built for the World Cup, juxtaposed with the poor quality of public transport, health provision and schools. Mass protests over corruption occurred in Mexico and Honduras, and helped to topple the president in Guatemala, as well as in Brazil. In Chile in 2006 and again in 2011–12, tens of thousands of students repeatedly took to the streets in protest over the high cost and poor quality of higher education. Bachelet tried to placate them by promising to make university education 'free' (i.e. taxpayer funded). But her second presidency never recovered from her clumsy handling of a scandal over a dubious property development by her son and daughter-in-law.

The problem of corruption, especially in public contracting, had become systematic. Odebrecht, a Brazilian firm that was Latin America's biggest construction company and was at the centre of the Petrobras scandal, admitted to paying bribes to politicians and officials in nine other Latin American countries totalling $436 million between 2000 and 2015, according to documents released by the US Department of Justice as part of the settlement of the largest-ever lawsuit under the Foreign Corrupt Practices Act. That was in addition to $349 million in bribes it paid in Brazil.[6]

There was an additional cause of voter discontent: the chronic insecurity of everyday life in a region where criminal gangs came to operate with impunity in many countries in the face of ineffective and often corrupt police forces and judiciaries. Proportionately, Latin America suffered more murders than any other part of the world (barring war zones). With only 8 per cent of the world's population, it accounted for about 37 per cent of total homicides in 2012, when 145,759 people were murdered in the region, according to the UN. Worryingly, despite the region's social progress, the murder rate rose.[7] A poll commissioned by the UN Development Programme suggested that nearly two-thirds of Latin Americans avoid going out at night for fear of crime, and one in eight had moved house in order to feel more secure.[8] No wonder that (at least until the economic slowdown set in) polls found crime had overtaken money worries as Latin Americans' top concern. Crime was an issue that few governments of either the left or the right got to grips with.

The combination of austerity and corruption was politically toxic. It brought about a demand for the alternation of power that is normal in democracies but that was a relative novelty for Latin America. Indeed, it was this combination and the anti-incumbent mood it engendered that had brought about the region's left turn in the first place.

Between progress and the populist temptation

In the dying years of the Cold War, Latin America had undergone a historic transformation, with the seemingly definitive establishment of democratic government. In 1978, outside the English-speaking Caribbean, only three countries in the region were democracies; by 1994, all except

Cuba and Mexico were (and Mexico would soon become one).[9] This democratic wave swept away some of the bloodiest and nastiest dictatorships the Latin American countries had seen in their long – though far from continuous or generalised – history of authoritarian rule. It went hand in hand with a surge of free-market economic reform after half a century of statist protectionism. Dubbed the 'Washington Consensus' or, if you prefer, 'neoliberalism', this prompted much optimism that Latin America had finally embarked on what some in the financial markets thought would be a seamless path of sustained growth and development.[10]

Those eager expectations turned out to be over-optimistic. History, as so often, took a more complicated course. The initial fruits of economic reform were mixed. Inflation, so long a Latin bugbear, was tamed. Growth picked up at first, as foreign investment poured in. But it was checked, and in several countries reversed, as it became clear in a string of wrenching financial crises that foreign capital could leave as fast as it had arrived. Between 1998 and 2002, the region suffered what the UN Economic Commission for Latin America and the Caribbean (better known as CEPAL, from its initials in Spanish) called 'a lost half-decade' of economic stagnation.[11] This disappointing record meant that the free-market reforms fell into widespread disrepute, albeit often unfairly. Privatisation was particularly abhorred, partly because it was associated in a few cases with corruption or the substitution of public monopolies for private ones. Moreover, the policies of the Washington Consensus were widely – if mistakenly – blamed for Argentina's economic and financial collapse in 2001. The 'lost half-decade' not only paved the way for the 'left turn', as electorates soured on centre-right incumbents. It brought political instability, too: eight presidents failed to complete their terms between 1997 and 2005.

The arrival of the left in power evoked widespread hopes of progressive reform. The left-wing leaders were united in their rhetorical opposition to what they called 'neoliberalism', an often-meaningless term of political abuse which exercises a baleful influence in the region. It is often used simply to denounce an open, capitalist economy.[12] I will use 'neoliberal' far more narrowly to refer to those who believe that macroeconomic stability, free markets and free trade *on their own* are sufficient to achieve economic development, rather than being necessary conditions which require the complement of an effective state.

Despite their shows of backslapping solidarity at frequent regional summits, there were important differences among the various left-of-centre presidents. Some were, broadly speaking, Latin American social democrats, while others were closer to the region's tradition of populism.[13] Lula and the Chilean socialist presidents – Ricardo Lagos (2000–06) and Michelle Bachelet (2006–10 and from 2014) – and Uruguay's Frente Amplio were examples of the first variant. The second was represented by Chávez, the Kirchners, Correa and, to a lesser extent, Morales. The first group were reformists; some in the second group talked of 'refounding' their countries' political systems. The attitude towards the institutions of liberal democracy was one dimension of difference. The social democrats represented more established political parties and came to power in countries with stronger institutions, of which they tended to be respectful. The instinct and practice of the populists, who tended to be political outsiders, was to concentrate power in their own hands, to override checks on executive power and to rule in a more plebiscitary and majoritarian fashion.[14] But leaders and parties evolved over time. Thus, Morales, who owed his rise to autonomous social movements, became more populist while in office, and Brazil's PT sought to bend the rules of liberal democracy through systematic illegal party financing. Cristina Fernández was more intransigent than her husband (who died in 2010). Chávez, a former army officer who had attempted a military coup against an elected government in 1992, stood in the classic Latin American tradition of the populist *caudillo* or strongman, but then, under the influence of Fidel Castro, veered towards a tropical Stalinism, while preserving merely the outward trappings of democracy.

Populism is a political phenomenon that has recently received much attention. The label has been attached to anti-establishment political movements in Europe both of the far right (such as Britain's UK Independence Party, Alternative für Deutschland in Germany and France's more longstanding Front National) and of the far left (Syriza in Greece and Podemos in Spain), as well as to Donald Trump's successful campaign for the US presidential election of 2016. In Latin America, populism has a long history. Like 'neoliberalism', it is a word that has become a loaded, normative term.[15] So here is my own definition. By 'populism', I mean two things: first, a brand of politics in which a strong, charismatic leader appeals to 'the people' by counterposing it to a rhetorical oppressor such as the 'oligarchy' or 'establishment' (or 'Washington' in Trump's case). He or she purports to be a saviour, blurring the distinction between leader, government, party and state, and ignoring the need for the restraint of executive power through checks and balances. Secondly, populism has often, but not always, involved redistribution of income and/or wealth in an unsustainable fashion. Populism is mistakenly assumed by some commentators to be synonymous with the left. That is not so. Thus, had the financiers of Wall Street correctly identified the fact that Brazil's Lula was a social democrat, not a populist, they might not have panicked at the thought of his election in 2002. The classic populist leaders included Juan Perón in Argentina and his second wife, Eva Duarte, and José María Velasco in Ecuador, while Brazil's Getúlio Vargas embraced populism in his final years. Conservatives, such as Peru's Alberto Fujimori and Colombia's Álvaro Uribe, governed in some respects as populists. In some of its past manifestations, Latin American populism was a creative political response to inequality and the dominance of powerful conservative groups. In others, it was a vehicle for authoritarianism. In many cases, it left countries, and especially the poor (whom it claims to champion), worse off, in economic terms at least.

Why is populism, nevertheless, so attractive to Latin American voters? Because, as Luis Rubio, a Mexican political scientist, points out 'people remember the years of economic growth, not the years of paying the bill'.[16] In the same vein, Argentina's Juan Perón became a symbol of 'the only period in which the worker was happy', according to John William Cooke, a leader of the Peronist left in the 1960s.[17] Having appeared to fade away in the 1960s, populism's return owed much to the persistence of Latin America's extreme inequalities of income and wealth. This reduced the appeal of incremental reform and increased that of messianic leaders who promised a new world. A second driver of populism has been Latin America's wealth of natural resources, from gold to oil. Many Latin Americans are taught at school that their countries are rich, whereas in truth they are not. If it were natural resources rather than hard work and effective institutions that made countries wealthy, Singapore and Switzerland would be destitute. Populists blame poverty on convenient scapegoats: corruption, 'the oligarchy', American 'imperialism' or multinational oil or mining companies. Third, as the politics of class has faded, it has been partly replaced by a new politics of identity. Not all Latin American populists are Amerindian or *mestizo* (of mixed race). Nevertheless, the appeal of men like Chávez, Morales or Peru's Ollanta Humala (who campaigned as a populist, but as president in 2011–16 did not govern as one) was partly one of ethnic identification, a sense among poorer and darker-skinned Latin Americans that they were 'one of us'. In that sense, such leaders helped to make their democracies more representative, even if they might have impaired them in other ways.

This populist challenge to liberal democracy is thus part of the high price that Latin America continues to pay for its failure to overturn at an earlier point in its independent history the two great structural causes of its socio-economic inequality, which were closely linked: on the one hand, unequal land distribution, whose origins in many cases lay in the colonial period, and on the other hand slavery (finally abolished only in 1886 in Cuba and 1888 in Brazil) and discrimination against the indigenous Amerindian population. In Latin America, unlike in the United States or apartheid South Africa, racial mixing has long been the norm. The *conquistadores* were overwhelmingly male, and so were the colonists who followed them, at least until independence. Most Latin Americans are now *mestizo* (of mixed European and Indian race) or *mulato* (black and European). But the poor still tend to be of darker skin than the rich.

Although several of the left-wing governments ruled pragmatically for many years, in the end many of them ended up jeopardising or destroying their own achievements in an exercise of hubris. Too often they claimed to be leading 'revolutions', with an implicitly irreversible freehold on power, rather than recognising that they were the ephemeral beneficiaries of democratic alternation in office. That led many to try to cling on either by rigging the rules of democracy or by subordinating the sound management of the economy to short-term popularity, or both. The most brazen example was Venezuela, which under Maduro slid into outright dictatorship and into what Ban Ki-moon, the UN secretary general, called a 'humanitarian crisis' (see Chapter 7). Nicaragua's president, Daniel Ortega, used his control of the electoral authority to expel the opposition from the Congress and deny his chief opponent the right to run in a presidential election in 2016. He named his wife, Rosario Murillo, as his running mate. He was thus establishing a dynastic dictatorship, like that of the Somozas which he had overthrown in 1979 as a leader of the Sandinista revolution. An example that was both sinister and farcical was the attempt by Cristina Fernández to conceal inflation and exaggerate economic growth by publishing bogus statistics. In Ecuador, Correa was heavy-handed in his harassment of the media.

Continuities and divergences

By the middle of the second decade of the twenty-first century, it seemed that, as in a Gabriel García Márquez novel, Latin America had come full circle. While many Asian countries continued to forge ahead economically, Latin America risked a renewed period of stagnation and perhaps of political instability and global irrelevance. But the commodity boom and the left turn had changed the region significantly. In many countries, there was more continuity and underlying progress than met the eye.

With 630 million people in 2015, Latin America and the Caribbean is an almost uniformly middle-income region, with annual income per person of almost $9,000 (in current US dollars). Taking into account purchasing power, that figure rises to over $15,000, ranging from almost $23,500 in Chile to just $1,750 in Haiti.[18] On most social indicators Latin America does better than other parts of the developing world, but has recently been overhauled by East Asia (see Table 1).

In the past few decades, the region has undergone several overlapping sets of powerful changes. The first is that of democracy itself, which could draw on a long, if truncated, tradition of constitutionalism, but had to grapple with ingrained undemocratic habits and practices. Despite clear regress in Venezuela and Nicaragua, elsewhere the pendulum between dictatorship and democracy that marked much of the twentieth century in Latin America has stopped. Coups are largely a thing of the past: the exception that proves the rule was a conflict of powers in Honduras which ended with the army, acting at the request of Congress and the Supreme Court, ejecting the president, Manuel Zelaya and installing another civilian in his place. No military officer on active duty has served as the president of a Latin American country since 1990.[19]

Second, since the 1960s the region has gone from being predominantly rural to mainly urban – a transformation that was much more gradual in Europe. Cities grew explosively: the population of greater São Paulo leapt from 69,000 in 1890 to 12 million in 1976 and 21 million

Table 1: **Socio-economic indicators**

Comparative, by region

	Life expectancy at birth, 2015 (years)	Infant mortality rate per 1,000 live births, 2015	Proportion of people living on less than $1.90* a day, 2013, %	Proportion of people with access to improved water source, 2015, %
East Asia & Pacific	75	14	3.5	94
Europe & Central Asia	77	10	2.2	98
Latin America & Caribbean	*75*	*15*	*5.4*	*94*
Middle East & North Africa	73	20	2.1	93
South Asia	68	42	15.1	92
Sub-Saharan Africa	59	56	41.0	68

Source: World Bank, World Development Indicators 2016   *In 2011 dollars at purchasing-power parity

today. Similarly, the population of Lima grew almost eightfold in the four decades to 1981.[20] Not surprisingly, urban growth on this dramatic scale overwhelmed governments, and public services failed to keep pace. So Latin American cities typically reflected in concrete and cardboard the injustices of the wider society: they were marked by large pockets of poverty, as well as ostentatious wealth. Much of the urban population lived in self-built dwellings lacking clear legal title: in Peru, for example, more than half at the turn of century, while in Haiti the figure was as high as 68 per cent.[21] But over time, most of these settlements acquired many of the comforts of urban life: electricity, water, sewerage, paved roads and parks – and, over the past decade or so, modern retailing and multiplex cinemas.

Third, in the 1980s and 1990s Latin American economies shed a dense cocoon of protection, statist regulation and costly economic distortions. The most visible of these was inflation, in which the region was long a world leader. The market reforms of the 1980s and 1990s coincided with – and in some ways were made possible by – the onset of a new period of globalisation which brought many benefits to Latin Americans, in the form of export and income growth, as well as access to cheap imported consumer goods. Even as the Washington Consensus was routinely denounced, so its central tenets – of macroeconomic stability and open, market economies – became an enduring part of the scenery in many countries of the region. Certainly, mistakes were made in implementing the market reforms (see Chapter 6). But the main failure was that the state and public institutions were left largely unreformed. More effective states, and better public policies, are the key to reducing inequality and to enabling Latin Americans to compete more effectively in the world.

A fourth transformation was in the region's societies, which have seen, on average, a dramatic improvement in housing conditions and access to basic services. Latin Americans are less badly educated, enjoy better health and are less poor and more middle class than ever before (see Chapter 9). Their societies are more dynamic, more demanding and more complex than they were in 2000, let alone in 1980.

Many deep-rooted difficulties remain, and I discuss these in detail in the chapters that follow. Five sets of problems stand out. The first is inequality. At the start of the twenty-first century, the richest 10 per cent took on average 43 per cent of the pie of total income from labour, while the poorest 20 per cent got just 3.1 per cent. By contrast, in the United States the richest 10 per cent got 31 per cent and the poorest 20 per cent got 5 per cent; while in Italy the figures were 27 per cent and 6 per cent, respectively. By 2013, the share of the richest 10 per cent in Latin America had fallen to 38 per cent and that of the poorest 20 per cent had risen to 3.9 per cent.[22] The fall in income inequality over the past decade was welcome, and ran counter to the trend in many developed countries. Even so, Latin America still vied with sub-Saharan Africa as the most unequal place on the planet.

Secondly, regular and generally clean elections and a far greater respect for human rights than in the past have not been sufficient to ensure the universal application of the rule of law or effective government. Crime and insecurity are the most visible manifestations of this. Justice is too often slow, venal, arbitrary or simply non-existent. In those circumstances, equality before the law remains a distant prospect: the powerful can usually find ways to protect themselves; the poor often cannot. In other ways, too, creating a democratic society and equal citizenship has remained a work in progress. Another symptom of the malfunctioning of the law and its institutions is the pervasiveness of the informal economy in Latin America. In many countries, the central institutions of democracy – Congress, political parties, the courts – are viewed with contempt rather than respect. Politicians are derided as corrupt and self-serving – and all too often they are.

Third, the commodity boom concealed big underlying weaknesses in Latin America's economic performance. These are revealed by the low productivity of many of the region's firms and workers, and the lack of competitiveness of many of its businesses. Addressing that is vital if the region is to continue to progress in a less helpful global environment. Adding to the urgency is the fact that Latin America is swiftly going through a demographic transition: by the mid-2020s, the size of the labour force will start to shrink in relation to the dependent population.[23] In other words, Latin America is starting to grow old before it grows rich. The causes of low productivity are multiple: they include widespread informality, lack of education and skills, and deficient or non-existent infrastructure. It doesn't help that many of the region's big cities are chaotic, polluted and choked with traffic, meaning that many workers face a daily two-way commute of three hours or so, cooped up in overcrowded buses or, in fewer cases, trains.

Fourth, politics may well become more difficult, too. That the hegemony of the left, both institutionalist and populist, lasted so long owed much to the commodity boom. This gave left-wing leaders increased tax revenues to spend on expanding social provision and on redistribution, without necessarily having to resort to money-printing and inflation, as was the case in the 1980s. In countries with many poor people and yawning income inequality, such policies were popular. Now the years of easy growth are over. The slowdown threatens the social progress of the past dozen or so years. Research by the World Bank has found that most of the fall in poverty came from faster economic growth (through the expansion in employment and higher wages) rather than from redistributive social policies. In harder times, the politicians will have to try to satisfy the expanded middle class, whose frustrations have potentially explosive implications for political order.[24] According to a study by the UN Development Programme, up to 30 million Latin Americans who left poverty are now at risk of falling back into it; many of them are young people and women with precarious jobs in services.[25]

It doesn't help that in many countries, political resources are under strain. Those dynamic societies are often governed through fossilised political systems. As traditional parties have declined, so politics has fragmented. Fears about 'governability' receded when incumbents were popular. Now the region may see shorter political cycles, with a risk of renewed turbulence or gridlock. It may help that the ideological polarisation that characterised Latin America in the Cold War, and which was revived by Chávez and his friends, seemed to be diminishing in intensity in favour of a pragmatic centrism. One welcome sign of that was that in Colombia in September 2016, after four years of hard negotiation with the government of Juan Manuel Santos, the Stalinist guerrillas of the so-called Revolutionary Armed Forces of Colombia (FARC) agreed to end their armed insurgency, which began in 1964. Another was that politicians of the centre-right, such as Macri and Kuczynski, recognised the need for social policies and fairer societies. The populist virus continues to be present in the Latin American body politic, but at least in many countries it appears to be going into remission.

Lastly, in marked contrast to recent decades, perhaps the biggest problem now facing the region is an external one. The liberal world order and the era of globalisation that held sway between the fall of the Berlin Wall in 1989 and the financial crisis of 2008 provided Latin America with a favourable and predictable environment in which to pursue democratisation and economic reform. Today the international outlook is far cloudier and more uncertain. If it is to return to faster economic growth, Latin America needs to boost its exports. But since the financial crisis, growth in world trade has slumped, and protectionist sentiment is on the rise. It was an irony that just as Latin America started to emerge from its most recent populist cycle, the rest of the world was discovering the dubious charms of populism. Three Latin American countries – Chile, Mexico and Peru – were signatories of the Trans-Pacific Partnership, a 12-country trade agreement championed by Barack Obama and rejected by Trump. For Mexico, President Trump represents a potentially grave danger, if he carries out his threats to wall the country off and undermine the North American Free Trade Agreement (NAFTA), which links the two countries and Canada. And Trump's expansionary fiscal promises hold out the likelihood of much tighter monetary policy in the United States, thus ending the era of cheap credit that began with the financial crisis and raising the cost of borrowing for Latin American governments and companies.

Why Latin America matters

It is fair to say that Latin America is a little less 'forgotten' by the outside world than it was when I began to work on the first edition of this book in the early 2000s. (The sense in which I meant 'forgotten' was overlooked rather than neglected.)[26] That is partly for the political and economic reasons that I have explained. It is also because of the steady rise in its cultural prominence. Its music, dance, films, novels and visual art have edged into the mainstream in the United States and Europe. Spanish is firmly established as the second international language of the western world. Taking into account use as both a first and second language, according to one estimate Spanish is spoken by perhaps 560 million people, making it the fourth most-spoken tongue after Mandarin, English and Arabic. Spanish is the second most-studied foreign language, after English, with 21 million students, up from 14 million a decade ago.[27] Portuguese, spoken in Brazil, is in eighth place, with 250 million speakers, behind Hindi, Russian and Bengali, but ahead of German and French.[28] Some Latin Americans have long claimed superiority in cultural production over their materially more successful northern neighbours. Yet, paradoxically, the region's enhanced cultural prominence stems in part from the increasingly audible and dynamic presence of 50 million Latinos in the United States. It also reflects globalisation and one of its consequences, the rise in tourism to Latin America. That has exposed more and more people to the region's awe-inspiring geography, the magnificent artefacts left by the ancient civilisations of the Aztecs, Mayas and Incas, and the personal warmth and relaxed approach to life that characterise the average Latin American.

There are, in fact, other reasons apart from culture and language why Latin America, a region of more than 630 million people, matters to the rest of the world. Despite the recent slowdown, Brazil and Mexico are among the world's 15 largest economies, and a further five Latin American countries (Argentina, Colombia, Venezuela, Chile and Peru) make it into the top 50. The region is not just a source of migrants and illegal drugs – though it is that. It boasts some of the world's most ecologically important, biodiverse and endangered natural environments, from the Amazon rainforest to the Andean glaciers and the Galapagos Islands. Brazil has more 'environmental capital' than any other country in the world: it has the most biodiversity and its river systems contain more fresh water than those of any other country (almost three times more than those of the United States).[29] All this puts Latin America on the front line of the global battle to impede and mitigate climate change. It is becoming a leader in renewable energy. Brazil has been a pioneer in policies to halt deforestation. The region has the world's largest reserves of arable land, and is a storehouse of many important commodities, from oil to metals and foodstuffs. If rich countries were ever to make a serious effort to dismantle agricultural protectionism, it could supply much of the world's food. In 2015, it held 20 per cent of the world's proven oil reserves (17 per cent lies in Venezuela alone, though much of that is heavy oil in the Orinoco belt which is expensive to process).[30] The region has become the site of many conflicts between mining and hydrocarbons companies and local people; sometimes difficult trade-offs are required between economic growth and environmental and social considerations.

In recent decades, outside interest in Latin America has been only intermittent. Back in 1994, Bill Clinton, then newly elected to the presidency of the United States, invited 33 other heads of government from the Americas (all of them except Castro) to a summit in Miami. Remarkably, it was the first such meeting ever held. It appeared that the two halves of the Americas, for so long locked in tensions and misunderstandings, had embraced diplomatic – as well as political and economic – convergence. NAFTA had just come into effect. At the specific request of the Latin Americans, the assembled leaders in Miami pledged to work for a hemisphere-wide Free Trade Area of the Americas (FTAA). That vision of hemispheric unity was not fulfilled. Lula, Kirchner, Chávez and the United States itself combined in different ways to kill off the idea of the FTAA. In its place, the United States built a web of bilateral trade treaties, encompassing Central America, the Dominican Republic, Chile, Peru and Colombia, as well as Mexico. Perhaps because of China's closer ties with Latin America, the US took a renewed interest in Latin America during Barack Obama's second term. Obama's boldest stroke was to negotiate a restoration of diplomatic relations with Cuba after a freeze lasting 54 years. That was warmly received throughout the region. After the Cold War ended, Latin American governments of all political stripes had restored ties with Castro's regime and began to oppose the American economic embargo against the island.

Both Obama and his vice-president, Joseph Biden, began to speak with increasing warmth of the ties that bound both ends of the Americas, and the opportunities they saw to deepen them. 'Canada, Latin America and the Caribbean have an outsize impact on our domestic security and prosperity, and in the twenty-first century, the Western Hemisphere should figure prominently among our top foreign policy priorities', Biden declared.[31] Whatever happens under Trump, the forces that link the two halves of the Americas – migration, trade, investment, tourism, religion and culture – are likely to endure.

The overlooking of Latin America by the outside world is in part benign. No news is good news, after all. Most Latin American countries are no longer home to dictators or death squads, and they pay their debts. Yet issues of much wider import are at stake in Latin America today. Along with Europe and North America, the region can claim to form the world's third great group of democracies.

So its attempts to make democracy work in a context of inequality and still widespread poverty, and to use it to create fairer and more prosperous societies, carry wider significance – especially given the setbacks to democracy elsewhere in the world. As had happened in the 1960s in the aftermath of the Cuban Revolution, outsiders began to pay attention once again to policy innovations emanating from Latin America, such as conditional cash transfer schemes like Brazil's *Bolsa Família* or Mexico's *Oportunidades* (now called *Prospera*) and the 'participatory budgeting' pioneered by municipalities in southern Brazil. On the other hand, Latin America offers lessons to the outside world on populism and its perils. When Latin Americans contemplated Trump, many found him uncannily familiar. Maybe, in an unexpected fashion, the United States was at last joining the Americas.

This book is a progress report from this laboratory of democracy that is Latin America, on the region's quest to achieve the twin goals of effective and equitable political institutions on the one hand, and sustained economic growth and development on the other. It is first and foremost a reporting job, drawing on almost 35 years of observation of the region. But it is also an attempt to convey the complex realities that can often elude journalism.

To the extent that outsiders have a view of Latin America, it is one that is heavily influenced by the region's inequalities and injustices, and of romanticised struggles against them. This mental picture is peopled by guerrillas, obscure and quixotic revolutions, drug barons and political machismo, set against a colourful background of imposing geography, quaint costume, grasping foreigners and grinding poverty. Like all cliches, this picture contains a grain of truth. Yet it is anachronistic. In many countries, though not everywhere, Latin American realities have changed substantially. Nowadays, the typical Latin American (if such a person exists) lives in a city, has access to basic services and to much more information about the world than his or her parents. Despite many wants and problems, she or he can aspire to material progress, can vote freely and, through a host of civil-society groups, can influence public policy.

Both left and right in Europe and the United States have tended to treat the region with condescension. Rich-world leftists, while enjoying the freedoms and prosperity of capitalist democracy, worshipped vicariously the defiance of the United States by Castro and Chávez, presuming that benevolent socialist strongmen were a worthy solution for what they saw as the corruption and poverty of capitalism in the rest of Latin America. On the other hand, some 'neoliberals' failed to grasp that small and weak states in Latin America were a formula not just for locking in extreme inequality, but for generating a Hobbesian dystopia of criminal violence. Conservatives often seemed to believe that Latin Americans were a poor, disorganised and hot-headed lot, too immature for democracy and in need of the smack of firm government from a capitalist strongman, a Pinochet or a Fujimori. All the evidence is that most Latin Americans, for their part, want what most people elsewhere want: freedom, security, clean and effective government, social provision and a vigorous capitalism that creates jobs, opportunities and prosperity. It is the purpose of this book to show why this deceptively simple combination has proved so elusive in the region – but also why for at least some Latin American countries it is within closer reach today than at any time in their history.

The main argument of the first edition of this book, published in 2007, was that for the first time in Latin America's history, genuine and durable mass democracies have become the norm in the region. This has far-reaching consequences. In some countries, the process is turbulent and chaotic, and democracy is still capable of being reversed. But in many others, in my view, democracy has either been consolidated or is close to becoming so. That said, Latin American democracy will always have some characteristics that are its own, just as French or Italian democracy differs from that in Britain or the United States. But it will be democracy. The subtitle of the first edition, 'The Battle for Latin America's Soul', referred to the contest between populism and reform. Though both strains of politics have suffered setbacks, I think reformism has clearly won the intellectual battle.

Much can still go wrong. Latin America's history since independence is by turns one of hope and despair, progress and reaction, stability and disorder, dictatorship and freedom. When Stefan Zweig, an expatriate Austrian author who had fled Nazism for Brazil, declared in delight that his new home was 'a land of the future', it was not long before popular humour added the bitter rider 'and it always will be'.[32] Even in the most hopeful view, several countries are likely to remain trapped in a vicious circle of poverty, populism and instability. The coming few years will be more challenging for the region than the past decade, and the international climate is less supportive of both democracy and development. Nevertheless, democracy is becoming increasingly rooted in the region, and some Latin American nations are within striking distance of achieving the status of developed countries in the next few years, with incomes close to those of Southern Europe in the 1970s. For the region as a whole, the challenge is to escape what some economists call 'the middle-income trap'.

One and many Latin Americas

Before proceeding, another definition is in order. What does one mean when one talks of 'Latin America'? The term itself is a relatively recent invention, and it is fraught with difficulties. It was popularised by José María Torres Caicedo, a Colombian writer, in 1856.[33] It was quickly taken up by French propagandists, ever conscious of Anglo-Saxon power and keen to stake out a claim for their country's influence in the 'other America' (a claim that Louis Napoleon pushed beyond prudence with a tragic attempt to install Maximilian, a Habsburg prince, as emperor of Mexico). Unfortunately, it is geographically vague. *Pace* my own misuse of the word in the title of this book, Latin America is not itself a continent. Clearly it includes South and Central America, but most of Mexico is in North America (geographers normally place the sub-continental divide at the Isthmus of Tehuantepec). And what of the Caribbean? Cuba, the Dominican Republic and Haiti clearly qualify. But Puerto Rico has been part of the United States since the Spanish–American war of 1898. And the English-speaking Caribbean (along with Belize and Guyana), though included with Latin America in many international bodies and sharing some of its problems (e.g. the drug trade), constitutes a distinct sub-region. On the mainland, French Guiana is a *départment* of France; Suriname, a former Dutch colony, is independent but separated from the other republics by language. But language is not a defining criterion either. While Spanish is the official language of 18 republics spread across Central and South America and the Caribbean, Portuguese is spoken in Brazil. As well as in Haiti, French Guiana, Guadeloupe and Martinique, French is spoken in Quebec and New Brunswick in Canada and Dutch in some Caribbean islands, as well as Suriname. And a number of indigenous languages remain important, each spoken by several million people. They include Quechua in the countries of the former Inca empire (Peru, Bolivia and Ecuador, where it is called Quichua); Aymara, too, is spoken widely in Bolivia and around the Peruvian shore of Lake Titicaca; Guaraní is the lingua franca of Paraguayans, spoken at home even by members of the country's elite; a score of Mayan languages are spoken in Guatemala and parts of southern Mexico. In all, Mexico has more than 50 Indian languages in current use, including Nahuatl, the tongue of the Aztecs.

For the purposes of this book, I will use Latin America to refer to the Spanish-speaking countries and Brazil (and only occasionally to Haiti). But even in this more restricted universe, there are obvious differences. The problems of Haiti are more akin to those of Africa, whence most of its inhabitants originally came against their will, than to those of Chile, a Europeanised country whose income per head is six times as large. Brazil is a country of continental scale; El Salvador is the size of Wales or Massachusetts. Peru and Mexico were the seat of sophisticated ancient civilisations; Brazil and Argentina are 'new' countries.

Such diversity defeats some casual generalisations. Latin America is far from being a monolith. But it is built from many common materials. The former Spanish and Portuguese colonies of Latin America share more than the same corner of the world. They have a shared experience of Iberian colonialism, of Catholicism, similar languages, and, with many variations, similar ethnic identities. Indeed, early and systematic colonialism, with the collapse of the prior civilisations, and precocious independence mark Latin America out from other regions of the developing world.[34] As already noted, that legacy has involved a further shared characteristic: deep inequality in the distribution of income, wealth and (until recently, at least) political influence. Many, but not all, of the larger countries suffer from challenging geography. One of the most striking differences in Latin America, as elsewhere in the world, is between coastal and mountain peoples, irrespective of country. The coast tends to be more outward-looking, commercially minded and racially *mulato*, while people of the mountains are more conservative and more Indian. This similarity has led Sergio Ramírez, a Nicaraguan writer and politician, to describe Brazil as a 'Caribbean country' despite its purely Atlantic seaboard.[35]

But all Latin Americans share to a greater or lesser extent some social attitudes and a common culture. Many of those who can afford to do so work to live rather than live to work. Many of Octavio Paz's observations regarding the central place of the fiesta in Mexican life apply to the region as a whole, and along with the fiesta goes the importance of music and dance.[36] Despite their prowess at football, a team sport, Latin Americans are torn between gregarious and anarchic impulses. Across the region, the family functions as both a powerful bulwark of social stability and an economic network. Until recently, there was a striking absence in the region of the kind of voluntary civic groups that Alexis de Tocqueville so admired in the United States. Polls regularly show that Latin Americans stand out from the rest of the world in their low levels of inter-personal trust, which is probably a product of the lack of the rule of law.

Brazilian pop music and Mexican *rancheras*, along with *telenovelas* from both countries, are popular throughout the region. So are the novels of García Márquez (a Colombian who lived mainly in Mexico and Cuba) and Mario Vargas Llosa (a Peruvian who lives in Spain). The love poems of Chile's Pablo Neruda have been recited by several generations of adolescents across Latin America. There have been other shared ways of thinking as well. From the Jesuits and scholasticism, to liberalism and positivism, corporatism and Marxism – and liberalism again – Latin American countries have drawn from the same European political philosophies and often adapted them to the conditions of the New World in similar ways.[37] Broadly speaking, their economic and political histories since independence have been similar. It is not coincidental that events have sometimes been strikingly synchronised across the region. Thus, Cuba and the Dominican Republic apart, all the Latin American countries gained independence between 1810 and 1830. Once independent, the Latin American republics have often copied from each other. Thus, six South American republics completed the abolition of slavery in 1851–54, while five expelled the Jesuits between 1848 and 1859.[38] There have been several waves towards and away from authoritarianism. In the wake of the Wall Street Crash of 1929, and the resulting world economic depression, no fewer than 16 countries suffered military coups or authoritarian takeovers of other kinds. That democratisation and liberal economic reform in the 1980s and 1990s took the form of a regionwide wave was thus far from coincidental.

Indeed, some writers have argued that so great are the similarities among the Latin American countries, and so great their differences with other parts of the world, that the region constitutes a distinct civilisation. Samuel Huntington, a conservative American political scientist, is the most prominent proponent of this view. 'Latin America has a distinct identity which differentiates it from the West . . . it has a corporatist, authoritarian culture', he argued.[39] However, as a result of their history, most Latin Americans would see themselves as part of the 'western world'. That in itself distinguishes Latin America from other developing regions. Latin American cultures are a unique mix of European, indigenous and African elements. But there is nothing in the historical record to suggest that Latin America is intrinsically incapable of following Europe and the United States down the path of democracy and capitalism – even if both will be of a distinct, Latin American kind. Alain Rouquié, a French political scientist and former diplomat, seems near the mark when he describes Latin America as the 'far west'[40] – its most challenging frontier of democracy and development.

CHAPTER TWO

The Latin American Conundrum

Until at least the middle of the eighteenth century, the southern part of the Americas was on most counts far more developed than the English-speaking colonies of the north.[1] By 1551, universities had been founded in the Dominican Republic, Peru and Mexico, almost a century before Harvard. Though the economies of the Spanish colonies and Portuguese Brazil were dominated by plantation agriculture, subsistence farming and mining, they also boasted handcraft workshops. Some of these, especially for textiles, qualified as rudimentary factories. But in the second half of the eighteenth century, the soon-to-be United States experienced incipient industrialisation and rapid economic growth. Some scholars reckon that by 1800 its income per head was twice that of Latin America, while others say that it was broadly similar, though income and wealth were much more unevenly shared out in Iberian America, which lacked the puritan egalitarianism of New England. Either way, there is consensus that at that point Latin America was the richest region of what is now called the 'developing world'.[2] It retained that status until fairly recently. At various times, its economic prospects have inspired the kind of excitement now reserved for China and other Asian countries. An observation typical in its tone, and in its self-interest, was that of Thomas Ashe, a Briton who in a work published in 1812 saw Latin America as 'embracing the finest country of the same magnitude in the world, peopled by 40,000,000 of inhabitants, abounding in riches, and wanting only our manufactures to possess every comfort of life'.[3] On the eve of the First World War, a similar enthusiasm was again widespread. In the 1960s, and again in the first decade of the twenty-first century, Latin America seemed to be 'catching up' with the developed world. Yet development has proved a tantalising mirage – more so, even, than the quest for democracy. The diverging fortune of the two halves of the Americas has generated a deep and abiding sense of failure.

That failure has been relative. According to calculations by Angus Maddison, an econometrician, income per head in Latin America in 1820 was roughly half that of the United States and Western Europe, similar to that of Eastern Europe and somewhat larger than the average in Asia. By 1998, he calculated, Western Europe was three times as rich, and the United States more than four times, as Latin America. In that year, income per head in Latin America was still higher than in Eastern Europe and Asia, if Japan is excluded (see Chart 1).[4]

Economic performance in Latin America varied sharply in different periods and between different countries. Much of the *widening* of the gap with the rich countries derives from two periods in which the region as a whole fared badly: the first half-century after independence, when political turmoil and internal warfare caused economic havoc, and the years since the debt crisis of 1982. Maddison found that between 1820 and 1870, income per person in Latin America grew by just 0.1 per

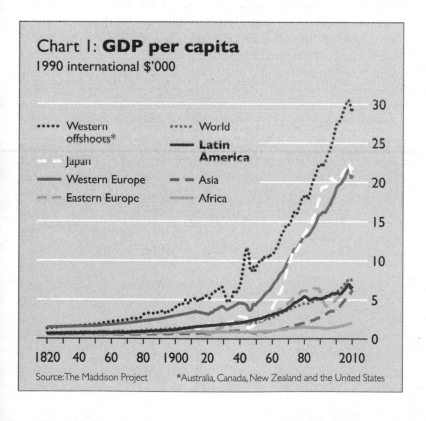

Chart 1: GDP per capita
1990 international $'000

Western offshoots*
World
Japan
Latin America
Western Europe
Asia
Eastern Europe
Africa

1820 40 60 80 1900 20 40 60 80 2010

Source: The Maddison Project   *Australia, Canada, New Zealand and the United States

cent a year. Between 1870 and the end of the Second World War, the eight biggest Latin American economies grew faster than the average of the rich countries that would make up the Organisation for Economic Co-operation and Development (OECD). Thereafter, growth remained respectable until 1982, but lagged behind that of the rich world. It has been disappointingly weak since then, until the 'golden decade' lasting until 2012 (see Table 2). In other words, Latin America fell behind in the first two-thirds of the nineteenth century, then held its own but failed to converge – as economic theory suggests it should – with countries that did achieve developed status. The upshot was that income per person in Latin America was about a quarter of that in the United States in 1900 and remained so a century later.

Most accounts of Latin American economic history from 1870 to 1982 divide the period into two. Until 1930, the region sought export-led growth. The industrial revolution in Europe and the United States, its technological application to transport, combined with the development of capital markets, led to unprecedented growth in world trade and a first period of what would later be called globalisation.[5] Demand boomed for Latin America's minerals (from Chilean nitrates to Bolivian

Table 2: **Growth of per capita GDP**
By region, annual average, %

	1820–1870	1870–1913	1913–1950	1950–1973	1973–2010
Western Europe	0.64	1.29	0.70	4.09	1.66
Western offshoots	1.25	1.81	1.56	2.45	1.64
Japan	na	1.48	0.88	8.06	1.78
Asia	−0.15	0.54	0.10	3.88	3.58
Latin America	*0.42*	*1.63*	*1.30*	*2.60*	*1.10*
Eastern Europe & former USSR	0.67	1.39	1.21	4.13	1.07
Africa	0.57	0.79	− 0.06	1.95	1.04
WORLD	**0.44**	**1.30**	**0.84**	**2.92**	**1.77**

Source: The Maddison Project

tin and Mexican and Peruvian silver) and for many of its food products (from Brazilian and Colombian coffee to Central American bananas, Cuban sugar and Argentine beef and wheat). From 1930, many of the larger countries pursued *desarrollo para adentro* (inward-looking development), with greater tariff protection and state intervention in an effort to industrialise. Though the Wall Street Crash and the depression which followed had an important impact on Latin America, much recent research finds that 1930 was less of an economic turning point than previously thought: industrialisation and more interventionist policies go back before the First World War, while some smaller countries continued to pursue export growth after 1930.

Some countries in the region did better than others in different periods. Victor Bulmer-Thomas, an economic historian, uses slightly different criteria from Maddison. Since income per head in the United States grew at 1.5 per cent a year in the nineteenth century, and population in Latin America expanded by 1.5 per cent a year in this period, to narrow the gap the region's economies would have to grow by more than 3 per cent a year. He calculates that this would require export growth of at least 4.5 per cent a year. For the period from 1850 to 1912, only Argentina and Chile managed this. Uruguay may have met the target because of the strength of its non-export economy.[6] During the second period, from 1928 to 1980, income per head in the United States grew at a faster annual average rate of 2 per cent. Bulmer Thomas finds that in this period, Brazil, Costa Rica, Cuba, Mexico, Peru, Puerto Rico and Venezuela all narrowed the gap by achieving growth in income per head of more than 2 per cent per year (and Colombia exactly that).[7] The successful countries of the first phase performed poorly. What is galling for Latin Americans is that many countries in Asia and Southern and Eastern Europe have pulled ahead over the past two generations. In 1966, Mexico was richer than Portugal, and Brazil richer than South Korea. By 2002, income per head in Portugal and South Korea was roughly double that of Mexico and Brazil, respectively.

A similar sense of thwarted possibility applied, at least until recently, to Latin American democracy. Unlike Asia or Africa, Latin America has a history of liberal constitutionalism spanning almost two centuries. It is a troubled history, in which constitutionalism has often been truncated or merely served as a mask for tyranny. Nevertheless, it should not be lightly dismissed. A century ago, most of the main Latin American countries had achieved civilian constitutional rule under the auspices of restricted or 'oligarchical democracy', to use a helpful oxymoron.[8] The franchise and participation were limited, but these incipient democracies were broadly comparable to those of much of Europe in the same period. Yet after 1930, nearly all countries in the region suffered repeated military interventions in politics. Dictatorship and brief periods of civilian rule alternated in pendulum swings; by the 1970s, the generals were in charge nearly everywhere. In the past three decades or so, Latin America's restored democracies have struggled with institutional failings, poverty and economic instability. By contrast, new European democracies, such as Spain and Portugal (though not Greece or some in Eastern Europe), appeared more solid than many in Latin America. Relative though it may be, Latin America's development failure and its difficulty in consolidating democracy have given rise to a large and almost obsessive literature. There are three main schools of thought: dependency theory; cultural explanations; and geography and institutional weakness. Let us examine them one by one.

Dependency: a theory in search of facts

The dependency school, composed mainly of left-wingers, blames United States intervention and Latin America's 'subordinate' role in the world economy as an exporter of raw materials both for its failure to achieve development and for its history of political authoritarianism. Dependency theory grew out of a marriage between Marxist sociology and an economic doctrine known as structuralism, associated in Latin America with CEPAL. Structuralism was formulated in the late 1940s by a group of economists led by CEPAL's first secretary general, Raúl Prebisch, an Argentine. Prebisch's basic argument was that Latin America suffered from a structural decline in its terms of trade: its exports of primary products got ever cheaper because a surplus of labour held down wages, while its imports of manufactures from rich countries became more expensive because productivity gains were pocketed by increasingly monopolistic industrial firms, rather than passed on as lower prices.[9] It followed from this that free trade would not enable Latin America to accumulate the surplus capital required to industrialise. Instead, governments should intervene to do the job, promoting industrialisation through protective tariffs, subsidised credit and a host of other incentives, and with the state itself setting up basic industries where private initiative could not or would not. This was the rationalisation for the policies of *desarrollo para adentro*.

Structuralism was soon taken up by sociologists, and turned into a broader theory of 'dependent development'. Their central argument was expressed by Fernando Henrique Cardoso, a Brazilian, and Enzo Faletto, a Chilean, in 'Dependency and Development', a slim volume first published in 1969. Between developed economies (which they called 'central' or 'metropolitan') and their underdeveloped ('peripheral') counterparts, they wrote, 'there is not just a simple difference of stage (of development) or of state of the productive system, but also of function or position within a single international economic structure of production and distribution. This presupposes, on the other hand, a defined structure of relations of domination.' In other words, poor countries are poor because others are rich, rather than because they have failed, for whatever other reason, to develop.[10] Dependency applied, too, they argued, to social and political systems. In an economy dominated by industrial monopolies, mainly foreign owned, the masses were excluded from employment ('development . . . is done by intensifying social exclusion').[11] The result was 'urbanisation without industrialisation'. At the same time, in return for their investment, foreign capitalists demanded of the state action to discipline the wage demands of the workers. That, it was held, led inevitably to military dictatorships.

The argument of Cardoso and Faletto contained some nuances. They accepted that there were important differences between foreign investment in industry and earlier foreign 'enclaves' in mines and plantations. 'Peripheral industrial economies' could achieve a considerable degree of development and autonomy in relation to 'the centre', they conceded. In a memoir published in 2006, Cardoso, who would serve as Brazil's president from 1995 to 2002, argued that 'the primary message of "Dependency and Development" was that the people of Latin America had control over their own fate . . . The problem faced by Latin America was political in nature rather than economic. Our backwardness was our own fault, not anybody else's.'[12] But that was not the way it was interpreted at the time, as Cardoso concedes. In other hands, there was no place for such nuances in dependency theory. It quickly became a dogma – heavily influenced by Marxist class analysis – according to which capitalism, foreigners and their local allies were directly responsible for Latin America's poverty and failure.[13]

Dependency theory was – and still is – enormously influential. At the beginning, it seemed to chime with its times. In the 1960s, American multinationals set up shop in many Latin American countries – sometimes displacing local firms that were unable to compete. The cities were swelling with rural migrants, who gathered in squalid shanty towns at the gates of the elegant residential districts of the better-off. Urbanisation certainly outpaced industrialisation. During the Cold War, the United States preferred reactionary military dictators to reformist democrats. To varying extents it backed military coups, from Guatemala to Argentina. The emergence of military juntas in some of the most developed countries in the region appeared to contradict standard modernisation theory.[14] This holds that, as countries industrialise and become richer, so they become more socially varied, with a middle class that pushes for mass education and political pluralism, gradually but inevitably creating the conditions for democracy.

Students and academics, part of a rapidly expanding middle class, seized upon dependency theory as an explanation for Latin America's relative backwardness – and as a justification for revolution. This movement found its evangelist in Eduardo Galeano, a Uruguayan Marxist journalist. As its subtitle makes clear, his popular economic history, *Open Veins of Latin America: Five centuries of the pillage of a continent*, is a scorching denunciation of foreign exploitation. First published in 1971 by Siglo XXI, a Mexican publisher, it was in its eighty-fifth edition in Spanish in 2016, having sold over a million copies, as well as having been liberally pirated across the region and widely translated. The book began by stating: 'to each area has been assigned a function, always for the benefit of the foreign metropolis of the moment'.[15] Its basic, oft-repeated, theme was that 'underdevelopment in Latin America is a consequence of development elsewhere, that we Latin Americans are poor because the ground we tread is rich, and that places privileged by nature have been cursed by history. In this world of ours, a world of powerful centres and subjugated outposts, there is no wealth that must not be held in some suspicion.'[16] Galeano bracketed as identical 'agents of plunder' both 'the caravelled conquistadors and the jet-propelled technocrats; Hernan Cortés and the [US] Marines; the agents of the Spanish Crown and the International Monetary Fund missions; the dividends from the slave trade and the profits from General Motors'.[17]

Galeano was a writer of brilliance and passion. But his history is that of the propagandist, a potent mix of selective truths, exaggeration and falsehood, caricature and conspiracy theory.[18] At bottom, his message is one of anti-capitalism, as well as anti-imperialism. He seems to reject all possibility of reform; local capitalists are dismissed as mere sepoys in the service of foreign masters. Latin America, because of its mineral and agricultural wealth, is rich. If most of its people are poor, it follows that someone must be stealing the wealth. These messages still echo across Latin America today, especially in the mouths of the leaders of radical social movements and populist politicians. The notion that Venezuela and Argentina are rich countries impoverished by foreigners, capitalism and corruption, lies at the root of the peculiarly powerful appeal of populist politicians in both these countries – Perón and Peronism in Argentina, and Hugo Chávez in Venezuela. When they met for the first time at a regional summit in 2009, Chávez gave Barack Obama a copy of *Open Veins of Latin America*. No matter that Galeano himself, shortly before he died in 2015, let slip at a book fair in Brasília that he would by then have found the book unreadable. He added that when he wrote it, he lacked 'sufficient knowledge of economics and politics' and that it belonged to 'a past era'.[19]

Paradoxically, given structuralism's disdain for commodity exports, dependency theory has served to sustain in Latin America what economists call 'the natural-resource myth' – the view that what makes countries rich is what lies below their soil, rather than the work and productivity of their inhabitants. This belief lies behind much of the recent opposition to foreign investment in mining and oil and gas in countries such as Bolivia and Peru. Burned on their collective memory was the fabulous wealth extracted by the Spanish Crown from the Potosí silver mine and how little of it was left behind. Dependency theory also nourished a view of trade as a zero-sum game, rather than a source of mutual profit. This is strikingly similar to eighteenth-century mercantilism – or indeed to the views of Donald Trump.

The view of foreign investment in Latin America as malign is widely propagated. It was given credence in a second book, which, along with Galeano's, had a fundamental role in fixing the mental picture of the region's history carried by Latin Americans and outsiders alike. But this one was a novel. In the climactic scene of *One Hundred Years of Solitude*, Gabriel García Márquez describes a massacre of striking workers by troops acting at the behest of an American banana company whose plantations are held to have replaced a prosperous Eden with an oppressive monoculture. More than 3,000 workers, women and children are cut down by army machine guns, their bodies are loaded onto a train and thrown into the sea, as the government silences news of the outrage. These scenes were loosely based on a strike in 1928 against the United Fruit Company in Magdalena department, on Colombia's Caribbean coast. But the actual events were very different. Historians estimate that no more than 75 people were killed (an appalling enough figure in any event).[20] Before the United Fruit Company's arrival, Magdalena had been one of the poorest and most backward departments of Colombia. The banana industry paid above-average wages, and attracted thousands of migrants.[21] Of course, the massacre was reprehensible, as was much else in the record of the United Fruit Company elsewhere in Latin America (see Chapter 4). But by exaggerating its scale, García Márquez distorted its historical import and created a myth.[22] Since the novel's publication in 1967, the figure of 3,000 dead has taken on a life of its own. In his memoirs, García Márquez noted that 'not long ago, on one of the anniversaries of the tragedy, a speaker in [Colombia's] Senate asked for a minute's silence in the name of the 3,000 anonymous martyrs slaughtered by the security forces'.[23]

Albeit in more scholarly form, dependency theory remains an important prism through which Latin American studies are taught in the United States and Europe. Certainly, the dependency school can point to a few basic historical truths: the asymmetry of power between rich and poor countries, and between the United States and Latin America. Foreign firms have sometimes behaved abusively; the United States has often bullied Latin American countries, from its 1846–48 war of annexation with Mexico to its encouragement of coups to its contemporary 'drug war'. Latin American economies have often found themselves vulnerable to sudden changes in a world economy over which they have little or no control.

But dependency does not stack up as an explanatory theory – especially as an economic one. For a start, it is unable to explain what is without doubt the most significant development in the world economy of the past 40 years: the journey towards development through the medium of capitalism and international trade of many Asian countries. That explanatory failure is hardly surprising. Dependency theory rests on flimsy foundations, as Stephen Haber, a historian at Stanford University, has pointed out.[24] It employed ad hoc reasoning, such as the notion that foreign investment decapitalised Latin America because the value of repatriated profits over time might exceed the value of the original investment. This confused a stock and a flow, and failed to take into account the creation of value in the host country in the form of jobs, demand for inputs, and transfer of technology (and tax revenues).

The main tenets of dependency theory have been disproved by later empirical research. For example, contrary to Prebisch's assertion, recent econometric work shows that commodity prices and Latin America's terms of trade have not suffered secular declines, but rather have shown cyclical swings and no clear overall trend. That became obvious with the commodity boom of 2002–11, as China's industrialisation and entry into the world economy pushed the prices of raw materials to unprecedented heights. Ironically, those governments that subscribed to the rhetoric of dependency theory, such as those in Bolivia, Ecuador and Venezuela, were among the biggest beneficiaries of its negation.

There is much evidence that local capitalists were powerful, independent and innovative, and that governments often regulated foreign capital to serve the interest of national development.[25] Similarly, recent research has demolished the notion that Latin American economies were 'underdeveloped' by free trade. In fact, the region has been the most protected in the world for most of its history. Even as they paid lip-service to free trade in the nineteenth century, governments levied tariffs on imports because foreign trade was the handiest source of revenue, and the wars and internal strife of 1810–70 needed to be paid for. As early as the years preceding the First World War, governments raised import tariffs, switching from revenue-maximising protectionism to explicit industrial protectionism. The agro-export 'oligarchy' had less political clout or was less committed to free trade than is often asserted. Urban artisans and workers gained increasing political influence as the cities grew. Contrary to the arguments of protectionists, those countries with the highest tariffs grew slowest, while those with the lowest tariffs grew fastest.[26]

Overall, it is fair to conclude, with Haber, that 'in retrospect, dependency thinking about foreign capital and national sovereignty might have had a good deal of accuracy in regard to the smaller countries of Latin America, such as Honduras, Guatemala or Cuba, but held limited explanatory power for the larger countries of the region'.[27] The same goes for politics. The smaller countries of the Caribbean rim suffered repeated American intervention. The larger countries of South America, and Mexico, have generally gone their own way. True, the United States encouraged coups, especially during the Cold War. But in nearly all cases those coups were internally generated, and external support, while sometimes important, was not decisive (see Chapters 4 and 5). Apart from being wrong, dependency theory had the unfortunate consequence of encouraging Latin Americans to blame all their woes on outsiders, rather than to take a closer look at themselves. (Conversely, many American academics and pundits appear to suffer from a guilt complex that leads them to exaggerate the scale and impact of US intervention in the region as a whole.) As David Landes, an economic historian at Harvard who is by no means a slave to neo-classical economics, noted: 'Cynics might even say that dependency doctrines have been Latin America's most successful export . . . They are bad for effort and morale. By fostering a morbid propensity to find fault with everyone but oneself, they promote economic impotence. *Even if they were true, it would be better to stow them.*'[28]

A reactionary culture – but what if it changes?

Dependency theory has been mirrored among some conservative commentators by an alternative explanation for Latin America's woes – one that is very different in content but is similar both in inducing impotence and in being based on assertion more than empirical testing. This school holds that Latin America has been doomed by its culture, and in particular an Iberian, Catholic tradition of social organisation and political thought which, it is argued, is both anti-capitalist and inimical to democracy. The most elegant and erudite expression of this viewpoint is to be found in the writings of Claudio Véliz, a Chilean historian. In *The New World of the Gothic Fox*, he adapted an ancient Greek metaphor previously employed by Isaiah Berlin, an Anglo-Russian liberal philosopher, to distinguish between two groups of Western thinkers. In the metaphor, the hedgehog is said to know one big thing, while the fox knows many small things. Berlin called 'hedgehogs' those thinkers, such as Plato and Marx, 'who relate every-thing to a single, central vision', as against 'foxes', such as Aristotle, Erasmus, Shakespeare or Goethe, whose 'thought is scattered and diffused, moving on many levels'.[29] In other words, the hedgehog way of thinking carries the seeds of authoritarianism and totalitarianism, while that of the foxes embodies liberal pluralism. Véliz argues that Latin American culture is like a 'hedgehog': he sees it as marked by a mono-lithic, ordering vision composed of centralisation, civil law, Baroque classicism, and a notion of society as a hierarchical, organic whole, in which each person has his or her place. For Véliz, English-speaking North Americans, by contrast, are 'foxes'. Their culture has featured decentralisation, the common law, romanticism and the Gothic. Another hedgehog-like characteristic of the Ibero-American peoples, he notes, is their capacity to resist change, and especially the transformations asso-ciated with the Industrial Revolution in the Anglo-Saxon world. The reward for this stubborn Catholic conservatism is that values of family and community have been better preserved.

The architects of this Iberian cultural edifice were the theologians of the Counter-Reformation, 'the greatest and most enduring achievement of [Spain's] impressive imperial moment', according to Véliz.[30] Its driving spirit was provided by the teachings of St Thomas Aquinas, which became entrenched at the University of Salamanca. Aquinas held that human society was an organic hierarchy governed by natural (i.e. divine) law. This view of the world was inimical to individualism, pluralism or the clash of competitive interest groups; the only restraint on absolute power was the duty of *noblesse oblige*, not that of man-made constitutions.[31] The mania for central control generated a habit of obsessive regulation which began with Philip II, the austere monarch at the zenith of Spanish power, who sat for long hours in his forbidding monastery-palace of El Escorial, in the hills outside Madrid, penning detailed ordinances to his viceroys across the ocean with only his impressive collection of Titian nudes for relief.

The 'culturalists' hold that this mindset still governs Latin America. Thus, Véliz says of the Counter-Reformation: 'the stability of its uncom-promising symmetries largely dominates, even to this day, the lives of the Spanish-speaking peoples almost as convincingly and pervasively as the dynamic asymmetries of the Industrial Revolution preside over the English-speaking world'.[32] Sometimes the rejection of capitalism and industrialisation has indeed been turned into an explicit virtue by Latin American thinkers. In *Ariel*, a hugely influential book published in 1900, José Enrique Rodó, a Uruguayan journalist and man of letters, argued that Latin America, inspired by Hispanic Christianity and classical antiquity, should pursue the ideals of beauty and truth. He admired the vigorous prosperity of the United States, but saw that country as the source of a vulgar utilitarianism. Like some of today's critics of globalisation, he feared that the United States wanted to impose its ideas on everybody else. Rodó accepted democracy as inevitable, but called for its 'regeneration' by an aristocratic intellectual elite.[33] Rodó was writing in the aftermath of Spain's comprehensive military defeat by the United States in the Spanish–American War of 1898. This entailed the loss of Cuba and Puerto Rico (as well as the Philippines) and thus the end of the empire begun by Columbus. Paradoxically, after a century in which many of Latin America's leaders had imbibed and propagated a *leyenda negra* (black legend) which attributed all of their countries' ills to the colonial power, Spain's defeat in 1898 prompted an outpouring of sympathy in its former territories. *Arielismo* gave rise both to a conservative and almost racist Hispanicism and, on the left, to a new Latin American nationalism, which included a pronounced anti-*Yanqui* element. It would not be the last time that leftists and conservatives found common inspiration in an anti-liberal agenda, and one that seemed to justify the conditioning of democracy to other, allegedly higher, values.

Those writers who stress the influence of Iberian culture argue that when Latin American leaders have seemed to embrace change and democracy, it has been, as with the Sicilian aristocrat of Lampedusa's novel *The Leopard*, in order that everything should remain the same. Latin American democracy has always been more formal than real, they say. Absent, the argument goes, was the tradition of Anglo-Saxon liberal democracy, associated in particular with John Locke, who stressed the importance of the rights of the citizen and checks on an over-mighty executive. Rather, the notion of democracy that has prevailed in Latin America, it is said, has been one derived from French political philosophy, and especially that of Jean Jacques Rousseau, who argued that the ruler would be legitimated by interpreting the 'general will'.[34] This is at once both a defence of popular sovereignty and the perpetual excuse of the tyrant. Similarly, when Latin America appeared to embrace capitalism and democracy, during what Véliz has called 'the liberal pause' from 1870 to

1930, in many countries it did so under the auspices of positivism. Not only was this another French doctrine, but it was one which essentially justified enlightened despotism or top-down reforms, separating economic freedom from political freedom. In this view, Latin America's industrial bourgeoisie, far from challenging an aristocratic, authoritarian state as their European counterparts did, allied with it. In this unflattering portrait, Latin American capitalists were rent-seekers rather than entrepreneurs, soliciting the comforts of protection, subsidies and privileges from the state, rather than risking the bracing challenge of unfettered competition. The result, it is argued, is a prevailing corporatist culture, in which Latin Americans see success as deriving not from individual merit but from patronage and personal contact – know-who rather than know-how. Behind a façade of constitutionalism and democracy, hierarchical domination and corporatist anti-individualism are held to thrive.

There is some truth in this explanation of the failure of capitalist democracy to flourish in Latin America. In particular, it is not hard to see in the Iberian legacy the origins of the mania for regulation and red tape that burdens business in the region. It is undeniably true that corporatism – an idea that emerged from late-nineteenth-century Catholic thinking and which favours government through a concert of functional interest groups, such as business and labour – has been influential in Latin America, bringing with it the comfortable monopolies granted to many businesses or trade-union confederations. It is true, too, that politics in Latin America has long been marked by undemocratic practices, such as 'patrimonialism' and 'clientelism'. The former refers in essence to the hijacking of the government, or bits of it, by powerful private interests. The latter term defines a pattern of politics in which local or national notables or political bosses extract votes and political loyalty from groups of poorer and less powerful followers, in return for offering a degree of protection and access to state resources.[35]

But ultimately, the 'cultural explanation' fails to convince as an overarching theory. First, it cannot account for the diversity of outcome within the region. Why have some countries been so much more successful than others at different periods? Given a presumed cultural heritage in common, why is Chile so different from Argentina, Colombia from Venezuela, or Brazil from Peru? Second, it is simply nonsense to claim that the influence of French political philosophy is self-evidently inimical to democracy per se. Thus, Mario Vargas Llosa, a Latin

American liberal democrat *par excellence*, professes himself a passionate admirer of French culture. From it, he says, he has learned above all 'to love liberty over all other things and to fight everything that threatens and contradicts it'.[36] Thirdly, in the two centuries since independence, Latin America has been shaped and enriched not just by its indigenous peoples and the Iberian legacy, but by migration from other parts of Europe and from Asia, as well as from Africa. Some of those migrants have adhered to authoritarianism, just as many Iberians have been democrats. As Alain Rouquié, a distinguished scholar of Latin American militarism, asked mischievously: 'How much do generals Stroessner, Geisel, Médici, Leigh and Pinochet owe to Castile?'[37] It is, however, also true that a disproportionate number of Latin America's business leaders and entrepreneurs are non-Castilian immigrants.

Above all, the 'cultural explanation' cannot explain recent, dramatic change in Spain itself. For much of the past two centuries, Spain was notorious for political instability, authoritarianism and economic backwardness. Since the end of the Napoleonic invasion, Spain saw six constitutions, seven military *pronunciamientos*, two periods of monarchy (and four abdications), two dictatorships, four civil wars and, finally, the 36-year dictatorship of General Francisco Franco. Yet 40 years later, Spain has become a consolidated democracy. Its vigorous export-led recovery from the financial crisis of 2008 and the related housing bust, and its preservation of political stability despite the rise of a populist far-left party in Podemos stands in marked counterpoint to the travails of Italy. If culture was the problem, clearly the culture has changed. And if it can change in Spain, then it can change in Latin America. The Spanish transition was still fresh in the mind when the democratic wave swept over Latin America in the 1980s. It is true that the prospect of entry to the European Economic Community (as it then was) was a powerful incentive for democratisation. Nevertheless, Spain's experience showed that culture is not the main obstacle either to democracy or to development.

Of geography and institutions

So what is? In recent years, economists have played a prominent role in the great debate about why some groups of countries around the world have proven to be so much more successful than others. One school, identified with Jeffrey Sachs, stresses the influence of geography. They are not the first to do so. French Enlightenment thinkers, such as Montesquieu and Rousseau, thought that tropical climates discouraged the hard work required for development. Adam Smith pointed to the relative prosperity of coastal regions compared to inland ones. Work by Sachs and his colleagues confirmed that countries that are landlocked and lack access to navigable waterways face a development handicap, while global production is highly concentrated in the coastal regions of temperate climate zones.[38] In tropical zones, the prevalence of diseases and the greater vulnerability of crops to pests are further disadvantages. Landlocked areas face higher costs of trade. But in recent decades, better health care and technological advances (such as air conditioning, air freight and, especially, scientific progress in tropical agronomy) have whittled away these handicaps. In Mato Grosso, deep in Brazil's tropical interior, farmers are now as productive as those in Iowa or Kansas (though their transport costs are higher). Sachs concedes that geographical factors are 'only part of the story', and that 'social and economic institutions are critical to long-term economic performance'. That contention has driven much recent work on development.

By institutions, economists mean any kind of rules, formal or informal, that constrain human behaviour, though these are normally embodied in political structures. They usually focus on formal rules, such as legal systems, and protection for private property and investment. An exhaustive study of Latin America's economic history by Rosemary Thorp and others stresses the interplay between institutions, geography and natural resource endowments.[39] It also notes that institution-building – the development of markets and a modern state – was crucial in determining the Latin American economies' 'capacity to change'. By that they mean the capacity both to absorb new technologies and to innovate and respond to shifting external conditions. A large cross-country econometric study, by Dani Rodrik, an economist at Harvard University, and two colleagues, found that institutional quality – measured by the perceptions of investors regarding the effectiveness of contract enforcement and protection of property rights – has a big impact on the income level of a country.[40] Deficient legal institutions do much to explain the shape of Latin American businesses, in which the family-owned diversified conglomerate has long been the dominant force and Anglo-Saxon-style entrepreneurship has struggled to take off. As Hernando de Soto, a Peruvian economist, argued in the 1980s, they are also the main explanation for the swollen 'informal' sector of unregistered businesses in Latin America.[41]

In a sense, it is a truism to say that institutions are crucial to development. A market economy is impossible without such institutions as a state, property rights and a legal system. Behind economic institutions lie political ones. As Francis Fukuyama explains in his magisterial two-volume study on political order:

> The difference in economic outcomes corresponds to a difference in political institutions. There is a strong correlation between the richest countries, in per capita terms, and those that have the strongest institutions: countries with effective, relatively uncorrupt states; enforceable, transparent legal rules; and open access to legal and political institutions.[42]

Fukuyama stresses that the evolution of modern democratic societies required the creation of an effective state, the rule of law and accountable government – and a balance between them. These are far from automatic: 'patrimonialism', or the natural human tendency to favour family or friends, is 'the default form of social organization' and constantly reasserts itself in the absence of strong countervailing incentives.[43]

Why does Latin America suffer from weak states and deficiencies in the rule of law? Many accounts seek the explanation in geography or history. Two American economists, Stanley Engerman and Kenneth Sokoloff, argue that different 'factor endowments' (meaning climatic suitability for particular crops, natural resources and the relative abundance of labour) played a crucial role in the different ways in which institutions were structured in the two halves of the Americas, and that this in turn had an effect on growth.[44] Thus, in Brazil and the Caribbean, the soils and climate favoured sugar, cotton and coffee, which were all of high value and attracted economies of scale. These crops stimulated the formation of large plantations and estates, and the import of slaves to work them. In Mexico and Peru, wealth came from exploiting mines and the initially large population of sedentary Indians. Again, large landholdings were the rule. In both cases, extreme inequalities of wealth and power were the norm. The institutions of colonial Latin America served to protect those inequalities. By contrast, in Canada and the northern British colonies (not the pre-Civil War South, whose economy was similar in many ways to those of Latin America), climatic conditions favoured mixed farming of grains and livestock, with no economies of scale. So, small family farms became the norm, there was less demand for slaves and a more equal society emerged. The authors argue that the more egalitarian society of the United States encouraged early industrialisation by providing a market and by making technical innovation easier.

Aníbal Quijano, a Peruvian Marxist sociologist, has argued that the Iberian conquest bequeathed a lasting power structure based on racial division. Political independence did not 'decolonise' Latin American societies; rather the continuing 'coloniality of power' in the region prevented the emergence of 'a genuine nation state' or democratic socie-ties.[45] There is some truth in this, especially for the nineteenth century, but considerable exaggeration: Quijano's argument denies the wide-spread *mestizaje* that has been a characteristic of Latin America, and the slow-burning social democratisation that has taken place in the region over the past century, accelerating in the past 30 years.

In *Why Nations Fail*, a best-selling work about development, Daron Acemoglu and James Robinson also stress the colonial legacy. They distinguish between 'inclusive' economic and political institutions, which protect property rights and foster innovation and technological change, and 'extractive' economic and political institutions which 'are designed to extract incomes and wealth from one subset of society to benefit a different subset'. In Latin America, they claim, 'the extractive political and economic institutions of the Spanish conquistadors ... have endured, condemning much of the region to poverty'.[46] This idea has some attraction in explaining both Latin America's inequality and the tendency of its businesses to 'rent-seeking' (i.e. the extraction of extra profits from monopolies). However, *Why Nations Fail* overstates its case. Its authors assert, for example, that the province of Acomayo in Cusco, Peru, is poorer than Calca, a neighbouring province, because it was subject to the *mita*, the forced-labour draft imposed by the conquis-tadors in the colonial period, while Calca was not.[47] In this case, geog-raphy supplies a much more powerful and obvious explanation: Calca includes the fertile valley of the Urubamba river (the 'Sacred Valley' of the Incas) and has good roads, while Acomayo is higher, bleaker and more remote. *Why Nations Fail* has little to say about why some Latin American countries are much more successful than others, or about why the region has changed so dramatically in recent decades. The authors accept that Latin American countries might develop inclusive political institutions through a process of citizen empowerment. In this regard, they cite Brazil, where they credit the Workers' Party (PT) with 'a sort of revolution in governance throughout the country'.[48] In fact, the crucial factors in creating a more inclusive democracy in Brazil were much broader democratic currents, embodied in the 1988 constitution (which the PT's representatives voted against, though they later signed it). Sadly, the Workers' Party, for all its earlier achievements, has become notorious for its role in a vast scheme for securing bribes from construction companies, a literally 'extractive' regime.

Not one explanation but several

It is a mistake to seek a single, overarching explanation for Latin America's relative failure, as the dependency theorists, the advocates of cultural explanations and the institutionalists all do in their differing ways. Much of the answer to the Latin American conundrum surely lies in the interplay between several sets of factors. History (the circumstances in which Latin America was colonised, became independent and related to the world economy), geography (climate, obstacles to transport, the presence of a large indigenous population) and political institutions have all contributed to moulding the region's fate. So have ideas and policies and social structure – the region's longstanding inequalities of income, wealth and power.[49]

These may have restricted growth not so much because they generated poor institutions per se but rather because they unleashed economically costly political conflicts which the region's political systems were unable to manage. After all, the two periods when the gap in average incomes between Latin America and the United States *widened* were during the wars of independence and their aftermath in the first half of the nineteenth century and the period from 1970 to 2000, when political conflicts engendered dictatorship and poor economic policies.[50]

Of course, the colonial order embodied inequality. But according to John Coatsworth, an economic historian, the extreme concentration of land, wealth and power in Latin America did not date from the colonial period, but rather from the second half of the nineteenth century, when the region's economies began to grow as a result of being drawn into the world economy in a first period of globalisation.[51] Inequality, he notes, did not in itself impede economic growth: governments cut deals with local and foreign investors in a kind of 'crony capitalism'. Yet those political arrangements condemned Latin America to a series of vicious circles. Perhaps the most important example concerns the labour market. In Latin America, as in the United States, land was abundant and labour was scarce. That should have led to higher wages and labour-saving innovations to increase productivity. This is what happened in farming in the United States. In Latin America, on the whole it did not (Argentina was a partial exception). Perhaps because of the prevalence of slavery and forced Indian labour during the colonial period, Latin American landowners were reluctant to pay higher wages, preferring continued coercion. There was a profusion of different forms of servitude associated with the *haciendas* or large estates. Indeed, the desire to gain control of labour, rather than the accumulation of land itself, was probably the main factor driving the expansion of *haciendas* at the expense of communal landholdings in the nineteenth century. These patterns in land and labour markets discouraged both innovation and the growth of the domestic market, and thus were an important factor delaying industrialisation.[52] Yet the diversity of experiences across the region is a caution against the notion of inevitability. To take just one example, Colombia's coffee boom rested in large part on family farmers: in 1932, 60 per cent of the country's production of coffee beans came from farms smaller than 12 hectares.[53]

In Europe and the United States, the benefits of industrialisation and economic growth were eventually widely spread because as productivity increased, trade unions secured higher wages and democratic governments established welfare states. That did not happen to the same degree in Latin America, where political leaders often blocked the incorporation of representatives of new social groups. Import-substitution industrialisation may have created a working class, but it also served to reduce competition and to maximise the gains and privileges of the politically well-connected. Inequality remained high and poverty widespread. The beneficiaries of the established order blocked the adoption of the reforms – of landholding, trade, taxes, credit and, above all, investment in education and health – which might have promoted greater equity. Yet such arrangements became harder and harder to sustain, leading to an increase in political instability and populist attempts to remedy inequality by expropriations of land or businesses (or the rhetorical threat of them).

The historical evolution of political institutions in Latin America has been unusual. In many parts of the world, effective states and the rule of law pre-dated accountable government. In East Asia, 'developmental states' in countries such as South Korea and Singapore drove surges of economic growth under regimes that were still authoritarian. In many Latin American countries, by contrast, to this day the state is weak and ineffective, partly because it is subject to patrimonial cronyism rather than the meritocratic bureaucracy proclaimed by Max Weber, the great German sociologist, as the hallmark of the modern state. One reason that Latin American states failed to modernise was the relative absence of wars between them; the region's conflicts have tended to be domestic.[54] As already noted in the previous chapter, the rule of law remains a work in progress in the region. But because most of Latin America became independent some two centuries ago, broadly speaking, under the aegis of the ideas of the European Enlightenment, constitutional government was, at least in theory, present at the creation of the new nations.

Laurence Whitehead argues that Latin America's unique history – of early colonialism, the collapse or obliteration of the prior indigenous political order, precocious independence, and relative isolation from geopolitical conflicts – generated among the region's elites both a 'bias toward modernity' and a tendency to promote innovations 'from above and without'. This orientation towards modernity was often conceived in terms of 'catching-up' with the United States or, recently, East Asia. Because of the existence of competing elites, specific modernising projects are often abandoned or simply deflected, rather than meeting frontal resistance. This leads to policy zig-zags and has turned Latin America into what Whitehead calls a 'mausoleum of modernities'. 'Because of the greater plasticity of institutional practice' in Latin America, compared with other regions of the world, 'a prevalent pattern is to launch an entirely new cycle of [policy] innovations and where possible to press them to the limit (or beyond).'[55] This formulation helps to explain why Latin America often seems to take policies to extremes, ranging from its dalliance with guerrilla warfare to its embrace of exaggerated levels of protection during the period of 'inward-looking development', its penchant for high inflation and the fervour with which it adopted the Washington Consensus. But it also highlights the region's openness to new ideas and the sense that it is always pregnant with possibility.

The burden of history is great in Latin America, but it is far from absolute. The advent of increasingly established and durable mass democracies in the region over the past 30 years has overturned much conventional wisdom. True, democracy involves particular problems of collective action. But at least in theory, it holds out the possibility of the peaceful resolution of conflicts, of lasting political stability, of swift problem-solving, and the speedy copying of successful models within the region. It thus offers Latin America an unprecedented opportunity to combine faster growth with greater equity. Rather than being determined solely by external, cultural or institutional factors, it is more fruitful to see Latin American history as a contest, between modernisers and reactionaries, between democrats and authoritarians, between the privileged and the excluded. That contest is the subject of the next three chapters.

CHAPTER THREE

The Seed of Democracy in the Land of the Caudillo

'Weapons have given you independence. Laws will give you freedom.' This pledge to his fellow countrymen from Francisco de Paula Santander, a Colombian independence leader, is inscribed above the doorway of the Palace of Justice in Bogotá's Plaza Bolívar, its paved main square. The inscription has an unintentionally ironic ring to it – and not only because freedom and the rule of law long proved elusive in Colombia and throughout Latin America. The current version of the palace, of blonde stone blocks, dates only from the 1990s. The previous building was destroyed by fire after guerrillas from the nationalist M-19 movement seized it in 1985, taking the Supreme Court hostage. The army, deploying armoured cars, retook the palace after hours of fighting; 95 people, including 11 Supreme Court justices, died in the confrontation, some executed after they had surrendered.[1] Not far away from the palace are other reminders of the violence that has intermittently dogged Colombia. Near the Congress building on the Carrera Septima, the city's main artery, a plaque marks the spot where General Rafael Uribe, a Liberal leader of the civil war of 1899–1902 – chronicled in García Márquez's *One Hundred Years of Solitude* – was assassinated a decade after he had made peace with a Conservative government. Half a dozen blocks to the north along the same avenue, a similar plaque marks a still more controversial assassination: Jorge Eliécer Gaitán, a crowd-pulling populist Liberal who seemed assured of victory in Colombia's 1950 presidential election, was shot at point-blank range by a lone assassin as he left his lawyer's office. His murder on 9 April 1948 triggered a yet bloodier civil war, known simply as *la violencia*, which claimed perhaps 180,000 lives. It is still debated whether the killer acted alone or at the behest of the Conservative opposition.

Though falling short of the abysmal standard set by many other parts of the world, notably Europe, political violence has been all too commonplace in Latin America over the past two centuries. In that regard, Colombia occupies a prominent role, though it is unusual partly because armed conflict continued into the twenty-first century even as it has died away everywhere else in the region over the past decade. It was only in 2016 that the Revolutionary Armed Forces of Colombia (FARC), a stubborn Stalinist insurgent group with links to drug trafficking, agreed to lay down its arms and demobilise (see Chapter 10). Paradoxically, Colombia has another claim to exceptionalism – one for which Santander and his followers can take much credit. The country has an unusually long democratic tradition: with only one brief exception, it has elected civilian governments since the 1830s, with suffrage arrangements that compared favourably with much of Europe. That statement requires one or two caveats. There were periodic civil wars, mainly between the Liberals and the Conservatives. The murder of Gaitán plunged the country not just into *la violencia*, but also into a short military dictatorship. Civilian rule was restored under a power-sharing pact between the two main parties. This lasted from 1958 to 1974; it brought stability, but restricted political competition. And the writ of government has never extended over the whole of a huge and fragmented territory with poor internal communications. Even so, Colombia, along with Costa Rica and Uruguay, stands out from the rest of Latin America: in all three countries, authoritarian dictatorships have been brief and rare. In much of the rest of the region, periods of civilian rule alternated with dictatorship; in some countries authoritarian rule was the norm at least until the 1980s.

As Santander's injunction makes plain, some of Latin America's independence leaders of the 1820s wanted to lay the foundations of democratic government. So why has democracy fared so poorly? This chapter will explore that question by surveying the region's history for the first century or so after independence. History still hangs heavy in Latin America: it is the stuff of contemporary politics, constantly invoked by Hugo Chávez or Mexico's Zapatista movement or by Argentina's Peronists, recalled in street names and statues. As Enrique Krauze, a Mexican historian, has said of his country, 'the weight of the past has sometimes been more present than the present itself. And a repetition of the past has sometimes seemed to be the only foreseeable future.'[2] That is especially true in Mexico, but it applies in many other Latin American countries, too. It is hard to analyse the prospects for consolidating democracy without regard to this history, to the lessons that Latin Americans draw from it, and the institutions, political traditions and economic practices which it has bequeathed to the region.

Independence at a price

The revolt of the 13 British colonies against King George III firmly planted democracy and Enlightenment republicanism in the western hemisphere. Along with the writings of the French *philosophes* and British economic liberalism, the political example set by the founding fathers of the United States exercised a strong intellectual appeal for many of the independence leaders in Latin America. It would not be until the end of the nineteenth century, the age of *arielismo*, that 'anti-Americanism' would take a firm hold in the region. Yet several things would hold the newly independent Latin American nations back, and impede them from following the United States on its path of democracy and development. These started with the nature of the independence struggle itself and the socio-economic order bequeathed by colonialism.

By comparison with the war of American Independence of 1776–82, the fight for independence in Spanish America was longer, bloodier and more destructive. It differed, too, in being triggered by events on the other side of the Atlantic. Napoleon Bonaparte's invasion of Iberia in 1807–08 and his overthrow of the Spanish Bourbon monarchy created a power vacuum at the heart of the empire. In 1808, as news of these developments reached first Caracas, and then Buenos Aires and other colonial centres, juntas were formed to exercise power. They proclaimed a nominal loyalty to Fernando VII, who was a captive in a French chateau. But discontent among the *criollos*, as American-born whites were known, had been building for at least a generation. At the start of the nineteenth century, they made up some 3.3 million of Spanish America's total population of 16.9 million.[3] They were outnumbered by 7.5 million Amerindians and 5.3 million mixed-race *mestizos*; there were also 776,000 blacks. Many *criollos* formed part of an incipient middle class of managers, lawyers and other professionals. Others formed part of the economic aristocracy of Spanish America, the owners of the great estates (*haciendas*) and the mines and the merchants and traders. But all of them were excluded from political power.

During his reign from 1759 to 1788, Carlos III, Fernando's grandfather, had made a vigorous effort to halt his country's long decline, and to reform its system of colonial rule. These 'Bourbon reforms' were in part a reaction to military defeat in the Seven Years' War (in which British fleets had captured Havana and Manila) and partly the result of new ways of thinking. The rationalism of the French Enlightenment had an important influence in Iberia. It challenged – albeit moderately at first – the Catholic conservatism that had held Spain and its colonies in its thrall since the Counter-Reformation. In place of the Habsburgs' 'composite monarchy', with its space for local autonomies, the Bourbons created a unified and centralised nation state. In Spanish America, the reforms involved more open trade (but only between ports within the empire, not, at least officially, with third countries), the weakening of the power of the Church (the Jesuits were expelled, for example), and a modest opening to new ideas. Above all, the reforms involved more efficient administration. But that meant a tightening of the control of Madrid over local affairs. In particular, the Bourbons restored a near monopoly of political and judicial office in the Americas to Spanish-born *peninsulares* (who numbered no more than 40,000 in the empire as a whole around 1800). Of 266 appointments to *audiencias* (high courts) from 1751 to 1808, only 62 were of *criollos*.[4] The *corregidores*, local *criollo* officials, were replaced by *intendentes*, a new corps of professional bureaucrats. And the Crown increased taxes, whose burden fell on the Indian population.

These reforms had two unintended effects. First, they helped to divide the rich and powerful in both Spain and its colonies into liberal and conservative camps – a division that would last in both places until at least the early twentieth century. In Spain itself, liberalism first showed its hand when the opponents of Napoleon convened in Cádiz in 1810 a parliament or *Cortes* – an institution with medieval origins but which had been snuffed out by centuries of absolutism. A majority of the members of the *Cortes* were reformers: they called themselves 'Liberals', the first time anywhere that the word was used as a political identity.[5] The *Cortes* proceeded to declare itself sovereign and issue a constitution which called for a parliamentary monarchy and wide male suffrage. Second, in Spanish America, the reforms rammed home to the *criollos* that they lacked the political power to defend their economic privilege. That gave rise to grievance, over the trade monopoly and taxes, for example. It also bred disquiet: some *criollos* came to see Spanish weakness as being as big a threat to their interests as Spanish power. They worried that a power vacuum at the top would threaten social order and private property.

They were haunted by a two-headed spectre of popular rebellion. In 1780, in the mountains south of Cusco, the former Inca capital, an Andean Indian *cacique* (local boss) and muleteer called José Gabriel Condorcanqui rebelled against the viceroy in Lima. He took the name of Túpac Amaru II, after the last Inca. His demands were a vague mixture of opposition to the Bourbon reforms, Inca revivalism and independence. After six months, he was captured and, along with his wife and co-leader of the rebellion, Micaela Bastidas, was executed with great cruelty in Cusco's main square. His insurgency, the largest rebellion in Spanish colonial history, extended over much of the southern half of the viceroyalty of Peru, as far as northern Argentina. Some 100,000 people died, and there was much destruction of property. Although Condorcanqui himself had stressed that his movement was a multiethnic one, it quickly degenerated into a race war. 'What began as an uprising developed into a guerrilla war and then deteriorated into a vicious bloodbath', according to Charles Walker's recent study.[6]

In 1791, inspired by the principles of the French Revolution, the black slaves of the sugar territory of Saint-Domingue, France's richest colony, revolted. 'It was a terrifying revelation of the explosive force of stifled savage hatred', as one account puts it.[7] In the first two months, 2,000 whites (or one in five) were killed, 180 sugar plantations and 900 coffee and indigo farms were destroyed and 10,000 slaves died in fighting, repression or famine. After a dozen years of violence and warfare, in which they successively defeated armies sent by Republican France, Spain, Britain and Napoleon, the former slaves triumphed, and in 1804 Saint-Domingue became Haiti – the second independent nation in the western hemisphere. But such was the destruction and the infighting among the patriots that the victory was a pyrrhic one.[8]

The memory of both these events meant that many *criollos*, especially in Peru and Mexico with their large Indian populations, did not at first favour cutting the link with Spain. Even Simón Bolívar, the great Liberator of northern South America, worried about the sheer numbers of the slaves and the mixed-blood *pardos* in his native Venezuela, stating: 'A great volcano lies at our feet. Who shall restrain the oppressed classes?'[9] Many historians have thus seen independence not as a progressive revolution in the mould of that of Washington and Jefferson, but rather as a conservative reaction. It was that – but it was more than that. Motives and interests within Spanish America varied, but the desire for the removal of colonial restraints was strong. It expressed itself first in Venezuela and the River Plate region, in part because they were the first to hear the tumultuous news from Spain, and in part because, as trading colonies, they had been hit hardest by the Bourbon reforms. In both places, the *criollos*, invoking a Spanish tradition of communalism with strong medieval roots, called a *cabildo* (town meeting), deposed the colonial authorities and proclaimed a governing junta. In Caracas, independence was declared in 1811; in the United Provinces of the Río de la Plata, from which would emerge Argentina, the declaration came five years later. Only in Mexico did the cry for independence come from below, from Miguel Hidalgo, a parish priest in the central Bajío region, who raised an Indian horde.

The struggle was almost everywhere protracted and convoluted, taking on the character of a civil war. The patriots were often divided, by local interest as much as by ideology. Social disorder, or the fear of it, caused many *criollos* to hesitate before breaking the bonds with Spain. The defeat of Napoleon saw Fernando restored to the Spanish throne in 1814, able to dispatch reinforcements to America. An expedition of 10,000 seasoned troops reached Venezuela in 1815, the darkest period for the patriot cause across the region. These were partly offset by the arrival of 6,000 mainly British and Irish volunteers who fought as mercenaries with Bolívar's armies. This force apart, Latin America lacked the kind of external support that France had offered to Washington in the United States.

Two things combined finally to prise South America from Spain's grasp. The first was better strategy and organisation on the patriot side. In southern South America, José de San Martín, an Argentine who had served for two decades as a regular officer in the Spanish army before joining the patriot cause, pulled off a bold strategic move. He organised and led a force of 5,000 troops across the Andes to Chile, through snowy 4,000-metre-high passes, and surprised the Spanish forces there. Having secured Chile, he embarked in the ships of Thomas Cochrane, a swashbuckling British admiral who served the patriot cause as a mercenary, and landed his army in Peru. He (temporarily) freed Lima, which until the Bourbon reforms had been the capital of the whole of Spanish South America and remained a royalist bastion. San Martín's forces joined up with those of Simón Bolívar. Bolívar himself had recovered from a rout in his native Venezuela in 1812. By allying with the *llaneros* (cowboys) of the Venezuelan plains, and through indefatigable generalship, including a march up and over the Andes to Bogotá even more demanding than that of San Martín, he had freed northern South America. Spain's last redoubt in Peru was surrounded and would fall to a multinational army under Bolívar. In 1826, the last remaining Spanish troops surrendered to his forces in Upper Peru (soon to become Bolivia).

The second factor was the twists and turns of peninsular politics, as power in Spain's restored monarchy oscillated between incipient parliamentary liberalism and absolutist reaction. Spanish strategy was misguided as well as confused. The liberals failed to seek compromises, such as home rule, until it was far too late. Royalist repression was often self-defeating. The Spanish forces sequestered the property of their opponents and, in Colombia for example, executed a number of patriots. On the other hand, the advent of a liberal government in Spain after 1820 prompted the conservative *criollos* of Mexico to opt for independence. The disorderly Indian armies led by Hidalgo and another radical priest, José María Morelos, had rampaged across half the country to the alarm of the *criollos*, before being defeated and their leaders killed. In 1821, Agustín de Iturbide, a *criollo* general who had fought for Spain, made common cause with the remaining rebel leaders, proclaimed independence and ruled briefly as emperor of Mexico.

Only in Brazil was independence a less-than-traumatic affair. When Napoleon invaded Iberia, Britain arranged to ship the Portuguese monarch and his court across the Atlantic to Rio de Janeiro. After hostilities ceased in Europe, King João VI returned, with some tardiness, to Lisbon. His eldest son, left behind as regent, quickly realised that the price of maintaining monarchy in Brazil was independence, which he himself declared in 1822. Though war with Portugal followed, it was brief and mainly settled at sea by the skill of Cochrane.[10]

The armies involved in the independence wars were not large: Bolívar never led more than 10,000 men into battle. But in some places almost two decades of near-continuous fighting exacted a heavy toll. Mines had been flooded, farms looted and bridges destroyed. In 1821, the coin produced by the mint in Mexico City from the country's silver mines totalled just 6 million pesos, down from 26 million pesos a year before the wars.[11] Recovery would take decades. With elegance but perhaps some exaggeration, Felipe Fernández-Armesto, an Anglo-Spanish historian, has recently summarised the comparative impact:

> the independence wars were, in short, the making of the United States and the ruin of much of the rest of the Americas . . . To fight the wars, all the affected (Spanish-American) states had to sacrifice liberties to *caudillismo* and civil values to militarism . . . People in the Americas often speak of the chaotic politics, democratic immaturity, and economic torpor of Latin American tradition as if they were an atavistic curse, a genetic defect, a Latin legacy. Really, like everything else in history, they are products of circumstance, and of the circumstances, in particular, in which independence was won.[12]

The colonial inheritance

Apart from its costly birth, the second handicap faced by newly independent Latin America was the legacy of the Iberian colonial order, which ill-equipped it for democracy and development. Colonial Latin America differed radically from New England or Canada (though less so from the more southerly of Britain's American colonies). In the sixteenth century, the *conquistadores* had brought with them a kind of militarised feudalism. This had been honed in the *reconquista*, the seven centuries of intermittent war that had driven the Moors from Spain. In 1492, in one of history's more striking coincidences of date, Columbus made his first landfall in the 'new world', just as the Muslim emirate of Granada, the last Moorish foothold in Iberia, was overrun, completing the *reconquista*.[13] The Spanish took two other sixteenth-century philosophies across the Atlantic. One was a militant, intolerant Catholicism, derived partly from the *reconquista* but given more force by the Counter-Reformation with its Inquisition and apparatus of censorship. The Spanish Crown exercised strict control over who settled in the Americas – indeed it went so far as to obtain a papal bull to uphold its authority to do so. In sharp contrast with English-speaking North America, no heretics, dissidents or freethinkers needed to apply. The second guiding philosophy was mercantilism. This doctrine held that gold and silver bullion was the ultimate source of wealth – and not merely another commodity – and that trade was a zero-sum game. So Spain imposed a rigid monopoly of trade with its colonies, and discouraged the production of items that might compete with its own farmers and artisans. The backbone of the colonial economy became the *hacienda* (the large landed estate with resident serfs), the plantation and the mine. The Crown had swiftly imposed central authority on the *conquistadores*. The principal institution of government was the *audiencia*, a judicial body but one that was presided over by the king's representative – the viceroy or captain general – whom it also advised. Though there were also town councils (*cabildos*), their responsibilities were minor. During the seventeenth century, cash-strapped monarchs resorted to the sale of office to raise funds. What had been an impressively 'modern' structure of government under Philip II degenerated into a patrimonial arrangement in which rich *criollos* came to dominate, in their own interest, the *audiencias* and many administrative posts in the Americas. Several familiar characteristics of Latin American government thus date from the colonial period: centralisation, patrimonialism and the blurring of executive and judicial authority.[14] To this list one might add a regulatory mania. The Crown issued a constant flow of decrees – over 400,000 by 1635, though they were later codified into 6,400.[15] Legislation in Latin America often embodies an ideal world, impossible to carry out in practice. That gave rise to a famous response among colonial officials: *obedezco pero no cumplo* (I obey but I do not comply). The result was less the rule of law than the realm of discretion, giving rise to corruption and politically influenced justice.[16]

Unlike the Pilgrim Fathers (and the Portuguese in Brazil), the Spaniards conquered territories with large populations of native Americans. In Mexico's central plateau, in Guatemala and in Peru, these had formed sophisticated and wealthy societies based on sedentary farming. At the time of their respective European conquests, Latin America may have contained some 20 million people, compared with some 3 million spread across what would become Canada and the United States. Millions of native Americans died, above all from disease, but also from forced labour and conquest itself. But one of the enduring differences between the two Americas is that many more Amerindians survived in Latin America. The Spaniards quickly realised that they needed Indian labour. Colonial Spanish America became a caste society: a small group of large landowners, officials and clergy ruled over a much larger population of Indians. Spanish absolutism recognised some rights (known as *fueros*) for its subjects, but these were exercised by groups, not individuals. The Church, the army and militia, some professions and the Indians had their own *fueros*. Indeed, the Spaniards found it convenient to administer the Indian population through *curacas* or *caciques*, local Indian leaders, many of whose privileges were left intact (this arrangement came to be known as the *República de Indios*). Many of their charges suffered servitude in mines and *haciendas*. Others continued to live in traditional communities, whose lands were given some legal protection, but they paid tribute to their new overlords. Nevertheless, as J.H. Elliott points out in his masterly comparative study, indigenous people in Spanish America 'were given at least a limited space of their own' in a philosophically inclusive society, while their counterparts in British North America were simply excluded.[17]

This arrangement was basically stable. Pre-conquest Indian societies were themselves rigidly hierarchical: the Indians thus swapped a local master for a European one – although the Incas, in particular, had been more paternalist rulers than the Spaniards. The Conquest had involved the brutal imposition of a new ideological order, as well as a political one. In Mexico City, recent excavation has revealed how the Spaniards built their cathedral on top of part of the Aztec *Templo Mayor*; in Cusco, a Dominican monastery stands on top of the *Koricancha* (the temple of the sun), the holiest shrine of the Inca empire. The Indian gods had failed, and that of the *conquistadores* had triumphed. No wonder the Indians would embrace the Catholic religion, while seeking to infuse it with their own practices, beliefs and images (such as Mexico's Virgin of Guadalupe). No wonder, too, that some of Latin America's Indian peoples to this day remain suspicious of change and modernisation. Their history since the Conquest has been one of enforced submission, followed by more or less successful adaptation, punctuated by occasional outbursts of rebellion, often of great violence. In places where the Indian population was wiped out (Cuba, Hispaniola), or where Indians were relatively few, nomadic and difficult to subjugate (Brazil), the colonists turned to the mass import of African slaves instead.

Inequality was a fundamental and integral aspect of colonial societies, whether they were based on serfdom or slavery or both. 'Perhaps nowhere is inequality more shocking', noted Alexander von Humboldt, an aristocratic German scientist and traveller, in his essay on New Spain (Mexico) published in 1811. 'The architecture of public and private buildings, the women's elegant wardrobes, the high society atmosphere: all testify to an extreme social polish which is in extraordinary contrast to the nakedness, ignorance and coarseness of the population.'[18] Spanish colonial theory did not entertain the idea of racial integration. It envisaged racial separation, partly in order to protect the Indian population from the *criollos*. Spaniards, *criollos* and Indians lived under separate laws. Yet over the centuries, much racial mixing occurred. Men always greatly outnumbered women among Iberian colonists, and overwhelmingly so at the start. Miscegenation resulted in a large number of *mestizos* and *mulatos*, *pardos* and *zambos*. In that sense, Spanish colonial society was more fluid than that of British North America. The colonial period saw 'the incomplete development of a heterogeneous hispanic-indigenous-*mestizo-criollo* society, which to this day exists in ferment', in the words of Jorge Basadre, Peru's greatest historian.[19] This was even more the case in Mexico.

Even so, the underlying socio-economic divides, broadly speaking, ran along racial lines. The fears, resentments and ignorance which racial difference generated made that divide all the harder to break down. At the heart of the history of Latin America since independence has been the tension between the beneficiaries of that divide and the gathering forces of socio-political *mestizaje*.

The challenge of geography

While Brazil remained intact, by 1830 mainland Spanish America had fragmented into 15 separate countries.[20] Given its size, this was inevitable. The new republics extended over an area stretching from the borders of Oregon and Oklahoma to the stony desert of Patagonia. But while some of the new countries, such as those in Central America, looked too small to be viable, others were too big and unwieldy quickly to become coherent nation states. The most obvious example was Mexico. It would lose half its original territory, as first Texas declared itself independent and then the United States waged a successful war of conquest in 1846–48, seizing northern Mexico in the name of its 'manifest destiny' to occupy the North American continent.[21] Meanwhile,

Yucatán was for practical purposes all but independent during the first half of the nineteenth century. In 1849, it asked to be annexed by the United States, but was turned down. It had no road or rail link with Mexico City until as late as the 1950s. Until then, its ties with New Orleans and Havana, via steamer services, were closer than those with the Mexican capital.

Geography placed huge obstacles in the way of development. Distances are vast: Brazil is as large in area as the continental United States, while Argentina (with 37 million people today) is almost as big as India (with 1 billion). The Andes are a formidable barrier to communication, as is the Amazon basin. Most of the more populated parts of Latin America lack navigable rivers. There are no significant ones on the Pacific Coast at all. In South America, three mighty river systems – the Amazon, the Paraná and the Orinoco – traverse the continent from the Andean watershed to the Atlantic. Only in the twenty-first century have the Paraná-Paraguay and stretches of the Amazon been turned into reliable waterways for the transport of bulk cargoes.[22] In the high altitudes of the Andes, life is harsh.[23] To survive, farmers must exploit microclimates at varying altitudes, as well as grapple with erratic rainfall. To do so demands a high degree of collective organisation – a world away from the family homestead of bucolic New England. Tropical lowlands pose a different set of challenges, including disease, flooding and hurricanes. While some parts of Latin America get little or no rain, others get far too much: some 70 per cent of Mexico's total annual average rainfall lands on the state of Tabasco, for example. To cap it all, earthquakes are relatively common along the region's western mountain spine, and so are volcanic eruptions. Mexico, Central America and the Caribbean suffer frequent hurricanes.

Yet Latin America also possesses geographical advantages. These include abundant natural resources and much good land. The Pampas of Argentina, Uruguay and southern Brazil form some of the world's most fertile farmland, blessed with a temperate climate. For much of the nineteenth century, land was abundant in relation to population (which is variously estimated to have totalled only 15–20 million at independence). But transport difficulties only began to be eased by the coming of railways in the second half of the nineteenth century, and later by air transport, which flourished as early as the 1920s in countries such as Brazil and Colombia. Contrary to nationalist myth, the railways did much to develop the domestic economy, as well as exports. In southern Brazil, for example, railways gave a big boost to commercial farming aimed at supplying the growing cities.[24] Even so, in the larger countries, communications between the capital and outlying areas often remained poor until the mid-twentieth century. This stimulated regional political movements and engendered persistent localism, as well as impeding internal trade. 'Its own extent is the evil from which the Argentine Republic suffers . . . wastes containing no human dwelling are, generally speaking, the unmistakeable boundaries between its several provinces', complained Domingo Faustino Sarmiento, later president of Argentina, in *Facundo*, his mid-nineteenth-century tract against the evils of *caudillismo*.[25]

Caudillos and modernisers

Spain's monopoly of trade and high political office during the colonial period meant that the new republics had no experience of self-government, as Bolívar bitterly complained. It would take many of them half a century or more to achieve a degree of stability. Intermittent internal conflict added to the damage inflicted by the independence wars. When they were not merely struggles for local or national power, these battles were over how the new republics should be governed – and by and for whom. Early efforts to establish a degree of popular sovereignty failed almost everywhere. Most of the new republics lapsed into three decades or more of rule by *caudillos* or strongmen, most of them army officers of the independence campaigns. Some were enlightened; more were not.

Many writers on Latin America, of both left and right, have stressed the continuities rather than changes associated with independence. Rule by a small 'white' elite and the basic inequalities of colonial society were preserved. In some ways they were aggravated: the liberal commitment to private property weakened some of the legal protections for Indian communal land. In many countries, that would allow some degree of land grabbing by *hacendados* throughout the rest of the nineteenth century. Together with mine owners and large-scale traders, the landowners would form an oligarchy, holding political as well as economic power. Yet to stop there is misleading. The removal of the Spanish monopolies on political office, trade and the economy did usher in a new order, but this happened gradually and by no means smoothly. Overall, 'Latin America was a far more egalitarian place after independence than before. Indians and *mestizos* rose to positions of power all over Spanish America', in the words of David Bushnell and Neill Macaulay, two historians of the nineteenth century in the region.[26] The newly independent countries all adopted constitutions based, broadly speaking, on liberal principles. This in itself was notable, given that most of Europe was still under the sway of absolutism. The constitutions were heavily influenced by that of the United States, by its Bill of Rights and the Declaration of the Rights of Man of the French Revolution. Though suffrage was limited by property qualifications, usually to only a small percentage of adult males, so it was in Britain and the United States in this period.

In Brazil, Dom Pedro I established a liberal constitutional monarchy which included elements of representative parliamentary government. This involved indirect elections – deputies were picked by provincial electors, and senators chosen by the emperor. Suffrage was relatively wide for the times, with some 11 per cent of the total population able to vote for the provincial electors in 1872.[27] According to Bolívar Lamounier, a Brazilian political scientist, the grafting of this representative element onto the remnants of Portuguese absolutism was essential to maintain government control over such a large country, riven with bloody local rebellions in the first 30 years after independence.[28] Under the first emperor's long-reigning and Brazilian-born son, Dom Pedro II (1831–89), this incipient parliamentary system worked well for several decades. In the view of Thomas Skidmore, a scholar of Brazil, it offered a political environment comparable to that of Victorian Britain in a much poorer and less developed country.[29] The emperor was a fair and honest ruler, an urbane and learned man who took the trouble to learn Guaraní, the most widely spoken indigenous language. But the last two decades of his rule, following war with Paraguay which he pursued implacably, was marked by political stagnation. In 1868, Dom Pedro dismissed a Liberal administration, replacing it with a Conservative one. Thereafter, the emperor increasingly became a hostage to advisers who were bent on delaying change – and the abolition of slavery in particular – as long as possible. This doomed Latin America's only experiment with monarchy. But the Brazilian empire's notable achievement was to keep the vast country united – it was potentially as fissiparous as Spanish America – and to implant a representative tradition.

In the new Spanish-speaking republics, as in Brazil, the basic political split was between liberals, like Santander, who wanted to move swiftly to dismantle the colonial order, and conservatives, such as Bolívar became, who were worried about instability and disorder ('governability', one might say). Across the region, the role of the Church became a battleground. It was seen by liberals as a reactionary bastion and as an obstacle to new ways of thinking, and by conservatives as a powerful force for social order. Another divide was over federalism: liberals tended to favour decentralisation. Argentina was an exception: there federalism was seen as a way of recognising regional differences, and of neutralising the overweening economic power of Buenos Aires, home of liberalism and jealous monopoliser of lucrative customs revenues. Looked at through another optic, liberals were standard-bearers of modernisation and of French and British Enlightenment thought, while conservatives defended a paternalist social order derived from Church and colony. Such divisions cut across class: artisans and Indians were as likely to support conservatives as liberals, partly because liberals tended to oppose communal ownership of land and to favour lower tariffs on imports. This division is an enduring one. It is reflected in part in two archetypal figures in Latin American politics: the *caudillo* and what one might call the modernising technocrat. The modernisers were not always liberals, though they often were, while the *caudillos* were characteristically, but not necessarily, conservatives, and some (though by no means all) were social paternalists.

Many elements of both these archetypal figures were awkwardly united in the person of Simón Bolívar. He was 'an exceptionally complex man, a liberator who scorned liberalism, a soldier who disparaged militarism, a republican who admired monarchy', in the view of John Lynch, one of his biographers.[30] Bolívar was a cultivated man. He had spent several years in Europe – he famously swore to liberate South America while visiting Rome with his tutor and friend, Simón Rodríguez. While on campaign, his aides lugged around a large trunk of books: Voltaire and Montesquieu were among his favourite reading, but the trunk also included Locke and Bentham.[31] He was a great correspondent, and wrote with clarity and vigour. He admired the systems of government of both the United States and Britain, the most democratic of the day. He found slavery personally abhorrent. He argued passionately for co-operation among the new republics, and is rightly invoked today as a precursor of Latin American integration. He attempted to maintain Venezuela, Nueva Granada (present-day Colombia) and Ecuador united as a single country, Gran Colombia. And yet his chief political legacy is a yearning for strong government and paternalist authoritarianism. He was insistent that without a strong central authority the new republics would fall apart. Though he subscribed to Montesquieu's doctrine of the separation of powers, what he most liked about the French philosopher was his insistence that laws and institutions should be adapted to a country's geography and culture. From Rousseau, he took the idea that it is the role of the leader to interpret and represent 'the general will'. In other words, strong and effective leadership is self-legitimating and when necessary should override institutions that guarantee individual liberty. Thus, much as Bolívar admired the United States, he once said that he would rather see the Latin American republics adopt the Koran than US federalism, which was 'too perfect'. In South America 'events . . . have demonstrated that perfectly representative institutions are not appropriate to our character, our customs, and our current level of knowledge and experience', he wrote in 1815.[32]

The definitive statement of Bolívar's political thought came a decade later, when he was asked to write a constitution for a new republic which had taken his name: Bolivia. This document had some features of liberal democracy: nominally at least, the executive, legislature and judiciary were to be separated, and were to be complemented by a fourth 'moral' power, a 'chamber of censors' with a scrutinising function. But Bolívar also included a hereditary senate and a president for life, who would have far-reaching emergency powers and the right to name his successor. This is constitutional monarchy in all but name. This document was swiftly discarded by Bolivia. In 1828, Bolívar assumed the dictatorship of Gran Colombia. He proceeded to undo some of the liberal reforms introduced during his long absence campaigning in Peru by Santander, his vice-president, from whom he had become estranged. Bolívar restored the Indian tribute and the privileges of the Church and banned the works of Bentham. Despite his own views on the matter, he never tried to force through a ban on slavery. After Gran Colombia split into its three constituent parts in 1830, Santander, a pragmatic liberal, was elected president of Colombia and is the founder of its democratic tradition. But he is long forgotten outside his own country. It is the great Liberator who still casts a shadow today.

Bolívar was not himself a *caudillo*: he always sought to institution-alise authority.[33] But his name has long been invoked and misused by authoritarian rulers of far less noble qualities, and far less sense. Venezuelan dictators, starting in the late nineteenth century, found it expedient to establish an official cult of Bolívar. His remains were repatriated in 1842, and in 1876 placed in a giant casket which rests in the national Pantheon, a former church a few blocks up the hill from his birthplace in the centre of Caracas. The latest exponent of the cult was Hugo Chávez, who claimed to be implementing a 'Bolivarian revolution' in Venezuela. Chávez included some elements from the Bolivian constitution (such as the 'moral power') in Venezuela's charter of 2001. He showed a Bolivarian disregard for checks on executive power.[34] But there is no reason to believe that Bolívar, the patrician aristocrat, the instinctive liberal turned pragmatic conservative who admired British parliamentary monarchy, the man who tried to sell his mines to British investors, would have felt represented by Chávez's militarist populism. This, Lynch observed tartly, was a 'modern perversion of the cult' which distorted Bolívar's ideas; at least past dictators 'more or less respected the basic thought of the Liberator, even when they misrepresented its meaning.'[35]

Where Bolívar was arguably too deferential to what he saw as Latin American weaknesses, the modernising technocrats paid insufficient heed to local realities. They wanted to make the new republics in the image of Europe or the United States. One of the first to try to do so was Bernardino Rivadavia in the province of Buenos Aires, the most important of the (still dis-) United Provinces of the Río de la Plata, the forerunner of Argentina. Rivadavia, a merchant and lawyer, was an admirer of Jeremy Bentham's utilitarianism. He dominated Argentine politics for much of the 1820s, first as chief minister and then as president of Buenos Aires province. He and his supporters founded the University of Buenos Aires and other educational establishments, endowing them with a scientific bias absent from Spain's scholastic educational tradition. He promoted the theatre and other cultural enterprises. Rivadavia abolished the ecclesiastical and military *fueros*, restricted church landholdings, transferred some church welfare activities to a state-sponsored body, established freedom of worship, and cut the size of the army. He signed a trade treaty with Great Britain. In a debate that echoes to this day, his critics blamed the problems of the textile and wine producers of the interior on Rivadavia's commitment to free trade. But the problems of these rudimentary local industries had more to do with inefficiency and distance from markets than with imports. When Juan Manuel de Rosas, a dictator, increased tariffs in 1835, the response of local industries was 'slow and feeble'.[36] From 1870 onwards, policies of Rivadavian inspiration aimed at promoting trade, foreign investment and European immigration would eventually see Argentina become one of the richest countries in the world. Less happily, Rivadavia's government contracted a loan from Britain, spent it on war with Brazil over Uruguay, and quickly defaulted. His liberalism was tinged with elitism. He tried to control wages, rather than leave them to the market. And he handed out the best lands of the Pampas on long leases which in practice became grants. Intended to create a middle class of farmers, the measure had the opposite effect: by 1830, just 538 beneficiaries had received a total of 20 million acres (8 million hectares) of some of the world's best farmland. Rivadavia drew up a constitution that would have given Argentina a strong central government – something that conservative federalists in Buenos Aires province, and especially beyond it, were not prepared to accept. In 1827, he headed into exile – like so many subsequent would-be reformers.

Liberal achievements and frustrations

The Rivadavians failed partly because they had little understanding of the difficulties of the Argentine interior, and partly because they were simply ahead of their time. Across many of the Spanish-speaking republics, the Liberals' day would not dawn again until after the 1848 revolution in Europe, which had almost as great an impact in Latin America as in the old continent. In the following three decades, the Liberals – and by now they called themselves thus – would return to power in many countries and carry through much of the unfinished business of independence. They laid the basis for republics based on civilian democratic politics and popular sovereignty, even if much of the population was still excluded. In many countries, slavery and the Indian tribute were finally abolished, along with the *fueros* of the Church and the army. Elected civilian presidents began to replace the *caudillos*, although the vote was generally restricted to adult men and subject to property and literacy qualifications.[37]

This new flowering of liberalism in the third quarter of the nine-teenth century was generally pragmatic and reformist. It coincided with, and was strengthened by, the emergence of Latin America from its post-independence economic torpor. Innovations in transport and commu-nications begat a first age of globalisation, in which the region enjoyed sustained export-led growth as a supplier of commodities to the indus-trial world. Coffee transformed the economies of Brazil, Colombia, Venezuela and Central America; grain, meat and wool did the same for Argentina and Uruguay; oil for Mexico and Venezuela; mining for Chile, Peru, Bolivia and Mexico; and sugar for Cuba, Mexico and Peru. A new urban middle class arose – of merchants, lawyers and doctors – which, though still numerically small, was socially significant.

In Mexico, where the mark of Church and colony went deeper than almost anywhere else, the Liberal triumph was heavily contested. In the wake of military defeat by the United States in 1846–48, Benito Juárez, a Zapotec Indian from Oaxaca, beat Bolivia's Evo Morales to the title of Latin America's first elected president of indigenous descent by more than 150 years. Juárez's Liberals abolished the military and church *fueros*, and banned the Church from owning property. Their Conservative opponents made the fatal mistake of appealing for outside help: France's Louis Napoleon responded by installing Maximilian, a Habsburg prince and his distant relative, as emperor. The Liberals won the resulting civil war, and the hapless Habsburg perished by firing squad.

Even in Peru, where military men had been politically dominant, in 1872 Manuel Pardo, a young businessman, was elected as the country's first-ever civilian president, at the head of a promising Civil Party. His election marked the triumph of a new generation of liberals, exempli-fied by Francisco Laso, a painter and writer. In a country that had preserved much of the caste society of the colonial period, Laso chal-lenged racial exclusion. His painting *The Three Races, or Equality before the Law*, which today hangs in Lima's Museum of Art, shows a rich young white boy playing cards with two girls, one black and the other Indian. The girls are presumably servants. Cards in hand, they watch with quiet resignation. But the message of the picture is that they are all equal players of the game. Pardo cut the military down to size, reformed taxes and began to give Peru the rudiments of a modern state. But much of this progress was undone when Chile declared war on Peru and Bolivia in a scramble for the nitrates of the Atacama. Chile won partly because it had British support, but mainly because it was a better-organised state. That achievement was the legacy of Diego Portales, a conservative, who, like Bolívar, favoured strong government. Portales was a minister, but never sought the presidency: he believed in the rule of law rather than of individuals. In the 1830s, he laid the foundations of a stable political system.

Portales's work was continued and humanised by Andrés Bello (1781–1865), a tough-minded Liberal who, in a remarkable life, did more than anyone to create the software of nation-building in Latin America.[38] Born in Venezuela, Bello was a polymath who was briefly Bolívar's tutor and then his colleague in a mission in 1810 to seek British support for the patriot cause. Bello stayed on in London for the next 19 years, serving as an often-unpaid envoy for Latin American independence. He spent the second half of his life in Chile, where he ran the foreign ministry and was the founding rector of the University of Chile. He drew up the country's civil code, which proclaimed the equality of citizens before the law. It was quickly copied in half a dozen countries in the region. Bello also wrote an influential treatise on international law, arguing for the equal status of nations, and a best-selling Spanish grammar for Latin Americans. Like Bolívar, Bello believed that strong political institutions were essential to thwart anarchy and for liberty to flourish. But whereas Bolívar argued that the new republics needed the discipline of top-down authority, Bello thought that to succeed they needed to create citizens, through universal public education and, above all, the rule of law ('our true *patria*', he once wrote).

The Liberals did not hold sway everywhere. In Colombia, Conservative governments held power from 1885 until 1930. Venezuela and several Central American countries remained in the grip of dictators, although several of these claimed allegiance to liberalism. In many countries, *caudillos* survived as local strongmen. Much as some Liberals regretted this, they could not be wished away. The *caudillos* embodied 'the will of the popular masses, the choice of the people'; they were the 'natural representatives' of the 'pastoral classes', according to Juan Bautista Alberdi, the pragmatic architect of Argentina's 1853 constitution (which remains largely in force today).[39] Although this constitution gave the federal government the power to intervene in the affairs of the provinces in exceptional circumstances, the long-term price of Argentine unity and internal peace was to allow the *caudillos* to preserve their fiefdoms in the poorer provinces of the interior. That price would prove a heavy one. Much the same went for several other countries.

The liberal era lasted, broadly speaking, from the mid-nineteenth century until 1930. For all its limitations, the liberal order represented important progress. In many countries, relatively enlightened civilian governments made efforts to tackle Latin America's huge deficit in education and transport infrastructure. Even so, in 1900 three-quarters of the 70 million Latin Americans still lived in the countryside, three-quarters were illiterate and average life expectancy was only 40 years.[40] Shaky as they were, from these foundations there was certainly a chance that Latin America might have gone on to create genuine democracies and sustained development. Yet three things were to conspire to frustrate that chance. First, before it could consolidate its triumph, Latin American liberalism mutated into a new and more authoritarian political philosophy: positivism. Second, Latin America's underlying inequalities meant that the benefits of economic growth did not reach much of the population. And third, from the outbreak of the First World War, the world economy entered upon three decades of turbulence, while economic development and incipient industrialisation in the Latin American countries brought new social tensions.

Order and progress

In the history of political ideas in Europe, positivism is little more than a footnote. In parts of Latin America, it looms large. It is derived chiefly from Auguste Comte, a French social theorist of the early nineteenth century. He saw the key to progress as lying in order and 'scientific development', to be implemented by an enlightened intellectual elite. This would be echoed in Rodó's elitist 'regeneration'. And it suited the privileged groups of Latin America admirably, seeming as it did to justify restrictions on popular sovereignty. Positivism did promote industrial development, foreign investment and reforms, for example, of education. But like Bolívar's thinking, it was another version of enlightened despotism and provided a new justification for authoritarianism. Not for the last time in Latin America, economic and political liberalism were divorced, as modernising technocrats were happy to serve conservative dictators who gave them a free rein in economic policy. Like General Augusto Pinochet, Chile's dictator, or Alberto Fujimori,

Peru's ruler from 1990 to 2000, the positivists championed economic freedom, but not political freedom.

When linked to the social Darwinism of Herbert Spencer, positivism seemed to provide a scientific justification for inequality – and indeed for racism.[41] In the late nineteenth century, conventional wisdom among educated Latin Americans was that the region's Indian and black peoples were a brake on progress. One consequence was the promotion of immigration from Europe, though there were other, more powerful motives for that: South America in particular was sparsely populated. 'To govern is to populate', declared Alberdi. Between 1880 and 1915, Argentina received 4.2 million immigrants (chiefly from Spain and Italy) and Brazil 2.9 million (mainly from Italy and Eastern Europe). Though this represented only 23 per cent of the 31 million migrants who crossed the Atlantic in this period (70 per cent went to the United States), it was a significant number for the receiving countries. In 1914, around 30 per cent of Argentina's population was foreign-born, a much higher percentage than in the United States.[42]

Positivism was especially influential in the two largest countries of Latin America. In Mexico, it buttressed ideologically the long dictatorship of Porfirio Díaz (from 1884 to 1910), who had first been elected in 1876 as a Liberal. A tough and shrewd *mestizo*, from Oaxaca like Juárez (for whom he had fought against the French), Díaz gave Mexico its first period of stability since the viceroyalty. During the 'Porfiriato', a team of modernising technocrats known as the *cientificos* (scientists) proceeded to provide Mexico with the rudiments of a modern economy and railway system. Díaz respected constitutional forms, duly having himself elected president every four years. But in the words of a contemporary observer, he had 'demolished the apparatus of government and concentrated all the subdivided power into his own hands'. Another contemporary, Justo Sierra, an educationalist, gave Díaz a friendly warning: 'there are no institutions in the Republic of Mexico – there is a man'.[43] Díaz expanded and professionalised the national police force, the *rurales*, who pacified the countryside. But he visited terrible repression on Indians, in the far north-west and the south-east, who stood in the way of progress. Social conditions remained grim: in 1900 one child in two died in its first year, while 84 per cent of Mexicans were illiterate.[44]

In Brazil, positivism inspired the very creation of the republic. As Dom Pedro II clung to his coterie of conservative landholding advisers, agitation against slavery increasingly took on republican tones under the aegis of a group of positivist lawyers and writers. Their leader, Benjamin Constant, lectured in the military academy and influenced a generation of army officers. When Dom Pedro finally yielded and agreed to abolition in 1888, it was too late. His action alienated conservatives from the monarchy, while coming far too late to satisfy liberal elements in the growing cities. Within months, a bloodless military coup ushered in a republic. Brazil adopted a new flag emblazoned with the positivist slogan 'Order and Progress'. Though the new republic was nominally a civilian democracy, it was a disappointingly elitist affair, dominated by the newly rich coffee barons of the two most prosperous states, São Paulo and Minas Gerais. Though voting became direct, suffrage was more restricted than under the empire. At the local level, positivists dispensed with many of the trappings of democracy. State governors gave unconditional support to the federal president; in return, their local Republican parties were given a free hand. Two positivists, Júlio de Castilhos and his disciple, Antônio Augusto Borges de Medeiros, ran the southern state of Rio Grande do Sul from 1893 to 1928. They left as their monument in the state capital, Porto Alegre, a fine collection of public buildings in the French *belle époque* style – a provincial version of the architectural splendour of Porfirian Mexico City and oligarchical Buenos Aires. These buildings were doubtless intended to persuade the *gaúchos*, as the local inhabitants call themselves, that they were well on the way to creating a new Paris in the Pampas. But positivist certainties were to suffer a bruising encounter with social realities in Brazil. In 1899, a revolt by an obscure millenarian preacher, Antônio Conselheiro, at Canudos, in the parched interior of Bahia state, mushroomed into a tragic confrontation between modernising technocracy and the traditionalism of the neglected poor. Conselheiro's makeshift army of cowherds and peasants defeated three military expeditions, including a column of a thousand crack federal troops backed by field artillery. Canudos was finally quelled only after a four-month siege and weeks of house-to-house fighting involving half the Brazilian army. This episode left 15,000 dead, including some prisoners garrotted after they had surrendered.[45] From this tragic clash, some members of Brazil's political elite drew the conclusion that their country's common people were too 'backward' to benefit from democracy. But others recognised the need to spread public education and the benefits of economic growth.

Argentina was less influenced by positivism. It had embarked on a golden age of economic growth and civilian rule. In 1862, the country had finally achieved internal unity. It quickly acquired the rudiments of a nation state: a national legal system, a bureaucracy, a tax system, a national electoral law, a new national army and two national newspapers.[46] From 1890, Argentina advanced steadily towards democracy: in 1916, Hipólito Yrigoyen, a Radical representing a growing middle class, became the first president to be elected under universal male suffrage (though the many foreigners were not allowed to vote). Yet Argentine democracy was being erected on somewhat shaky foundations. The Pampas, whose development was the source of the country's headlong economic growth, had been fully settled by the First World War. Between them, Buenos Aires and the Pampas accounted for more than 90 per cent of Argentina's cars and telephones in the early 1920s, two-fifths of Latin America's railways, half of the region's foreign trade and three-quarters of its educational spending.[47] Beyond lay a vast and less prosperous territory. Liberals from Rivadavia to Alberdi and Sarmiento had supported American-style homesteading policies, but had been unable to impose them in the face of oligarchical opposition. The Pampas had been divided up very unequally: according to the 1914 census, the largest 584 farms occupied almost a fifth of the total area, and those of over 1,000 hectares (2,470 acres) more than 60 per cent. The mean average landholding in Argentina was 890 acres (360 hectares), compared with 175 acres (70 hectares) in New South Wales and 130 acres (53 hectares) in the United States.[48]

Across the River Plate in Uruguay, the rise of Montevideo as a port serving parts of Argentina and Brazil similarly spawned a vigorous middle class, reinforced by European migration. Through the medium of the Colorado Party, leaders of this social group struck a political alliance with the sheep farmers of the interior. Under José Batlle y Ordóñez (president, 1903–07 and 1911–15), Uruguay established the foundations of a modern democracy and one of the world's first welfare states. The death penalty was banned and divorce legalised. Legislation imposed the eight-hour working day, social insurance and free secondary education. In a foretaste of policies that would be adopted more widely in the region two decades later, state monopolies were created to run services from the port to electricity generation and insurance. Thanks to this social contract forged by *batllismo*, as it was called,

Uruguay, the smallest country in South America, has also long been the most egalitarian. Elsewhere, things were very different.

Land but not liberty: a revolution creates a corporate state

In September 1910, delegations from across the world came to Mexico City to celebrate the centenary of Mexican independence – and a quarter-century of 'peace, order and progress' under Porfirio Díaz. Within months, the appearance of stability was shattered. After Díaz had claimed to a North American journalist that he would 'bless' an opposition, Francisco Madero, the austere scion of a wealthy northern business family, stood for the presidency against the dictator under the banner of 'effective suffrage, no re-election'. After mobilising support in rallies across the country, he was arrested. Bailed, he escaped to the United States, and re-entered Mexico in February 1911 at the head of 130 armed men. Other rebels launched local risings, many of them unconnected. By May, Madero's troops had captured Ciudad Juárez, the most important customs post on the border with the United States. Faced with a national rebellion that he could not defeat, Díaz finally resigned.

Madero was a liberal democrat, an eccentric spiritualist and medium who believed himself chosen to redeem Mexico, and a man of great personal integrity and decency.[49] But he was politically inept. He disbanded his own troops, while allowing supporters of the dictatorship to cling to positions of power. He failed to reach agreement with Emiliano Zapata, an Indian peasant leader who had launched his own localised revolution in Morelos, a small central state whose modernised sugar mills had made voracious encroachments on peasant land. In 1913, Madero was overthrown and murdered in a coup led by Victoriano Huerta, an army commander backed by the Porfirians and by Henry Lane Wilson, President William Howard Taft's meddling ambassador in Mexico City. This coup served only to intensify discontent. In 1915, Huerta would in turn be defeated by revolutionary armies sweeping down from the north. They were led by Francisco Villa, a bandit turned follower of Madero, and Álvaro Obregón, a farmer from Sonora, an important centre of commercial agriculture in the north-west, who emerged as the revolution's most gifted and ruthless military commander. Venustiano Carranza, another northerner, a pre-revolutionary state governor but an admirer of Juárez, became president.

The revolution had long since acquired its own momentum: it had become a confused and prolonged series of local and national struggles over power and land. Zapata had raised the ancestral Indian demand for land restitution, under the banner (borrowed via a Mexican anarchist intellectual from Alexander Herzen, a Russian liberal) of 'Tierra y Libertad' ('Land and Freedom'). But Zapata lacked interest in forging national alliances, or in venturing far beyond the villages of Morelos. He would be betrayed, and then shot by federal troops working for Carranza's government. In 1916, Carranza convoked a constituent assembly in Querétaro, north of Mexico City, to draw up a new constitution. The resulting document remains in force, though much amended. It was a compromise between Carranza, a liberal in the nineteenth-century tradition but an authoritarian one who believed in a strong executive, and radical social reformers, some of whom had advised Zapata and who had the backing of Obregón. Notably, the constitution declared both land and the sub-soil to be the property of the nation – provisions which sounded socialist, but were also a throwback to the colonial period, when they were vested in the Crown.[50]

It would be another two decades before local rebellions and violent power struggles among the commanders of the victorious revolutionary armies died away. What eventually emerged was a more broad-based nation state, but one in which power was ruthlessly centralised – not the liberal democracy of which Madero had dreamed. The post-revolutionary state was largely the creation of three men: two Sonorans, Obregón and Plutarco Elías Calles, a conservative former teacher and local police chief; and Lázaro Cárdenas, the last of the revolutionary generals to become president and a reformer with socialist leanings. The great achievement of the post-revolutionary system was to bring lasting stability by institutionalising political conflict and allowing for regular political renewal. Thus, almost uniquely in Latin America, in Mexico the army was politically neutralised. In 1928, Calles created an official hegemonic political party, known (after 1946) as the Institutional Revolutionary Party (PRI). The PRI system was a civilian one. It gave the president the powers of an absolute monarch – but only for six years. Though he was allowed to choose his successor, once out of office the president was a political nobody. He could not be re-elected. The constitution was nominally federal. During his presidency (1934–40), Cárdenas suppressed the remnants of the separation of powers: he purged the Congress and the state governors, and scrapped Carranza's idea of appointing judges for life. After Cárdenas, the president had all the levers of power. Congress and governors did his bidding, but they did form channels through which grievances could be funnelled upwards to the president. All this was carefully legitimated through elections. The PRI ruled by consent and co-option when possible, and by electoral fraud and violence only when necessary. The system paid more than lip-service to the myths of the revolution. Its rule was less elitist than the Porfiriato. Its main characteristics were a corporate state, social reform and nationalism.

Cárdenas reorganised the ruling party, as a mass organisation on functional lines, with sections for peasants and workers (and later for middle-class professionals). He put into practice many of the social aspirations of the radicals in the Querétaro assembly. He distributed 18.4 million hectares of land among 1 million peasants in the form of *ejidos*, a term which dated from pre-Hispanic communal landholdings. But the land was not owned directly by the communities and individual farmers, as Zapata had wanted. Under Cárdenas's system, while the community enjoyed the use of *ejido* land, the state remained its owner. The peasants were tied into the PRI system. They were demobilised, not empowered. They had won land, but not freedom.[51] Nor did many of them escape poverty. Cárdenas also set up a national trade-union confederation. The PRI guaranteed to private industrialists and other capitalists political stability, subsidised credit and an expanded and protected domestic market – provided they played the rules of the political game. The Church, too, was subordinated to the state: the 1916 constitution echoed the fierce anti-clerical laws of Juárez, though these were applied with decreasing severity after the 1920s.

If the PRI had an ideology, it was nationalism – the party even adopted the national flag and colours as its own emblems and Mexico came to define itself in rhetorical opposition to the United States. During the revolution, the United States twice sent troops to Mexico: in 1914, President Woodrow Wilson sent marines to Veracruz, to prevent arms from reaching Huerta; when, in March 1916, Villa, resentful at American recognition of the Carranza government, briefly raided the border town of Columbus, New Mexico, Wilson dispatched a futile 'punitive expedition' under General John Pershing (who the following year commanded a much more significant force in France). Even so, in the view of Alan

Knight, a historian of the revolution, 'at no point can it be said that US policy . . . was primarily responsible for making or breaking a regime south of the border. Still less could Standard Oil, or any other corporation, make a similar claim.'[52] But the generous concessions made by the Díaz regime to foreign capital, especially in mining and oil, angered the revolutionaries. They argued that the oil companies, both Standard Oil and the British-owned El Águila, operated as states within a state, and evaded taxes. In 1938, Cárdenas acted: he nationalised the oil industry, declaring '*el petróleo es nuestro*' ('the oil is ours'), though he did pay compensation. A state company, Petróleos Mexicanos (Pemex), was given a monopoly over the industry. Post-revolutionary ideology also embraced *indigenismo* – an intellectual current that called for the integration of the Indian into the mainstream of society.

At several junctures, Mexico might have taken the more democratic road espoused by Madero. In the early 1920s, a Liberal Constitutionalist Party pushed for municipal autonomy and the separation of powers. Such sentiments inspired some of the backers of a failed rebellion in 1923 by Adolfo de la Huerta, yet another Sonoran general. In 1929, José Vasconcelos, the philosopher of *indigenismo* who, as Obregón's education minister, had been a patron to Diego Rivera and his fellow muralists, stood for the presidency on a platform of *maderista* democracy. But he was defeated by Calles's machine, which employed the electoral fraud and strong-arm tactics that would become the PRI system's less attractive trademarks.[53] In the event, under the PRI, Mexico adopted many elements of corporatism, the ideology championed and discredited by Southern European fascism in Mussolini's Italy, Franco's Spain and Salazar's Portugal. But the PRI was not grossly repressive, and it was essentially pragmatic, not revolutionary. Some of its presidents, like Cárdenas, veered left. Others were right wing: Miguel Alemán (1946–52) was friendly to private business. The PRI co-opted the left – especially writers, artists and academics – but it was also anti-communist. The PRI's rule gave Mexico stability, and laid the basis of a modern nation state and an industrialised economy. From 1930 until at least 1968, it was highly successful. The economy grew at an annual average rate of 4 per cent from 1929 to 1950, accelerating to 6.4 per cent from 1950 to 1980.[54] On the whole, there was social peace. The PRI system mimicked the outward forms of liberal democracy. But in reality, it was 'the perfect dictatorship', as Vargas Llosa, the Peruvian novelist, said in

1990. The system had huge defects: corruption, lack of political and media freedom, massive waste and inefficiency, all of which became more important as time went by.

Building the popular nation

The Mexican Revolution and its aftermath had a singular political influence in much of Spanish-speaking America. Other countries faced the same challenges as Mexico, of consolidating a modern nation state, of industrialisation, the growth of cities, the emergence of an organised working class; they, too, saw the rise of new political currents, such as nationalism, socialism and corporatism. One early admirer was Víctor Raúl Haya de la Torre, an exiled Peruvian student leader. He founded the Alianza Popular Revolucionaria Americana (APRA) as a continental movement in Mexico City in 1924, and then as a political party in Peru in 1930. APRA's founding 'international maximum programme' called for action against Yankee imperialism, the political unity of 'Indo-America' (as Haya called Latin America in deference to its indigenous peoples), the nationalisation of lands and industries, the internationalisation of the Panama Canal, and international solidarity.[55] This smacked of radical socialism, but Haya favoured a broad non-communist front, in which the middle class would take the lead, along with workers and indigenous peasants. In his long life – he died in 1979 while president of a constituent assembly preparing the return of democracy to Peru – his ideas went through various evolutions. 'Since its creation, APRA has been a study in contradictions', as Julio Cotler, a Peruvian sociologist, has put it.[56] In Peru, APRA would at first flirt with revolutionary violence, and always retained a conspiratorial flavour. But Haya's preference, if allowed, was to compete for power through elections. He said that APRA would respect democratic liberties. Haya became increasingly conservative, but many in his party yearned for a Mexican-style corporate state and nationalisation of American mining companies in Peru.[57] The army repeatedly intervened to prevent APRA winning power; it would take office for the first time only in 1985, under the inept leadership of Alan García (who won the presidency again in 2006, this time governing as an economic liberal with far more success than in his first term). Even so, Haya was a hugely influential figure in his country's politics and beyond. He supported the campaign in Nicaragua of Augusto Sandino, a dissident Liberal general, against a government backed by American marines.[58] APRA became the transmission belt conveying the ideas of the Mexican Revolution to South America.

The liberal order lasted for two decades longer in South America than in Mexico. Its death knell was sounded by the Wall Street Crash of October 1929 – as it was in Europe. If the Great Depression did not amount to a decisive turning point in Latin America's economic history, it certainly marked a sharp political rupture. The impact of the depression on employment and living standards was severe. Ten countries in the region saw the value of their exports fall by more than half between 1928 and 1932. No other country in the western world was as badly affected by the crash as Chile, whose trade fell by 83 per cent between 1929 and 1932. In Chile and Cuba, income per head fell by a third.[59] Many governments defaulted on their foreign debts for the first time since the mid-nineteenth century. Across the region, the depression prompted discontent and agitation by fledgling labour unions, many of anarcho-syndicalist persuasion, and small left-wing political parties. In El Salvador, an attempt at an insurrection by the small Communist Party was crushed in a bloodbath. In Peru, risings by APRA and the communists were repressed. In Chile, a brief socialist republic was declared by Marmaduque Grove, an air force officer and uncle of Salvador Allende. Cuba saw a short-lived revolution by radical students and army sergeants.

Conservatives felt threatened by mass demonstrations and the new left-wing parties. Some looked to military rule to save them from the masses. Some were attracted by fascism, especially in its Mediterranean form of corporatism. Many on the left, too, would be attracted by corporatism. In Latin America, Mussolini and Franco were more influential than Marx and Lenin. Within two years of the Wall Street Crash, army officers had sought or taken power in Argentina, Brazil, Chile, Peru and three Central American countries (Guatemala, El Salvador and Honduras).[60] In 1933, the army took power in Cuba. In Argentina, the crash ended 50 years of broadly stable civilian rule. It found the second administration of Hipólito Yrigoyen, the elderly leader of the Radical Party, fiscally exposed: his efforts to cut a vast budget deficit undermined his political support. In September 1930, a military junta took power. It was not particularly repressive, and it presaged a decade of civilian–military rule. But in deciding that it would accept as legal the junta's edict, the Supreme Court elaborated a dangerous doctrine of *revolución triunfante* – or might is right.[61] For half a century after 1930, that doctrine brought Argentina instability and the subordination of civilian politics to the armed forces. In Chile, the lasting impact was in reverse: a wave of protest and anti-militarism swept away Carlos Ibáñez, a moderate conservative military dictator. Two brief military interventions followed. But exceptionally, democratic and constitutional rule was strengthened, lasting until the overthrow of Salvador Allende in 1973. Even more exceptional was Colombia: in an election in 1930, the Liberals ended 50 years of Conservative rule, helped by the impact of the crash and their opponents' divisions. A period of vigorous social reform followed. Many of the Latin American economies recovered fairly swiftly from the depression, thanks both to renewed export growth and Keynesian measures of state intervention and import-substitution industrialisation. But politics had changed forever. Only in a few smaller countries did 'oligarchical' liberalism survive the crash.

Mexico was unique in institutionalising corporatist nationalism. But its revolution was strongly echoed four decades later in Bolivia. In 1951, the National Revolutionary Movement (MNR), a mainly middle-class party but with support among miners, workers and peasant farmers, won an election. Robbed of power by a military coup, in 1952 it staged a popular rising. For three days, the MNR's urban militias fought army conscripts in La Paz. The battle was turned in the MNR's favour by the arrival of a contingent of armed miners, and by splits in the security forces. Some 500 people died, but the old order had been toppled.[62] The MNR's leader, Víctor Paz Estenssoro, a university teacher of economics, was installed as president. His government enacted universal suffrage, nationalised the tin mines (which provided the main export), and broke up most of the *haciendas* on the Altiplano, handing over the land as family plots to the Indian resident serfs. A serious effort was made to provide universal education, at least at primary level. And for the first time, Indians were allowed to enter the Plaza Murillo, La Paz's main square and the site of the cathedral, the presidential palace and the Congress. The MNR would be the dominant political force in Bolivia for the next half-century, but it neither achieved the supremacy of the PRI nor did it tame the armed forces.

Elsewhere, corporatism tended to be articulated by charismatic nation builders – old-fashioned *caudillos* in a new, more powerful incarnation. In this form, political scientists have often preferred to label corporatism as populism. The most prominent nation builder was Brazil's Getúlio Vargas, who, as governor of Rio Grande do Sul, was heir to that state's positivist tradition, and who became president through a civilian–military coup in 1930. Vargas ruled as dictator from 1937 to 1945, and then was elected president again in 1950. Strictly speaking, it was only in this last phase that he acted as a populist.[63] In Argentina, Juan Perón, an army colonel, ruled from 1946 to 1955; the movement he founded has remained the dominant political force in Argentina to this day. But Perón did not hold a monopoly on Argentine populism: Yrigoyen's Radicals also had strong populist streaks. In Venezuela, Acción Democrática (AD), with which Peru's APRA had especially close links, evolved from populism to social democracy. AD dominated Venezuelan politics for much of the period between the 1940s and the rise of Hugo Chávez. There were some differences between these movements. For example, Perón's government of 1946–55 was the closest Latin America came to a fascist regime. It gave refuge to at least 180 Nazis and their collaborators, including such notorious figures as Adolf Eichmann, Eduard Roschmann, Josef Mengele and Klaus Barbie (who moved on to Bolivia).[64] During the dictatorship of the *Estado Novo* (New State), Vargas also flirted with fascism. Haya de la Torre was, at least for parts of his career, closer to democratic socialism, though APRA was organised on corporatist lines. Of the larger countries, only Colombia and Chile remained relatively aloof from populism.

In Latin America, unlike in Russia and the United States, populism was an overwhelmingly urban movement and ideology.[65] It was, above all, a political response to urbanisation, and to what was seen as the elitist and exclusionary politics of the pre-1930 'oligarchical' republics. It reflected what Jorge Castañeda, a Mexican writer and politician, has called the 'unfulfilled Latin American dream of painless modernity'.[66] The original populist movements flourished from the mid-1920s to the mid-1960s – though populism has enjoyed an unanticipated recent revival in the region. They promoted industrialisation, a policy on which local industrialists, the middle class and organised labour could all agree. Populist movements were multi-class electoral coalitions. Their leaders deliberately talked of *el pueblo* (the people) rather than, say, *la clase obrera* (the working class). As well as nationalism, they injected the concept of *lo popular* into Latin American political vocabulary (meaning 'for and by the people'), as in their claim to lead 'popular' governments. Their programme involved protection and subsidies for local industry, and political representation and welfare provision for the urban masses. This in turn involved an expansion of the role of the state in the economy and society, which generated new jobs for the middle classes. Populist movements opposed foreign domination and the power of what they called the agro-export 'oligarchy'. These movements were reformist – unlike parties of the Marxist left, they aimed to mitigate class conflict, rather than stimulate it. Even so, populist movements were often seen as a threat by conservative agro-exporting interests (and by the United States). In a way, they were: they sought to redistribute resources from farming to the cities. The result was that populists were often the target of repression. Another distinguishing characteristic of populist movements was their reliance on charismatic leadership. The populist leaders were often great orators or, if you prefer, demagogues. Ecuador's most emblematic populist leader, José María Velasco, famously said: 'give me a balcony and I will become president'. This was no idle boast: his campaigning skills saw him elected president five times – though his lack of governing skills, and the fierce opposition he generated among conservatives, saw him ousted four times by the army. Such leadership exalted an almost mystical bond between leader and masses. This sometimes involved the use of religious imagery or techniques, as with Haya de la Torre.

For better or for worse, populism was the political vehicle through which many Latin American countries entered the modern era of mass politics and bigger government. Its achievements included a boost to industrialisation, and an improvement in social conditions for favoured sectors of the urban workforce. Workers received tangible benefits, such as paid holidays, pensions and health provision. Those benefits were sufficient to encourage remarkably durable loyalty among the beneficiaries, as the longevity of the PRI and Peronism, in particular, illustrate. Perón's social reforms deprived Argentina's small socialist and communist parties of working-class support; they were never to regain it. The populists did help to build nation states that were still very much a work in progress. Whereas liberals and positivists had often looked abroad for inspiration, populists promoted a 'national culture', rescuing indigenous people and their cultural artefacts from official neglect.

In these respects, populism played an analogous role to social democracy in Europe. But there were important differences. Overall, populism had a negative impact on Latin American democracy and development. Four defects stand out. First, although it employed electoral means, populism was in many ways less than democratic. As Paul Drake puts it, populist leaders 'were devoted to expanding popular participation but not necessarily through formal, Western democratic mechanisms'.[67] Perón, Vargas and Haya 'repeatedly exhibited dictatorial propensities toward their followers and opponents. They apparently favoured controlled, paternalistic mobilization of the masses more than uninhibited, pluralistic, democratic competition'.[68] In fairness, their conservative opponents, too, were often less than democratic. In Argentina, even a liberal such as Jorge Luis Borges, the writer, came to believe that Peronism showed that his country was not 'ready' for democracy. He argued at one point that military dictatorship was a necessary evil to prevent Peronism from remaining in power.

A second, linked failing was the reliance on charismatic leadership. Max Weber, the German sociologist, defined charismatic authority as being exercised by an individual who is 'considered extraordinary and treated as endowed with supernatural, superhuman, or at least specifically exceptional powers or qualities'.[69] As Weber's definition makes clear, charismatic leadership is inimical to the rule of law – or indeed the separation of powers and the construction of democratic institutions. Populist leaders relied on a direct bond between themselves and the masses: not for nothing did they emerge simultaneously with the radio and the cinema. Eva Perón had worked as an actress in radio soaps; like FDR in the United States, Getúlio Vargas made regular radio broadcasts. They established political clienteles, rather than creating citizenship. Benefits came from loyalty, not as a matter of right. The reliance on charisma was one reason why populism was inherently unstable. Another was its assault, often rhetorical but sometimes real, on property rights.

Thirdly, perhaps the most disappointing feature of populism was its failure to make a serious attack on inequality. In contrast to Mexico and Bolivia, where revolutions broke the political power of the traditional *hacendados*, other populist leaders usually excluded the poorest sections of the masses – the peasantry – from their coalitions. Populist governments made no attempt to extend the franchise to illiterates, nor to implement land reform. And in attempting to transfer resources from agriculture to industry, such as by controlling food prices, they were impoverishing peasant as well as landlord. Their reliance on inflation, rather than thoroughgoing tax reforms, to finance government hurt the poor disproportionately, too. This was but one aspect of a fourth defect of populism: its economic policy. Populist governments were not alone in pursuing statist protectionism: by the 1960s, many military dictatorships did, too. But the constant tension in populist governments between industrialisation and welfarism (as Drake puts it) led them to rely on over-expansionary macroeconomic policies and made them prey to extreme economic volatility. While claiming to champion the creation of a modern state, the clientelist approach to politics adopted by many populist leaders led them to create inefficient public bureaucracies stuffed with their supporters.

Some of these weaknesses, combined with the opposition that populists aroused among some powerful conservative groups, meant that from the 1930s on, Latin America's incipient democracies were subject to chronic instability, and to what came to be known as the pendulum effect, as civilian governments alternated with dictatorships. In the aftermath of the Second World War, an external conflict would intensify these political battles in Latin America, to tragic effect.

CHAPTER FOUR

Cold War and Revolution

Guatemala is the saddest country in Latin America. The beauty of its verdant highlands dotted with whitewashed colonial towns, its shimmering lakes overlooked by soaring volcanoes and its Mayan ruins half-buried in rainforest cannot conceal the ancestral oppression of its indigenous majority. It has had an elected civilian government since 1986. But a guerrilla war lasting almost three decades was settled only in 1996. It cost some 200,000 lives; most of the victims were Mayan Indians killed by the army.[1] The war continued to cast a dark shadow. Guatemala's democrats must struggle against what some have called *los poderes fácticos* – shadowy networks linking corrupt former army officers and organised criminal gangs of drug traffickers, and powerful business oligarchs. In the twenty-first century there were some grounds for hope. Efforts were made to cut Guatemala's army down to size and to liberate democracy from military tutelage. A UN-sponsored International Commission against Impunity (known as CICIG) helped to punish misdeeds by the powerful and empower the country's prosecutors and judges. But the progress was fragile.

The CIA snuffs out the Guatemalan spring

And yet Guatemala might have developed into a far more robust democracy much earlier. That it did not do so is in large part the fault of the United States: more than anywhere else in Latin America, Guatemala was a victim of American intervention. In 1954, the Eisenhower administration organised a coup to topple the democratic, reformist government of Jacobo Árbenz, which the American president alleged to be a possible 'communist outpost on this continent'.[2] Though the enterprise was initially hailed as a success by its authors, in the words of one historian sympathetic to them, 'in light of subsequent events it might reasonably be considered little short of disaster'.[3] Not only did Guatemala itself pay a high price for the American intervention: the lessons drawn by the United States and by Latin Americans of both left and right had tragic consequences in other countries, handicapping democracy in the region for a generation or more. How was it that Guatemala came to be the first battle in the Cold War in Latin America?

Central America was an underdeveloped backwater throughout the nineteenth century. After independence in 1824, the United Provinces of Central America soon fragmented into five separate countries, of which Guatemala, the seat of the colonial captain-generalcy, was the largest. Except in Costa Rica, an unenlightened despotism was the norm in the isthmus.[4] In Guatemala, a long line of brutal dictators went through the motions of legitimating their rule through elections; but these were farcical affairs in which opposition was rarely registered. An oligarchy of coffee planters dominated the republic; they assured themselves of a seasonal Indian workforce through debt peonage. In 1934, Jorge Ubico, a dictator even more repressive than his predecessors, decreed a vagrancy law under which all males without either a profession or four *manzanas* of land (2.76 hectares) were required to work between 100 and 150 days each year on the plantations on pain of jail.[5] As in apartheid South Africa, the Indians had to carry a labour card on which their forced labour was recorded.

When the Second World War drew to a close, democratic eddies washed across Latin America. Several dictatorships fell, to be replaced by governments elected on a reasonably broad franchise. Labour unions expanded, and flexed their muscles in a strike wave. Communist parties grew rapidly, from a total membership of less than 100,000 in 1939 to 500,000 by 1947.[6] In Latin America, as elsewhere in the world, there were expectations that a new era of democracy was beginning. This opened up an opportunity for Latin American countries to move towards social democracy – as much of Western Europe would do in the aftermath of war – through an alliance between industrialists and the emerging middle and organised working classes.[7] But the opportunity proved tantalisingly brief. In Latin America, the rural landlords had not been hurt by war, and they still exercised a powerful political grip, while the trade unions were still weak. By 1948, in most places, the progress towards democracy had been rolled back, and communist parties had been banned in most countries. By then, the Cold War had begun. It did not create anti-communism in Latin America. This had been espoused by conservatives and the Catholic Church since the Russian Revolution and the formation by Lenin in 1919 of the Third Communist International (Comintern) with its brief of world revolution. So most Latin American governments were happy to line up with the United States in the Cold War. For Washington, it began to matter more that those governments should be reliably anti-communist rather than democratic.

In Guatemala, the post-war democratic spring lasted longer. In 1944, protests by students, teachers and other members of an incipient middle class prompted Ubico to step down. Three months later, junior officers rebelled against his chosen successor. This 'October revolution' was carried out in the name not of Bolshevism, but of 'constitution and democracy'. Both were quickly achieved. Juan José Arévalo, a mild-mannered teacher of philosophy who had returned from years of exile in Argentina, was elected president in the freest vote Guatemala had seen. Arévalo claimed inspiration from Franklin Roosevelt's New Deal and from the Four Freedoms – of speech and religion, and from want and fear – for which the American president had fought the war. A new constitution extended the franchise to all except illiterate women, created elected local authorities, made racial discrimination a crime and banned military men from standing for office. Arévalo's government abolished the vagrancy law, gave rights to trade unions, established a social security system, central bank and statistical office, and built hundreds of new schools. It brooked no restrictions on political or press freedom, despite suffering frequent plots from conservatives.

In 1950, Jacobo Árbenz, a leader of the 'October revolution', was elected to succeed Arévalo, with 65 per cent of the vote. While Arévalo had established democratic freedoms, Árbenz promised 'to convert Guatemala from a backward country with a predominantly feudal economy into a modern capitalist state'.[8] His plans to do this centred on agrarian reform and public infrastructure projects, several of which had been proposed by the president of the World Bank. On both counts, that meant a confrontation with the United Fruit Company, an American firm based in Boston. Known to Central Americans as *el pulpo* (the octopus) because of its all-encompassing tentacles, in 1899 United Fruit had obtained a 99-year concession over a vast tract of jungle from Guatemala's then dictator – and with it, the right to finish and operate a railway to the Caribbean coast. The company thus obtained a monopoly over much of Guatemala's trade: its port at Puerto Barrios was the country's only Atlantic port, and its railway the only means of transport to and from the port. In return, it paid only a small tax on banana exports.[9] Árbenz proposed to build a public port next to Puerto Barrios and a highway to it; United Fruit, which had already seen a rise in trade-union organising, became the main target of his land reform.

Even by Latin American standards, land distribution in Guatemala was highly unequal: 2 per cent of landowners held three-quarters of all cultivable land, while more than half of all farmland was made up of large plantations (above 1,100 acres/445 hectares). Much of this land was left fallow. Árbenz's reform affected farms larger than 670 acres (271ha) whose land was not fully worked (or those above 223 acres (90ha) where a third of the land was uncultivated). Compensation was paid in interest-bearing bonds, according to the land's declared taxable value. In two years, a million acres – a third of this from German-owned farms nationalised at American insistence during the war – were distributed to 100,000 families. Árbenz ordered the expropriation of 380,000 acres (154,000ha) of United Fruit land – a substantial chunk of its holdings, of which 85 per cent was left fallow, supposedly in case of banana diseases. The government offered compensation of $1.1 million; the company claimed the land was worth $16 million, thus revealing the scale of its tax evasion. Its claim was backed by the US Department of State.

By then, the Eisenhower administration was bent on overthrowing Árbenz, whom it accused of presiding over a communist takeover. With support from Nicaragua's notorious dictator, Anastasio Somoza, and his counterpart in Honduras, the CIA trained and armed a force of 170 men, and assembled a dozen planes. Their 'invasion' was a halting affair. But bombing and strafing from the air, combined with disinformation broadcasts suggesting a force of thousands, caused the army high command to oblige Árbenz to resign. Through a mixture of threats and manipulation, the Americans quickly secured the appointment as president of Carlos Castillo Armas, the undistinguished retired colonel they had chosen to lead the 'invasion'. Guatemala's ten-year democratic spring was over.

Ever since, controversy has raged over the American action. Was the coup an enterprise of crude economic imperialism, in which the Eisenhower administration was acting as enforcer for United Fruit? Since the days of Arévalo, the company had conducted an effective propaganda campaign in the United States, painting Guatemala as being in the grip of communists. The family of John Foster Dulles, the secretary of state, and his brother Allen, the CIA director, were shareholders in the banana company. But J.F. Dulles insisted: 'if the United Fruit matter were settled, if they gave a gold piece for every banana, the problem would remain as it is today as far as the presence of communist infiltration in Guatemala is concerned'.[10]

In recent years, as official archives have been opened, historians have come to accept Dulles's contention. But many question his verdict on Árbenz. Not for the last time in Latin America, the critics argue, the United States failed to distinguish between a nationalist reformer and a communist. The Guatemalan Labour Party, as the communist party was called, was tiny; it never had more than 2,000 activists. Though an enthusiastic backer of Árbenz and the land reform, it was the smallest of the four parties in the governing coalition. It won only four of the 56 seats in Congress in an election in 1953, had no Cabinet members, and fewer than ten senior government jobs. Guatemala had no diplomatic relations with the Soviet Union and the eastern bloc. Until the late 1950s, the Soviet Union had only three embassies in the whole of Latin America, a region which Stalin had dismissed as 'the obedient army of the United States'.[11] Dulles made great play of an arms shipment from Czechoslovakia received a month before the coup. But the United States had maintained an arms embargo on Guatemala since 1948, and the Czech arms were of limited use. Árbenz's coalition was fractious, the army restless and the middle class became disillusioned as tensions with the United States rose. The president did come to depend on the communists, who alone could mobilise popular support for the government. His wife is alleged to have been a communist sympathiser. The CIA feared that land reform would create a base for the communists in the countryside. Even so, it is hard to see the army or the civilian politicians acquiescing in a communist takeover.

In the event, in Guatemala the US crushed democracy, not communism. Castillo Armas swiftly reversed the agrarian reform, reached agreement with United Fruit, and restored the old order of corrupt dictatorship. In 1960, junior army officers would rebel in the name of nationalism, angry that Guatemala was being used by the CIA to train anti-Castro Cuban exiles. The rebellion failed, but two of its leaders went on to found Guatemala's first guerrilla group. This was crushed after right-wing death squads murdered thousands of civilians, many of whom had no connection to the guerrillas. In the mid-1970s, new Marxist guerrilla groups established a presence among the Mayan Indian communities of Guatemala's western highlands. That prompted the army to undertake a scorched-earth campaign that saw scores of Indian villages wiped out, their inhabitants butchered and the survivors forcibly relocated and conscripted into army-backed auxiliary forces called 'civil patrols'. Of all the counter-insurgency campaigns in Latin America during the Cold War, only that in Guatemala merits the much-abused term of genocide. Repression by dictatorships in Chile and Argentina, where most of the victims were middle class, attracted far more outside attention. But in the deliberate infliction of mass terror, the massacres of Mayan Indians in the Guatemalan highlands in the late 1970s and early 1980s had no parallel in the region. Those excesses caused Jimmy Carter to cancel the United States' previous aid to the army. Another Democratic president, Bill Clinton, made a formal apology for that aid on a visit to Guatemala in 1999. But by then the Cold War was long over.

The ease with which Árbenz was overthrown would lead policy-makers in Washington to adopt 'regime change' as their standard response to perceived communist threats in Latin America. A few years later, another such attempt – on a much larger scale – would end in disaster at the Bay of Pigs in Cuba. Thwarted, President John F. Kennedy would launch the Alliance for Progress in an attempt to stall the spread of communism in Latin America by encouraging democratic reform. 'Those who make peaceful change impossible make violent change inevitable', Kennedy declared. Indeed, had Árbenz's agrarian reform taken place a decade later – or a decade earlier, when FDR was preaching freedom from want – it might well have drawn applause from Washington.

The Latin American left, too, drew lessons from Guatemala. A young Argentine doctor, Ernesto Guevara, had arrived there on New Year's Eve 1953 and witnessed the fall of Árbenz. By the time he was given safe conduct from the Argentine embassy to Mexico, he had acquired the nickname 'Che', bestowed by leftist exiled Cubans he met in Guatemala.[12] According to one of his most perceptive biographers, Guatemala was Che Guevara's 'political rite of passage'. Guevara thought the coup showed that the United States 'was *a priori* ruthlessly opposed to any attempt at social and economic reform in Latin America'. So he inferred that the left should be prepared to fight US interference, rather than try to avoid or neutralise it.[13] He also thought that Árbenz had allowed his enemies too much freedom, especially in the press, and had erred in not purging the army. As Hilda Gadea, Guevara's first wife, wrote: 'It was Guatemala which convinced him of the necessity for armed struggle and for taking the initiative against imperialism.'[14]

From the Monroe Doctrine to the corollary of intervention

The overthrow of Árbenz was far from the first intervention by the United States in Latin America. Yet Guevara's analysis was flawed: interventionism was by no means constant, and it was almost wholly confined to the Caribbean basin. The policy of the United States towards its neighbours went through several contrasting phases. In the century following George Washington's presidency, his successors had two main foreign policy priorities. One was to prevent European involvement in the Americas. The second was to expand their own territory across North America. The first aim was expressly formulated by President James Monroe in 1823, when he warned the European powers: 'we should consider any attempt on their part to extend their system to any portion of this hemisphere as dangerous to our peace and safety'.[15] The Monroe Doctrine, as it came to be called, was defensive in inspiration. In opposition to the restored absolute monarchies of continental Europe, it envisioned a commonality of liberal economic principles and civil, political and religious freedom across the republics of the Americas.[16] Thus, President Harry Truman would say in 1947: 'there has been a Marshall Plan for the Western hemisphere for a century and a half. [It is] known as the Monroe Doctrine.'[17] In any event, the United States long lacked the power to enforce it; throughout the nineteenth century, European powers would occasionally intervene in Latin America, pursuing trade or protecting the lives and investments of their citizens.

The second aim came to be known as the pursuit of the United States' 'manifest destiny' to occupy North America from the Atlantic to the Pacific seaboard, a term coined by John O'Sullivan, the editor of the New York *Morning News* in 1845. The process began with the purchase of Louisiana and Florida. It continued with the admission to the union of Texas, which had declared its independence from Mexico in 1836. This was followed swiftly by an expansionary war with Mexico in 1846–48. To the victor went the present-day states of Arizona, California,

Colorado, Nevada, New Mexico and Utah, in return for a payment of $15 million.

Cuba and Central America were the focus of the next phase of American expansionism, from the 1890s to 1930. In this period, successive presidents – not just Theodore Roosevelt, the rough-riding conservative, but also Woodrow Wilson, the idealistic democrat – concluded that control of the Caribbean basin was of crucial strategic importance for the defence of the homeland and its commerce. This control was challenged by Germany and, to a lesser extent, Britain. Kaiser Wilhelm II believed that Germany should be the 'paramount power' in Latin America, and that Cuba should be a 'European state'. Germany sought a naval base in the Caribbean. Against the background of 'a scramble for Africa' among the European powers, many influential Americans reckoned that the United States had to assert a policing role in its 'sphere of interest' in the Caribbean and Central American region – or risk seeing another power do so.[18] The chaotic misrule afflicting many of the small countries in the area provided ready pretexts for intervention in the name of stability. In 1904, Theodore Roosevelt summed up the new policy thus:

Chronic wrongdoing, or an impotence which results in a general loosening of the ties of civilized society, may in America, as elsewhere, ultimately require intervention by some civilized nation, and in the Western Hemisphere the adherence of the United States to the Monroe Doctrine may force the United States, however reluctantly, in flagrant cases of such wrongdoing or impotence, to the exercise of an international police power.[19]

This became known as the 'Roosevelt corollary' to the Monroe Doctrine. It was an ex-post justification for American intervention in Cuba.

Since the 1850s, American policymakers had made it clear that Cuba's transfer to any other European power would be unacceptable. By 1898, Spanish control over its 'ever-faithful isle' was tenuous. When the USS *Maine*, an American battleship on a visit to Havana, exploded, killing 266, a clamour for American intervention followed. (That the explosion was almost certainly an accident, caused by a fire in a coal bunker that ignited the forward magazines, was ignored.) The four-month war that followed shattered the remnants of Spanish empire and signalled the advent of the United States as a world power; it annexed Puerto Rico, the Philippines (for which it paid $20 million) and the Pacific island of Guam. It had gone to war in support of *Cuba Libre* (Free Cuba), but opted to make the island a protectorate. Roosevelt turned a minor role as a cavalry officer in the expeditionary force in Cuba into a national legend that swept him to the White House. Two years later, he created a new country in Central America. The United States had negotiated a treaty with Colombia, allowing it to build a trans-isthmian canal at Panama. When Colombia's Senate was slow to ratify this (partly because of the Thousand Days' War), Roosevelt organised and financed a revolution for Panamanian independence. Panama, like Cuba, became a de facto American protectorate. 'I took the isthmus', Roosevelt would subsequently boast.[20]

Under Woodrow Wilson, American imperialism took on a more idealistic tinge, influenced by the Progressive reform movement. The man who joined the First World War 'to make the world safe for democracy' claimed a similar motive closer to home. 'We are the friends of constitutional government in America; we are more than its friends, we are its champions', he said.[21] Yet American views of the neighbourhood were coloured by a racism akin to that of the positivists in Latin America in that period. The countries of the Caribbean basin, many assumed, were not ready for democracy. Wilson dispatched the marines for what turned into lengthy sojourns in the Dominican Republic (1916–24) and Haiti (1915–34), where they built roads and health clinics, as well as imposing order. In Nicaragua, the marines stayed from 1912 until 1933 (apart from a brief interval from 1925 to 1927). But instead of building nations, they built *gendarmeries*. It would be a recipe for trouble. In Nicaragua, the marines trained a National Guard, which suppressed Sandino's low-level guerrilla campaign. After Sandino made peace with the government, he was murdered on the orders of Anastasio Somoza, the guard's commander. Somoza went on to seize power in 1936, inaugurating a kleptocratic family dynasty that would last until 1979, when it was overthrown by leftist revolutionaries who claimed inspiration from the memory of Sandino. In the Dominican Republic, Rafael Leónidas Trujillo would use his command of the American-created army to impose a personal tyranny from 1930 until he was murdered in 1961, by which time this tropical *generalísimo* had become an embarrassment to his former sponsors.

From the First World War onwards, the United States began to displace Britain and Europe as the main source of trade and investment in the northern part of the region, though not in Argentina or some other South American countries. In the 1920s, intervention went hand in hand with commercial aggrandisement and 'dollar diplomacy', as American banks lent to eager but cash-strapped governments. This often-inglorious period in the United States' relations with Latin America was caustically summed up by General Smedley Darlington Butler, who was said to be embittered at having been passed over for the job of commandant of the US Marine Corps:

> I spent thirty-three years . . . being a high-class muscle man for Big Business, for Wall Street and the bankers. In short, I was a racketeer for capitalism . . . I helped purify Nicaragua for the international banking house of Brown Brothers in 1909–12. I helped make Mexico and especially Tampico safe for American oil interests in 1916. I helped make Haiti and Cuba a decent place for the National City [Bank] boys to collect revenue in. I helped in the rape of half a dozen Central American republics for the benefit of Wall Street.[22]

In all, between 1898 and 1934, there were some 30 separate military interventions by the United States in nine countries of the Americas – all of them in the Caribbean basin. Most of these exercises were self-serving, even if they were driven, too, by a high-minded sense of the United States' improving mission in the world (what would today be called 'liberal interventionism'). On the other hand, interventionism was restrained both by a desire to avoid foreign entanglements and by the moral rejection of imperialism on the part of a former colonial people.

These interventions impregnated the popular view in both halves of the hemisphere of US policy towards Latin America. It was captured by Rubén Darío, a great modernist poet from Nicaragua, in his ode of 1904 'To Roosevelt':

> *Eres los Estados Unidos,*
> *eres el futuro invasor*
> *de la América ingenua que tiene sangre indígena,*
> *que aún reza a Jesucristo y aún habla en español.*

[You are the United States,
you are future invader
of the guileless America of Indian blood
which still prays to Jesus Christ and still speaks Spanish]

As well as such eloquent statements of *arielismo*, this bullying provided fuel for dependency theorists, especially when they were repeated in Central America in the 1980s. Yet they applied to only a small part of the region. And intervention is only one motif in the pattern of hemispheric relations. Another is a search for peaceful co-operation. At the first Pan-American Conference, held in Washington in 1889, James G. Blaine, the US secretary of state, proposed a hemispheric customs union and arbitration mechanisms to settle disputes between nations. These ideas were not adopted, because of opposition led by Argentina and Chile. But they set the stage for increasingly busy hemispheric diplomacy – and would find an echo in the Miami summit of 1994. A similar approach would be followed by Franklin Roosevelt. On taking office in 1933, he proclaimed his administration's intention to be a 'good neighbour'. Roosevelt read Spanish; he had visited both Central and South America, and gave the region great importance in foreign policy (until the Japanese attack on Pearl Harbor in 1941 imposed other priorities). The United States committed itself not to intervene in the affairs of other countries. But that also meant it made no effort to promote democracy. Haya de la Torre, the leader of Peru's APRA, noted pointedly that Roosevelt was 'the good neighbour of tyrants'.[23] However, the famous comment attributed to FDR concerning Somoza ('He's a son of a bitch but at least he's our son of a bitch') was probably apocryphal. With the advent of the Second World War, the administration's main concern was to ensure access to Latin America's raw materials. The 'good neighbour' began to dispense economic aid, such as a cheap loan to enable Brazil's government to build a large, integrated steel mill at Volta Redonda.

Until the Spanish–American war, anti-Yankee feeling had not been the norm in Latin America. When the Monroe Doctrine was first enunciated, some in Latin America, such as Santander, saw it as a useful commitment by the United States to buttress still-fragile independence against Spanish and European covetousness. But Bolívar, for all his admiration of the United States, was wary. In a prescient phrase, he said it was destined to inflict on Latin America 'torments in the name of freedom'. (Instead, he wanted an alliance with Britain.) To this day, Latin American leaders remain torn between these two impulses. Brazil, for example, enjoyed a special relationship with the United States, which lasted until the 1970s. The Baron of Rio Branco, whose career as Brazil's premier diplomat spanned the empire and the early republic, argued that:

> Latin America has nothing to fear from Anglo-Saxon America . . .
> Nothing, absolutely nothing, in the policies of the United States would be able to cause uneasiness to the national sensitivity of the other American countries. Just the opposite, these nations find in the preponderance of the first nation of the continent support for their causes and aspirations.[24]

But some other countries, especially Argentina – whose special relationship with Britain endured until the Second World War – saw Pan-Americanism as limiting their options. As more confident nation states emerged in Latin America, they began to elaborate diplomatic defences. In the last decades of the nineteenth century, an Argentine diplomat, Carlos Calvo, had argued for a strict version of national sovereignty. He rejected the notion that foreign governments had the right to intervene to protect the lives and property of their citizens abroad, as both the European powers and the United States frequently did in Latin America. The 'Calvo Doctrine' held that foreigners, including investors, should be treated exactly the same as nationals, with no right of appeal to foreign governments even if host nations unilaterally changed the rules under which investments had been made.[25] This principle was adopted by Carranza in Mexico's 1917 constitution, and found adherents elsewhere in the region – including Néstor Kirchner, Argentina's president in 2003–07, in his handling of foreign investors in his country's privatised utilities. A second principle, known as the 'Drago Doctrine' after another Argentine, held that debts owed by one nation to another should not be collected by force. Again, its target was mainly European powers.

By the end of the Second World War, Latin America's mighty northern neighbour had become a superpower, while Europe, immersed in its own reconstruction, was temporarily disabled and permanently weakened. As the United States embarked on the Cold War, it dusted off the

Monroe Doctrine and applied it to the Soviet Union's efforts to spread communism around the world (cautious though these were in the Americas). That was one inspiration behind what came to be called the Inter-American system, comprising the Rio Treaty of mutual defence and, in 1948, the establishment of the Organization of American States (OAS). In deference to Calvo, the OAS Charter emphasised the principle of non-intervention. Nevertheless, to obtain diplomatic cover for the Guatemalan coup, J.F. Dulles spent a fortnight personally arm-twisting his Latin American counterparts at an OAS Assembly in Caracas in 1954. Only with great reluctance did they accept Dulles's proposition that 'the domination or control of the political institutions of any American state by the international communist movement' would constitute a threat to the Americas as a whole and would require 'appropriate action'. This would be the guiding principle of American foreign policy in the western hemisphere until the fall of the Berlin Wall. At first, Latin America was a minor theatre in the global rivalry between the United States and the Soviet Union. That would soon change.

The 'sugar prison' changes jailers

Like the island of Hispaniola and Brazil's north-east, Cuba was shaped and distorted by sugar. The cane plantations and sugar mills depended on slave labour. Between 1820 and 1865, up to 500,000 African slaves were imported; by 1841, they made up 43.5 per cent of the population.[26] Such was Spain's desire to maintain Cuba's sugar wealth that it hung onto the island through the nineteenth century by means of an implacable dictatorship. In the words of Hugh Thomas, a British historian, Cuba was 'a sugar prison rather than a sugar palace'.[27] A prolonged guerrilla war from 1868 until 1878 failed to dislodge Spanish rule. After the abolition of slavery in 1886, a more powerful independence movement emerged. Its leader was José Martí, a writer and political activist who founded the Cuban Revolutionary Party (PRC). Martí had spent 15 years living in New York. He was just one among many Cubans, both white and black, who had migrated to the United States. They were the forerunners of a large Cuban–American community that has endured to this day, while undergoing many changes. Martí admired the United States' democracy, but was a critic of some aspects of its capitalism, and deeply mistrustful of its intentions towards Cuba. In his last letter, written in 1895 after he had landed on the island as part of a liberating expedition and two days before he was killed, Martí declared:

> Every day now I am in danger of giving my life for my country and for my duty . . . in order to prevent, by the timely independence of Cuba, the United States from extending its hold across the Antilles and falling with all the greater force on the lands of our America. All I have done up till now and all I will do, is for that . . . I lived in the monster and I know its entrails – and my sling is the sling of David.[28]

Martí's fears were soon justified by the aftermath of the Spanish–American War. The rebel army that had fought the Spaniards to a stand-still in 1895–98 – many of whose members were black – was disdained by the Americans. After four years of American military rule, Cuba emerged independent in name, but a protectorate and economic colony of the United States in practice. Into Cuba's constitution were inserted restrictions known as the Platt Amendment (to the Army Appropriations Act of 1901). These limited the Cuban government's freedom to contract debt and make military alliances; required it to grant bases to the United States (one was promptly set up at Guantánamo Bay, which has recently become notorious);[29] and allowed the US the right to intervene in Cuba to ensure 'the maintenance of a stable government adequately protecting life, property and individual liberty'.[30] Although abrogated in 1934, the Platt Amendment served merely to inflame Cuba's frustrated search for nationhood. During the first 30 years of the new republic, government was generally corrupt and elections rigged; the losers would rise in arms and appeal for American intervention, which was often forthcoming. Political gangsterism was common.[31] Gyrations in the world price of sugar served to consolidate the control of deeper-pocketed American companies over the economy. Some 60 per cent of rural properties came to be owned by Americans. Cuban society was less racist than that of the southern United States, but power lay firmly with the whites.

The Great Depression hit Cuba very hard, prompting a collapse of sugar prices – the value of the island's sugar crop plunged from $199 million in 1929 to $42 million in 1932.[32] The resulting hardship and discontent brought down the repressive regime of Gerardo Machado, an elected dictator (dubbed a 'tropical Mussolini' by one of his opponents). An attempt by Sumner Welles, the American ambassador, to select a new government was thwarted by a rebellion of army NCOs led by Sergeant Fulgencio Batista, a handsome *mulato* stenographer. Batista allied with students and university professors, who formed a revolutionary government of socialist and radical-liberal inspiration. It decreed the nationalisation of the American-owned electric company and of several sugar properties. But Welles withheld recognition of the government, and Batista withdrew his support. Subsequent democratic governments were marred by corruption, and the chance of reform was lost. Batista would remain the dominant figure in Cuba for the next quarter of a century, ruling as an elected president in 1940–44 and returning as a dictator in 1952. Within a year, his dictatorship was challenged by Fidel Castro, a young lawyer, former student leader and member of the radical Ortodoxo Party (which claimed descent from Martí's PRC). Acting in the Cuban tradition of violent risings, he organised an attack on the Moncada army barracks in Santiago, Cuba's second city. It failed, but Castro survived. He was sentenced to 15 years, but was soon released under a general amnesty. Having made his way to Mexico, in December 1956 he tried again, landing with 82 guerrillas (including his younger brother, Raúl, and Che Guevara) in Oriente province, many of whose people were black and poor. Against all odds, the guerrilla force established itself in the mountains of the Sierra Maestra. The rest is history – but history wrapped in many myths.

There is, of course, a vast literature on the Cuban Revolution. The main question that need concern us here is why Castro and his fellow-revolutionaries did not restore democracy, but opted instead to extinguish capitalism. After all, less than a year before Castro marched into Havana, across the Caribbean in Venezuela an alliance of civilians and dissident army officers had ousted another dictator, Marcos Pérez Jiménez, but had established a democracy under a pact which excluded the Communist Party from power. The answer has much to do with Castro himself and with Cuban history, in which his revolution was grounded. As a student leader at Havana University, Fidel claimed to have read Marx and to have become a 'utopian communist'.[33] Never an ideologue, he was always a man of action, a political and military strategist; he wanted and understood power above all else. As a young lawyer, he was a rising star of the Ortodoxo Party; he would almost certainly have been elected as a deputy in the 1952 election, had this not been cancelled by Batista's coup. Even before the coup, disillusioned by what he saw as the betrayals of the democratic governments of the 1940s, he had decided that Cuba needed a revolution and that he would lead it. But what sort of revolution? The manifesto of Castro's 26 July Movement (named after the date of the assault on the Moncada barracks) issued at the outset of the guerrilla war was couched in moderate terms: it called for the restoration of the 1940 constitution, agrarian reform and nationalisation of public utilities. Several of Fidel's inner circle were communist sympathisers. Raúl Castro had been a member of the Communist Youth, while Che Guevara was a self-taught Marxist and fellow-traveller of communism, but not a party member. According to Tad Szulc, a well-informed biographer of Fidel, 'the historical [sic] decision that the revolution should lead to the establishment of socialism and then communism in Cuba was reached by Castro alone in the late spring of 1958.[34]

That decision was carefully concealed. As Batista fled Havana on New Year's Eve 1958, Castro named Manuel Urrutia, a provincial judge, as president; the cabinet was drawn mainly from the moderate, non-communist, wing of the 26 July Movement. But power lay with Fidel, who made himself commander-in-chief of the armed forces and established what Szulc calls a 'parallel' government, based on the new National Agrarian Reform Institute. He and Guevara applied the lessons they had learned from Guatemala: Batista's army was destroyed; an alliance with the Popular Socialist Party (as the old Communist Party called itself) was struck, but was concealed for two years until Castro had full political and security control. The Eisenhower administration was not persuaded by the democratic façade: although Castro would not nationalise all American businesses in Cuba until October 1960 and would not declare himself to be a communist until December 1961, as early as March 1959 the National Security Council began to review how 'to bring another government to power in Cuba'.[35] The CIA began sabotage operations: in March 1960, it blew up a Belgian freighter unloading a shipment of rifles in Havana harbour, killing a hundred people. When the invasion by a force of 1,500 Cuban exiles organised by the CIA came at the Bay of Pigs in April 1961, Castro, the master strategist, was ready as Árbenz had not been. The invasion was crushed on the beach by Castro's militias, partly because Kennedy refused to commit American air power or other forces. In October 1959, just nine months after entering Havana, Castro had already begun the contacts with the Soviet

Union that would lead to a full-scale military and economic alliance. In 1962, the Soviet Union's decision to station missiles on Cuban soil brought the world close to nuclear war. Kennedy and Khrushchev negotiated the withdrawal of the missiles in return for a guarantee that the United States would not again invade Cuba. Castro, who had wanted a military pact with the Soviet Union but not the missiles, was furious at being excluded from the negotiations, and at what he saw as Khrushchev's climbdown.[36]

The evidence suggests that those who have argued that Castro was somehow pushed into the arms of the Soviet Union and communism by the American economic embargo imposed, in stages, in 1960–62 are mistaken. The Cuban government's decisions were of its own volition.[37] It is safe to say that two political impulses drove Fidel Castro. The first was Cuban nationalism and anti-Americanism: he was determined to end US influence over the island's affairs. The other was the permanence of his revolution and of his personal control over his country.[38] Communism provided the tools to satisfy both impulses, rather than being an end in itself. Fidel always claimed primary inspiration from Martí – the nationalist, anti-imperialist Martí, rather than the democrat – not Marx. 'The intellectual author of this revolution is José Martí, the apostle of our independence', he said at the Moncada trial in 1953.[39]

It may not be coincidental that in both Cuba and Mexico revolutions whose aims included the consolidation of the nation state in the face of what was perceived to be a threat from the United States led to the establishment of one-party regimes. Yet democracy is far from incompatible with national self-determination, as many other countries have demonstrated. Castro drew on Cuba's traditions of guerrilla warfare and revolutionary violence, and its long struggles for nationhood and racial and social justice. The extent to which he came to embody that struggle explained the affection and respect many Cubans held for him despite their privations. But Fidel was also a Latin American *caudillo*, who militarised Cuban society as never before and ruthlessly crushed dissent. Especially in the 1960s, he incarcerated tens of thousands of political prisoners, often under appalling conditions – for much longer than would have been the case under the most repressive of South American dictators, as Jorge Domínguez, a Cuban–American political scientist, has pointed out.[40] The American economic embargo, and the countless failed assassination attempts against Castro by the CIA, served only to

aggravate this. They allowed Castro to claim that Cuba was in a permanent war with American imperialism.

The left turns against democracy

As well as awakening outside interest in Latin America, the Cuban
Revolution inspired a generation of young Latin American radicals.
Ultimately, it would have less impact on the region than the Mexican
Revolution, but that would not be for want of trying. Its appeal to the
Latin American left was enormous – and tragic. Before the Cuban
Revolution, the left was fairly weak in most countries. Its three main
components were anarcho-syndicalists, many of them European immigrants; communist parties, formed in most places in the 1920s and
subservient to the Comintern in Moscow; and thirdly, the more radical
supporters of populist leaders. In some countries, the communists had
achieved a small but significant following, especially in trade unions. In
Brazil, they had some support among army officers and conscripts. In
1935, the party attempted a coup against Getúlio Vargas, with a rising at
three army bases. It was crushed, and gave Vargas a pretext to declare
the *Estado Novo*, a quasi-fascist dictatorship.[41] Everywhere, the left faced
a structural problem: how to make a revolution where its main presumed
protagonist, the urban working class, was small and its trade unions
weak. It was for this reason that populists – with their appeal to a
broader, multi-class coalition – rather than social democrats, had been
the midwives of mass politics in Latin America. (The main exception
was Chile, whose mining industry, isolated in the distant Atacama
desert, generated a powerful union movement, and socialist and
communist parties.) The communists' answer would eventually be a
cautious one: that they should first ally with the 'national bourgeoisie'
against the 'feudal' agrarian oligarchy and 'imperialism' in order to create
a 'bourgeois-democratic' (i.e. capitalist) revolution. Only then would
socialism be on the agenda.

A dissenting and creative response came from José Carlos Mariátegui,
a journalist and essayist who founded what would become Peru's
Communist Party. His thought combined Marxism and *indigenismo*,
which, inspired by the Mexican example, took powerful root among
Peruvian writers and painters alike in the 1920s.[42] Mariátegui argued
that in Peru, at least, the source of revolution would be the peasantry in

alliance with the workers. This was because Peru's history was very different from that of Europe. He saw in the Andean Indian community 'elements of practical socialism' and of 'agrarian communism'. At the same time, the prevalence of the *latifundio* (large landholdings with indentured serfs) militated against capitalist development. 'Democratic and liberal institutions cannot flourish or function in a semi-feudal economy', he wrote.[43] Only socialism could bring development to Peru, he argued, but it would be not 'a tracing or copy' of its European models, but rather 'a heroic creation'. Mariátegui wrote in *Amauta*, the politico-cultural monthly journal he founded: 'We have to bring to life, with our own reality, in our own language, Indo-American socialism.'[44] This was a long-term task and would require a mass movement from which would emerge a revolutionary party.

Mariátegui was opposed from two sides. In Peru, it was Haya de la Torre and APRA, not the socialists, who led the opposition to the modernising dictatorship of Augusto Leguía of 1919–30. Abroad, at the first Latin American Communist Conference, held in Buenos Aires in 1929, unimaginative bureaucrats from the Comintern imposed orthodoxy.[45] Months later, Mariátegui, long an invalid, died at the age of 35, probably from the consequences of childhood diabetes. He seemed to have lost the argument. Yet his thought is reflected in several of the traits that came to distinguish the Latin American left, such as the importance given to nationalism, popular religiosity and social movements. It was not surprising that in Peru, unlike the rest of Latin America, Maoism, which also gave a pre-eminent role to the peasantry, should find adherents. The fundamentalist Maoist guerrillas who terrorised Peru from 1980 to 1993, claimed inspiration from Mariátegui: their full name was the Partido Comunista del Perú – Por el Sendero Luminoso de José Carlos Mariátegui (Peruvian Communist Party – for the Shining Path of José Carlos Mariátegui). In fact, Mariátegui, the most free-thinking of Marxists, had almost nothing in common with Abimael Guzmán, the sectarian and dogmatic terrorist who founded the Shining Path.

Mariátegui's vision of an indigenous Andean utopia, menaced by capitalism and imperialism, is today echoed by radical leaders such as Bolivia's Evo Morales. It was, however, based partly on myth. Mariátegui had little knowledge of the Andean world; his illness prevented him making more than one visit to the Peruvian sierra, and not a single peasant was among the founders of his party. 'He had constructed the image of an egalitarian and conflict-free [indigenous peasant] community which had never existed and still less at that time', admitted Alberto Flores Galindo, a Peruvian historian sympathetic to Mariátegui.[46] But Mariátegui had offered the most creative attempt to adapt Marxism to Latin American realities.

Thirty years later, the Cuban Revolution seemed to many on the left to offer the solution to their frustrated quest – a 'revolution in the revolution', as Régis Debray, a French theorist, put it. In the view of Che Guevara – whose writings on the Cuban campaign in which he fought achieved wide circulation – the only thing that had been missing previously was the courage of revolutionaries. In *Guerrilla Warfare*, a slim but enormously influential volume published in 1961, he stated:

> We consider that the Cuban Revolution contributed three fundamental lessons to the conduct of revolutionary movements in America. They are:
>
> (1) Popular forces can win a war against the army.
> (2) It is not necessary to wait until all the conditions for making revolution exist; the insurrection can create them.
> (3) In underdeveloped America the countryside is the basic area for armed fighting.[47]

This seemed to make sense. There were, after all, tens of millions of poor peasants in Latin America, and Mao Zedong's revolution in China had successfully based itself on the peasantry and rural warfare. Yet Guevara's message found its most receptive audience among the middle-class youth of Latin America, which was expanding rapidly as a result of economic growth and urbanisation. Many of them were acutely conscious of the injustices in their societies, and saw in the Cuban Revolution an effective way to tackle them. At the same time, the Catholic Church had an attack of conscience. Stimulated partly by the reforms of the Second Vatican Council and Pope John XXIII, a new current emerged which preached that the Latin American Church should concern itself primarily with helping the poor. The main impact of liberation theology, as it was called, was to form a network of grass-roots 'base communities' that agitated for change. But some of its proponents flirted with Marxism and violence. Nearly a thousand priests submitted a manifesto to a conference of Latin American bishops, held at Medellín in Colombia in 1968, in which they differentiated between the 'unjust violence of the oppressors' and 'the just violence of the oppressed'.[48] That stance would create many martyrs, both among priests and nuns and their followers. As Cardinal Óscar Andrés Rodríguez Maradiaga, a Honduran archbishop, put it: 'there were many priests in Central America who supported violent change . . . There was a big temptation to try and change things through violence, and what did we get? Only dead people.'[49]

For the best part of three decades after 1959, across Latin America a radicalised left committed itself to revolution. Rural guerrilla *focos* soon appeared in more than half a dozen countries, including Guatemala, Colombia, Venezuela and Peru. Yet Guevara's prescription for the *foco* – the Spanish word means 'focus' or 'centre', but also 'light-bulb' – had two fatal flaws. The first was that, like Mariátegui's vision, it involved a mythologised rewriting of history. Recent research has underlined that Fidel Castro's rebel army did not make the Cuban Revolution alone. It depended for its survival, and for its eventual victory, on a broad range of alliances with groups of middle-class professionals, the churches, labour unions and various revolutionary organisations. Strikes, agitation and sabotage in the cities were important in wearing down the will to fight of Batista's army, allowing the guerrillas to triumph.[50] The second flaw in Guevara's argument was even more serious. There was a world of difference between an armed rising against a corrupt and brutal dictatorship in an American neo-colony, such as Cuba, and attempting guerrilla warfare against the more powerful armies of the larger, independent nations of South America. That was especially so where governments enjoyed legitimacy and had carried out significant, if inadequate, social reforms. Guevara himself half-recognised this. In *Guerrilla Warfare*, he had written: 'where a government has come into power through some form of popular vote, fraudulent or not, and maintains at least an appearance of constitutional legality, the guerrilla outbreak cannot be promoted, since the possibilities of peaceful struggle have not yet been exhausted'.[51] But in practice, he would ignore this rider. His central message was that 'it is the duty of the revolutionary to make the revolution'. The voluntarism of a self-appointed revolutionary elite and a murderous militarism would thus come to act as a substitute for any missing political conditions.

Guevara was right, however, that after the Cuban Revolution, 'imperialism' (i.e. the United States) 'will not allow itself to be caught by surprise'; the same went for the 'higher bourgeoisie' in the region (i.e. Latin American business and governments).[52] After 1959, it was a basic tenet of United States policy towards Latin America to prevent a 'second Cuba'. That led successive administrations into alliances with some brutal or unsavoury dictatorships, and in turn served to stoke the fires of nationalist anti-Americanism in the region. In Washington's eyes, the first candidate for the role of another Cuba was the Dominican Republic. Following the assassination of Trujillo, an election in 1962 was won by Juan Bosch, an ineffectual social democrat. Bosch was soon overthrown by a military coup. When a subsequent government collapsed, a 'constitutionalist' group of army officers and their civilian allies attempted to restore Bosch to power. In fighting in Santo Domingo, the capital, they drove back conservative military officers who opposed them. The administration of Lyndon Johnson feared that communists were behind Bosch. It dispatched the marines as the spearhead of a force that would total 23,000 American troops – the lesson of the Bay of Pigs was thought to be not to do such things by halves. Their ostensible mission was to protect American civilians from chaos. In an echo of the Roosevelt corollary, Johnson claimed in justification of his action that there were 'headless bodies lying in the streets of Santo Domingo'. When opponents challenged this, he is said to have called the American ambassador, enjoining him 'For God's sake see if you can find some headless bodies.'[53] The outcome was the defeat of Bosch's supporters, and the installation in a less-than-free election of Joaquín Balaguer, a quiet and reliably anti-communist lawyer and amateur poet who had been Trujillo's amanuensis and, at the end, his frontman as president for a couple of years. He would win five more increasingly rigged elections. Though the outcome was less tragic than in Guatemala, the Dominican Republic would not become a democracy until well into the 1990s.[54]

For his part, Fidel Castro saw 'exporting the revolution' as a way to defend it on his island. Cuba trained, armed, financed and advised thousands of revolutionaries from other Latin American countries. In turn, the sudden advent of an increasingly loyal ally in the Caribbean caused the Soviet Union to take a much more active interest in Latin America. 'Cuba forced us to take a fresh look at the whole continent, which until then had traditionally occupied the last place in the Soviet leadership's system of priorities', according to Nikolai Leonov, who was long the KGB official closest to the Castro brothers.[55] In 1961, the Soviet leadership adopted a KGB plan to 'activate . . . armed uprisings against pro-Western reactionary governments' around the world, placing Central America at the top of the list.[56] The KGB had a habit of overstating its powers, and the Soviet Union became increasingly cautious about provoking the United States in its 'backyard'. Internal factors were almost always more important than external factors in the conflicts which played out in Latin America after the Cuban Revolution. But the recent availability of archive material from the former Soviet Union underlines the fact that outside intervention in the region during the Cold War was not a game played only by the United States.[57]

The main outcome of the first wave of rural guerrilla movements in the 1970s was the slaughter of some of the best and brightest among a generation of idealistic middle-class youths – and of the peasants and conscripts who were unlucky enough to get in their way. Guevara himself famously practised what he preached, going first to the Congo and then to Bolivia in answer to his own call to create 'two, three . . . many Vietnams'. His Bolivian venture summed up the arrogant futility of his quest. Although he had spent several weeks there on his way to Guatemala, he seemed oblivious to the fact that Bolivia's 1952 revolution had granted land and appreciable benefits to many peasants.[58] To compound his difficulties, most of Bolivia's communist leaders were unenthusiastic about Guevara's plan for a guerrilla *foco*, and steered him to barren and remote territory near Vallegrande in the south-east, far from the country's mines and their powerful trade-union movement. Not a single peasant joined the guerrillas, and several passed on information to the army, so the *foco* was quickly detected. A score of Green Berets from the United States swiftly trained a new Ranger unit of the Bolivian army in counter-insurgency. Together with regular army troops, within months they annihilated the *foco*, and captured and shot Guevara.

The manner of his death, at the age of 39, would make Guevara a universal icon. He had three times risked his life to bring revolution to countries that were not his own. That quest turned Guevara into a symbol of romantic rebellion everywhere. Thus, Diego Maradona, Argentina's troubled multi-millionaire football hero, explained his tattoo of Che: 'He was a rebel. So am I.'[59] To others among his acolytes, it seemed that Guevara, an ascetic, symbolised a selfless quest for utopia – that mirage which has dazzled so many Latin Americans and those who are drawn to the region. As Jorge Castañeda points out in his biography of Guevara, the photos of the dead guerrilla portrayed him as 'the Christ of Vallegrande' whose eyes expressed 'the tender calm of an accepted sacrifice'.[60] The stubborn, dogmatic and militaristic Argentine Marxist-Leninist thus became transubstantiated into a figure akin to that of a Christian martyr. His image not only adorns the most unlikely products of global capitalism, from bars to coffee mugs, but it takes its place in the gallery of popular saints with which Latin America's truck and bus drivers choose to adorn their vehicles to ward off the demons of the road.

Only in Nicaragua would something resembling the Cuban Revolution be repeated, with the Sandinista insurgency of 1979. Not by coincidence, Nicaragua, like Cuba, had suffered American intervention, was ruled by a corrupt dictator, and its army was a US-created gendarmerie that lacked legitimacy. The Sandinistas were a far from cohesive coalition of Marxists, liberation theologians, nationalists and social democrats. Some Sandinista leaders and many of their supporters had an idealistic commitment to social justice. The Reagan administration saw in the Nicaraguan Revolution the nightmare of a 'second Cuba'. It moved to overthrow the Sandinistas by organising the *Contra* guerrillas. The Sandinistas were determined to avoid the fate of Árbenz. With support from Cuba and the Soviet Union, they created a 100,000-strong army and an increasingly militarised state – 'a Central American Sparta', as Castañeda puts it.[61] The Reagan administration was hamstrung by opposition in the United States Congress, and further embarrassed by the exposure of its illegal efforts to funnel to the *Contras* the proceeds of clandestine arms sales to Iran. As a result, the *Contras* were no match militarily for the Sandinista army. But the Sandinistas' economic mistakes, their arrogant treatment of the peasantry and the hardships imposed by an American trade embargo and the *Contra* war engendered a growing groundswell of discontent. By then, Mikhail Gorbachev was acutely aware of the bankruptcy of the Soviet economy: after providing $1.1 billion in mainly military aid, the Soviet Union told the Sandinistas that they were on their own.[62] That encouraged the Sandinista leadership to embrace a peace plan authored by Óscar Arias, Costa Rica's president, and backed by the rest of Latin America, involving a free election. Eventually this was supported by George H.W. Bush, who had replaced Reagan; he was eager to turn the page on Iran–*Contra* and involvement in Nicaragua. After electoral defeat, the Sandinistas left power voluntarily in 1990. The revolution's 'most obvious legacy' was thus to create a democracy 'although this was not its most passionate objective', as Sergio Ramírez, the Sandinista vice-president and a novelist, wrote in a memoir.[63]

In 2006, Daniel Ortega won power again in a presidential election. He gradually turned Nicaragua into an elected dictatorship and the Sandinista party into his personal fiefdom. Thanks to a pact with a corrupt Conservative leader, he took control of the Supreme Court and the electoral authority, and in 2016 dissolved the main opposition. Only one among the six other surviving commanders of the revolution still supported him. Unlike in the 1980s, Ortega cosied up to the private sector; economic growth and Venezuelan aid made him popular. His intention appeared to be to create a dynastic regime, in an ironic echo of the Somozas: in 2016, he installed his wife, Rosario Murillo, who already ran the government behind the scenes, as his vice-president and putative successor.[64]

In neighbouring El Salvador, another small Central American country with a dire history of dictatorship, a powerful left-wing movement based on trade unions, radical priests and peasant groups emerged. In 1972, a reformist coalition was denied victory in a presidential election by fraud at the hands of the military party, whose only platform was anti-communism.[65] Thereafter, El Salvador spiralled into civil war between leftist guerrilla groups and the armed forces, some of whose leaders formed death squads. The United States pumped in military aid, while coaxing the generals towards democracy. The guerrillas of the Farabundo Martí National Liberation Front (FMLN) enjoyed considerable popular support; they fought the army to a standstill over a decade. By then, the Cold War was over. A peace agreement signed in Mexico in 1992 turned El Salvador, like Nicaragua, into a democracy. For two decades the right-wing Arena party, which built a powerful political machine, held power. Since 2009, El Salvador has been governed by the FMLN, now a peaceful political party of the left. It must grapple with a lacklustre economy, a weak tax base, organised crime and youth gangs, which have turned El Salvador into the most violent country in the Americas.

As the Cold War ended, the saga of US interventions in the Central American isthmus that had begun in Guatemala in 1954 closed with the invasion of Panama in 1989. At a cost of some 500 to 1,000 Panamanian dead (civilians and soldiers) and 25 American troops killed, this over-threw Manuel Noriega, a thuggish strongman, but one who was no nastier than many American allies (which he himself had been for much of his career as intelligence chief of the Panama Defence Forces).[66] Noriega had annulled an election which appeared to have been won by a large margin by the opposition candidate, Guillermo Endara, whom the American troops went on to install in office. Noriega was a trouble-some figure in a country to which the US was committed to turning over the Panama Canal ten years later. But in the end he was overthrown because of his links with drug traffickers at a time when the 'war on drugs' was as all-consuming in Washington as the 'war on terror' would become a dozen years later. Noriega was arrested and jailed on charges of aiding drug traffickers.[67]

If revolution and American pressure helped in the end to democra-tise Central America, that was not what Guevara and Castro had fought for. Under their influence, a generation of leftists gave priority to social justice, nationalism and anti-capitalism, and disdained democracy and the rule of law.[68] Not all of the myriad 'new left' groups – of Maoist, Trotskyist and nationalist inspiration, in addition to Guevarists – that sprang up across Latin America embraced violence and *la lucha armada* (the armed struggle). But many were equivocal on the matter; some would even welcome the arrival of dictatorships, in the deluded belief that repression would arouse the masses.

The long twilight of the Castros' Cuba

Halfway along Calle Obispo, a long street that connects the tourist haunts of Old Havana to the crumbling tenements of the nineteenth-century city, a garish placard advertises the museum of the Committees for the Defence of the Revolution (CDRs), the neighbourhood networks set up by Fidel Castro in 1960 to be the grassroots of his revolution. On the walls are blown-up extracts from Castro's speeches, and a chart showing the growth of membership in the CDRs, which by 2007 had reached 8.4 million of Cuba's 11 million people. The highlight, on the first floor, is a scale model in plaster of a typical Cuban street, the houses fronted with the Greek-revival columns that past sugar wealth bequeathed to the island's architecture, the façades painted in shocking pinks, lime green, toothpaste blue, peach and lemon. This remarkable exhibit of revolutionary kitsch goes unregarded. On a Saturday afternoon early in 2008, shortly after it opened, the museum was empty. One of the bored women attendants, with the mix of friendly warmth and necessary opportunism that characterises Cubans nowadays, asked if her only visitors could spare any antacids, saying 'medicines are very scarce'.

Fidel Castro ruled Cuba for almost half a century through the unbridled exercise of his massive ego. He centralised all power in his own hands, imposing utopian egalitarianism, a sclerotic centrally planned economy and a police state.[69] Even as he expropriated almost all property, he poured resources into social programmes that reached from cradle to grave, providing free world-class health care and education, as well as free housing, pensions and funerals. Life expectancy and many other social indicators rose above those in the United States. During his cold-war heyday Fidel turned his island into a pocket superpower, dispatching armies to Africa to fight apartheid and to support nominally Marxist tyrants, as well as fomenting revolution across Latin America. Yet Cuba would find that national self-determination again proved elusive. It became a Soviet satellite, a producer of Caribbean sugar for the eastern bloc in return for some $4 billion a year in economic aid.

The collapse of the Soviet Union and the disappearance of its subsidies had an impact on the island comparable only to that of the Great Depression: the economy contracted by a third and discontent grew. Many believed that Castro's revolution was bound for swift extinction.[70] To save it, he enacted economic reforms for what he called 'the Special Period in Peacetime'. He encouraged foreign investment, especially in the tourism industry. He gave state enterprises much more autonomy over their trade and finances. He allowed the use of the American dollar, to attract remittances from Cuban Americans. And he gave the smallest of nods to private enterprise in the form of peasant markets and small, family-run private businesses, such as restaurants and plumbers. After more than two centuries, sugar was finally eclipsed – by tourism and remittances – as Cuba's main source of foreign exchange, as it has been across the Caribbean. In 2002, the government decreed the closure of almost half the island's 156 sugar mills; half of the land under sugar was to be turned over to other crops, and at least a quarter of the 400,000 workers in the industry lost their jobs (officially, they were to be retrained).[71]

Many in Cuba and beyond hoped that economic reform would lead to political liberalisation. Yet the concessions turned out to be strictly tactical. At the start of the twenty-first century, Castro at last found replacements for his Soviet sponsor – in China and, especially, in Hugo Chávez's Venezuela. China provided Cuba with cheap loans for infrastructure and some consumer goods. Venezuela gave Castro all the oil he needed at a heavily subsidised price, as well as other goods. In return, some 16,000 Cuban doctors (a quarter of the island's total complement) worked in Venezuela, and Castro provided Chávez with political advice and security and intelligence advisers. Thus fortified, in 2005 Castro declared the 'Special Period' over. With it went many of the reforms. The previous year, he had banned the use of the dollar, and reimposed central control over state companies. By mid-2005, half the 800 foreign investors had gone, while only 140,000 small businesses remained, down from 240,000 a decade earlier.[72]

A mild relaxation of political control during the 'Special Period' was reversed, too. In April 2003, while the world was distracted by the start of the war in Iraq, Castro's secret police rounded up 78 dissidents. After summary trials, they received jail sentences averaging 28 years. More than two-thirds of the detainees were independent journalists and/or activists for the Varela Project, a pro-democracy group of Christian democrat inspiration, which in 2002 presented to the National Assembly a petition, signed by more than 11,000 people, calling for democratic elections. The regime responded by organising a referendum backing a change to the constitution that declared 'socialism' (i.e. communism) irreversible. The Varela Project was based inside Cuba, not in Miami. Its leader, Oswaldo Payá refused help from the United States and condemned the American trade embargo.[73] That made him especially dangerous to Castro's autocracy. In 2012, Payá was killed in a car crash, the cause of which is disputed.

Rather than dissent, it was what Cubans called 'the biological factor' that brought about the start of a slow and gradual transition on the island. In 2006, Fidel, needing urgent abdominal surgery, handed over his powers to his brother, Raúl, who formally replaced him as president in 2008. Raúl was temperamentally Fidel's opposite, an orderly and practical family man, lacking his brother's messianic streak. He was Sancho Panza to Fidel's Don Quixote; they even looked the parts (Raúl is said to keep statues of Cervantes's characters at his house). He launched a systematic programme of economic reform (officially 'updating') that revived many of the measures of the 'Special Period' and went beyond them. He abolished many of the petty restrictions suffered by Cubans, who could once again buy and sell houses and cars and stay in tourist hotels. He abolished the hated exit visa. By 2016, a third of Cuba's labour force of 5 million worked in a budding private sector of small businesses, co-operatives and private farms. Some 500,000 of them were owners of small or micro businesses – the most visible were restaurants and guest houses, but they included all manner of services.[74] Many relied on income from tourists and remittances from Cuban Americans. They faced many difficulties: the government wanted them to exist, but not to grow.

Change stirred across the Florida straits as well. Barack Obama loosened the embargo's restrictions on remittances and tourism, and authorised limited trade. After 18 months of secret negotiations, in December 2014 Obama and Raúl Castro surprised the world by announcing that their countries had agreed to restore diplomatic relations, frozen since 1961. The reopening of embassies followed. Obama called for the lifting of the embargo, though only Congress can approve that. In doing so, he was recognising the futility of a policy that had merely served as an ideological prop for Fidel's regime, while penalising American companies and tourists. He was also paying heed to the longstanding view of Latin American governments of both left and right.

In March 2016 came the historic sight of Air Force One flying low over Havana, bringing Obama and his family for a three-day visit. He stressed that he had come to 'bury the last remnant of the Cold War in the Americas' and 'to extend a hand of friendship to the Cuban people', but he also called for change on the island. In a speech in Havana's ornate and newly restored Grand Theatre, televised live to the nation, he voiced his support for the right of the Cuban people 'to speak their mind', 'to protest peacefully' and 'to choose their governments in free and democratic elections'.[75] Raúl soon made clear that this was not his intention. A month later, at the Seventh Congress of the Cuban Communist Party, he declared, with reference to free elections, 'if they manage some day to fragment us, it would be the beginning of the end . . . of the revolution, socialism and national independence'. Even the modest hopes in Havana that the congress might approve a limited electoral reform or a bigger role for the rubber-stamp parliament were dashed. While Raúl repeated that he planned to step down as president at the end of his second term in 2018 (when he will be 86), the congress reappointed him for a second term as first secretary of the Communist Party, until 2021.

Fidel's death, in November 2016, may in time free the way for faster economic reform. Unlike his brother, Raúl praised the 'market socialism' of China and Vietnam. He has been withering in his intellectual critique of the shortcomings of Cuba's centrally planned economy. Cuts in aid from Venezuela, as its own economy imploded, added to the urgency for change. Announcing that Cuba's GDP would shrink by 0.9 per cent in 2016, the government said that shipments of oil from Venezuela had fallen from a peak of 108,000 barrels per day in 2008 to some 40,000 by the end of 2016. Despite Fidel's pouring of resources into industries like biotechnology, Cuba was nowhere near being able to make its way in the world economically. Capital investment, at 7 per cent of GDP in 2011, was a third of the Latin American average, according to Carmelo Mesa-Lago, a Cuban economist at the University of Pittsburgh.[76] Thanks to the inefficiencies of the state agricultural system, the island imports 70 per cent of its food. Cuba also faces a demographic threat. It is the only Latin American country whose population is falling, because of both a low birth rate and emigration. The government's hopes of attracting investment were for a time pinned on a 'special development zone' around a new deep-water port at Mariel, west of Havana, built by Odebrecht of Brazil. Partly because of the American embargo, but mainly because of bureaucratic obstacles to foreign investment, three years after its creation, fewer than a dozen ventures there had been approved.[77] The reforms got bogged down over the complexities involved in scrapping Cuba's dual currency system, the regime's fear that change would create losers before winners and its residual fear of loss of control.[78] Uncertainty regarding the future of American policy towards Cuba under Donald Trump reinforced the regime's naturally cautious instincts.

Raúl has groomed Miguel Díaz-Canel, a 56-year-old former education minister, as his successor, appointing him vice-president (but not second secretary of the party, a post retained by José Ramón Machado Ventura, an elderly Stalinist ideological enforcer). It remains unclear how big a role the armed forces will play in the transition. As defence minister, Raúl moulded them into the island's most effective institution.

They run around 60 per cent of the economy. General Luis Alberto Rodríguez, Raúl's former son-in-law who heads GAESA, a state holding company that operates much of the tourism industry, is a powerful figure.[79]

With the death of Fidel and the eventual departure of Raúl, the regime will no longer lay claim to the legitimacy bestowed by many Cubans upon the generation that made the revolution. Their successors will be judged strictly on results. After almost six decades of the Castros, Cubans both long for and fear change. The social contract Fidel established in the Soviet period has frayed, as health services and living conditions have deteriorated. And Cuba is in some ways coming to resemble the rest of Latin America, but without political or much economic freedom. Critics have noted that back in 1959 Cuba was already one of the top five Latin American countries on a wide range of socio-economic indicators.[80] True, the distribution of income, schooling and health was highly unequal then. A third of the workforce lived in severe poverty, dependent on seasonal work on the sugar harvest; most of these Cubans were black. But in terms of average life expectancy, Cuba in 1959 was close to the United States, and it had more doctors per head than Britain and France. Between 1989 and 1993, social spending per person in Cuba was slashed by 78 per cent in real terms.[81] Though it has since recovered somewhat, by 2016 countries such as Chile, Costa Rica or Uruguay were close to matching Cuba in life expectancy and health outcomes, but their citizens were much more prosperous. Cuba was becoming Latin American, too, in its growing inequality. The Gini coefficient of income inequality rose from 0.24 in the late 1980s to 0.41 a decade later, according to *Espacio Laical*, a magazine published by Cuba's Catholic Church.[82] A confidential later study put the figure at 0.5, similar to the Latin American average of 0.53 in the mid-2000s.[83]

In many of the eulogies to Fidel when he died in November 2016, he was referred to as 'the father of his people'. In a sense that was true: he infantilised Cubans. Those with any initiative departed – more than a million of them. Miami is a tribute to their entrepreneurial drive. Those left behind eked out a living. The streets around Havana's Parque Central heaved with vendors, hawking snacks and tourist trinkets. Many of these *cuentapropistas*, or workers on their own account in the official jargon, were teachers, accountants or doctors who had left their ill-paying jobs for a more lucrative, if precarious, life in the incipient private sector. One was a woman who gave her name as Grisel. As a family doctor, she earned $23 a month in 2012; working in an improvised handcraft shop she made $40. She had two small children. A pair of children's shoes cost $13. 'I faced a choice of buying shoes or eating', she said.[84]

For those who remained in state jobs, petty pilfering and absenteeism was the norm. This half-life of the revolution carried a certain stability. Cuba's island status delayed change, just as it allowed Spain to retain its 'ever-faithful isle' long after losing its colonies on the American mainland. Obama's policy switch recognised that change could only come to Cuba from within. But the sense of inevitability about democratic transitions in the world that accompanied the fall of the Berlin Wall has gone.

Every evening, hundreds of Cubans hunch over smartphones, tablets and laptops on La Rampa, the avenue between the Habana Libre hotel and the Malecón, the seafront boulevard, as they do at other points around the country, after Raúl at last announced plans to hook the island up to the internet. The regime has lost its monopoly over information, just as it has lost its monopoly over the economic lives of Cubans. The younger generations have very different expectations from their parents and grandparents. The regime will ignore them at its peril.

CHAPTER FIVE

Failed Reformers, Debt-Ridden Dictators

On the Rua do Catete, a busy commercial street that connects Rio de Janeiro's central business district with the southern beaches of Copacabana and Ipanema, stands a neo-classical mansion whose exuberant external embellishment bespeaks its tropical location. Built by a coffee baron, it served as the residence of Brazil's presidents from the foundation of the republic until the move to Brasília in 1960. It is now a museum. On the top floor, faithfully preserved, is the bedroom where, early in the morning of 24 August 1954, Getúlio Vargas reached for his revolver and shot himself through the heart. 'I gave you my life. Now I offer my death', he wrote in a last letter to the Brazilian people.[1] After ruling from 1930 to 1945 mainly as a dictator, Vargas had reinvented himself as a populist democrat, winning a presidential election in 1950. He had been ground down by bruising battles with a powerful conservative opposition, first over the setting up of Petrobras, the state oil firm, then over the minimum wage and a government-backed attempt to bring trade unionism to the *fazendas* of the countryside. When an aide, acting apparently without the president's knowledge, arranged a botched murder attempt against one of Vargas's chief tormentors, the army demanded that the president resign. In choosing suicide, Vargas, ever the political survivor, made himself a martyr and ensured that his brand of developmentalist politics would predominate in Brazil for another decade. But it would be a struggle. Across much of South America in the quarter-century after the Second World War, reformers would try and achieve peaceful, democratic change. They had to chart a narrow and treacherous course between public expectations and entrenched land-owning oligarchies, and between restless armies and radicalised left-wing movements. They were not helped by the inflation and volatility generated by their economic policies. Few succeeded for long.

A decade after the coup in Guatemala, this contest again reached a denouement, this time in Brazil. Vargas was succeeded by Juscelino

Kubitschek, a genial medical doctor and skilled political deal-maker who had been governor of the large state of Minas Gerais and mayor of its capital, Belo Horizonte. Kubitschek promised 'fifty years' progress in five', to be achieved through a combination of state and private, especially foreign, investment. Deep in the *cerrado*, Brazil's great inland savannah, he built Brasília, a previously unfulfilled mandate of the 1891 constitution – one much desired by nearby *mineiros*, not a few of whom grew rich on the building contracts for the new capital. Under his presidency, foreign firms set up from scratch what would become a fully integrated car industry. Kubitschek formed a development agency for the backward north-east and gave a decisive push to Brazil's industrialisation. The economy grew at an annual average rate of around 9 per cent from 1957 to 1961. But all this came at a price. Opponents jibed that Kubitschek had notched up 'fifty years' inflation in five', while the current account plunged deep into deficit.[2] He called in the IMF, but then refused to implement a stabilisation programme. That allowed him to pose as a champion of national independence and leave office more popular than he had entered it. Indeed, Kubitschek was the first president in Brazil's new democratic era to complete his term – and the only elected one to do so until Fernando Henrique Cardoso served two full terms from 1995 to 2002. But the economic problems he had left unresolved would defeat his successors. Jânio Quadros, an eccentric anti-corruption campaigner from São Paulo, resigned after less than seven months in office. That prompted a constitutional crisis, since the vice-president was elected separately, and Quadros's running-mate had been narrowly defeated by João Goulart, a populist who was Vargas's former labour minister and political heir. Goulart, an essentially moderate but ineffectual politician, was distrusted by the right, which saw him as pro-communist. The army, then the ultimate arbiter of power in Brazil, was divided. A compromise was reached: Goulart would take office, but for two years many of his powers would be vested in Congress, creating a semi-parliamentary government.

Goulart's political base lay in the unions, but he was also backed by the Communist Party and newer left-wing forces, such as peasant leagues in the north-east. The Communist Party was fairly strong: it had won 10 per cent of the vote in the 1945 elections (it was banned three years later). It also had support in the armed forces, especially among the lower ranks; in addition, some 20–30 senior officers were party members.[3] Goulart steered a vacillating course. In just 30 months in office, he had no fewer than five different finance ministers. He twice appointed competent economic teams, but shrank from backing the stabilisation programme that Brazil clearly required if growth was to resume. In mid-1963, he veered left, frustrated by conservative opposition and egged on by his brother-in-law, Leonel Brizola, the governor of Rio Grande do Sul and an irresponsible demagogue. Facing an opposition majority in Congress, the government organised a series of mass demonstrations at which Goulart announced a programme of 'basic reforms'. These were to be carried out by decree, and included some land expropriation and the nationalisation of privately owned oil refineries. He fatally antagonised a pivotal group of moderate army commanders by supporting the unionisation of the lower ranks of the armed forces, encouraging a communist-supervised mutinous movement of army sergeants and navy petty officers.[4] As a result, these moderate commanders threw their decisive weight behind a rising against the president. On 1 April 1964, Goulart fled to one of his ranches in Rio Grande do Sul (whence he would seek asylum in Uruguay). Later that week, the Congress elected Humberto Castelo Branco, a moderate general, as president. To legitimise itself, the new government, mainly made up of civilian technocrats from the conservative União Democrática Nacional (UDN) party, issued an 'Institutional Act'. Its main author was Francisco Campos, who had drafted the constitution of Vargas's dictatorship, the *Estado Novo*. As in Argentina in 1930, the Act relied on the dubious juridical principle of *revolução vitoriosa* – or might is right. It gave the regime the power to purge Congress.

The armed forces thus extinguished two decades of civilian democracy in Brazil. They claimed to be acting in the name of legality, and many believed them. The coup was almost bloodless. It was supported by the elected civilian governors of the three most powerful states, two of them from the UDN. Castelo Branco, a moderate, said he would serve only for the rest of Quadros's original term. It was widely expected that Kubitschek would win the election due in 1965. But the armed forces were split between moderates and hardliners. They would end up staying in power for two decades. The left claimed that Brazilian democracy was overthrown because Goulart had used it to challenge, on behalf of the poor, the interests of Brazil's landowners and bankers. They also argued that the United States had helped to organise the coup. Certainly, the conservatives in Congress were implacably opposed to even moderate reforms. Yet Goulart could have survived, had he heeded the pleas of the military moderates to break with the far left and to assert rather than subvert military discipline. In the end, the coup happened because Brazilian politics had become too polarised and because too many politicians of both left and right concluded that they could not achieve their aims through democracy. Goulart's opponents were convinced that the president himself was using his military and union supporters to seek dictatorial powers, in the mould of Vargas in 1937 or Perón in Argentina. In the view of Lincoln Gordon, the American ambassador to Brazil, 'it had become a choice between populist coup from the top down and preventative counter-coup from the mainstream military. The latter prevailed.'[5] The United States supported this outcome, but did not organise it. The Brazilian armed forces had had a vigorous anti-communist tradition since the uprising of 1935. Elio Gaspari, a distinguished Brazilian journalist, recently concluded after an exhaustive investigation of the matter: 'not a single Brazilian, civilian or military, took part in the deposing of João Goulart because the United States desired it.'[6]

A coup in Chile

The events in Brazil acquired greater resonance as further military coups followed elsewhere. In all, there were nine between March 1962 and June 1966; all but one were against governments seen as weak in the face of communist and Cuban influence.[7] Moderately reformist govern-ments were toppled in Bolivia in 1964, in Argentina in 1965, in Peru in 1968, and in Ecuador in 1962 and again in 1972. Even Uruguay's democ-racy, one of the most robust in the region, succumbed. It had been built on an unusual combination of rural *latifundia* and urban socialism.[8] The harmonious process, in which farm exports paid for a paternalist state and a large public sector, broke down. On the one hand, the world market for wool collapsed in the 1950s; on the other, public employ-ment had become a tool for rewarding party loyalty and grew inexo-rably, with no corresponding increase in the output of public services.[9] Between 1960 and 1970, income per head barely grew, inflation rose and strikes became common. Compromise gave way to polarisation: ranchers sought to curtail the public sector, whose workers and pensioners resisted. The Tupamaros, an urban guerrilla movement of Guevarist inspiration, further inflamed matters by killing military men and policemen. In what one historian called the 'longest coup d'etat', civilian presidents first decreed a state of siege, and then placed the armed forces in charge of internal security, unleashing a murderous wave of repression against the law-abiding left, as well as the guerrillas.[10] Finally, in 1973, President Juan María Bordaberry dissolved Congress and ruled as the civilian face of a dictatorship. Three years later, the armed forces pushed him aside, even though they had already crushed the Tupamaros.

It was the coup in Chile in 1973 that shocked the world. Since 1932, Chile had appeared to offer a model of political stability and civilian democracy. But problems, including chronic inflation, were accumulating. With a small domestic market, the prevailing economic policy of industrialisation behind high tariff barriers produced disappointing results in Chile. Private investment was feeble; the economy was uncomfortably dependent on the export of copper. In the 1960s, Chile saw a determined attempt to remedy these problems through moderate reform. Eduardo Frei, a Christian democrat elected in 1964, promised a 'revolution in liberty'. This was based on Catholic social doctrine. It also received enthusiastic backing from the United States, which saw Frei as an exemplar for the Alliance for Progress. Frei's government negotiated the partial nationalisation of the American copper companies. It also pushed through a radical land reform, limiting farm size to just 80 hectares, and encouraged the unionisation of rural labourers. Some 22,000 families got land, but implementation of the reform did not satisfy the exaggerated expectations it had aroused. That went for the government's overall performance. Frei's achievements were real, but they alarmed the right, while failing to satisfy the left or the more radical elements in his own party. A policy of inflationary wage increases led only to an increase in strikes. The search for compromise which had traditionally marked Chilean democracy was giving way to polarisation, as in Brazil. And as in Brazil, that process would intensify with the arrival of a left-wing government with a narrow electoral mandate.

The victory in the 1970 presidential election of Salvador Allende, a socialist doctor of great personal charm, did not represent a big underlying swing to the left among Chileans.[11] Allende, in his fourth presidential campaign, won with just 36 per cent of the 3 million votes cast – or only 39,000 more than were received by Jorge Alessandri, a former president who stood for the right-wing National Party. Allende proposed a democratic but revolutionary government. The main aim of the programme of his six-party Popular Unity coalition was 'the search for a replacement of the present economic structure, doing away with the power of foreign and national monopoly capital and of the *latifundio* in order to initiate the construction of socialism.'[12] The government proposed to nationalise 76 companies (accounting for 44 per cent of total manufacturing sales), enact a more radical agrarian reform, redistribute income and promote 'popular participation' in the economy, politics and the administration of justice. Implementing this 'Chilean Road to Socialism' without violating the law or the constitution, as Allende proposed, would have been hard, even if he had enjoyed majority support and a cohesive coalition. He had neither. The opposition had majorities in both houses of Congress. And Popular Unity was deeply divided. On the one hand, the communists, the small Radical Party and Allende himself wanted to move cautiously and seek agreements with the Christian democrats. On the other, a large section of the Socialist Party had become enamoured of the Cuban Revolution and, at least in theory, armed struggle. At its 1967 congress, a majority of the party declared itself Marxist-Leninist and backed the *vía insurreccional* (the insurrectional road) to socialism. A far-left socialist splinter group, the *guevarista* Movement of the Revolutionary Left (MIR), was outside the Popular Unity, but its commitment to direct action exercised a gravitational pull on some of the coalition's grassroots. These anti-democratic elements on the left were mirrored on the far right by Patria y Libertad (Fatherland and Freedom), a small fascist group, by hard-line elements in the National Party and by a minority of military officers.

In office, Allende quickly completed the nationalisation of copper, with unanimous opposition support. Far more controversially, the government also took over 507 industrial and commercial firms; these included 80 large concerns, and nearly all of the banks. In the case of the takeover of industrial firms, it resorted to legal chicanery or to the punitive application of price controls. An obscure 1940s law allowed the government to intervene in firms facing an industrial dispute, so officials encouraged strikes in firms they wanted to nationalise.[13] Allende also drastically sped up implementation of Frei's agrarian reform, and did nothing to discourage land seizures by peasants. By 1973, about 60 per cent of

Chile's farmland had been transferred; two-thirds of these transfers happened under Allende. Taking into account the compensation paid, landowners suffered a net capital loss of up to $1.6 billion (a sum equal to 130 per cent of Chile's GDP at the time), according to one estimate.[14] The main beneficiaries were the resident labourers on the *haciendas*; there was nothing for the numerous *minifundistas* (small-scale farmers) or day labourers.

The government's macroeconomic policy was recklessly populist, designed to increase public support for Popular Unity and thus for socialist structural changes in the economy. The government granted big wage increases, cranked up public spending and public employment (which increased by almost 40 per cent in three years),[15] maintained an overvalued currency, printed money on a massive scale and imposed price controls. The result was predictable. At first, the economy grew rapidly, as unused capacity was brought into play; unemployment and inflation fell. But big distortions soon appeared: the trade account moved from surplus to deficit and the government was forced to suspend debt payments. Predictably, too, private investment dried up, since business was scared of expropriation. State and nationalised firms were badly run, requiring huge subsidies. By 1973, Chile was in the grip of shortages, rationing and black markets. As the public sector deficit reached 30.5 per cent of GDP, inflation climbed to 605 per cent, growth gave way to recession, and international reserves were enough to cover only three weeks of imports.[16]

The economy's initial expansion did help to produce an increase in support for the government. In a municipal election in April 1971, Popular Unity won 48.2 per cent of the vote. But this share then fell to 44.2 per cent in a congressional election in March 1973. The speed of the state takeovers intensified opposition and polarised the country. Congress refused to approve tax reforms to plug the fiscal chasm, and did its best to make life difficult for the government. Bosses' strikes, such as a month-long stoppage by truck owners, compounded the economy's problems. Much of the press was hostile to the government and was partisan. The United States helped the opposition. The CIA had spent $425,000 on anti-communist propaganda during the 1970 election. On the other hand, it now appears that the KGB spent some $500,000 in support of Allende's presidential campaign – including $10,000 to dissuade a potential left-wing rival from standing, which might just have tipped the result.[17] After the election, President Richard Nixon authorised the CIA to spend up to $10 million to try to prevent Allende from taking office. In the hope of provoking a coup, the agency organised a bungled attempt to kidnap General René Schneider, the army commander, which ended in his murder. Nixon then told Richard Helms, the CIA director, to 'make [Chile's] economy scream'.[18] After Allende took office, the administration blocked loans to Chile by the IMF and the World Bank. Allende's refusal to pay compensation to the copper companies (alleging 'excess profits') aggravated relations. The CIA gave money to the truck owners, other opposition groups and *El Mercurio*, a conservative newspaper. The KGB countered, though probably less lavishly, giving further funds to Allende and to publications sympathetic to him, as well as its regular stipend to the Chilean Communist Party.[19]

In the end, American machinations were less important in the destruction of Chilean democracy than economic chaos and the political intransigence of both Popular Unity and its opponents. Efforts to broker an agreement between Popular Unity and the Christian democrats, which might have saved democracy, foundered because too many on both sides opposed a compromise. The Christian democrats then joined the National Party in opposing Allende. But between them they lacked the two-thirds majority in Congress needed to impeach the president. Allende himself was powerless to restrain Popular Unity's left wing and the MIR, which pushed ahead with takeovers of land and of even small and medium businesses, and set up parallel political structures known as *poder popular* (popular power). Popular Unity was fatally divided between those trying to make a socialist revolution and those attempting radical reform within democracy. Finally, on 22 August 1973, the Chamber of Deputies declared the president to have violated the constitution and, by a vote of 81 to 47, invited the armed forces to defend it.[20]

More surprising than the coup that followed three weeks later was that the armed forces had not intervened earlier. They had a long tradition of respect for the constitution and the law. In 1972–73, several military commanders served as ministers. Allende, unlike Goulart, did not intervene in military matters. The army put down at least five coup attempts.[21] But its involvement in government dragged it into politics. The army commander, Carlos Prats, and the other Popular Unity supporters among the generals became increasingly isolated within the officer corps. On 23 August, Prats resigned, convinced that his replacement by his loyal deputy, Augusto Pinochet, offered the only hope of averting what seemed an imminent coup.[22] At the last minute, Pinochet joined a coup plot that was about to be unleashed by conservative members of the armed forces. On 11 September 1973, as the air force bombed La Moneda, the presidential palace, Allende committed suicide. The armed forces faced little resistance; subsequent claims by apologists of General Pinochet that Chile suffered civil war are false. The coup enjoyed the support of many Christian democrats, as well as of the National Party, the far right, and probably a majority of Chileans. Most expected the army to restore order and call fresh elections. Most were surprised and dismayed by the scale of the violent repression that followed the coup, and at Pinochet's determination to stamp out not just Popular Unity but Chilean democracy.

Was the coup inevitable? On its eve, Allende told several of his aides that to thwart it he was planning to announce a plebiscite on his rule, which he expected to lose. But by then it was too late.[23] Today, a statue of Salvador Allende stands in the square behind La Moneda, which has been restored. The man who put it there, Ricardo Lagos, Chile's president from 2000 to 2006, did much to reconcile his country to its past. A moderate socialist, his judgement on the Allende period in which he was a government official, carries weight: 'No country can survive when dreams spill over, when polarisation exacerbates differences, and when the authority doesn't govern. Those were the mistakes. But after September 11th, 1973, came the horror.'[24]

Political failure in Argentina

If Chile had seemed a model of democratic stability, Argentina had become a pathological case of political failure. The passions surrounding Juan Perón's decade in power and his overthrow in a military coup in 1955 had produced a political stalemate. The country was divided into two, incompatible halves – the larger one made up of Perón's supporters. The army's solution was to proscribe Peronism and exercise tutelary power over the republic. This produced only instability – between 1955 and 1973, Argentina had eight presidents, of whom only three were civilians – and, eventually, political violence on a scale not seen for a century or more. Peronism itself became fractionalised. With their chief in exile, Augusto Vandor and other trade-union leaders attempted to mould a Peronism without Perón. Had this project succeeded, it might have produced a moderate labourism and an accommodation with the armed forces that might have permitted a return to stable civilian rule.[25] But it did not succeed, partly because it was opposed by a growing Peronist left wing. This was drawn mainly from middle-class youths; paradoxically, in some cases their political roots lay in violent right-wing Catholic nationalism.[26] Out of this milieu would come Latin America's most powerful urban guerrilla movement, the Montoneros (founded in 1968), along with a slew of violent *grupúsculos*. Generally anti-Marxist, but not anti-Guevara (an Argentine after all), the Montoneros drew together 'radical Catholicism, nationalism and Peronism into a populistic expression of socialism', according to a historian of the organisation.[27] They received encouragement from Perón, because he saw them as a counterweight to Vandor. Perón was at heart a corporatist: he chose Franco's Madrid as his place of exile. But to keep control of the self-contradictory movement which claimed loyalty to him, he played its warring factions off against each other. In 1970, he told Tomás Eloy Martínez, an Argentine novelist, that when he was visited by supporters from the right or left of his movement, he talked to each 'in the language they wanted to hear'.[28] It was a game which would end explosively. At first, the Montoneros concentrated on spectacular acts of 'armed propaganda' against a military dictatorship reeling from the *Cordobazo* – in 1969 two days of rioting by striking workers in the industrial city of Córdoba ended with 14 killed by the army. Three years of low-level warfare by Peronism's armed gangs delayed, but did not reverse, a retreat by the armed forces, whose commanders concluded that only Perón's return could pacify the country. Restored to office with 60 per cent of the vote in 1973, an old (aged 78) and ill Perón had no use for the Peronist left. The Montoneros and their allies began to kill 'corrupt' trade-union leaders (Vandor had been murdered in 1969), managers at businesses facing strikes, as well as policemen and army officers. Perón and, after his death, his third wife and successor, María Estela 'Isabelita' Martínez, a former nightclub dancer, unleashed against the Montoneros the indiscriminate violence of the Argentine Anti-Communist Alliance, or Triple A, a death squad made up mainly of policemen.

Most Argentines saw the military coup that overthrew 'Isabelita' in 1976 as inevitable, and many at first welcomed it.[29] The country was suffering galloping inflation, a political killing every five hours and a bomb explosion every three hours.[30] The violence of Argentina's guerrillas was far from trivial. By 1975, the Montoneros comprised some 5,000 people under arms (though many were not full-time fighters) and had extorted $60 million by kidnapping a leading businessman, Jorge Born (a sum equal to a third of Argentina's defence budget, as Born pointed out). They began to flirt with regular warfare, attacks on army bases and terrorism (a bomb in an army cinema wounded 60 among a group of retired officers and their wives).

The scale of Montonero violence goes some way to explaining, without in any way justifying, the unprecedented wave of terror unleashed by the military junta of 1976–83. General Jorge Videla, its head until 1981, declared: 'a terrorist is not just someone with a gun or a bomb but also someone who spreads ideas that are contrary to Western and Christian civilization'.[31] The armed forces proceeded to institutionalise the methods of the Triple A. Victims included not just guerrilla suspects, but also their relatives and friends, peaceful dissidents and innocent bystanders. The methodology involved abduction, 'disappearance', lengthy and unrestrained torture, murder and then the disposal of the body at sea or in secret graves. Military installations were turned into clandestine concentration camps. An investigative committee set up by the democratic government of Raúl Alfonsín later found that at least 8,960 people had disappeared in this 'dirty war' – almost three times the number killed by the Pinochet regime in Chile.[32] Within two years of the coup, the Montoneros and many of their sympathisers had been wiped out.

From *caudillos* to bureaucrats of repression

From 1930 to the early 1970s, across much of Latin America civilian governments and dictatorships interrupted each other in what came to be called the pendulum effect. By the mid-1970s, dictatorship had become the norm. In 1977, more than two-thirds of Latin Americans – and eight out of ten South American republics – lived under the heel of the armed forces. Add Mexico's civilian authoritarianism, and democracy appeared to have failed completely in the region. It survived only in

Costa Rica, and in Colombia and Venezuela. In the latter two countries, pacts between the main political parties allowed for varying degrees of power-sharing and fixed limits to political competition. This guaranteed stability, though at some cost to democracy itself; in both countries, opponents would claim, more or less plausibly, exclusion from the democratic process as a justification for taking up arms.

The dictatorships of the 1960s and 1970s were different from those of the past. On the whole, armies were no longer the vehicles through which *caudillos* could construct personal dictatorships – though Pinochet would be an exception while, in Paraguay, the lengthy tyranny of General Alfredo Stroessner (1954–89) was a throwback to an earlier era. Nor did these new regimes merely back one civilian faction against others. They were more ambitious, seeking a permanent reordering of society. To eliminate communism, General Pinochet declared, required ending democracy, since this had shown itself 'no longer able to confront an enemy that has destroyed the state'.[33] The terror they meted out was far more intense and systematic than that to which most of South America (though not Central America) was accustomed. What explained this new brand of dictatorship and the failure of democracy? It is as well to start with the armies themselves. Many on the left pinned the blame on the United States and the training in anti-communist soldiering it imparted to Latin American officers at places such as the School of the Americas, in Panama. Certainly, after Guatemala, the United States had in effect given the green light to coups in the name of anti-communism. The Cold War was an important factor in the rise of the dictatorships, yet it is patronising, as well as false, to assume that Latin American armies required lessons in anti-communism – or in coups. One of the few empirical studies of such matters, of the coup which overthrew a populist government in Ecuador in 1963, found that the US-trained officers involved were no more anti-communist than the others.[34] National security doctrines, under which the armed forces saw themselves as fighting a total war against communism that involved politics and the economy, as well as military confrontation, were home-grown products rather than American imports.[35] And not all armies behaved in the same way. The Venezuelan army, which traditionally had close links with the United States, yielded to a democratic regime in 1958.

Other analysts attributed democratic breakdown to the contradictions of 'dependent capitalism'. Guillermo O'Donnell, an Argentine political scientist writing in the midst of the political violence and state terrorism in his country in the 1970s, described the new breed of dictatorships in Brazil and the Southern Cone as 'bureaucratic-authoritarian' regimes, a term that gained wide currency. By that he meant that they had arisen to enforce the dominance of a 'highly oligopolised and internationalised bourgeoisie' (i.e. local business magnates and multinational firms). They did this by excluding from power 'popular sectors' (such as workers and peasants), restoring political order and stabilising the economy in ways that benefited large companies at the expense of workers.[36] There seemed to be much truth in this. The military dictatorships typically banned political parties, trade unions and other grassroots groups, often hunting down and killing or imprisoning their leaders. They sometimes handed over economic policy to conservative technocrats. Strikes were normally banned, and military governments often tried to impose wage cuts as part of efforts to stabilise the economy. A partial exception was Brazil's regime: more politically sophisticated than its peers, it purged Congress, but did not shut it down, and allowed (heavily controlled) elections for state governors. But most senior government jobs went to generals or technocrats.

Yet the facts do not support the notion that the dictatorships' primary purpose was to impose 'neoliberal' economic policies. Only in Chile would the dictatorship impose comprehensive and far-reaching free-market economic policies. A telling counter-example was Peru's dictatorship of 1968–80, especially in its first phase under General Juan Velasco. Like the 'bureaucratic-authoritarian' regimes, it was a government of the armed forces as an institution. Yet it enacted a radical agrarian reform, expropriated foreign oil and mining companies and the fishmeal industry. It set up a host of new state companies and co-operatives, and required private firms to grant workers a share of the profits and a place on the board. It was not particularly repressive, but it did limit freedom of expression, seizing control of the press and television. The regime declared itself 'neither capitalist nor communist'. But despite Velasco's nationalisation of American firms (for which Peru eventually paid compensation), his government did not attract outright hostility from Washington. That was partly because it signed new contracts for private foreign investment in oil and mining, and partly because it was accurately seen as staunchly anti-communist, even though it was supported by the local Communist Party and bought large quantities of military hardware from the Soviet Union. Indeed, the 'Peruvian experiment' was an attempt to prevent future social conflict, and to deter the rise of the left, by implementing much of Haya de la Torre's populist programme of the 1920s and 1930s. Even by regional standards, landholding in Peru was highly unequal: fewer than 10,500 big *haciendas* (or 1.2 per cent of the total number of farms) accounted for more than half of all farmland. Some of Velasco's reforms were overdue, but many were heavy-handed or poorly executed, and some created new problems, such as a bloated state. His government failed to create an organised base of civilian support, and the military regime was eventually undermined by debt and popular protest against consequent austerity measures.[37]

In retrospect, it is clear that some fairly straightforward factors lay behind the genesis of the 'bureaucratic-authoritarian' regimes. Depending on the country, guerrilla action, the breakdown of order, extreme political polarisation, the discontents and disorders generated by inflation and stop-start economic policies – and usually a combination of several of these things – prompted military officers to believe that the survival of the state itself was at risk. They were often encouraged to step in by civilians, and not just businessmen. Just as sections of the left turned their back on democracy, so did many on the right (some conservatives, of course, had never embraced democracy). They feared that they would lose the game of mass politics. In Argentina, the Peronists seemed electorally unbeatable. In Brazil, the anti-Vargas UDN despaired of its inability to win the presidency democratically. Business groups feared expropriation or punitive policies by elected populist or leftist governments. Together with parts of the middle class and of the poor, they came to value order and economic stability above democracy and liberty. Politicians failed to find compromises. Above all, the economic policies of state-led industrialisation and protectionism were limping into more and more problems. It is not coincidental that these policies had been pursued with particular fervour in Brazil, Argentina, Chile and Uruguay – and that in the three countries of the Southern Cone they had produced disappointing growth rates. Political instability and breakdown were indeed a faithful reflection of economic disorder and the distributional conflicts which this generated. Since the prevailing economic policies gave such a vast role to the state, it is not surprising that the battle for control of the state became so desperate.

The rise and indebted fall of statist protectionism

After the Second World War, many Latin American governments had adopted the policy recommendations of CEPAL in an attempt to speed industrialisation. In addition to raising tariffs on imports, governments added many non-tariff barriers (including outright bans) against goods which competed with local production, and gave soft loans and subsidies to favoured industrial firms. They also used the state aggressively to promote development, through state-owned companies and regulation. This effort was partly successful: by the end of the 1960s, Brazil, Mexico and Argentina were at least semi-industrialised, and Chile and Colombia were not far behind.[38] But because they were over-protected, many industrial firms were very inefficient. Some of the main beneficiaries of protection were multinationals, which set up factories behind the tariff barriers where they could often get away with using old technology. State-owned companies multiplied, partly because of the reluctance or inability of the private sector to make large industrial investments. By the end of the 1970s, Brazil had established no fewer than 654 state firms, including 28 of the 30 largest companies in the country.[39] The proprietorial state in Latin America owed as much to Mussolini as to Marx. It was supported by private business (which saw state companies as a source of padded contracts or subsidised raw materials) and by the armed forces (which favoured it for reasons of national security), as well as by trade unions and the left.

In sharp contrast to industrialising countries in Asia, Latin America neglected exports. The region deliberately turned its back on the world economy just as international trade began its long post-war boom. In 1946, Latin America (with 6.5 per cent of world population) accounted for 13.5 per cent of world exports, a figure that had fallen to just 4.4 per cent by 1975.[40] But the new industries relied on imported machinery and components, so periodic balance-of-payments crises became the norm. By the mid-1960s, it was clear that the policy formula needed adjusting. The *cepalistas* argued that the key to making the model work was to expand the size of the domestic market. To do this, they favoured structural reforms, such as agrarian reform and tax changes. Yet such reforms were fiercely opposed by the landed oligarchy and others, and governments normally shrank from them; even where they were adopted, they had only a marginal effect. Regional free-trade schemes provided some additional markets for manufactures, but their implementation was patchy.

All too often, governments resorted to fixes. The tools of choice for market expansion were unsustainable wage increases and printing money to cover the subsidies and losses of state-owned companies. These expedients fuelled two characteristic Latin American economic vices: inflation and sickening boom-bust cycles, ending in currency devaluation (which in turn fuelled inflation). And they did nothing to reduce income inequality. Workers lost out from inflation, while businesses reaped exaggerated profits (called 'rents' by economists) from government protection from competition. The system thus rewarded businesses for their effectiveness at lobbying, rather than for their efficiency in production. Governments often resorted to multiple exchange rates, under which importers of goods deemed essential by the bureaucrats and planners would get artificially cheap dollars. This encouraged corruption and the misallocation of resources.

When oil prices rose sharply in the 1970s, East Asian countries such as South Korea responded with fiscal retrenchment and redoubled their export drive. Latin America responded by borrowing, in a desperate attempt to keep the state-led model on the road. Commercial banks in the United States, Europe and Japan, flush with petrodollars, were eager to lend. Their loans came without the strings attached to those from the IMF. The catch was that they also carried higher, and variable, interest rates. When the Iranian Revolution of 1979 triggered a second 'oil shock', the subsequent stagflation in rich countries drove up international interest rates (to 16 per cent by 1981), while causing export earnings to fall in many Latin American countries. In a financial merry-go-round, the banks made fresh loans to cover the interest payments on previous ones. Between 1979 and 1982, Latin America's total debt rose from $184 billion to $314 billion, while the ratio of debt payments to exports jumped from 26.6 per cent in 1975 to 59 per cent in 1982.[41] Richer and smarter Latin Americans used this expensive hiatus to get their money out before the crash. Estimates of the money that went abroad range from $50 billion to $100 billion, with Argentina, Mexico and Venezuela the most affected.[42]

The tone was set by Mexico. Flush with new oil discoveries, President José López Portillo threw aside a cautious economic programme, proclaiming that Mexico's challenge was now to 'administer abundance'.

A binge of spending, pharaonic investment and corruption ensued. When the oil price fell again and interest rates rose, López Portillo pledged to defend the peso 'like a dog'. A fortnight later, the Bank of Mexico gave up trying to defend the exchange rate, which plunged from 26 to 45 to the dollar. Six months after that, in August 1982, the government stopped payments on Mexico's $80 billion foreign debt and suspended foreign-exchange transactions. In a last, destructive throw, López Portillo nationalised the banks. Over the next 12 months, debt defaults ricocheted across Latin America. It was by no means Latin America's first debt crisis: most countries in the region had defaulted in the 1820s and again in the 1930s (some had done so at other times, too). Just as on those previous occasions, default marked the end of an era and the start of a new one.

Neither Che nor Pinochet: the democratic wave

In 1977, all but four Latin American countries were dictatorships. By 1990, only Cuba was, while Mexico had begun to move along its slow road to democracy. Even as academic treatises were being published, claiming that Latin America suffered from 'blocked societies', incapable of democratic modernisation, winds of change blew through the region. The democratic wave began in Ecuador, where a civilian government was elected in 1978, and moved quickly to Peru and beyond (see Table 3). At first, some analysts saw this as just another swing of the pendulum. Yet it soon became clear that several deeper factors were at work. The first was that the international climate was changing. In the late 1970s, Jimmy Carter had proclaimed the importance of human rights in American foreign policy, especially as regards Latin America. That led to friction between the United States and some of the dictatorships. As importantly, in Spain and Portugal, mortality put paid to the longstanding fascist dictatorships of Francisco Franco and António de Oliveira Salazar. The Iberian transition to democracy in the 1970s was highly influential across the Atlantic.

Second, state terror and long years of exile caused the left to reflect on the folly of its conduct in the 1960s and 1970s. Many left-wingers came to accept the value of civil liberties and of democracy – without the derogatory adjectives, such as 'bourgeois' or 'formal', with which they had previously vilified it.

Table 3: **The democratic wave**

A chronology

1977: only Colombia, Costa Rica and Venezuela	Had democratic governments.
1978: Domincan Republic	Opposition victory in presidential election ended 12 years of rule by Joaquin Balaguer. (Subsequent elections, three of which were won by Balaguer, were marked by fraud. Since 1996, elections have been free and fair).
Peru	Military government calls elections for a Constituent Assembly.
1979: Ecuador	Presidential election ends seven years of military rule.
1980: Peru	Presidential election ends 12 years of military rule. (In 1992 President Alberto Fujimori dissolved Congress; a Constituent Assembly was elected later that year. In 2000, Fujimori fled the country after winning an unconstitutional third term in a fraudulent election; democracy was again restored in 2001).
1981: Honduras	Presidential election ended ten years of military rule (but government remained under military tutelage until 1984).
1982: Bolivia	Civilian government elected in 1980 but blocked by military coup. Military takes office.
1983: Argentina	Presidential election ends seven years of military rule following defeat in Falklands/Malvinas war.
1984: El Salvador	Presidential election ends half a century of military-dominated government. Civil war continues until 1993 peace agreement.
Uruguay	Presidential election; restoration of democracy in 1985 ends 12 years of military rule.
1985: Brazil	Congress elects a civilian president, as part of a gradual transition to democracy; the armed forces return to barracks having seized power in 1964.
Guatemala	Presidential election restores civilian government after three decades of military-dominated rule. Civil war continues until 1996 peace agreement.
1989: Chile	Election of civilian government ends General Augusto Pinochet's dictatorship (begun in 1973), flowing his defeat in a referendum in 1988.
Paraguay	Presidential election after General Alfredo Stroessner, dictator since 1954, is ousted in a coup.
1990: Haiti	First-ever free presidential election won by Jean-Bertrand Aristide; overthrown by military in 1991; restored to power by US invasion in 1994; and resigned in 2004 following armed rebellion and US and French pressure. Free presidential election held under UN supervision in 2006.
Nicaragua	A free and fair election, held as a result of US pressure and a regional peace agreement, ends 11-year Sandinista regime, which had overthrown the dictatorship of Anastasio Somoza in 1979.
Panama	Civilian government takes office following US invasion of December 1989 which overthrew the authoritarian regime of General Manuel Antonio Noriega; free and fair election takes place in 1994.
2000: Mexico	Victory of Vicente Fox in presidential election ends seven decades of rule by the Institutional Revolutionary Party.

An analogous re-evaluation took place on the right and among businessmen. Many of them had assumed that dictatorships, free of the need to satisfy voters, would be able to take the unpopular decisions required to put in place policies that would guarantee faster economic growth in the medium to long term. Yet it had not turned out like that – and this was the third and most important factor behind the turn to democracy. Most of the dictatorships had proved as incapable of grappling with the economic challenges facing the region as their civilian predecessors had been. Military officers around the world tend to be hostile to free-market economics.[43] In Latin America, in addition, the armed forces themselves had a vested interest in a large state, since this provided jobs for officers and subsidies for military enterprises such as arms factories. Many military governments in the 1960s and 1970s began stabilisation programmes that involved a retreat from *cepalista* policies of state-led industrialisation, but few sustained the effort. Contrary to conventional wisdom, dictatorships, lacking an electoral mandate, depended on short-term economic success for legitimacy.

The exception was General Pinochet's Chile.[44] In 1975, he appointed a team of liberal economists (known as the 'Chicago Boys' after the university where many of them had imbibed the teachings of Milton Friedman as doctoral students). They carried through a drastic programme of reform. They cut tariffs from a peak of 750 per cent under Allende to a flat 10 per cent; used a strong peso to fight inflation; implemented large-scale privatisations; cut the fiscal deficit; and began a compulsory private pension system. Their policies had some heterodox elements: they did not privatise the state copper company, partly because the armed forces took a share of its profits for arms purchases. Pinochet was able to impose this free-market programme because, uniquely among his dictatorial peers, he managed to concentrate absolute power in his own hands. Chile's armed forces lacked the interservice rivalry and politicisation of those in Argentina, Peru and elsewhere. Pinochet appointed a team of civilian liberal economists – partly in order to cement his own power and autonomy in relation to the armed forces.[45]

Elsewhere, when the 1982 debt crisis broke, the dictatorships suffered the opprobrium of economic failure. They had not broken decisively with the *cepalista* policies. Some had faced mass protests, such as the strikes in the São Paulo car factories that would first bring a bearded trade-union leader called Luiz Inácio da Silva (or Lula) to the attention of Brazilians. The generals had found that governing urbanised societies and increasingly complex economies was not simple. Rather than risk their professional cohesion, Latin America's armies sat down with the civilian politicians and negotiated a return to the barracks. The first task facing the newly established democracies was thus to deal with the economic wreckage left behind by the dictatorships. Only in Argentina did military retreat turn to rout, and that was thanks to the dictators' folly in invading the Falkland Islands (Islas Malvinas) in a desperate attempt to whip up popularity. Like so many other things in Argentina over the previous decades – and over the decades to come – it reflected the delusions of grandeur of a country that neither understood nor was reconciled to its puzzling decline.

CHAPTER SIX

From the Washington Consensus to the Commodity Boom – and Bust

The Casa Rosada, Argentina's presidential palace, turns its back on the estuary of the River Plate and looks out over the Plaza de Mayo, the heart of Buenos Aires during the centuries of Spanish rule, when it was no more than a small muddy settlement for the trading of hides. The present palace was built in the 1870s in an eclectic mixture of the Florentine and French styles, just as Argentina was beginning its rise to fleeting greatness. From its balcony, Juan and Eva Perón conducted their love affair with the *descamisados* (literally, 'shirtless ones'), the masses of industrial workers and migrants from the interior who crowded into Buenos Aires in the 1940s – a scene recreated by Madonna in the film *Evita*. On an overcast October day in 2001, in the southern-hemisphere spring, the Casa Rosada looked unusually gloomy, its appearance not helped by a short-lived official decision to paint the frontage a garish puce instead of the previous gentle pink. The mood within was scarcely more cheerful. The previous Sunday, the battered centre-left governing coalition had suffered a swingeing defeat in a mid-term congressional election, at which almost half the electorate was so disillusioned with politicians of all stripes that they either stayed away from the polls or cast spoiled or blank ballots. In a small sitting room on the first floor of the palace, lined with smudgy scenes of the port and the Pampas by local impressionists, Fernando de la Rúa, the president, did his best to sound upbeat, but managed merely to suggest that he was in denial. The election was 'not a vote against the government but against the political class', he explained over a cup of tea. 'The electoral results, given the [austerity] measures I've taken, are excellent.'[1]

De la Rúa, a cautious lawyer, took pride in his public image as a boring but honest administrator. He had stuck doggedly to the conservative economic policies of his predecessor, Carlos Menem. These centred on an arrangement known to economists as a currency board, and to Argentines as *convertibilidad* (convertibility). This involved fixing the peso – by law, not just policy decision – at par to the dollar, abolishing all exchange and capital controls, and restricting the money supply to the stock of hard-currency reserves. The effect was that Argentina renounced both exchange-rate policy and monetary policy. The interest rate for borrowing by both the government and ordinary Argentines would, in effect, be that of the US Federal Reserve plus a risk premium (known to Argentines as *riesgo país*, or 'country risk'). The currency board, together with an array of free-market reforms, brought rapid growth in the 1990s. But then capital suddenly stopped flowing to emerging-market economies, plunging Argentina into a recession which, by October 2001, was entering its fourth year. The confidence that foreign financiers and locals had shown in the country for a decade turned to a stampede for the exit. Despite two IMF loan packages in nine months, totalling \$22 billion, a run on deposits saw some \$15 billion leave the banks between July and November 2001. Much of this money left the country. Under the currency board, the resulting fall in the Central Bank's reserves automatically translated into a monetary squeeze which throttled the economy: in the second half of 2001, Argentina's GDP shrank at a rate equivalent to 11 per cent a year. Every day, Argentine newspapers would report anxiously on the oscillations of *riesgo país*. By July 2001, it had climbed to 16 percentage points – a rate at which the government's debt was unpayable under any reasonable assumptions. Even so, de la Rúa rejected calls for a change in economic policies. 'There will be no [debt] default, no devaluation . . . We will fulfil our obligations', he insisted.[2]

Out in the rustbelt suburbs that ring Buenos Aires to the south and west, the mood among the descendants of the *descamisados* was turning from despair to anger. At dusk in a backstreet in Mataderos, a district of shuttered cold stores that once supplied the world with chilled beef, a ragged line of several hundred people spilled out from a charity soup kitchen. They were queuing for an evening meal, a thin stew of rice with small lumps of sausage and carrot and, on this occasion, a rare handout of flour, pasta and a few oranges. Many in the queue said they had not had a job for years. In what had long been Latin America's richest country, 'each year, there's more and more hunger and less and less hope', said Mónica Carranza, who ran the soup kitchen and a hostel for destitute young women.[3]

When the run on deposits threatened to bring down the two biggest local banks, on 1 December the government imposed restrictions on withdrawals, in effect freezing most savings. This enraged the middle class, and seemed to undermine the whole point of convertibility. It prompted the IMF to pull the plug on Argentina, halting disbursement of its loan. A fortnight later, angry mobs began to loot supermarkets, at first in the interior and then in Buenos Aires. On 19 December, de la Rúa went on television to declare a state of emergency. That night, Buenos Aires echoed with the sonorous roar of a *cacerolazo* (mass pot-banging), a traditional form of protest among the Latin American middle class. The next day tens of thousands of mainly unemployed protestors, many of them organised by the Peronists, converged on the Plaza de Mayo. After 29 people were killed, most when police opened fire on demonstrators, de la Rúa resigned. He was spirited away from the Casa Rosada by helicopter.

Over the next week, as power passed to the deeply divided Peronists, three provisional presidents came and went. One of them declared a default on $81 billion in foreign-currency bonds issued by the government – the biggest sovereign debt default in world history. The announcement was greeted with cheers in the Congress and shouts of 'Argentina, Argentina' – as if the national team had just won a football match. Congress then installed Eduardo Duhalde, the Peronist boss of Buenos Aires province, as president. He decreed the end of the currency board. 'Argentina is bust. It's bankrupt. Business is halted, the chain of payments is broken, there is no currency to get the economy moving and we don't have a peso to pay Christmas bonuses, wages and pensions', Duhalde declared with grim realism.[4] He devalued the peso, which quickly sank to three to the dollar.

Argentina suffered a national catastrophe in 2001–02, a collapse that was economic, financial, political and social. In the year to March 2002, the economy shrank by 15 per cent and unemployment climbed to 21 per cent. The number of Argentines living below the official poverty line rose from 38 per cent to 58 per cent.[5] Although a vigorous recovery followed, it would be mid-2005 before the economy regained its size of 1998. Until the 1970s, Argentina had boasted a European-style society, in which some 60 per cent considered themselves to be middle class.[6] Now, the social pyramid resembled the rest of Latin America.

The Washington Consensus on trial

For many in Argentina and beyond, this collapse became the prime exhibit in the case against 'neoliberalism', the Washington Consensus and the policies pursued by the IMF in Latin America. These policies, it was asserted, led to an increase in poverty, inequality, unemployment and the informal economy across the region; through privatisation and free trade, they enriched a few at the expense of the many; they benefited multinationals at the expense of national enterprise, especially small and medium firms; they led governments to give priority to debt payments instead of social spending; and they were foisted on Latin America in a doctrinaire 'one size fits all' manner by the IMF, the World Bank and the United States, and by Latin American presidents who employed undemocratic methods. One popular text attacking the reforms concluded: 'although the rich have had a vintage two decades, most of the region's people are poorer and more insecure: their homes, communities, schools and hospitals are collapsing around them'.[7] If nothing else, the Washington Consensus had clearly become a 'damaged brand', as Moisés Naím, a former Venezuelan trade minister, noted.[8]

Before assessing to what extent, if at all, such charges are true, given the severity of the Argentine collapse it is important to explain why it happened and who or what was to blame. The first point is that convertibility was a purely Argentine invention. It was not imposed on the country by outsiders. Rather, it was a desperate home-grown remedy for Argentina's chronic instability and decline. Between 1976 and 1989, first under dictatorship and then democracy, income per head had shrunk by an average of 1 per cent a year. A bout of hyperinflation and two banking collapses destroyed confidence in the peso and in economic policy. In Argentina, the old model of state intervention and protectionism had led to economic distortions on a pathological scale. Government, especially at provincial level, had become a vast employment agency, incapable of delivering basic services efficiently.[9] State-owned companies were no better: between 1983 and 1988, their losses averaged 5.6 per cent of GDP per year.[10] The state railway company employed 95,000 people, but only half of its locomotives were in working order.[11] The telephone system was especially notorious: the waiting list for a line was more than six years, and businesses employed staff whose sole job was to hold a telephone handset for hours on end until a dialling tone appeared.[12]

Menem's predecessor, Raúl Alfonsín, a Radical and an exemplary democrat but a poor economic manager, had tried to tackle inflation using 'heterodox' methods, such as price controls. When these failed, discontent boiled over, with lootings of supermarkets on a larger scale than in December 2001. Alfonsín was forced to step down several months early. In 1989, the economy shrank by 6 per cent, inflation climbed to 200 per cent a *month*, the consolidated public-sector deficit had reached the incredible figure of 21 per cent of GDP, the foreign debt had not been serviced for a year and national morale was on the floor.[13] Inflation cut the value of state pensions to just $26 a month. Just as happened in 2002, an army of the destitute toured the streets picking over rubbish for items to sell. The difference was that in 1990 it was made up of pensioners, rather than the unemployed. The public administration was close to collapse: in ministries, typewriters, photocopiers and toilets were broken and unrepaired; in the economy ministry, only one of the 12 lifts worked.[14]

When campaigning for the presidency, Menem, a traditional Peronist political boss from the backward Andean province of La Rioja, criticised the free-market reforms sweeping across the region. Once in office, a second burst of hyperinflation changed his mind. In setting up the currency board, Menem's economy minister of 1991–96, Domingo Cavallo, a Harvard-trained economist, deliberately harked back to Argentina's golden age. For much of the period before 1935, the country had operated a currency board, under which a body known as the *Caja de Conversión* was charged with maintaining the peso's value in gold.[15] The purpose of convertibility was to restore economic stability and confidence in the currency by making it impossible for the government to print money and debauch the peso, as it had done so often before. But linking the peso to the dollar was rash: only 15 per cent of Argentina's trade was with the United States in 2001.

Menem also dismantled barriers to trade and privatised nearly all of the state's vast holdings, from the oil company to the railways and the post office. He fired 100,000 state employees, causing hardship for those involved, but with no discernible effect on the efficiency of administration. Capital flooded in from abroad, the economy grew fast and the number of Argentines living below the national poverty line fell from 41.4 per cent in 1990 to 21.6 per cent in 1994.[16] Officials at the IMF swallowed their previous doubts about the currency board. Few at the

Wall Street investment banks had held such doubts: for foreign inves-
tors, convertibility seemed conveniently to have removed all risk of
devaluation. Argentina became a poster child for free-market reform in
Latin America. In a rare accolade, Menem was invited to join the host,
Bill Clinton, in opening the IMF's annual meeting in Washington in
October 1998.

Yet by then, several officials at the Fund were privately expressing
grave doubts about Argentina's policies.[17] They worried specifically that
the government's relatively loose fiscal policy meant that public debt was
rising despite rapid economic growth.[18] The government's deficits were
not as large as they had been in the 1970s and 1980s. They were partly
the result of the transitional cost to the government of a pension reform,
which saw future provision pass from the state to private funds. But part
of the deficit came from Menem's profligacy. Instead of pressing on with
further structural reforms to make the economy more efficient, he tried
to buy political support for an unconstitutional third term. The underlying point was that to sustain convertibility, the government needed to
notch up fiscal surpluses in good times. And it wasn't doing so.

The miracle formula becomes the perfect trap

Bad times soon came. They exposed Argentina's lack of policy flexibility. First, the devaluation of the Thai *baht* in July 1997, and then
Russia's debt default of mid-1998, prompted a retreat by foreign
financial investors from many emerging markets. In response, Brazil –
Argentina's largest market, accounting for 30 per cent of its exports –
devalued in January 1999. Convertibility prevented Argentina from
following suit, pricing many of its exports out of Brazil. To make matters
worse, the dollar, to which Argentina was tied, was appreciating against
other currencies, and world prices for the country's commodity exports
were falling. Under convertibility, the only way to restore competitiveness was deflation – driving *nominal* prices and wages down, something
which economists have long recognised is politically far more difficult
than allowing inflation to cut the real value of wages. (This was the
same drama that afflicted Greece and other Southern European countries after 2008.) The only way to restore growth was to attract renewed
inflows of foreign capital. But Wall Street finally woke up to Argentina's
fiscal fragility. To make matters worse, de la Rúa, a Radical who had

replaced Menem at an election in 1989, presided over a weak coalition government – a new experience in Argentina, where *caudillos* were the norm. De la Rúa's policies were more orthodox than Menem's: he tried to balance the budget and to change the law to make the labour market more flexible. But his coalition fell apart after it became clear that bribes had been paid in Congress to secure passage of the labour law. And balancing the budget required ever greater spending cuts, as recession ate into tax revenues. The miracle formula had become the perfect trap.

Ironically, it was Domingo Cavallo, recalled in desperation by de la Rúa as economy minister in March 2001, who delivered the coup de grâce to convertibility. He browbeat the IMF, against the better judgement of many of its officials, into a second loan of $8 billion in September 2001. Having laboured to establish the independence of the Central Bank, he proceeded to oust its governor, who opposed his policies. He strong-armed local pension funds into buying government paper and local banks into swapping their holdings of government bonds for low-interest loans. He thus weakened what had been seen as Latin America's strongest financial system. He also arranged a bond swap, whose only practical effect was to provide $90 million in fees to a group of Wall Street banks.[19]

Right to the end, polls suggested that convertibility retained the support of 70 per cent of Argentines (just as membership of the Euro area remains popular in Greece, despite the hardship it has entailed). Many had taken out dollar loans and mortgages. In retrospect, it is clear that the government should have voluntarily dismantled the currency board in the mid-1990s, when it could have done so from a position of strength. But why fix something that didn't appear broken? By 2001, the system could only be dismantled under duress, at a much higher cost. So it seemed reasonable to many officials to try and do everything possible to save the currency board, even though that had become impossible.

Many Argentines blamed the IMF when it pulled the plug on convertibility – but then came to blame it for not doing so earlier. They felt let down when the IMF did not rush to their aid after the currency board collapsed. Yet when Néstor Kirchner, who was elected president in 2003, called the IMF 'the promoter and vehicle of policies which provoked poverty and pain in the Argentine people', he was guilty of a wilfully misleading exaggeration.[20] The IMF was an accessory to the Argentine disaster, not its author. The economic policies that failed were of the government's own making. Rather, the Fund's mistakes were of omission. It should have pressed the Menem government much harder to adopt a responsible fiscal policy in the mid-1990s, and should have resisted Cavallo's demand for additional help to maintain the currency board after the failure of the first loan in 2001. And the Fund was wrong to have been such an enthusiastic public cheerleader for Menem's Argentina.

A second claim of the Fund's critics is that Argentina recovered after 2002 by ignoring the IMF's policy advice. That claim has a bit more plausibility, but is also exaggerated. Certainly, the hard line that the government of Néstor Kirchner, who replaced Duhalde, took on the restructuring of Argentina's debt – in defiance of the IMF and others – meant that debt repayments were not a fiscal drag on recovery. The government offered a tough take-it-or-leave-it deal to its bondholders, giving them only around 40 per cent of the face value of their bonds. Yet the recovery mainly stemmed from the success of Roberto Lavagna, appointed by Duhalde as economy minister in May 2002, in imposing relatively tight fiscal and monetary policies which brought stability to the exchange rate and choked off the threat of high inflation. The devaluation did its work, as exports boomed and local industry began to substitute for imports. Futhermore, luck finally turned Argentina's way again: soaring world prices for its commodity exports and strong growth in the world economy added up to the most favourable international conditions for half a century. Lastly, a decade of free-market reform bequeathed a more competitive economy, and one whose infrastructure had been modernised by Menem's privatisations. Certainly, the IMF might have done more to speed the recovery. In order to start negotiations on the debt, Lavagna wanted a medium-term agreement with the IMF sooner than he got one (in September 2003).[21] A senior IMF official conceded that outsiders were slow to recognise that Lavagna had put in place a coherent policy framework.[22] What delayed the agreement was chiefly an argument over fiscal policy, in which the IMF was too cautious, given the scale of Argentina's social problems.

For the first two and a half years of his presidency, Kirchner felt obliged to tolerate Lavagna at the economy ministry. Kirchner was weak: he was elected in April 2003 without a clear popular mandate, when Menem disgracefully pulled out of a run-off ballot that he was certain to lose. In a mid-term congressional election in October 2005, the president finally won that mandate. And the great commodity boom began to fill the government's coffers. Kirchner quickly sacked Lavagna, who wanted to cut energy subsidies and tackle rising inflation. He broke free of the IMF, paying off early the $9.8 billion that Argentina owed the Fund. In essence, Kirchner was betting on faster growth now at the price of higher inflation and fiscal disorder – a bet that Argentine rulers had often made, invariably to the country's cost. This time was no different.

What killed Argentina's economy in 2001 was not 'neoliberalism' or the free-market reforms, but a fiscal policy incompatible with the exchange-rate regime, and a lack of policy flexibility. That inflexibility meant that Argentina was worse-placed than others when the wave of financial crises hit emerging-market countries in 1997–98. Convertibility, with its emphasis on sound money at any cost, was a policy of conservative, not liberal, inspiration. Contrary to many claims, Argentina's policy mix was in direct contravention of the Washington Consensus. At least as conceived by John Williamson, the veteran British economist who coined the term, this called for a competitive exchange rate and sound fiscal policy.[23] Unfortunately, the debate over the Washington Consensus has been one of much heat and insufficient light – one in which the meaning of the term itself has mutated. So what exactly was it, and how did it come about?

A paradigm shift

The origins of the Washington Consensus lie in the debt crisis of 1982. Latin America had been living on borrowed money and time since the mid-1970s. The years of living beyond its means caught up with the region with a vengeance. Governments were forced into a savage economic adjustment, slashing imports, public spending and domestic demand in order to plug the payments gap and honour their rescheduled debts. The flow of money reversed: an average net *inflow* of capital of $12 billion a year between 1976 and 1981 turned into a net *outflow* averaging $26.4 billion a year over the next five years.[24] For ordinary Latin Americans, the cost was dramatic. In 1986, income per head in the region stood 0.7 per cent below its level of 1982; by 1992, it had still not recovered its level of ten years before. With reason, CEPAL spoke of a 'lost decade', though the picture varied from country to country. Some of the economic damage proved lasting. Investment, both public and private, took many years to recover.

Inflation, chronically higher in Latin America than elsewhere, took off as devaluation increased the price of imports and recession slashed tax revenues, leading many governments to print money on an unprecedented scale. The average annual inflation rate across 19 countries in the region rose from 33 per cent in the 1970s to 437 per cent in the 1980s.[25] Several countries would suffer devastating hyperinflation. Inflation acts as a tax on the poor: the better-off normally secure some degree of protection against the declining value of money through wage indexation, buying dollars or holding assets. The poor have no income protection. Since other taxes are collected in arrears, government revenues are also worth less in real terms. High and rising inflation destroys the possibility of financial planning, or agreeing long-term contracts. It triggers social conflicts, undermines trust in government and so tends to lead to political instability. Inflation led middle-class Brazilian families to invest in enormous fridges so that they could do a month's shopping before their wages lost their value. It meant that the profitability of businesses depended not on the quality and efficiency of their product or service, but on the nimbleness of their finance director. But taming inflation usually involved costs, as well as huge benefits, and was thus politically challenging.

Some economists of the structuralist persuasion argued that inflation was being caused not by the fiscal deficit, but by a combination of inertia (i.e. it was fuelling itself) and *insufficient* demand in the economy, which meant that producers were operating inefficiently. Under the influence of this thinking, so-called 'heterodox' stabilisation programmes were launched in the mid-1980s in Brazil (José Sarney's 'Cruzado Plan'), Argentina (Alfonsín's 'Austral Plan') and Peru (under Alan García). These involved an effort to break inflationary expectations through new currencies and price controls and, in Peru's case, a ceiling on foreign debt payments and measures to expand domestic demand.[26] In each case, after initial apparent success, the economy ended up worse than at the outset, as inflation soared still higher – mainly because of fiscal weakness.

The failure of these 'heterodox' plans gave force to a rethink that was already under way among many Latin American economists. Some of these economists had studied as postgraduates in American universities. They were influenced by the eventual success of Chile's market-based economic policies, as well as by the rise of the East Asian tigers. In 1985, Chile's reforms were imitated by a democratic government in Bolivia.

These economists concluded that Latin America required a radical change of course, abandoning the state-led protectionism of the previous half-century. In the 1980s, even CEPAL, the guardian of structuralist orthodoxy, had begun to shift towards these positions. By 1992, there was 'a trend towards convergence' around the new policies, according to Enrique Iglesias, who was CEPAL's boss from 1972 to 1985 and went on to head the Inter-American Development Bank from 1988 to 2005.[27]

It was this shift in the region's thinking towards the economic orthodoxies of the IMF, the World Bank and the OECD countries that Williamson intended to capture. In a background paper for a conference convened by the Institute for International Economics, a Washington think-tank that brought together policymakers from across Latin America, he summarised the new policies in a ten-point list. He called it the 'Washington Consensus' because his intention was to demonstrate to 'official Washington' that Latin America was reforming and deserved debt relief. As things turned out, the name 'was, I fear, a propaganda gift to the old left', he wrote later.[28]

Williamson's ten points were as follows:

1) Budget deficits small enough to be financed without recourse to the inflation tax.
2) Public expenditures redirected (from subsidies) toward fields such as primary education and health, and infrastructure.
3) Tax reform so as to broaden the tax base and cut marginal tax rates.
4) Financial liberalisation, involving an ultimate objective of market-determined interest rates.
5) A unified exchange rate at a level sufficiently competitive to induce a rapid growth in non-traditional exports.
6) Quantitative trade restrictions to be rapidly replaced by tariffs, which would be progressively reduced until a uniform low rate in the range of 10 to 20 per cent was achieved.
7) Abolition of barriers impeding the entry of foreign direct investment.
8) Privatisation of state-owned enterprises.
9) Abolition of regulations that impede the entry of new firms or restrict competition (including in the labour market).
10) The provision of secure property rights, especially to the informal sector.[29]

Williamson insisted that his formulation did not endorse 'neoliberalism' – if by that is meant 'monetarism, supply-side economics and minimal government', as advocated in the 1980s by some advisers to Ronald Reagan and Margaret Thatcher. That, however, was the meaning that many of its critics gave to the Washington Consensus.[30] Many of the ten points are basic principles of economic management which nowadays command wide consensus across the world. And the main thrust for the reforms came from within the region. In most cases, they were not imposed from outside. It is certainly true that the IMF, the World Bank and the US Treasury supported many of the reforms. Especially in smaller countries (such as those in Central America), the IMF and the World Bank made some of their loans conditional on the adoption of the new policies. But normally, such conditions were a matter of negotiation rather than of imposition – and Latin American governments had a long tradition of failing to comply with the conditions of IMF loans.

Williamson's list boiled down to three main elements. The first was the importance of achieving macroeconomic stability and taming inflation through the control of fiscal deficits. The second was dismantling protectionism and opening up to foreign trade, competition and investment. The third aspect was reforming the role of the state in the economy and promoting the role of markets in allocating resources and generating wealth. That meant getting the government out of producing goods through privatisation. The implicit idea was to focus the state's activity on regulation, social provision and poverty alleviation. But this was not made explicit.

The reform process varied hugely in timing, speed and extent from country to country. Most progress was made on the first point, macroeconomic stabilisation. Chile in the 1970s, and Bolivia and Mexico in the 1980s were the first to tackle inflation by closing the fiscal deficit. Unlike the 'heterodox' plans, these orthodox programmes brought more lasting success, and would be imitated across the region. They involved a combination of tax increases and spending cuts, though usually more of the initial burden fell on the latter. Privatisation helped, since many state-owned companies regularly recorded big losses. Governments moved to eliminate many across-the-board subsidies, such as those on petrol or foodstuffs, which had benefited rich and poor alike. In their place, social safety nets for the poor were set up, but far too slowly. Often, spending was cut indiscriminately, or the burden fell disproportionately on public investment. Monetary policy was reformed, too. Nearly everywhere, governments renounced printing money. Half a dozen countries moved towards giving their central banks legal or de facto independence. The upshot was that by the early 1990s, fiscal deficits and inflation had been brought down sharply almost everywhere.[31]

Stabilisation was helped, too, by a new approach to the debt problem. As debt service took an ever-larger slice of government revenues, this weakened the incentive to reform. Eventually – and later than was desirable – it came to be recognised that forgiving part of the debt was in the interest not just of debtor countries, but also of creditors, who might thus get at least some of their money back. Nicholas Brady, a former Wall Street banker who was the treasury secretary in the administration of George Bush Snr, put this idea into effect in 1989. Under the Brady Plan, countries had to show willingness to reform, and some action in that direction. The essence of the plan involved swapping the old, defaulted debt for new bonds that were either of lower face value or that paid a much lower interest rate. The new bonds were guaranteed by some $30 billion of US treasury bonds put up as collateral by the multilateral financial institutions and Japan. The Brady Plan worked, though more favourable conditions in the world economy helped, too. By 1994, there had been 18 Brady deals, covering $191 billion in debt, of which $61 billion was forgiven. Whereas Latin America had been locked out of capital markets for 40 years after the defaults of the 1930s, this time capital began to flood back to the region within a decade.[32]

Tearing down barriers

The record of structural reform was more mixed. It went furthest in trade policy and financial liberalisation. Given Latin America's long history of protectionism, the trade reform was dramatic. In the mid-1980s, barriers to imports in Mexico and Central America were greater than anywhere else in the world, while those in South America were surpassed only in Africa.[33] Since many exports, especially of manufactures, themselves included imported components, protection carried a strong anti-export bias. The reformers implemented a sweeping unilateral trade liberalisation. Average tariffs across the region fell from over 40 per cent in the mid-1980s to around 10 per cent. Nearly all quotas and import prohibitions were swept away. Tariff structures were radically simplified. Many countries joined the General Agreement on Tariffs and Trade (which became the World Trade Organization in 1996), from which Latin America had largely absented itself at its foundation in 1947. The upshot was that by the end of the 1990s, Latin America was the most open region of the developing world.[34] At the same time, free-trade agreements multiplied, and interest in regional integration schemes revived. Mercosur was founded in 1991 by Brazil, Argentina, Uruguay and Paraguay as a putative customs union in the mould of the European Union. Older schemes, such as the Andean Pact and the Central American Common Market, were relaunched. In the past, such arrangements had been an attempt to broaden the scope for import substitution and industrial planning. Now, they had a radically different aim. The 'new regionalism', as some called it, was 'an integral part of the structural adjustment process that is designed to make the economies more market-oriented, open, outward-looking, and internationally competitive in a modern democratic institutional setting'.[35] Further afield, Mexico and Chile led the way in striking bilateral free-trade agreements with the United States, the EU and Asian countries. Many of these trade agreements were aimed mainly at attracting foreign investment by 'locking in' the reforms by international treaty. The aims of liberalisation were to turn trade into a motor of economic growth and to increase the efficiency and competitiveness of Latin American firms. To an extent, it worked. In the 1990s alone, the total volume of Latin America's trade doubled.[36]

There were losers as well as winners. The process was made more costly than it might have been by the way in which trade liberalisation interacted with stabilisation and financial reform. Many governments tore down barriers to the movement of money as well as goods. That was partly because they saw exchange controls as ineffective and as sources of corruption, and partly because they hoped to attract foreign investment, both direct (in factories or business) and financial. But the resulting surge of money from abroad saw many Latin American currencies appreciate in the early 1990s. Strong currencies and cheap imports helped to get inflation down, and thus took some of the pressure off fiscal adjustment. But orthodoxy – and the Washington Consensus – held that trade reform should start with a big real-terms devaluation. When that didn't happen, it meant that some manufacturers and farmers who were reasonably efficient went under in the face of competition from cheap imports.

The combination of trade opening and overvalued currencies resulted in ballooning current account deficits. Pedro Aspe, Mexico's finance minister under Salinas, argued that these did not matter; they merely mirrored the inflow of foreign investment, he said. Aspe was unperturbed even as Mexico's current account deficit hovered around 7 per cent of GDP in 1992–94.[37] The problem was that much of this investment was 'hot' money, placed in shares and bonds. It could leave as fast as it came. That is what happened in Mexico in 1994, an election year and one of political turmoil. The new government promptly ordered a devaluation that quickly became a rout. This 'tequila crisis', as it became known, plunged Mexico into a deep recession (GDP shrank by 6 per cent in 1995, though recovery was swift).[38]

It was a foretaste of problems to come for Latin America. In 1998, when Russia's devaluation and default triggered what would become worldwide financial strain in emerging markets, the region's current account deficit stood at 4.5 per cent of GDP. Just as Mexico had four years earlier, the region suffered a 'sudden stop' in capital inflows.[39] This time the impact was particularly severe in South America. It forced Brazil into a disorderly devaluation; in all, half a dozen Latin American countries abandoned pegged exchange rates. The region faced a new round of economic adjustment. External factors – the dotcom crash of March 2001 in the United States – and turbulence within the region (including Argentina's collapse and its knock-on effects) meant that recovery did not come until 2003. CEPAL promptly dubbed this period the 'lost half-decade'.[40] Life in a world of free-flowing capital had proved to be something of a roller-coaster for Latin America.

In some cases, the ride was made choppier by flaws in banking systems. When the reformers took charge, in an attempt to get credit flowing, they freed interest rates, abolished rules on credit allocation for banks, and sharply reduced reserve requirements. In some countries, state-owned banks were privatised or wound up. Restrictions on foreign ownership of banks were removed. Efforts to improve banking supervision often proved to be belated and inadequate. Sudden stops in capital flows and interest-rate rises were followed by banking collapses in Mexico and, to a lesser extent, Argentina in 1995, and in the Andean countries three years later. These inevitably amplified recessions.

In Ecuador, political instability, flooding caused by the El Niño weather pattern, low oil prices, poor economic management and a dozen bank failures triggered a financial and economic collapse only slightly less severe than that of Argentina. As the country tottered towards hyperinflation, the government decreed that Ecuador would adopt the US dollar as its currency. It had little choice in the matter: Ecuadoreans showed no desire to hold the sucre, the debauched local currency. Dollarisation brought stability. But the cost was high: GDP shrank by 7 per cent in 1999. The bank collapses ended up costing the government $3.5 billion: it chose to repay depositors in full, but failed to recover many of the banks' defaulted loans, partly because of pressure from politically powerful debtors. A million Ecuadoreans migrated, many to Spain and Italy. In 2000, the daily Iberia flight, a big Airbus A340, would make its outward journey from Madrid to Quito almost empty, but be overbooked for the return leg. Stability and high oil prices eventually brought growth.

Even Colombia, long a paragon of effective orthodox macroeconomic management, succumbed to the credit bubble. It was the only Latin American country not to reschedule its debts in the 1980s and the proud possessor of an investment-grade credit rating. But when it opened its economy in 1990, capital inflows (including drug money) caused the peso to appreciate, and pushed up asset prices, especially for property. In part because of the spendthrift mandates of a new constitution, fiscal policy was uncharacteristically loose in the 1990s. In 1998, Colombia registered fiscal and current account deficits of 5 per cent of GDP. When the money stopped flowing, property prices crashed, several banks collapsed and the country suffered its first recession since the 1930s.

Public vices, private passions

Cochabamba, Bolivia's third city, sits at a comfortable altitude of 2,500 metres in a broad valley, where family farmers with small or medium-sized holdings provide much of the country's food. In 1980, it was a pleasant, rather sleepy place of some 200,000 people. At weekends, the *Cochabambino* middle class would head for the pavement restaurants of the Prado, a broad sunny avenue then on the outskirts, to eat roast duck washed down with lager from the local brewery founded by German migrants.[41] It was shaken out of its bucolic torpor by rising demand for cocaine in the United States. The city became the jumping-off point for the coca fields of the Chapare in the tropical lowlands to the east.

Swollen by migrants from the dying tin mines and the impoverished Altiplano – of whom Evo Morales was one – Cochabamba became a disorderly metropolis of some 600,000 people. The nocturnal calm of the Prado yielded to the thumping beat of Colombian *cumbias* blasting out from discos.

For the anti-globalisation movement, Cochabamba occupies a prominent place in the mythology surrounding the Washington Consensus. The city's chaotic growth put great pressure on water supplies. The reforming government of Gonzalo Sánchez de Lozada was keen to attract private investment to the water industry. In Cochabamba, the mayor reckoned the solution was to bring water to the city from the Misicuni river, on the far side of a mountain range. This involved building a 120-metre-high dam and boring a 19.5-kilometre tunnel through the mountains. The project would provide hydroelectricity as well, but it cost $252 million. The World Bank argued that it was unnecessarily expensive. It backed a cheaper option, under which no tariff increases for water would have been permitted for five years. The government, under pressure from the mayor, went ahead with the Misicuni scheme anyway, signing a contract with a consortium called Aguas del Tunari led by Bechtel, an American engineering giant, which took over Semapa, the municipal water company. To defray the cost of the Misicuni project, the consortium raised water charges by 43 per cent on average.[42] Charges doubled for a small number of very poor consumers; a few people found themselves paying a third of their income for water. The new charges drew protests in January 2000, in which a 17-year-old was killed by a soldier. The government of Hugo Banzer, a former military dictator turned conservative democrat, panicked. Instead of dealing with the injustices of the new system, it tore up the contract with Aguas del Tunari. Under a better-designed contract, Aguas del Illimani, a consortium led by Suez, a French utility, was administering and expanding water and sewerage services in the capital, La Paz, and its satellite city of El Alto. But because of the Cochabamba unrest, the government refused its request to raise tariffs, even though these were lower than those of publicly owned water companies elsewhere in Bolivia. Instead, the government raised charges for new connections by the company, to $450 for water and sewerage – or six months' wages for poorer Bolivians. The mayors of El Alto and La Paz called for the contract to be rescinded. In January 2005, the weak, interim government of Carlos Mesa did just that.

These 'water wars' were hailed by the radical left, in Bolivia and beyond, as proof of the iniquities of privatisation. Certainly, water is especially sensitive. Not only is its supply a natural monopoly, but in Andean Indian culture water is a divine gift that belongs to everyone, not a commodity. The livelihoods of farmers in much of Latin America depend on water for irrigation. But the Bolivian experience was a failure of government regulation, rather than of privatisation. Although Misicuni was a longstanding demand of civic leaders in Cochabamba, it should not have been approved. In La Paz and El Alto, Aguas del Illimani had a good record. It invested $63 million (though some of this was soft loans through the government). After years in which the state water company failed to keep pace with demand, the annual rate of new sewerage and water connections rose by two-thirds in the first three years of its contract. Thanks largely to private investment, many more Bolivians, and especially poorer ones, gained access to basic services. In 1992, only 50 per cent had piped water, while in 1997 only 45 per cent had electricity. In 2004, according to the World Bank, 70 per cent had water and 60 per cent had electricity.[43] In Cochabamba, six years after the water war, victory was hardly sweet. Semapa was under 'community control'. Half of the city's population still lacked piped water. For the other half, service was poor: some had running water for only three hours a day.[44] A decade later, in 2016, La Paz suffered prolonged water rationing, when a severe drought exposed the lack of investment by the nationalised water company.[45]

Across Latin America, those who lack piped water normally pay more for it – sometimes up to ten times more – than those with a mains connection. The unconnected get water from tankers, usually operated by private, informal businesses. This water is rarely clean. In some cities in Argentina, too, water was privatised in the 1990s. Suez took a controlling stake in Aguas Argentinas, which operated in Buenos Aires. By applying more efficient management, it was able to cut water tariffs, while extending service to an extra 3 million poor people (though connection charges were high).[46] According to one study, water connections increased more rapidly in provincial areas of Argentina where water was privatised than where it was not. The authors calculate that the increase in safe water supplies provided by privatisation cut child mortality rates by 5 per cent in the areas concerned.[47] In many parts of the region, there were valid reasons for water prices to rise, both to cover new investment and to discourage wastage. But the lesson from

Cochabamba was that if water privatisation is to be politically viable and socially just, it should go hand in hand with targeted subsidies (in the form of cash payments) for the poorest.

More than any other policy, the Washington Consensus came to be identified in Latin America with privatisation – and controversially so, as the 'water wars' exemplified. The sell-offs began in Chile in the 1970s, as the Pinochet regime handed back the companies nationalised by Allende (except Codelco, the state copper company), and then went on to imitate the sweeping privatisations of Margaret Thatcher in Britain. Privatisation spread to Mexico in the 1980s, and took off across the region in the 1990s. In Latin America as a whole, more than 2,000 enterprises were sold, ranging from steelworks to electricity companies, and banks to airlines. The state's share of production declined more in Latin America than in any other region, except the former communist countries of Central and Eastern Europe. In the 1990s, government receipts from privatisations in Latin America totalled $178 billion (of which $95 billion came in 1997–99), accounting for 55 per cent of the total in the developing world.[48]

The scale of privatisation was as much tribute to the multiplicity of state companies in Latin America as to reforming zeal. In Peru, for example, in the 1980s not only were the commanding heights of the economy largely in state hands – oil, mining, agriculture (in government-organised co-operatives), steel, fishmeal, a chunk of banking, utilities – but so, too, was the marketing of food staples and minerals (not to mention a pornographic cinema, a former asset of an insolvent banking group). Though there were islands of excellence – the public-utility company of Medellín in Colombia, for example – most state-owned companies were poorly run, and by the 1970s many were chronically loss-making. In Mexico, at the peak in 1982, some 1,155 state-owned companies received transfers and subsidies from the public purse, equal to 12.7 per cent of GDP, according to Jacques Rogozinski, who, as an official in Carlos Salinas's government of 1988–94, was involved in privatising many of them.[49]

Governments privatised for a mixture of ideological and pragmatic reasons. If one aim was to promote economic efficiency, another, often equally pressing, was to plug holes in the public finances. (Too often, governments used privatisation revenues for current spending, rather than to pay debt or for public investment, as they should have done.) In the first aim, privatisation was highly successful. A comprehensive analysis of the performance of privatised firms in seven countries showed that on average they increased output (by 40 per cent) and profits, while shedding labour (a quarter of the workforce on average).[50] Take Brazil's steel industry, sold as six separate companies in 1991–93. In state hands in 1990, it employed 115,000 people and produced 22.6 million tonnes of steel. By 1996, it produced 25.2 million tonnes with just 65,000 workers. In most cases, privatised firms increased sales and profitability. Labour productivity thus rose sharply; in some cases, such as in Argentina, firms also made big new capital investments. Above all, performance in privatised firms improved because of better management. The firms also paid more taxes when in private hands. Wages for workers who kept their jobs rose – in Bolivia they more than doubled.[51] In many cases, privatised firms subsequently expanded. For example, in the first eight years after its privatisation in 1997, Brazil's Companhia Vale do Rio Doce, an iron ore and transport group now known just as Vale, increased sales by 2.5 times and its profits by 13 times. It was transformed from a Brazilian conglomerate into one of the world's biggest multinational mining companies, employing 74,000 people in 2015, up from 14,000 at the time of privatisation.[52]

Despite the overall success of privatisation, it became very unpopular. After the Cochabamba water war, and a similar riot in Arequipa, Peru's second city, over the proposed sale of two small electricity companies in 2002, privatisation all but stopped in the region. Its unpopularity was mainly because the benefits to consumers and taxpayers were thinly spread and often not very visible. On the other hand, the losers tended to be vocal. In some countries, workers sacked as a result of privatisation found it hard to get other jobs. In Argentina, for example, the payroll in formerly state-owned companies fell from 250,000 in 1989 to around 60,000 in 1993.[53] Many of those laid off when YPF, the oil company, was privatised were in far-flung provinces with little alternative work. They tended to be older workers, with specific skills. Many spent the next decade living on government handouts and staging frequent protests.[54] There were some outright failures. Privatised airlines floundered in Argentina, Mexico and Peru. Salinas's privatisation of Mexico's banks turned into a costly boomerang: 12 of the 18 banks sold in 1991–92, mainly to stockbroking groups with little banking experience, had to be taken back a few years later when the 'tequila crisis' revealed the shakiness of their balance sheets. Mexico's pioneering effort to get private companies to build toll roads also stumbled. When a new motorway from Mexico City to Acapulco opened in 1993, the tolls for the five-hour journey totalled more than $100 – higher than the cost of a flight. To attract traffic, motorway tolls had to be cut sharply. Compensating the highway companies and bailing out the banks increased Mexico's public debt from 25 per cent to 50 per cent of GDP.[55]

Another reason for privatisation's unpopularity was that it became identified in the public mind with corruption, largely because some of the early asset sales in Chile, Mexico and Argentina were not carried out in an open manner. But the main target of public opprobrium was the higher tariffs charged by some privatised utilities.

Take telecoms, which were privatised in many countries starting in the late 1980s. At first, governments failed to build in competition, allowing public monopolies to become private ones. In the most egregious example, Telmex, the Mexican phone company, was granted a ten-year monopoly for many of its services after it was sold. It continued to have a dominant market position long after the formal monopoly ended. The profits from Telmex helped Carlos Slim, whose family owned 48 per cent of the capital and 71 per cent of the voting shares, to become the fourth-richest person in the world, with a fortune of $50 billion in 2016, according to *Forbes* magazine. Most of that fortune was the result of Slim's undoubted business acumen and skill at diversification. But Telmex's profits were partly the result of some of the world's highest telephone charges, as the OECD pointed out.[56] In several other countries, such as Argentina and Peru, Spain's Telefónica enjoyed a near monopoly of fixed-line telephony. Brazil, which privatised later, tried harder to ensure competition. Nevertheless, across the region telecoms privatisation brought new investment, technological modernisation and huge increases in coverage. One study found that in countries which privatised, over the next three years the rate of growth of coverage (in relation to population) of land lines and mobile phones combined rose from 5 per cent a year to 14 per cent a year, the waiting list fell by half and the quality of service improved.[57] Privatisation positioned Latin America to take advantage of the mobile and digital revolutions in telecommunications. By 2015, there were more mobile phone contracts than people in Latin America.[58] Internet usage rose fast: by June 2016, 62 per cent of the region's population was using the internet, higher than the world average.[59] In telecoms, Latin America was closing the gap with the developed world. But there were still concerns about the cost and quality of service, with mobile telephony in many countries subject to a near duopoly of Telefónica and América Móvil, controlled by Slim.

In all, from 1990 to 2001, private investment in infrastructure in Latin America totalled a whopping $360 billion, $150 billion more than in East Asia.[60] But in some sectors, especially transport and energy, the record of private investment was mixed. Chile used private finance to build a modern motorway network. Other countries, such as Colombia and Peru, have continued fine-tuning private–public partnerships in infrastructure in recent years. On the other hand, a study of more than a thousand concessions granted in Latin America in the 1990s to build and operate infrastructure, such as motorways or power stations, found that in more than 60 per cent of cases, their terms were substantially renegotiated within three years.[61] These addenda to contracts were sometimes a device to facilitate corruption: construction companies would make low bids, while bribing officials to accept later big increases in costs. It came to be recognised that private investment would have to be supplemented by a revival of public investment, especially in areas such as water and transport.

Nevertheless, on balance, privatisation of public services was clearly positive for Latin America. One detailed study concluded that infrastructure privatisations

> generally increased access to power, telephone services and water, particularly for the poor who, before privatization, often had no services or paid higher prices for private services (particularly in the case of water). Although some privatized firms have raised prices, which has burdened lower-income households, the bottom line is still one of absolute gains in welfare for the poor.[62]

A balance sheet of the reforms

What was the overall record of the Washington Consensus in Latin America? The first thing to say is that its impact on growth was relatively disappointing. Growth picked up from 1990 to 1997, stagnation followed from 1998 to 2002, but then there was strong recovery from 2003 onwards (see Chart 2). Measuring the impact of the reforms on

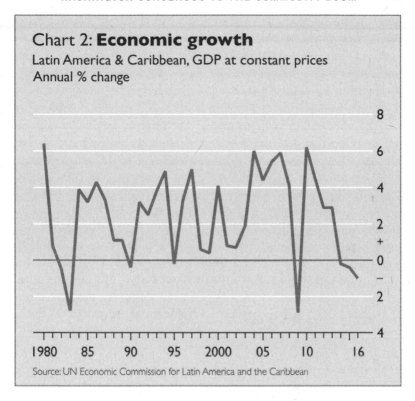

Chart 2: **Economic growth**
Latin America & Caribbean, GDP at constant prices
Annual % change

Source: UN Economic Commission for Latin America and the Caribbean

growth is not straightforward. As José Antonio Ocampo, a former secretary general of CEPAL, pointed out, stabilisation often is (but should not be) confused with reform.[63] Stagnation and the rise in poverty in the 1980s were the hangover from the debt-fuelled growth fiesta of the 1970s. Those who pin the blame for the 'lost decade' of the 1980s on stabilisation are merely stating a truism. The critics are unable to show that any alternative set of policies would have produced a better long-term outcome. Some early studies suggested that the reforms added 2 percentage points to annual growth rates in the early 1990s. A later study, by researchers at the Inter-American Development Bank (IDB), found that the reforms had only a temporary effect in accelerating growth. Even so, they concluded that per capita income in Latin America in 2000 was 11 per cent higher than it would have been without the reforms. In general, reforms delivered more growth in countries with better public institutions.[64] Just like the prior slowdown, recovery after 2003 owed much to external conditions. But it was not fanciful to imagine that after two decades of stabilisation and reform, the region's economies had emerged from the 'lost half-decade' in much better shape to take advantage of such opportunities. In other words, there was a lag before the full effect of reform was felt.

The outstanding achievement of the reforms was the taming of inflation, and greater macroeconomic stability (see Chart 3). The average inflation rate in the region fell from a peak of 1,206 per cent in 1989 to just 10 per cent by the end of the 1990s. By 2006, this average rate had fallen to 4.8 per cent, and for the first time since the 1930s no country suffered inflation of more than 20 per cent.[65] The average public-sector deficit in the region fell from 6.5 per cent of GDP during 1980–90 to 1.3 per cent of GDP by 2005.[66] Exclude interest payments on

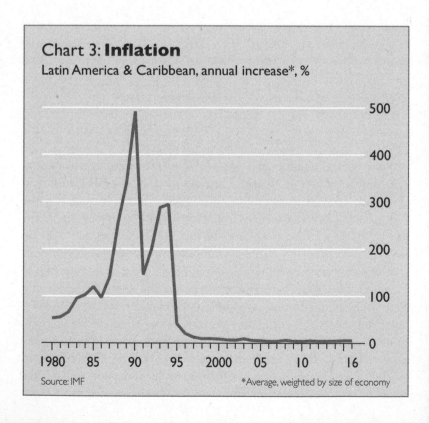

Chart 3: Inflation

Latin America & Caribbean, annual increase*, %

Source: IMF   *Average, weighted by size of economy

public debt, and the 2005 figure was a surplus, of 2.2 per cent of GDP. Low inflation opened up the possibility of bank credit and cheap mortgages for Latin Americans who had been denied them for a generation – or had never had access to them. There was strong growth in credit in Mexico and Brazil in the years after 2003, for example. Low inflation and reasonably disciplined fiscal policies served to boost the authority and credibility of economic policymakers in many countries in the region. The risk premium on Latin American government bonds fell sharply, and many of the larger economies achieved investment-grade credit ratings. For a while, at least, governments were able to reduce their dependence on foreign financing. By 2005, the governments of Mexico, Brazil and Colombia had switched more than half their debt to local currencies, as well as extending its term.[67] With surprising speed, they seemed to have overcome what Ricardo Hausmann, a Venezuelan economist at Harvard University, had dubbed 'original sin' – emerging-market countries' traditional inability to borrow long term in their own currency.[68]

There were three main problems with the reforms. First, the abrupt lifting of controls on capital movement, combined with inadequate supervision of the banks, paved the way for the renewed bout of instability of 1998–2002. Capital inflows contributed to currency appreciation and a loss of export competitiveness. An early warning – which went unheeded – had been provided by banking collapses in Chile and Argentina in 1982–83, which followed the lifting of capital controls and freeing of interest rates by military regimes. An early remedy, which could have been more widely copied, was Chile's subsequent imposition of a tax on short-term capital inflows (which also helped to prevent its currency from becoming overvalued). Williamson himself later accepted that he should have included effective supervision of banks as an essential concomitant of financial liberalisation.[69] On the other hand, retaining capital controls would have cut growth: unlike many Asian countries, Latin America does not save enough to finance growth internally. The gross national saving rate in Latin America was just 17.5 per cent of GDP between 1980 and 2014, compared with 34 per cent among Asian developing countries and 23 per cent in developed countries, according to the IDB.[70] Second, at least some of the increase in poverty in the 1980s might have been avoided, had governments been quicker to put in place social assistance programmes. And thirdly, macroeconomic reform was not matched by 'second-generation' reforms (as they came to be called) of markets, institutions and the state.

Joseph Stiglitz argued that gradual, carefully sequenced reform would have avoided the social cost and policy mistakes of 'shock therapy'.[71] That is true – in a perfect world. The problem in the Latin America of the 1980s and 1990s was that governments faced economic emergencies. Naím, the Venezuelan trade minister, points out that reformers in his country did not adopt swift, drastic reforms because of a 'theoretical preference for traumatic shocks', but because of 'the practical impossibility of doing otherwise given the deterioration of the state apparatus'.[72] In addition, past experience showed that gradual reform tended to peter out in the face of pressure from powerful local interest groups that benefited from the subsidies and rents of the old model.

Another criticism was that the reforms were imposed in a uniform fashion, which took no account of national circumstances, and that they were rammed through undemocratically. A cursory examination shows that this was not so.[73] Some countries reformed drastically and quickly (Argentina, Bolivia and Peru), while others did relatively little (Ecuador, Uruguay and Venezuela). In Brazil and in Chile (after democracy was restored in 1990), reform was more gradual, and was preceded by the slow building of political consensus. Mexico signed NAFTA, but retained state monopolies in oil and electricity and the labour laws of the PRI.[74] Even Chile kept its two largest firms – Codelco, the world's biggest copper producer, and Enap, an oil producer and distributor – in state hands. Brazil invited private investment in electricity and oil exploration. But the state retained majority ownership of its oil company, as well as three banks, including a development bank, which pursued industrial policies. The politics of stabilisation and reform varied widely, too. Certainly, in Mexico, Peru (under Alberto Fujimori) and, to a lesser extent, Argentina (under Menem), reforms were often decreed from on high, with little prior political debate. But both Fujimori and Menem were re-elected for second terms, as was Fernando Henrique Cardoso's reforming government in Brazil. Low inflation and rising social spending were democratic conquests, not dictatorial impositions. Although he is often approvingly cited by left-wing opponents of the reforms, Stiglitz himself concluded that 'the Washington Consensus policies were designed to respond to the very real problems in Latin America, and made considerable sense'.[75]

Nevertheless, the notion that the Washington Consensus involved external imposition and sado-monetarist shock therapy became part of the rhetorical critique deployed by many of the left-wing governments that came to power in the 2000s. Rhetoric aside, the 'lost half-decade' of 1998–2003 and the election of left-wing governments saw the emergence of a new, pragmatic 'Post-Washington' consensus. This included an adjustment in macroeconomic policies. In 1999, as capital flowed out of the region, half a dozen countries abandoned pegged exchange rates in favour of floating their currencies. Instead of using the exchange rate to control inflation, they entrusted the task to monetary policy, adopting inflation targeting. The 'tripod' of floating currencies, inflation targeting administered by more or less independent central banks, and a responsible fiscal policy was adopted in all the larger economies in the region, except Argentina and Venezuela, and some of the smaller ones. (Argentina began to adopt this tripod after the election of Mauricio Macri in 2015.) On the whole, it worked well – at least when followed rigorously, which after 2010 it would not be in Brazil, in particular. At the same time, the region began to redress its neglect of poverty and fairness and began, more or less cautiously, to experiment once again with industrial policies.[76] These adjustments aside, many governments continued to implement the main tenets of the Washington Consensus, whatever their rhetoric. And those countries that strayed from it, beguiled by the commodity boom, would later pay a price.

The great commodity boom – and bust

A four-hour drive north of Buenos Aires, Rosario is Argentina's third city, renowned as a centre of culture and nursery of footballers (including Lionel Messi, Ángel di María and Javier Mascherano, of the current crop of stars). Rosario sprang up from nothing in the mid-nineteenth century, thanks to its location where the railway across the *pampa húmeda*, the rain-fed heart of the world's most bounteous farmland, met the brown, broad and navigable waters of the Paraná river. The city's Bolsa de Comercio, with its dome and grand pillared entrance, harks back to Argentina's golden age. The original trading floor of circular wooden benches is preserved on the ground floor; upstairs, screens flash red and green, logging price movements. Nowadays Rosario's bourse is Argentina's biggest grain-trading and futures market.

Within a 300-kilometre radius of the city, 40 per cent of the country's wheat, maize and soya is grown. The world's biggest and most efficient cluster of oilseed-crushing plants stretches for 80 kilometres along the Paraná, either side of Rosario. At wharves on the river, oceangoing bulk carriers fill up with soya meal and oil.

As China industrialised and entered the world economy (it joined the World Trade Organization in 2001), its demand for foodstuffs, minerals and fuels pushed prices to record levels. That triggered a boom in South America. Between 1995 and 2015, Argentina's total production of grains and oilseeds expanded from 45 million tonnes to 120 million tonnes (despite the imposition of export taxes by Cristina Fernández). As well as Argentine and Brazilian soya beans, China gobbled up Brazilian iron ore, copper from Chile and Peru, and oil from Venezuela and Ecuador. Latin America's terms of trade (the ratio of the price of its exports to those of its imports) soared, triggering a surge in economic growth. Farmers and mining companies invested heavily in expanding output. It helped, too, that money was cheap, with international interest rates staying low for most of the early years of the twenty-first century. At first, governments and consumers reacted prudently. Between 2004 and 2007, for the first time in memory, rapid growth in Latin America went hand in hand with a surplus in the current account of the balance of payments and even, in 2006 and 2007, a fiscal surplus. Governments paid down debt: by 2008, the region's public debt stood at just 32 per cent of GDP, down from 45 per cent in 2005, according to CEPAL. This prudence paid off. When the follies of Wall Street and the City of London tipped the world into the 'great recession' of 2008–09, Latin America at first found itself in the unaccustomed position of being a bystander in a financial crisis that was caused, in the opinion of Lula, by 'the irrational behaviour of white people with blue eyes, who before seemed to know everything and now show that they knew nothing'.[77] However, as foreign banks tightened credit because of their difficulties at home, and as commodity prices plunged in late 2008, so did Latin American currencies and stock markets. But after a brief downturn, the region recovered swiftly (with growth of 6.2 per cent in 2010).

Better policies had proven their worth. Unlike in the past, currency depreciation did not trigger panic or an inflationary spiral. Governments had learned the lessons of the banking collapses of the 1990s; this time, financial systems did not buckle. Its greater financial and fiscal strength allowed Latin America to respond to the crisis with 'counter-cyclical' fiscal and monetary policies. Central banks cut interest rates without prompting a run on the currency. Several governments – notably those of Chile, Peru and Brazil – increased public spending to help offset the downturn. As money poured back into the region, soon finance ministers, in Brazil and Chile for example, were worrying about the overvaluation of their currencies.

Yet for Latin America, the world was changing once again. As China's growth slowed and its economic policy evolved, with less emphasis on investment and exports and more on services and consumption, commodity prices began to fall steadily from 2011 onwards. Latin America's currencies depreciated once again. A credit boom in the region tailed off, and companies and households had to devote more of their income to paying off debt. Investment fell, partly because much of it was linked to the production of commodities in mines, oilfields and farms. Latin America suffered a prolonged economic slowdown, one that was more pronounced than in any other developing region of the world and which forecasters repeatedly underestimated. In 2016, the region's economies, taken as a whole, shrank by 1.1 per cent, in the sixth successive year of deceleration. Forecasters expected a modest recovery in 2017.

Two divergent economic realities lay behind these figures. In one camp were the countries that managed their economies well, including Chile, Colombia, Mexico and Peru. Without structural reforms, they faced a 'new normal' of growth of 3 per cent or so (and Mexico had other problems). In the other camp were the countries that had repeated the mistakes of the late 1970s, of refusing to adjust to harder times. Venezuela entered a catastrophic slump (see the next chapter). Ecuador and Argentina suffered recessions. In Argentina, Cristina Fernández bequeathed to Mauricio Macri, her centre-right successor, a host of problems which she had stubbornly denied. These included phony inflation numbers, a gaping fiscal hole, indiscriminate subsidies for energy consumption and public transport, an artificial exchange rate and a festering dispute with opportunistic bondholders which cut Argentina off from international credit. Macri began tackling all of these problems, but the short-term cost was a rise in inflation and a fall in output.

Brazil's success in sailing through the great recession went to the heads of Lula and Dilma Rousseff, his successor and disciple. They appeared to think that the lesson of the crisis was that free-market capitalism had failed and that state capitalism was the future. Rousseff was far too slow to withdraw the fiscal stimulus Lula had applied in 2009. She began to interfere in the 'tripod' of macroeconomic policies which had served the country well, replacing it with what her advisers called 'the new economic matrix'. This involved disregarding fiscal responsibility and bullying the Central Bank into cutting interest rates and intervening to cut electricity prices and hold down petrol prices, for example. And she resorted to old-fashioned industrial policy, ramping up subsidised credit from state banks and announcing a barrage of tax breaks and tariff increases. Business lost confidence in government policy. All this served to win Rousseff, narrowly, a second term in 2014. But it soon turned an inevitable slowdown into a slump and would contribute to her losing her job. Brazil entered its deepest and longest recession since records began, as political turmoil hindered a recovery of consumer and business confidence (see Chapter 8).

Such ideological and policy errors aside, did Latin America squander its big commodity windfall? Not wholly so. Investment did edge up, social provision and education were expanded, and many countries achieved greater financial resilience, with stronger and better-regulated banks than in the past. But while Asian countries built factories, Latin America tended to erect shopping centres. The IDB warned that 77 per cent of the extra revenue from the commodity boom went on spending which involved permanent entitlements.[78]

The productivity puzzle

To return to faster growth, Latin America needs to address its chronic structural weaknesses. Put simply, it exports, saves and invests too little; its economies are not diversified enough; and too many of its firms and workers are unproductive.

To make matters worse, the rise of China (and India) served to exacerbate some of the region's economic weaknesses. Latin America's share of the world's manufacturing exports shrank, while its reliance on commodity exports increased.

There is nothing inherently wrong with exporting commodities. But demand for them tends to be more volatile than for manufactures. And a steep rise in their price tends to push up the value of currencies of commodity-exporting countries, undermining the competitiveness of other businesses in an effect known to economists as 'Dutch disease'.[79] In Latin America, this currency effect was exacerbated by the region's low savings and dependence on foreign capital. In the 1990s, the region had begun to diversify its exports, selling a bigger variety of products. But that has reversed since 2000. Only a small and declining percentage of the region's exports are of 'complex' (i.e. knowledge-intensive) products. This matters. Ricardo Hausmann found a close correlation between the diversity and complexity of exports and subsequent economic growth. Put another way, with the partial exception of Mexico, Latin America has failed to join what economists call 'global value chains' (though they are in fact mainly regional). Modern industry needs elaborate supply chains, with parts coming from several different countries.

Latin America now has a cohort of efficient home-grown multinationals. Many of these *multilatinas* are in services – Brazilian banks, Chilean retailers, Mexico's América Móvil and so on. Some are even in manufacturing, such as Brazil's Gerdau, a steelmaker, and Weg, which makes electric motors, or Mexico's Bimbo (a bakery giant) or Alfa, in car parts and infrastructure. But they are exceptions. Overall, the productivity gap between Latin America and much of the rest of the world has been widening. According to the IDB, Latin America's total factor productivity (the efficiency with which labour and capital work together) was slightly over half the level in the United States in 2010, compared with almost three-quarters in 1960. Over the same period, East Asia narrowed the gap from around half to a third.

Why are Latin Americans so relatively unproductive? Alejandro Valladares's garment-making business, in a quiet residential street in Huaycán on the eastern outskirts of Lima, offers some explanations. In a large room of bare breeze-block walls on the ground floor of his house, Valladares has installed a score of knitting machines. He makes around 12,000 pairs of baby socks, of cotton or nylon, a month. He sells most of them in the Lima wholesale garment market, but also exports some to Panama. The business employs four of Valladares's children and two hired workers. It makes them a living, but not much more. Peru produces top-quality natural fibres, such as pima cotton and alpaca wool, and has a tradition of textile manufacture that dates back to long before the Spanish Conquest. So what stops the business from growing? 'Chinese competition', said Berta Valladares, one of his daughters. 'Fifteen years ago, our sales were better, but we've stagnated for many years.' Expansion would require 'more capital', added Alejandro. He cherished his British-made Bentley-Komet knitting machines, bought second hand from factories, but they embodied technology pre-dating the Second World War. He has run out of space in his house. After falling behind on loan repayments, he sold his cars and sent his goods to market by taxi. He didn't do business with banks any more. 'I want a quiet life', he said. His daughter dreamed of studying business administration or accepting a job offer in a factory that would train her in computerised production. But she had to combine her work with looking after two young children. Public transport in the area consisted of slow and overcrowded buses. It was more convenient for her to work in the family home.

The Valladares family workshop, lacking scale, modern technology and professional management, is all too typical of Latin American businesses. Of 7 million businesses in Peru, only 60,000 had more than ten workers and annual sales of more than $100,000 in 2014. Latin American companies grow much more slowly than their counterparts in many other parts of the world.

There are multiple reasons for Latin America's poor productivity. They include the lack of transport and communications infrastructure, a deficit of education and skills, lack of competition in what in most cases are fairly small economies, legal and bureaucratic obstacles, a relative lack of credit, lack of childcare facilities and the congested and inefficient cities where most economic activity happens. Governments have failed to foster innovation and new businesses. It doesn't help that half the workforce labours in the informal economy – both a cause and a consequence of low productivity.

In some ways, in 2016 the region seemed to be back where it was in the aftermath of Argentina's 2001–02 collapse, looking for a new formula for economic growth. But much had been learned. Those countries whose governments were the most vocal critics of the Washington Consensus were in far worse shape than the average, having managed to prove, in different ways, that there was no viable radical alternative in macroeconomic policy. That pointed to the importance of moving beyond the tired ideological debate between market and state that still bedevilled Latin American politics. The region needs both better-functioning markets, with more competition, and smarter, more effective government. Some countries faced much bigger and more basic tasks.

CHAPTER SEVEN

The Venezuelan Disaster

In 2001, on one of his many foreign trips, Hugo Chávez visited the editorial offices of *The Economist* in London. Over coffee and biscuits, he expounded on his globetrotting diplomacy aimed at sustaining the oil price, which had only recently climbed from the low levels of the late 1990s. Asked for his response to criticisms in Venezuela that he was concentrating all power in his own hands, he suddenly unleashed a lengthy diatribe, accusing his enemies of lying and his questioner of being an opposition propagandist. Already running late, he stopped on the way out to chat up two young black women receptionists, as if they were Venezuelan voters. Across the road, in Lancaster House, several hundred people were waiting for him to give a lecture. By the time Chávez arrived, more than half an hour late, the British foreign-office minister deputed to welcome him was already halfway through his speech.

Hugo Chávez would become the best-known Latin American after Fidel Castro and the region's most controversial and polarising contemporary figure. Built like one of the tanks he once commanded, he was possessed of seemingly inexhaustible energy. He travelled incessantly, both around Venezuela and abroad. Each Sunday for most of his 14 years as his country's president, he would host a live television show lasting up to 12 hours. Blessed with *llanero* wit and charm, he achieved a unique bond with ordinary Venezuelans. He was a seducer of audiences in the manner of a televangelist, as Cristina Marcano and Alberto Barrera, two Venezuelan journalists, pointed out in a perceptive biography.[1] Chávez was also arrogant, prickly and paranoid – he was so even before a coup attempt against him in 2002. Like Fidel or Trump, he was a narcissist, and seemed to consider that his own interests and those of his country were synonymous. He believed in the accumulation of power through systematic confrontation. Even more than his bête noire, George W. Bush, Chávez took the view that people were either with him or against him.[2]

He was tactically reckless, but strategically cunning and calculating. His rhetoric was incendiary, but his actions were sometimes surprisingly timid. Some of these ambivalences were noted by Gabriel García Márquez, who interviewed Chávez shortly before he became president in 1998. He concluded that there were 'two Chávezes'. One was a potential saviour of his country. The other was 'just another despot'.[3] As Teodoro Petkoff, a newspaper editor and former planning minister, noted, Chávez also enjoyed that most precious of qualities for a politician – luck. This notably included the upswing in the price of oil. It was also his good fortune to be consistently underestimated by his opponents.[4] His death at the age of 58 of cancer on 5 March 2013 – at least that is when it was officially announced – meant that he escaped much of the opprobrium for the catastrophe that his misrule visited upon his country.

Chávez claimed that his 'Bolivarian revolution', which he saw as continental in scope, replaced a corrupt representative democracy with a superior 'participatory democracy', and was substituting 'twenty-first-century socialism' for 'savage capitalism'. His supporters argued that he successfully challenged globalisation and the hegemony of the United States, while offering a better life to his country's poor. They saw in him an echo of the Cuban Revolution.[5] On the other hand, many of his opponents saw Chávez as a dictator, albeit an elected one, and some of them repeatedly tried to oust him. In Venezuela and in Latin America, Chávez's opponents were by no means confined to the right. One of his leading critics at home was Petkoff, a guerrilla leader in the 1960s who went on to found a socialist party. Chávez, he said in 2005, represented 'a significant regression for democracy'. Outside Venezuela, his regime 'is seen as a government of the left because it faces up to the gringos. But it has fascistic elements and practices, such as the use of selective violence and repression to corner the opposition in a ghetto.'[6] Carlos Fuentes, the Mexican novelist and a persistent critic of George W. Bush, said of Hugo Chávez that 'he passes himself off as a governing leader of the left when in truth he is a tropical Mussolini, disposing benevolently of oil wealth while sacrificing the sources of production and employment'.[7] In the same vein, a liberal Mexican writer, Enrique Krauze, argued that Chávez subscribed to the 'cult of the hero', a fascist rather than a socialist tradition.[8]

Certainly, Chávez and his hand-picked successor, Nicolás Maduro, embodied the bluntest challenge to liberal democracy in Latin America so far in the twenty-first century. Like Vladimir Putin or Iran's Mahmoud

Ahmadinejad, they came to embody a new post-Cold War model of authoritarianism, which combined a democratic mandate, populist socialism mixed with crony capitalism, anti-Americanism and resource nationalism bound together by carefully calibrated repression. Whatever the defects of the prior regime in Venezuela – and they were many – Chávez's rule was less democratic, open and pluralist than that of his predecessors.[9] By the time he died, and even more so by 2016, it was clear that his regime had accelerated his country's decline, squandering a massive oil windfall and delivering misery on a scale previously unthinkable in what had been one of Latin America's richest countries.

The blessing and curse of oil

Modern Venezuela is built on a lake of oil. Foreign oil companies began pumping the black stuff during the First World War. In December 1922, while drilling beneath the shallow waters of Lake Maracaibo, engineers working for Shell stumbled upon a fountain of oil gushing forth at the rate of 100,000 barrels per day.[10] For the next four decades, Venezuela was the world's biggest oil exporter (until it was overhauled by Saudi Arabia). Thanks to oil, between 1920 and 1980, its economy grew faster than any other in the world, at an annual average rate of 6 per cent.[11] Oil money transformed what had been a sleepy, rural nation of coffee, cattle and cacao farms. Venezuela became the most 'Americanised' country in South America, the only one where baseball was more popular than football, its capital studded with skyscrapers and criss-crossed by urban motorways crowded with big Chevrolets and Fords. Venezuelans glimpsed prosperity: in 1970, income per head was the highest in Latin America, outstripping that of Argentina.[12] 'With a growing state presence, Venezuela became one of the most modern, egalitarian, urban and educated countries in the world', according to Margarita López Maya, a historian and sociologist.[13]

Venezuela was one of the five founding members of the Organization of the Petroleum Exporting Countries (OPEC). But higher and more volatile oil prices from the 1970s onwards proved to be as much a curse as a blessing. Oil gave Venezuela a chronic case of 'Dutch disease'.[14] Productivity languished and inefficiencies multiplied. Second, oil played havoc with fiscal discipline. Habituated to oil revenue, the government failed to collect taxes efficiently: by 1992, non-oil public revenue was just 5.6 per cent of GDP. When the oil price fell, governments turned to foreign loans and to debasing the currency, so that oil dollars went further in bolívares.[15] As a result, after decades of price stability, Venezuela caught the Latin American inflationary disease.

The third curse inflicted by oil was political. Oil rendered public opinion hostile to even the mildest of austerity measures or economic reforms. Venezuelans were convinced that they lived in a rich country. If they were poor, they believed that this was because someone – corrupt politicians or foreign multinationals – must be stealing their wealth, rather than because of misguided policies or weak and ineffective institutions. This would make them uniquely susceptible to populist political messages – especially because after the mid-1970s they did get steadily poorer. The long boom came to a painful and symbolic end on 'Black Friday' in February 1983, when the bolívar was devalued. Under the presidency of Jaime Lusinchi (1983–89), Venezuela drifted deeper into an economic abyss, exacerbated when the oil price halved after 1985. The government struggled to carry on servicing its debt, which absorbed up to 70 per cent of export earnings. It imposed exchange controls, under which importers of 'essential' goods were subsidised with cheap dollars. According to one estimate, over-invoicing or downright fraud under this scheme, known as Recadi, cost the state up to $11 billion, a colossal figure.[16]

Economic decline exposed political weaknesses. A popular revolution in 1958 had ushered in a seemingly solid democracy in a country that had seen an almost uninterrupted succession of dictators since Simón Bolívar. This democracy was moulded by a power-sharing agreement, called the Pact of Punto Fijo. It placed the two main political parties – the social-democratic Acción Democrática (AD) and the Christian democratic COPEI – at the centre of political life.[17] It was designed to exclude the Communist Party, and to set limits on political competition. Its authors wanted to avoid the polarisation that marked a short-lived democratic interlude from 1945 to 1948, when an AD-dominated government had pushed through modernising reforms, but its sectarianism had alienated business, the Church, the army and the other parties. Punto Fijo was similar to the National Front forged by Colombia's Liberal and Conservative parties in the same year.

For a quarter of a century, *puntofijismo* worked well. Both parties, and especially AD, were highly organised and disciplined. They controlled social organisations, such as trade unions and professional associations. Their leaders spun a vast web of patronage financed by oil revenue. The party in power would regularly consult the other, which functioned as a loyal opposition. Guerrilla movements were defeated and sections of the left brought into the system in a third party, the Movement to Socialism (MAS) founded by Petkoff. Both of the main parties backed the prevailing economic orthodoxy of state-led industrialisation. Business was fed cheap credit and tariff protection. Though generally speaking Venezuela aligned itself with the United States in the Cold War, its foreign policy displayed considerable autonomy. In his first term as president (1974–79), Carlos Andrés Pérez of AD began selling oil to Cuba, for example.

The system had several weaknesses which would eventually prove fatal. The armed forces were bought off with arms purchases, perks and a top-heavy command structure, and allowed to run their own affairs without civilian oversight. Political power was highly centralised: until 1989, state governors and mayors were appointed, not elected. Some social groups were not well represented by the two main parties. That was especially true of the urban poor. From the mid-1970s onwards, Venezuela's economy failed to create anything like enough jobs to employ a rising population. The swelling urban informal sector was in practice excluded from a social protection system administered through trade unions. The civil service was underpaid, poorly trained, corrupt and politicised. As Moisés Naím, a minister in Pérez's second administration (1989–93) has pointed out, Venezuela's democracy spent far more than the Latin American average on social programmes. But in 1988, infant mortality was three times higher than in Chile, which spent only a third as much. Vaccination rates were half the regional average. Every few years, hospitals had to be re-equipped because of theft or neglect. Above all, the system depended for its smooth functioning on a rising level of oil revenue. But the ratio of government oil revenues to population fell from a peak of $1,540 per person in 1974 to $382 in 1992 (and $315 by 1998).[18] By 1989, 53 per cent of Venezuelans lived in poverty, up from 32 per cent in 1982, and income per head had receded to its level of 1973.[19]

The rise of Hugo Chávez

Venezuelans quickly dubbed it 'the coronation'. For three days in February 1989, champagne flowed ceaselessly, as waiters circulated with plates of lobster for hundreds of guests thronging the brutalist concrete labyrinth of Parque Central, a complex of museums, office blocks and the Hilton Hotel in the centre of Caracas. Middle Eastern oil sheikhs rubbed shoulders with Fidel Castro, Spain's Felipe González and Dan Quayle, on his first foray abroad as vice-president of the United States. The motive was the inauguration of Carlos Andrés Pérez as president of Venezuela for the second time.[20] He had won AD's nomination against the wishes of the party hierarchy. Pérez was popular. Venezuelans remembered that in his first term (1974–79) he had nationalised the oil and iron-ore industries. He had poured oil profits into new state-owned heavy industries, including a Soviet-style complex comprising massive steel, aluminium and hydropower plants at Ciudad Guayana, deep in the interior. Those were the days when *Venezuela Saudita* (Saudi Venezuela), as it was dubbed, was the world's top importer of Scotch whisky and Concorde connected Caracas to Paris. Pérez had only narrowly escaped corruption charges after his first term.[21] Many voters took the cynical view that having already enriched himself, he would not need to steal. At a huge rally to close his campaign, he promised 'full employment' and insisted that 'we won't pay the debt at the cost of sacrificing welfare and development'.[22] He won 53 per cent of the vote.

Pérez inherited a bankrupt government and country where the price of everything from bank loans to medicines and staple foods was artificially held down.[23] To take one example, petrol, at the equivalent of just 20 US cents a US gallon, was cheaper than anywhere in the world except Kuwait. When spread across the nation's petrol consumption, the difference between this and the average world price – and thus the implicit, indiscriminate subsidy – was equal to 10 per cent of the national budget.[24] No matter that he had campaigned otherwise: Pérez suddenly realised that reform was unavoidable, as Fujimori in Peru and Menem in Argentina were to do shortly afterwards. He appointed a talented team of free-market technocrats, who launched a radical programme intended to shift Venezuela from state-led import substitution to export-led growth. But the president, a machine politician accustomed to 'administering abundance', as he had put it in the 1970s, proved a poor salesman for austerity and reform. And it soon became clear that the years of easy money had rotted the Venezuelan state to its foundations.

Within three weeks of the 'coronation', Venezuela was shaken by urban rioting on a scale hitherto seen in Latin America only in Bogotá in 1948, following the murder of Gaitán. The immediate trigger was a botched decision to double the petrol price. Not only did Pérez fail to explain the need for this, but officials also failed to enforce an agreement that bus operators would only raise fares by an initial 30 per cent.[25] On Monday, 27 February – the end of the month, when many people tend to be short of cash – commuters were faced with an abrupt doubling of fares. Small protests by radical students were joined by angry commuters. From the capital and its suburbs, the protests spread to a dozen other towns and cities, encouraged by live television coverage. By mid-morning, the crowds began to loot shops. The Caracas police had only just ended their first-ever strike, and stood idly by as the slums were enveloped by chaotic and leaderless rage. The government seemed paralysed. After 30 hours of chaos, Pérez ordered the army to restore order. Over the three days of what became known as the *Caracazo*, some 400 people were killed, according to a careful analysis by human-rights groups. Most were civilians shot by the security forces.[26] Some 3,000 shops, including 60 supermarkets, were destroyed in the Caracas area, most of them serving the *ranchos*, as the tightly packed slums that cling to the hillsides were called.

The *Caracazo* was a profound shock to a peaceful democracy. Pérez pressed on with the reforms, but he had been forced onto the defensive politically from the outset. The reforms did produce growth. But they were incomplete: inflation remained stubbornly high, the fiscal situation remained fragile and labour laws unreformed. The government was slow to put in place an effective anti-poverty programme. A much-needed reform of bank supervision was held up by opposition in Congress, including from Pérez's own party. The riots had another unexpected consequence. Hugo Chávez, an army major, concluded that the conditions were ripe for his longstanding dream of overthrowing what he saw as a corrupt democracy. 'It was the moment we were waiting for to act', he would say later.[27]

Chávez had long nurtured a sense of himself as a man of destiny. A typical Venezuelan *mestizo*, of mixed African, indigenous and European descent, he grew up in respectable poverty – though not in the 'mud hut' of the title of a hagiography – in Sabaneta, a small town in the depths of the Venezuelan *llanos* (plains) in Barinas state.[28] His father was a teacher, his mother a teaching assistant. Like so many other ambitious Latin Americans of modest provincial background, he joined the army as a way of getting ahead. Gradually, radical politics displaced baseball in his affections. But his initial inspirations were not Marx, or even Fidel Castro. As a young cadet, he travelled to Peru for the 150th anniversary of the Battle of Ayacucho and was received by the president, General Juan Velasco Alvarado. Chávez was a fervent admirer of Velasco's military socialism, as he was of Omar Torrijos, the Panamanian strongman who negotiated a 1977 treaty wresting ownership of the Panama Canal from the United States. Through childhood friends and his elder brother, Adán, Chávez met leaders of small left-wing groups founded by survivors of Venezuela's guerrillas of the 1960s. From one of them, Douglas Bravo, Chávez adopted the image of a 'three-rooted tree' of radical nationalism drawn from Venezuelan history – an inspiration to which he constantly referred when in power. The first root was Bolívar. What Chávez saw in the Liberator was not the conservative aristocrat who admired Britain and the United States. Rather, he imagined Bolívar as a radical anti-imperialist. The second root was Simón Rodríguez (who sometimes called himself Samuel Robinson), a tutor and friend of Bolívar and an eccentric educator, socialist and early champion of indigenous rights. The third was Ezequiel Zamora, a Liberal general in Venezuela's endless 'federal wars' of the mid-nineteenth century. One of Zamora's slogans was 'Lands and free men: horror to the oligarchy'. Chávez took him as a pioneer of agrarian reform, though he was a *hacendado*.[29]

In 1983, the year of the 200th anniversary of Bolívar's birth, with three other young officers Chávez formed the Bolivarian Revolutionary Movement-200 (MBR-200). On the date itself, they gathered under a celebrated saman tree near Maracay, where their hero had rested after a battle. There they repeated the oath of liberation that Bolívar had sworn in the company of Simón Rodríguez after they had climbed Monte Sacro in Rome. Two years after the *Caracazo*, Chávez and his friends were promoted to the rank of *comandante* (lieutenant-colonel). For the first time, they had command of troops – in Chávez's case, a parachute battalion at Maracay, the army's main garrison, just 110 kilometres south-west of Caracas. At last, they could put their conspiracy into effect. On the night of 3–4 February 1992, Chávez set off with 460 conscripts, telling them that they were going on a training exercise. In fact, their destination was Caracas and the exercise was a military coup, in which they were joined by four other lieutenant-colonels with some

1,900 further troops. The conspirators seized the Caracas military airport, the state television station and other positions in the capital, as well as in Maracaibo and Valencia, the country's second and third cities. But Pérez, their target, eluded them. The previous night, Pérez had returned from the World Economic Forum at Davos, where he had received the plaudits of international bankers and businessmen. He managed to broadcast a message denouncing the coup and rallying loyal troops. Ironically, given Castro's subsequent alliance with Chávez, one of the first messages from abroad supporting Pérez came from the Cuban leader.[30]

The coup failed. Chávez's bid to seize power from a democratically elected government had cost 20 dead (14 of them soldiers), and left several dozen wounded. But it turned into a political triumph. In a fatal mistake, Pérez's defence minister allowed a defeated Chávez to broadcast live a brief call to his supporters to surrender. For the first time, Venezuelans glimpsed Chávez's innate skill as a communicator: 'Companions, unfortunately, *for now*, the objectives that we set ourselves in the capital were not achieved . . . I assume responsibility for this Bolivarian military movement.'[31] This brief broadcast turned him into a hero to many citizens of an unhappy republic. The phrase 'for now', which he later said had been unconscious, seemed to signal a continuing movement. His ready acceptance of responsibility for his actions contrasted with the self-serving evasions of the politicians. He had crystallised popular disillusion with political leaders and corruption, which, in hard times, had suddenly become unbearable to previously complaisant Venezuelans. He had managed to identify himself in the public mind with the sainted Bolívar, Venezuela's only unquestioned hero. He had exposed the weakness of the Punto Fijo state. The MBR-200 had been almost reckless in its preparations, but had not been stopped – just as the interior ministry had failed to anticipate or respond to the *Caracazo*. The conspirators enjoyed much military sympathy. Officers' salaries had declined, so that they could no longer afford cars or decent housing: a lieutenant was taking home the equivalent of $200 a month in 1991.[32] Months later, a group of senior officers staged a second, bloodier rebellion. In several hours of fighting, in which Mirage fighter jets buzzed the capital, 142 civilians and 29 soldiers were killed. The rebels broadcast a tape recorded by Chávez in prison, in which he called for the population to join the rising.[33] Repelled by the violence, they did not. But that did not save Pérez. His approval rating had dipped into single figures in opinion polls. In 1993, the hapless president was impeached. Ironically, given Chávez's subsequent massive off-budget financing and use of billions of dollars of public funds for foreign diplomacy, Pérez was sentenced to 28 months of house arrest for misappropriating a mere $17 million, which he said he had used in part to help Violeta Chamorro win the 1990 presidential election in Nicaragua.

Another irony surrounding the collapse of *puntofijismo* was that its final gravedigger was one of its original authors – Rafael Caldera, an elderly COPEI leader who had been Venezuela's president from 1969 to 1974. The Punto Fijo Pact had taken its name from Caldera's Caracas house, where it was signed in 1958. In February 1992, in a special session of Congress, he expressed sympathy for the aims of Chávez's coup attempt, though not for the method. Breaking with COPEI, Caldera stood for the presidency in 1993 as an independent at the head of a coalition of 17 small parties, mainly of the left. He won, but with only 30.5 per cent of the vote. Caldera – who would be aged 83 by the time he left office in 1998 – tried vainly to turn the clock back. For the first two years of his government, he abandoned economic reform and reimposed controls. But within days of his taking office, the economy was dealt another heavy blow when Banco Latino, the country's second-largest bank, collapsed. That triggered a run on the financial system. Misguidedly, the Caldera government tried to keep the stricken banks alive, pumping liquidity into them, while leaving their owners in charge. In vain: much of the new money went swiftly abroad, while 13 banks (accounting for 37 per cent of total deposits) duly went bust in 1994. The bailout cost the state the equivalent of 21 per cent of GDP.[34] The bank bust wiped out an important segment of Venezuelan business, while further undermining the credibility of democratic government.

Caldera eventually realised that he had little choice but to relaunch Pérez's reform programme. It was implemented by Petkoff, whom Caldera had made planning minister. Given more time, this programme might have restored faith in the system. But it was too late. Desperate for change, in the 1998 presidential election Venezuelans turned once again to the candidate who expressed the most radical rejection of the status quo, as Caldera and Pérez had seemed to in 1993 and in 1988, respectively. This time it was Hugo Chávez, whom Caldera had pardoned after he had served just two years in prison. The former coup leader had been persuaded, reluctantly, that elections were a more effective route to power than force. To that end, he formed the *Movimiento V República* (MVR, or Fifth Republic Movement), which brought together his military and civilian supporters. He was backed, too, by several small left-wing parties. He promised a constituent assembly, action against corruption, and wage increases. He won 56.2 per cent of the vote.

The battle for Venezuela

In proclaiming a 'Fifth Republic' in Venezuela, Chávez was not invoking General Charles de Gaulle.[35] Rather he was signalling his intention to dismantle the Punto Fijo system. His first act as president was to order a referendum on convoking a constituent assembly, in which his supporters won only 52 per cent of the vote, but 95 per cent of the seats. On paper, the new constitution that the assembly wrote did not involve big changes. However, it did increase the powers of the president. It extended the presidential term from five to six years, and introduced the possibility of a second consecutive term. It scrapped some of the decentralising measures introduced after 1989. In economic policy, it was a bit more statist, reversing a partial privatisation of the pension system approved by the Caldera government. Above all, the assembly was a tool which enabled Chávez to take control of all the organs of state. The assembly proclaimed itself sovereign, replacing the Congress elected in 1998 and the Supreme Court. But in other ways, Chávez began cautiously, making few changes to economic policy. He even invited foreign bids to explore for natural gas, and completed the privatisation of telecommunications. He was very proud of his new constitution: he had it printed in a little blue book and would hand out copies to everyone he met.

At first, Chávez enjoyed overwhelming popular support. He headed a broad coalition, stretching from the centre to the left. The new government encouraged grassroots movements, in both the *ranchos* and the countryside.[36] In a fresh general election held under the new constitution in July 2000, he was re-elected with 59 per cent of the vote, while his coalition won 99 of the 165 seats in the new unicameral National Assembly. Yet in little more than a year thereafter, he managed to arouse a mass opposition movement bent on his overthrow. Several things contributed to this.

Chávez picked a series of verbal quarrels with interest groups, such as the media, the Catholic Church, the trade unions and private business. Despite his ample majority in the National Assembly, he sought and was granted extraordinary legislative powers. In December 2001, he used his legislative powers to issue, without prior consultation with those affected, 49 laws, including measures on land use and oil contracts. In themselves, these laws were not especially radical, although the land law gave the government power to determine what crops should be grown. But they crystallised fears that Chávez was bent on becoming a dictator. In November 1999, at a meeting with students in Havana University during his first state visit to Cuba, he had surprised Venezuelans by proclaiming that 'Venezuela is travelling towards the same sea as the Cuban people, a sea of happiness and of real social justice and peace.'[37] He publicly expressed sympathy for Colombia's Marxist guerrillas. In 2001, he launched the Bolivarian Circles, intended to be a paramilitary organisation to defend his regime, paid for out of public funds. Though probably modelled on the 'Dignity Battalions' of Panama's General Manuel Noriega, opponents compared them to Cuba's Committees for the Defence of the Revolution. He had already put the army in charge of a new social programme, the Plan Bolívar 2000, which quickly became the target of corruption allegations. Finally, Chávez sacked the board of Petróleos de Venezuela (PdVSA), the state oil company, appointing a new one headed by a leftist academic and made up of low-ranking employees picked for their political loyalty.[38] He accused PdVSA of having become a state within a state, acting in its own interests rather than those of Venezuelans. His opponents saw the company as a rare example of meritocratic efficiency and feared its subjection to political control.

The opposition staged a series of strikes and massive street demonstrations. Some sectors of the opposition were undemocratic or represented vested interests (such as business owners and the media), or the remnants of the old order resisting Chávez's determination to extinguish them. Many others were convinced democrats, battling against what they saw as imminent military or communist dictatorship. The government organised counter-demonstrations in support of the president. But Chávez's approval rating in opinion polls had sunk to around 30 per cent. He had lost the middle class and the political middle ground. Several of his closest allies turned against him, including two of his co-conspirators of 4 February 1992 and Luis Miquilena, an octogenarian former communist who had persuaded Chávez to contest the 1998 election and who had presided over the Constituent Assembly.

Events came to a head in April 2002. The unions and *Fedecámaras*, an umbrella private-sector lobby, declared an indefinite general strike cum lock-out, seeking the restoration of the PdVSA board. Unrest in the armed forces was palpable.[39] There is much evidence that a conspiratorial movement within the armed forces had been planning a coup for months. On 11 April, hundreds of thousands of opposition supporters marched through the centre of Caracas towards the Miraflores Palace. Gunmen opened fire on the demonstration, killing several people. Many senior army officers refused to obey Chávez's order – reminiscent of that of Pérez during the *Caracazo* – to put troops on the streets to repress the crowds.[40] On the evening of 11 April, the army command asked Chávez to resign. There is controversy as to whether he in fact did so. By one account, negotiations over his resignation broke down. Certainly, he did not submit a written resignation. But Chávez did take Fidel Castro's advice, delivered in a telephone call that night, and opted to surrender rather than to resist or to die in his palace, like Salvador Allende.[41] As he had done on 4 February, Chávez showed cold realism, choosing strategic withdrawal after losing a battle. Had the army turned power over to the National Assembly and agreed to Chávez's request to go to Cuba, he might today be little more than a footnote. But there was a 'coup within the coup'. Pedro Carmona, the president of *Fedecámaras*, proclaimed himself president, named an ultra-conservative cabinet which excluded even his labour allies, decreed the immediate closure of the National Assembly and the Supreme Court, and the abolition of the new constitution, which had been approved by a large majority in a referendum only 28 months previously. Carmona was backed by a coterie of senior generals and admirals. But they had no command of troops. Those who did withdrew their support. As diehard *chavistas* from the Caracas slums protested on the streets (something which the private television channels chose not to cover), General Raúl Baduel, the commander of the parachute brigade, sent three helicopters to collect Chávez from his confinement at a naval base on the Caribbean coast and return him to the Miraflores presidential palace.[42] In four days of chaos and confusion, some 50 people had died. In the end, it was the army that restored Chávez to power, just as it was the army that had eased him out days before.

The coup had been swiftly condemned by other Latin American governments – but not by the United States. Under George Bush, the United States had become increasingly supportive of the Venezuelan opposition, especially after January 2002, when Otto Reich was appointed to be the State Department's top diplomat for Latin America. Reich, who was born in Cuba, had worked in the Reagan administration, in an office conducting propaganda on behalf of the Nicaraguan *Contras*. Chávez had irritated the Bush administration not just with his anti-American rhetoric and his affection for Colombia's guerrillas, but by visiting Saddam Hussain in Iraq in 2000, and Iran and Libya the following year. Chávez's government would later go to great lengths to assert that the coup had been dreamed up in Washington – perhaps to try to distinguish it from his own effort of a decade earlier. The 2002 coup was 'manufactured by the CIA', claimed Chávez.[43] There is no evidence of this. But the United States knew that a coup was planned and did nothing to stop it, though Reich vehemently denied this. Certainly, the Bush administration was guilty of not condemning the coup – an extraordinarily short-sighted and selective failure to support democracy in Latin America which sent a dangerous message.

Chastened by the coup, Chávez temporarily backpedalled, restoring the old PdVSA board and making a half-hearted call for dialogue. But the coup weakened the opposition, undermining its international legitimacy, more than it did the government. Chávez moved quickly to strengthen his control over the armed forces. Seven months later, the opposition's most uncompromising leaders once again marched into the president's trap. Many of the military officers who had backed the April coup began a public protest in a square in Altamira, an upper middle-class district of Caracas. At the same time, *Fedecámaras* and the trade unions began an indefinite general strike. This was soon joined by PdVSA workers. Oil output plunged. The dispute cost Venezuela $50 million a day, and wreaked huge economic damage. But to the disappointment of the military rebels, the army sat on its hands. Chávez opted to sit out the strike whatever its costs. When it collapsed after two months, the president seized direct control of a shattered oil company, sacking 18,000 workers, including many experienced professionals. He replaced them with untrained loyalists.

In its quest to unseat Chávez, the opposition belatedly arrived where it should have begun. As the strike ended in February 2003, the opposition movement collected 3.2 million signatures for a referendum to recall the president – a device inserted into the constitution by Chávez. Had the referendum been held in mid-2003 (instead of finally in 2004), by his own admission Chávez would almost certainly have lost.[44] The economy was reeling: mainly because of the strike, by December 2003 GDP had shrunk to less than 85 per cent of its level of two years previously. Despite the rise in the oil price, poverty had continued to climb under Chávez, peaking at 60 per cent in 2004.[45] Opinion polls showed support for the president at only 30 per cent.

An elected autocracy

Three things came to Chávez's rescue. The first was the spectacular rise in the oil price, to which his own actions had made a modest contribution, but which was mainly attributable to war in Iraq and rising demand in China and India. By 2005, higher prices had quadrupled Venezuela's annual oil revenues, compared with 1998.[46] Second, with Cuban advice, Chávez finally came up with more effective social programmes. Third, Chávez used judicial manoeuvring and his control of the electoral authority to delay the recall referendum. The opposition was obliged to collect the signatures again, in December 2003. That the referendum was at last held, in August 2004, owed much to pressure from the Organization of American States (OAS) and other Latin American countries. By then the economy was recovering and the new social programmes, called 'missions', were up and running. Chávez survived the referendum, winning by 59 per cent to 41 per cent on a turnout of 70 per cent of registered voters (compared with an average of 55 per cent in previous elections). Opposition claims of fraud were not endorsed by observers from the Carter Center and the OAS.[47]

Buoyed by his referendum victory, Chávez moved quickly to consolidate an elected autocracy. He used his majority in the National Assembly to name 12 new judges to the Supreme Court and sack others seen as disloyal. Many opposition voters no longer trusted the electoral authority. The opposition boycotted an election for the National Assembly held in December 2005 – a strategic mistake which gifted Chávez all the seats in the legislature. A year later, he easily won a presidential election, with 63 per cent of the vote. It marked the zenith of his popularity.

Beginning a new six-year term, the president announced an acceleration of his drive to achieve 'twenty-first-century socialism'. He nationalised a slew of companies, including the main telecoms, steel and cement companies and a hypermarket chain. (In all, Chávez would expropriate or nationalise 1,200 companies.)[48] He merged most of the political groups that supported him into a single party, the United Venezuelan Socialist Party (PSUV). In 2007, he narrowly lost a referendum to change the constitution, to concentrate almost all power in the executive and abolish presidential term limits. He went ahead regardless. Behind the façade of the constitution, and out of key with its 'participatory' approach, he used decree powers to create a centralised autocracy and a parallel legal structure, featuring 'communal councils', which began to enjoy many of the powers and resources previously held by elected local governments.[49] The Central Bank's independence was abolished. The armed forces were turned into an instrument of 'the revolution'. Between a third and a half of state governors and ministers tended to be military men. Cuban intelligence and security agents surrounded Chávez; he would never again be caught off guard by street protests or military dissent. He created a 125,000-strong militia, directly answerable to the president. And in 2009, he won a fresh referendum abolishing term limits for all elected offices.

Venezuela still had some of the outward trappings of democracy. But little by little, freedoms were chipped away. The government controlled the courts and the electoral authority. A group of lawyers analysed more than 45,000 rulings issued between 2004 and 2013 by the constitutional, administrative and electoral chambers of the Supreme Court, and found that in no case did they rule against the government.[50] In violation of the electoral law, Chávez and the PSUV routinely used the machinery of the state, from vehicles to money, for campaigning, while opposition activists faced intimidation in some parts of the country. The regime harassed the media, many of which supported the opposition. It refused to renew the broadcasting licence of RCTV, the biggest opposition television station. Globovisión, a television channel, and El Universal, a newspaper, were bought by regime sympathisers and their journalism neutered. Petkoff's Tal Cual and El Nacional, another daily, and the remaining independent media were battered by specious law suits and regulations and denied access to the dollars required to import newsprint (which was later turned into a government monopoly).[51] The names of the 3.4 million people who signed the petition for the recall referendum were published; some found themselves sacked from government jobs or denied passports. Opposition political activities faced intermittent and selective violence from *chavista* gangs drawn from the slums. By provoking the opposition and polarising the country, Chávez had gained near-absolute power.

'We're starting to build our own socialist model', Chávez claimed in 2005. To get a glimpse of what this entailed, officials directed foreign visitors to Catia, a gritty district a few kilometres west of the Miraflores Palace. There, a defunct petrol-distribution depot had been turned into a 'nucleus of endogenous development'.[52] That meant a combination of workers' co-operative and social services, all paid for by PdVSA, which Chávez turned into a piggy bank and all-purpose instrument of his social programmes. Three new buildings surrounded a central meeting area. One housed a well-equipped health clinic. In a second, the government installed scores of sewing machines for a co-operative of 180 women. Their first contract, in 2005, was to make red T-shirts and caps for Venezuela's diplomats to wear on a May Day march. The third building was a co-operative making shoes. The hillside above had been planted with maize by another co-op, this one of market gardeners. Some 1,200 people worked in the 'nucleus', which cost $6.6 million to build. Across the road there was a small but well-stocked new supermarket run by Mercal, a state company set up by Chávez to provide cheap food for the poor. Mercal operated on largely commercial lines, but some of its prices were subsidised, at a cost of $25 million a month to the government. Nearby was a centre for the education 'missions' set up by Chávez. One programme taught adult illiterates to read. Two others allowed people to finish their primary or secondary education; a fourth gave cramming courses – and the promise of a place in an expanded university system – to 286,000 teenagers who had failed to complete secondary school. The first and perhaps most appreciated of the 'missions' was *Barrio Adentro*, under which 16,000 Cuban doctors and dentists, lent by Fidel Castro in return for cheap oil, worked as general practitioners in the *ranchos*, where medical services were all but non-existent. So the 'Bolivarian revolution' started to provide the urban poor with services that they had previously lacked. But it did so in a clientelistic fashion, in return for political loyalty.

The 'missions' represented a parallel state, accountable to nobody but Chávez. Their financing was opaque and, predictably, proved to be unsustainable.

Twenty-first-century corruption

For all the bombast, 'twenty-first-century socialism' failed to come up with an alternative economic model. Even more than its predecessor, the Fifth Republic was dependent on oil revenue. Thanks to the surge in the price, between 2000 and 2012 Venezuela's total oil revenues (of around $800 billion) were two and a half times as great in real terms as those of the preceding 13 years.[53] That was despite the fact that the country's oil output declined on Chávez's watch, because of the mismanagement of PdVSA and the cancellation of contracts with multinationals. By squeezing the private sector and maintaining a wildly overvalued official exchange rate, Chávez intensified the country's dependence on its oil rents. 'Dutch disease' became a plague. Non-oil exports all but vanished: they accounted for just 4 per cent of total exports in 2014; in current dollars, they were worth $2,165 million that year, down from $4,922 in 1999.[54] The economy ran on little more than oil and imports. Not sated by his oil windfall, Chávez went on a borrowing spree: between them, the government and PdVSA issued more debt in 2007–11 (a total of $66 billion) than any other emerging-market country.[55] On top of that, China lent Venezuela some $60 billion, in return for future oil shipments.

Where did all the money go? Public spending rose sharply, almost doubling as a share of the economy, from 20 per cent of GDP in the late 1990s to 38 per cent in 2006, some of it disbursed through opaque funds controlled by the president. Part of the increase went on social programmes, health and education, and infrastructure such as new roads and metro lines. But much went on creating client groups. Public employment more than doubled between 1999 and 2014, to 2.7 million, according to the National Statistics Institute.[56] PdVSA's payroll swelled from 38,000 in 2003 to over 100,000 by 2010. Chávez lavished new weapons systems on the armed forces. He set up new, loss-making state companies, such as an airline; companies he nationalised leached money. Even as the state grew, its administrative capability, never great, deteriorated and corruption increased.

Across Venezuela, large signs sprouted up, proclaiming revolutionary projects, including thousands of co-operatives. Behind the billboards, the waste, failure and frustration was palpable. Take, for example, a gleaming new fish-processing plant at Boca de Uchire, in Anzoátegui state. In 2007, it had stood empty for a year because a planned wharf remained on the drawing board, while just three carpenters worked on the beach, building the fishing fleet designed to supply it. Then there was a model collective farm near the village of Buenos Aires in the coastal plain of Barlovento, an area with a large black population east of Caracas. Set up in 2002, five years later it looked like a neat suburban estate, its bungalows for 144 families grouped in 12 circular cul-de-sacs. Three tractors, from China and Iran, were parked nearby. But farming the project's 108 hectares 'did not go as we wanted', said Jacobo Pacheco, one of the community's leaders, with quiet understatement. Wearing a red beret with an image of Che Guevara, Pacheco said he supported Chávez. But he painted a devastating picture of mismanagement. Agronomists, some Cuban, from the government's National Lands Institute, which was responsible for the project, advised the collective's farmers to plant half a dozen different fruits; all but the lemons failed, either because the land was unsuitable or because of defects in the irrigation system. The houses lacked water, because a pump was broken. None of six promised workshops, offering training and employment in carpentry, metalworking and the like, had been built. The would-be farmers had to take outside work to make ends meet. Pacheco said that collective farming didn't suit Venezuelans; he wanted the government to divide the land into individual plots. And he was fuming because the project's houses had been shoddily equipped. He had seen receipts for the equipment and said that between them the officials involved and a supplier had pocketed a billion bolívares (then $465,000).[57]

Venezuela came to be littered with unfinished or abandoned projects. Chávez awarded contracts totalling $11 billion to Odebrecht, a Brazilian multinational construction firm, which became notorious for its practice of paying bribes to secure work across Latin America and beyond. In a plea-bargain with the US Department of Justice in December 2016, Odebrecht admitted paying bribes totalling $98 million in Venezuela. Unlike the company's projects elsewhere in the region, few were completed in Venezuela. They included an abandoned 13-kilometre bridge across the Orinoco river and El Diluvio, a $2 billion agroindustrial commune, where in 2016, according to a report in the *Wall Street Journal*, a thousand concrete huts stood empty, while silos rusted and irrigation canals were choked with weeds. The government also gave billions to Belorussian, Iranian and Chinese contractors to build agricultural and industrial projects, none of which were finished.[58] Even where projects were completed, there were signs of waste. A 1.8-kilometre cable car built by Odebrecht, which opened in 2010 and whisked residents and workers up the hill from Parque Central in Caracas to the *ranchos* of Hornos de Cal, cost $318 million – over ten times as much as a longer line that opened in Medellín, Colombia, in 2004.[59]

Improbably, given the oil windfall, Venezuela began to run out of dollars. Perhaps mindful that the 'Black Friday' devaluation had marked the beginning of the end of the 'Fourth Republic', Chávez allowed the currency, the bolívar, to become wildly overvalued. When the oil price briefly crashed after the world financial crisis, the government disguised the magnitude of the inevitable devaluation by introducing a system of multiple exchange rates. It awarded dollars for priority imports, such as food and medicines, at a much lower exchange rate than for other purposes. Despite subsequent devaluations and the introduction of an intermediate rate at which the government auctioned dollars, the gap between the official rates and the black-market rate became an abyss.[60] Similarly, the government's determination to avoid a repetition of the *Caracazo* led it to freeze the price of petrol. Even after the administration timidly raised the price in 2016, for the first time in 20 years, it was still the cheapest petrol in the world, costing less than the equivalent volume of water. The government, which stopped publishing many economic statistics, ran a vast fiscal deficit; Ecoanalítica, a consultancy, estimated the deficit at 20 per cent of GDP in 2015, of which almost half was financed by printing money.[61] The dollar shortage and the printing of bolívares inexorably fuelled inflation, to which the government responded with price controls.

The exchange and price controls were an open invitation to corruption on a scale that dwarfed the notorious Recadi scheme of Lusinchi's presidency. The caste in power in Caracas helped themselves not just through padded public contracts, but also by exploiting the exchange-rate differential and the vast subsidies on petrol and food for smuggling and resale. Jorge Giordani, a monkish utopian who had been Chávez's economic supremo, complained that in 2012 alone, some $20 billion in subsidised dollars was stolen through fictitious companies, an allegation echoed by Edmée Betancourt, the president of the Central Bank, who was sacked shortly after speaking out.[62] In 2016, the finance committee of the (opposition-controlled) National Assembly claimed that $435 billion of public money was unaccounted for during the 17 years of *chavismo*.[63]

The decay of governance in Venezuela manifested itself, too, in an explosion in crime. The murder rate soared, from 20 per 100,000 people in 1998, prior to Chávez's election, to 70 per 100,000 in 2016, according to Luisa Ortega, the attorney general. That made Venezuela the second most violent country in the world (excluding war zones), after El Salvador. Most of the victims were the poor residents of the *ranchos*. Kidnapping and carjacking became common. Residents of Caracas stopped going out at night. By many accounts, Venezuela became a centre for the export of Colombian cocaine to the United States and Europe.[64] Prosecutors in the United States charged several senior Venezuelan officials with involvement in drug trafficking; the government's response was usually to promote them. In November 2016, two nephews of Cilia Flores, Maduro's wife, were convicted in a New York court of conspiring to import cocaine to the US. Prosecutors said the men planned to use the presidential hangar at Maiquetía airport near Caracas to send 800 kilograms of cocaine to Honduras, for onward shipment. Their lawyers said that they were set up by informants of the US Drug Enforcement Administration.[65]

Chávez's tomb

Just to the west of the centre of Caracas, a hillside overlooking the Miraflores Palace is crowned by a fort that was once the military museum and is now called the Cuartel de la Montaña. It was the post from which Chávez directed his failed coup of 4 February 1992. It has been turned into his mausoleum. In an arcaded courtyard, his body lies in a large coffin of purplish marble, flanked by busts of Simón Rodríguez and Ezequiel Zamora. It is attended by soldiers dressed in the scarlet, gold-braided uniforms of the war of independence. Every two hours, the guard changes, the soldiers taking turns to chant honours to Chávez. One refers to him as 'the Liberator of Modern Times'. A cornet plays the Last Post. The ceremonial is almost identical to that which nowadays takes place at Bolívar's tomb. One of Chávez's last projects was to commission an extension to the National Pantheon in Caracas, a sweeping sail-like white vault where Bolívar's wooden coffin is now displayed in solitary state, separated from those of his fellow liberators.[66]

In mid-2011, Chávez interrupted a Latin American tour to fly to Havana, where it was announced that surgeons had removed 'a baseball-sized tumour from his pelvic region'. Puffed up by drugs, he conducted his last campaign, winning another six-year term in an election in October 2012 with 55.1 per cent of the vote, against 44.3 per cent for Henrique Capriles, the opposition candidate. Though Venezuelans were kept in ignorance of his condition, their president was a sick man. Before returning to Cuba for yet another operation, he announced that his successor was Nicolás Maduro, his vice-president and foreign minister. Maduro, a former leader of the bus drivers' union, lacked his predecessor's charisma and political skills. In an effort to compensate, he presided over the consecration of the official cult of Chávez, a new God as well as a new Liberator. When I visited the mausoleum, the young guide repeatedly referred to Chávez's 'physical disappearance', never his death. As Maduro campaigned for a fresh presidential election, held in April 2013, he claimed that while he was praying in a small chapel he was visited and blessed by the spirit of Chávez, which took the form of a little bird.[67]

Maduro was declared to have won the election against Capriles, who was again the opposition's candidate, by just 1.5 per cent of the vote. The regime refused to investigate opposition claims of fraud. Maduro lacked his mentor's luck, as well as his political qualities: Chávez's rotten legacy was compounded by the plunge in the oil price. Instead of devaluing and seeking IMF support, Maduro intensified Chávez's lopsided economic policies. Desperate to avoid defaulting on the foreign debt, his government continued paying bondholders, but instead defaulted on its obligations to Venezuelans, as Ricardo Hausmann, the Venezuelan economist at Harvard University, put it.[68] The government applied a python squeeze to imports: having peaked at $66 billion in 2012, they were slashed to just $18 billion in 2016, when Venezuela made foreign debt payments of $17 billion, according to Maduro.[69] The economy fell into a deepening slump: having contracted by 4 per cent in 2014 and 5.7 per cent in 2015, in 2016 it shrank by 18.6 per cent, according to a Central Bank report. Venezuela was sliding towards hyperinflation: the Central Bank said inflation was

181 per cent in 2015 and 800 per cent in 2016.[70] By 2016, wealth per head had fallen below $5,000, placing Venezuela alongside only Bolivia and Nicaragua in Latin America, a group of African countries and India, according to a report by Credit Suisse, an investment bank.[71]

What all these numbers meant to Venezuelans was that they faced a choice between queuing for hours to obtain goods at controlled prices, or paying a fortune in the free market. By 2015, the government controlled the price of more than 1,400 pharmaceutical products, 140 food items and more than 240 personal hygiene items. Since the official prices were well below the cost of production, and the government often failed to provide the dollars required to make or import these items, this was a recipe for widespread shortages. Government hyper-markets featured kilometres of empty shelves and mad rushes for recently delivered goods. Venezuelans would abandon their offices in droves when they received news on social media of a delivery at a nearby supermarket of chicken, cooking oil or nappies. Faced with disorderly queues, the authorities resorted to rationing, allowing people to buy only on certain days of the week, according to the last number of their identity cards. In the mixture of the primitive and the sophisti-cated that came to characterise Venezuela, they then installed finger-printing machines at check-outs to track purchases. The system was an invitation both to panic buying and to resale on the black market. By one count, up to two-thirds of people in the queues were *bachaqueros*, or those engaged in resale, a Venezuelan term derived from *bachaco*, a large Amazonian ant.[72] Although they lost money producing controlled goods, private companies faced constant official harassment and some-times expropriation. The acute shortages of medicines and medical equipment was particularly devastating. Counter to the regional trend, the infant mortality rate began to rise sharply.[73] Faced with these condi-tions, many Venezuelans, especially those from the middle class, emigrated. Perhaps 2 million Venezuelans lived abroad in 2016, and could be found driving taxis in Buenos Aires, working as estate agents in Madrid and Miami or subsisting in Colombia.

Even the revolution's showcases lost their shine. In January 2016, an air of lassitude hung over the 'nucleus of endogenous development' in Catia. There was no longer any security on the gate. 'There's been a lot of changes here since Hugo Chávez died', said Osglen Rivas, a young *llanero* in a red windcheater, whose job it was to show visitors around.

'I feel everything's deteriorated a lot since 2013.' The textile and foot-wear co-ops had been absorbed into PdVSA, their workers turned into salaried employees. The textile workers were sitting around and chat-ting, their idle sewing machines covered with red cloths. 'I'm with the revolution, but not everyone here is', said Mirta Molina, the supervisor. 'Some voted for the opposition.' The footwear workshop was idle, too. Miguel Rosales, a manager from PdVSA's industrial division, said that it had run out of linings for the work boots it made. Another worker said they were waiting for an 'administrative procedure' to obtain the linings. Did this mean they had no money to pay for them? 'That's right', was the reply. The only elements of the nucleus that were operating normally were a market garden, a clinic and physiotherapy centre, run by Cubans.

Maduro claimed that Venezuela was the victim of an 'economic war' by the United States and the private sector. But this fiction, like the cult of Chávez, had worn thin. By 9.00 a.m. on a bright morning in January 2016, just six Venezuelans had turned up at the Cuartel de la Montaña for the tour of Chávez's tomb. Outside the gate, around 120 people were queuing for food at a government store, some since 3.00 a.m. 'We hope to get chicken, flour and cooking oil', said one. 'Sometimes there's food, sometimes there isn't, what with the situation of the country.'

The government's third fiction, developed in the aftermath of 2002, was that it constantly faced a coup. This was the threadbare justification for increasing repression. When Voluntad Popular (Popular Will) and others from the radical wing of the opposition organised weeks of protests involving street barricades in 2014, the government cracked down. In all, 42 people were killed (though not all by government forces) and some 3,000 were arrested. They included Leopoldo López, Voluntad Popular's leader, and Antonio Ledezma, the mayor of Caracas. By 2016, there were more than a hundred political prisoners, according to Foro Penal Venezolano, an NGO. *Chavismo* had lost its popular majority at last. In an election for the National Assembly in December 2015, the opposition gained a thumping victory. It won 56.2 per cent of the popular vote, against 40.9 per cent for the PSUV. The opposition's 7.7 million votes were 140,000 more than Maduro won in 2013. Despite government gerrymandering, the opposition won 112 seats in the National Assembly, against the PSUV's 55 – the two-thirds majority necessary to approve constitutional amendments and sack ministers. It had a bigger and fresher mandate than Maduro.

The regime's response was to throw the constitution – Chávez's once-precious little blue book – out of the window, in a coup by the state against democracy. Before the new Assembly took office, the regime arranged for the outgoing legislature to replace with its nominees 13 Supreme Court justices whose terms were due to expire over the coming months. It then used the court as a quasi-legislature, declaring void the election of three deputies, in order to deprive the opposition of its two-thirds majority. Maduro governed by decree; on bogus grounds, the court knocked down the assembly's measures, including an amnesty law that would have released the political prisoners. The opposition set in motion a recall referendum against Maduro, collecting 1.3 million signatures as a first step. Having dragged its feet for months, in October 2016 the electoral authority halted the procedures for the referendum, violating the constitution. Datanálisis, a pollster whose electoral surveys had proved to be accurate, found that 64 per cent of respondents wanted Maduro to go.

On Venezuela's streets, frustration boiled over in frequent incidents of looting. The regime had learned lessons from the *Caracazo*: the security forces swooped quickly to stamp out disorder. Having refused for years to accept inflation and issue banknotes of more than 100 bolívares, when at last it did so the government bungled the switch, withdrawing the old notes before the new ones were available. That prompted three days of rioting in Ciudad Bolívar, a city on the Orinoco, in which at least 350 shops were looted. The government sent in 3,000 troops; several hundred people were arrested. Many of the looted stores were run by Chinese immigrants.

Maduro's strategy appeared to be to play for time, in the hope that the oil price would rise again and rescue him. To this end, he recruited Ernesto Samper, a former Colombian president who was the secretary general of UNASUR (the South American Union), a regional body, and who claimed to believe that Venezuela's government represented the rule of law and was being undermined by undemocratic forces.[74] Samper, joined by José Luis Rodríguez Zapatero, a former Spanish prime minister, and two former Latin American presidents, tried to mediate a desultory dialogue between the government and the opposition during 2016. This acquired more credibility when the Vatican joined in, backed by the Obama administration, drawing up an agenda that included the release of political prisoners, the electoral calendar and humanitarian relief. Many foreign governments and international observers believed that the only alternative to a violent denouement or a consolidation of dictatorship in Venezuela was a negotiation that would see Maduro resign, yielding power to a moderate vice-president heading a government of national unity, backed by the armed forces and tasked with organising a transition back to democracy and a modern economy.[75] But Maduro had other ideas. The dialogue collapsed after he refused to free political prisoners, hold overdue local elections and return to constitutional rule. Instead, as his vice-president he appointed Tareck El Aissami, a hard-line *chavista* state governor, who saw his brief as being to crack down yet harder on the opposition.[76]

How did Maduro survive economic disaster, political defeat and public rejection? Despite the defection of some *chavistas*, both moderates and left-wingers, he retained the support of a core of around 20 per cent of the population, either out of conviction or self-interest. More importantly, he held a monopoly of hard power, controlling all the institutions of state, apart from the legislature. He coddled the army: in 2016 the armed forces had more than 4,000 generals, compared with fewer than 50 in 1993. Maduro created more than a dozen military-run companies. Senior officers received big salary rises and preferential access to housing, cars and food.[77] Nevertheless, the possibility that the army might refuse to repress looters and withdraw its support from the government was the biggest threat to Maduro.

His second advantage was a divided opposition. Although it formed an effective electoral and legislative coalition, the opposition was fragmented among 21 different parties, many of them small. It was split over strategy: Voluntad Popular put more emphasis on street protests, while Capriles and other more moderate leaders concentrated on trying to win over *chavista* supporters. And repression worked: Venezuelans were understandably scared of the bullets or beatings of armed *chavista* mobs and the National Guard and of the dungeons of the secret police.

Thirdly, the outside world and especially other Latin American governments failed to put effective pressure on the regime. For many years, Chávez could count on the support of many of the left-wing governments in the region. He set up Petrocaribe, a scheme which offered subsidised oil to energy-poor Caribbean and Central American states, in return for diplomatic support. He could count on the backing of Lula in Brazil and the Kirchners, partly out of ideological sympathy and partly because of money ties. Lula was close to Brazil's construction companies, who did good business in Venezuela. In 2007, an alert customs official at Ezeiza airport in Buenos Aires opened a suitcase with $800,000 in cash, brought in by a Venezuelan businessman, Guido Antonini Wilson, who had arrived on a plane belonging to PdVSA. Antonini, who lived in Miami, later said that the money was for Cristina Fernández's election campaign.[78] Apart from approving sanctions against half a dozen officials it accused of human-rights abuses, the Obama administration kept well away from Venezuela, on the basis that unilateral diplomatic interventions would be counterproductive.

By Easter 2017, Maduro's position was weakening. He tried to shut down the National Assembly through a court ruling, only to partially back down in the face of international protests and the public dissent of his attorney general, Luisa Ortega, previously a loyal *chavista*. In what looked like an effort to create a tame opposition, as Daniel Ortega did in Nicaragua, the government deprived Capriles of his political rights for 15 years on specious grounds. These moves prompted a renewed wave of opposition protests and their repression. Maduro was also losing much of his previous regional support. Political changes in Brazil, Argentina and Peru brought to office leaders who spoke out against the government's undermining of democracy. So did Luis Almagro, a former foreign minister in a left-wing government in Uruguay who became the secretary general of the Organization of American States in 2015. In a diplomatic defeat for Maduro, in 2016 Venezuela was suspended from membership of Mercosur, the trade bloc led by Brazil and Argentina, because it had failed to adopt the group's rules. But the new governments in Latin America were weak.

Unlike Fidel Castro, who had made a revolution, Chávez and Maduro derived their legitimacy from the ballot box. If a majority of Venezuelans supported Chávez in his heyday, it was because they thought he was broadening democracy, not extinguishing it, as Maduro did. By departing from constitutional rule, and refusing a serious dialogue to restore it, Maduro was closing off the possibilities of peaceful change. For all Chávez's claims to help the poor, they had become far more numerous. According to a regular survey carried out by three leading Venezuelan universities, 82 per cent of households lived in poverty in 2016, compared with 48 per cent in 1998, meaning that the *chavista* regime had wholly squandered the biggest oil windfall in history.[79] The 'missions' were set up alongside existing health and education provision; they were patchily implemented and many were abandoned. Social spending did go up, and some social indicators improved while the oil boom lasted. But the improvements were 'not exceptional' in Venezuela's recent history, according to an academic study.[80] They were quickly reversed. And they came at the cost of the destruction of Venezuela's democracy and social coexistence. The most modern country in Latin America had been reduced to a Zimbabwe.

CHAPTER EIGHT

The Stumbles of Reformers

Beside an urban motorway in Lo Espejo, a crowded working-class district of Santiago, builders were labouring in the chill and mud of the southern-hemisphere winter of 2009 to complete 125 new houses of brick and timber. They were the new homes of the families from the dilapidated huts that previously stood on the site, part of a government programme of publicly subsidised housing aimed at abolishing the last remaining shanty towns in Chile. There was another purpose to the builders' labours. When the great recession struck following the collapse of Lehman Brothers, the government of Michelle Bachelet responded with a $4 billion fiscal stimulus. This included ramping up the housing programme, thus giving employment to 125,000 building workers. It was able to do so because it had prudently saved some of the windfall from the commodity boom. The economy recovered swiftly, and Bachelet's popularity soared. It seemed to be a moment of triumph for what was widely seen as Latin America's most successful country.[1] In marked contrast to Venezuela, in differing ways Chile, Brazil and Mexico had all pursued a path of democratic reform. All would stumble, though not on Venezuela's scale.

Reform deepened by democracy

Over the two decades from 1987 to Bachelet's arrival in office in 2006, Chile's economy grew at an annual average rate of 6 per cent, more than double the figure for the region as a whole. Keep that up, and in another decade Chile would have achieved developed-country status, with income per head similar to Portugal, Greece or Spain today.[2] True, income distribution in Chile was much more unequal than in those countries. But poverty fell sharply, from a peak of 45 per cent of the population in the mid-1980s to 19 per cent by 2004 (and 11.7 per cent by 2015).[3]

What explained Chile's success? It was an uncomfortable fact for democrats that the foundations of the country's dynamic export-led economy were laid by the blood-stained dictatorship of General Pinochet – but only through an unnecessarily costly process of trial and error. Shortly after seizing power, Pinochet entrusted the economy to the 'Chicago Boys', a group of neo-conservative economists trained at Santiago's Catholic University and at the University of Chicago. They implemented a drastic squeeze, which saw the fiscal deficit fall from 25 per cent of GDP in 1973 to 1 per cent in 1975; large-scale privatisation (though the copper and oil firms were kept in state hands); the opening of a previously closed economy; and the lifting of all restrictions on the financial system. The Chicago Boys ignored the short-term social cost of their policies. They also made mistakes. In privatising, they paid no heed to competition or regulation, with the result that the economy came to be dominated by a clutch of highly indebted conglomerates centred on the privatised banks.[4] Worried that inflation was slow to fall, in 1978 the government fixed the exchange rate. The peso quickly became over-valued, prompting an import boom and allowing the conglomerates to borrow dollars cheaply abroad. In 1982, Chile went bust, hit harder by the debt crisis than any other Latin American country. The financial system collapsed, and was renationalised, lumbering the government with liabilities equivalent to 35 per cent of GDP. In the aftermath, a new economic team implemented more pragmatic, gradualist policies. Growth resumed, and this time it was sustained. By the early 1990s, Chile could be hailed as a 'textbook example of an open economy'.[5]

The dictatorship gave way to democracy after Pinochet lost a referendum in 1988 on staying in power. The governments of the centre-left Concertación coalition that ruled Chile between 1990 and 2010 kept the broad thrust of the dictatorship's post-1982 economic policies, deepened some of them and reformed others. This bestowed democratic legitimacy on the 'Chilean model'.[6] The Concertación governments, and especially that of Ricardo Lagos, a moderate socialist who was president from 2000 to 2006, placed greater emphasis on social policy, to repair the lack of social investment by the dictatorship and to try to reduce inequality. Their approach was cautious. In 2006, public spending in Chile was only 22 per cent of GDP – the same share as in 1987, pointed out Nicolás Eyzaguirre, a Harvard-educated former IMF official who was Lagos's finance minister.[7] But rapid growth and a reduction in military spending meant, for example, that spending on education tripled in the decade after 1990. Lagos introduced unemployment insurance and set out to abolish extreme poverty, through a programme called *Chile Solidario*.

The Concertación governments drew on private investment, operating under public contracts, to upgrade the country's infrastructure. More than 2,000 kilometres of motorways were built, and airport capacity tripled.[8] Chile acquired the most modern network of roads, ports and airports of anywhere in the region. Better transport links and economic development went hand in hand. Take the Casablanca valley: in the 1980s, it was a dusty place of sleepy farms through which traffic crawled on a narrow road linking Santiago with Valparaíso, Chile's main port. By 2006, the valley floor was carpeted with mile after mile of trim vineyards. They produced good-quality white wine in a country that had been known for cheap *vino tinto*. A fast new toll motorway snaked through the valley and over the dun-coloured hills to the coast. Wine was only one among several new export industries created in recent decades. Copper, the country's traditional mainstay, remained important, but only provided around half of total exports.

Chile's remarkable success was based on three factors. The first was good policies. Under the Concertación, the state concentrated on regulating markets, rather than intervening in them. Macroeconomic management was prudent. Public debt was negligible. Chile pioneered what economists call 'counter-cyclical' policies. When copper prices were higher than average, the government saved in a 'stabilisation fund', which it could draw on in recessions, as in 2009. Lagos codified this into a legal rule. Secondly, these policies were based, until recently, on a broad political consensus, forged in negotiations over the transition to democracy. This consensus generated policy stability. In Chile, unlike in many other countries of the region, businesses could afford to make long-term investments, knowing that political surprises were highly unlikely. A third factor was relatively solid institutions, such as the civil service and courts – a legacy of the country's long tradition of constitutionalism and the rule of law dating from Diego Portales. The core institutions of the Chilean state never became as subservient to political forces as in Peronist Argentina or in Venezuela.[9]

Contrary to the claims of critics, the 'Chilean model' wasn't 'neoliberal'. The state promoted economic diversification. CORFO, a state development agency founded in 1939, and other state bodies such as the Institute for Fisheries Development (IFOP), helped to develop new industries, such as fruit, forestry and fish-farming.[10] An important role, too, was played by Fundación Chile. This unique body was set up in 1976 as a joint venture between the government and ITT, an American conglomerate whose assets were expropriated by Allende. ITT's half of the Fundación's $50 million capital came from the compensation it was paid, and was an attempt to improve a corporate image damaged by allegations that it had conspired with the CIA against Allende. The Fundación helped develop the salmon and wine industries by bringing foreign technology and consultants and setting up laboratories for quality control. In 2004, the Lagos government pushed through a law setting up a national innovation fund, to be paid for with a royalty of up to 3 per cent on the profits of mining companies.

Chilean democracy became increasingly self-confident. For much of the 1990s, the Concertación had to govern in the shadow of Pinochet and his supporters, who exercised much influence over the army, business and the media. More than in most Latin American countries, the transition to democracy was a negotiation, as a result of which Pinochet stayed on as army commander for seven years, the civilian government was saddled with a military-dominated national security council, and former military commanders were among nine appointed senators who gave the conservative opposition a veto over constitutional change. Pinochet's arrest in London in 1998, at the request of a Spanish court, proved to be a turning point. After 16 months of house arrest, the British government sent him home, his aura of omnipotence gone. This emboldened Chile's judiciary to unpick parts of the amnesty that the dictatorship had granted itself for its abuses of human rights. By January 2005, some 300 retired officers, including 21 generals, were in jail or facing charges.[11] Pinochet's standing among his own supporters suffered when it was revealed that he had $27 million stashed away in foreign bank accounts, as well as several false passports. Lagos was both willing and able to adopt a more robust attitude than his two elected predecessors to making Chile 'a democracy above suspicion', as he put it. In 2005, the conservative opposition at last agreed to scrap the authoritarian clauses in the constitution. Talking in La Moneda, the palace where Allende had fallen, Lagos pointed to 'a wider, cultural change in Chilean society' and 'a greater openness'.

Those changes were symbolised by the election of Michelle Bachelet as president in 2006. A paediatrician, Bachelet came from the left wing of the Socialist Party. Her father was an air force general who sympathised with Allende. He died of a heart attack while in prison after the coup; both she and her mother were briefly detained and ill-treated in Villa Grimaldi, the headquarters of the DINA, Pinochet's notorious intelligence agency, before going into exile in Australia and then East Germany. Rather than her socialist politics, what made her election remarkable in a country long held to be the most socially conservative in Latin America was that she was an agnostic and had three children by two different men, neither of whom she lived with. In office, she got off to a shaky start. She soon faced protests by school students, backed by many parents and teachers, over the poor quality of education, in the biggest display of discontent since the end of the dictatorship. With the state's coffers overflowing with record copper revenues, they demanded that the government breach its fiscal rules and spend more on schools.[12] The government's firm stance was vindicated in the 2009 recession. But despite Bachelet's popularity, after 20 years in power, the Concertación looked increasingly stale. Its candidate in 2010, Eduardo Frei, was a solid but unexciting former president. He lost to Sebastián Piñera, a businessman, for the centre-right Alliance coalition, which included many former supporters of the dictatorship (although Piñera himself had campaigned for a 'No' vote in the 1988 referendum). With the alternation of power, Chile had at last become a normal country.

Normality and its discontents

That very normality would encourage an upsurge of discontent. In many ways, Piñera continued the policies of the Concertación. Helped by a recovery in the copper price, the economy grew strongly again. The president harvested national and worldwide acclaim when his government successfully organised the dramatic rescue of 33 miners trapped deep underground after a rockfall. But he was then faced with months of student protests over an education system that many Chileans saw as entrenching the inequality of opportunity that the dictatorship bequeathed. In 2010, nearly 40 per cent of education spending was made by households – by far the highest figure in the OECD, a group of mainly rich countries that Chile had joined. A small minority of rich children went to private schools. Almost half of pupils attended what were known as 'subsidised' schools – private, for-profit operations where costs were split between the state and parents, who paid on average $400 per child per year (in a country where the monthly minimum wage was $363).[13] Democracy brought a huge expansion in higher education: 1.1 million young people studied in universities or technical colleges by 2011, up from just 200,000 in 1990. Over 70 per cent of these students were the first from their families to do so. Privately run, for-profit universities had sprung up to meet the demand. Student tuition fees accounted for four-fifths of spending on higher education.[14] Many students took on debt to pay for their courses, but got a poor return on their investment. According to one study, two graduates out of five would find that their salaries would not compensate for the cost of their courses.[15]

In the end, Piñera addressed many of these concerns. He pushed through a law cutting the interest rate on student loans, while promising grants to the poorest two-fifths of students. He raised government payments to municipal schools, attended by the poorest children. His government also took steps to bust the business cartels and oligopolies which were characteristic of Chilean capitalism. But the president got little political credit for all of this. He had reacted to the student protests with political zigzags, sometimes undermining his ministers. Many Chileans saw him as arrogant. And as a billionaire who had made part of his fortune from Pinochet's privatisations, and many of whose ministers were drawn from the most privileged slice of society, he seemed to symbolise Chile's abiding inequalities.

Many on the left, seemingly including Bachelet, saw in the student protests a rejection of the 'Chilean model' and of the Concertación's gradualist, consensus-building approach. In 2014, after an interlude running the UN Women's organisation in New York, she swept back to office on the most left-wing programme Chile had seen since Allende. She remade the Concertación as a more left-wing coalition, called the New Majority, bringing in the Communist Party and some of the student leaders who were elected to Congress as independents. One of the coalition's leaders called for the government to use its legislative majority as a 'steamroller'; another wanted to deploy it as a 'retroexcavadora' (backhoe loader) to demolish the 'neoliberal model'. She proceeded to launch a wide-ranging programme of reforms. The aim, she said, was to 'struggle against inequality'.[16]

However laudable her intentions, she soon ran into trouble. A tax reform aimed at raising an extra 3 per cent of GDP to invest in education by abolishing credits for reinvestment was widely seen as bungled, creating an unwieldy system. Rather than starting by improving municipal schools, Bachelet's education reforms began by outlawing parent co-payments and the profit motive in taxpayer-funded schools. A promise to offer 'free' (i.e. taxpayer-funded) higher education to 70 per cent of students was branded by her opponents as both unrealistic and inequitable, since some of those it would favour were among the relatively better-off. A reform to give trade unions more power was partly blocked in the courts. She said she wanted Chile to have a new constitution by the end of her term, because the existing charter originated with Pinochet. However, it had been much amended, and carried the signature of Lagos, not the dictator, and few Chileans thought replacing it was a pressing need. More positively, an electoral reform introducing proportional representation in place of two-member districts (a Pinochet bequest which favoured the centre-right) was overdue. The government responded to revelations of illegal campaign financing with a raft of measures aimed at cleaning up politics.

Two things combined to weaken Bachelet. Her credibility was lastingly undermined when she was slow to react to revelations that her son had secured a $10 million loan from a large private bank for a dodgy deal by a small property company half-owned by his wife. And the uncertainty caused by the reforms and the prospect of a new constitution took its toll on investment and the economy. The slowdown was initially the result of the halving of the copper price between 2011 and 2015. But the longer it lasted, the clearer it became that in trying to change the Chilean model, Bachelet had damaged it. Economic growth during her term was set to average less than half the rate under Piñera. Some business people complained that the president was taking Chile down a path of Argentine-style populism. That was an exaggeration. To carry on growing, Chile needed better education and public services, more competitive markets, more meritocracy and less privilege. The sharpest critique of Bachelet's programme came from moderates in the New Majority, who lamented that her team was less technically competent than its predecessors, and that ideology had replaced consensus-seeking. They argued that the president had misdiagnosed Chile's problem: most Chileans did care about the lack of equality of opportunity and social mobility, but they wanted to share in 'the model' rather than to abolish it. Bachelet repeatedly claimed that if her programme failed, Chile risked falling into populism. Yet it seemed more likely that the presidential election in 2018 would see Piñera return.

Hubris and nemesis in Brazil

In June 2006, Luiz Inácio Lula da Silva, then Brazil's president, went to Itaboraí, a sleepy farming town nestled where the flatlands beside Guanabara Bay meet the coastal mountain range. He announced the building of Comperj – the Rio de Janeiro petrochemical complex, a pharaonic industrial undertaking of two oil refineries and a clutch of petrochemical plants. With forecasts of 220,000 new jobs in a town of 150,000 people, Itaboraí geared up for a boom.

In 2015, it had the look of a ghost town. An unopened shopping mall marked the point where Itaboraí's straggling main street turned off the highway from Rio de Janeiro. Near the town centre stood the similarly empty Hellix Business Centre, two ten-storey towers of sleek green glass with a heliport on the roof. Another score of office towers and blocks of flats punctuated the street, all recently finished and all plastered with 'For Sale' signs. 'A lot of people bet on this new El Dorado in Itaboraí and it didn't happen', said Wagner Sales, of the union of workers building Comperj.[17] What happened was that the private companies that were supposed to join Petrobras, the state-controlled oil giant, in investing in the petrochemical plants took fright when the shale-gas boom in the United States slashed the costs of their competitors there. A year after Lula's visit, Petrobras discovered vast new oilfields deep below the Atlantic Ocean. Lula and his successor, Dilma Rousseff, burdened Petrobras with developing the new fields as a monopoly operator, while also building three further refineries. They also imposed rigid national-content rules on the oil and gas industry, driving up costs. Then oil prices crashed; in addition, Petrobras and its supply chain were all but paralysed when the company was revealed to be at the centre of a vast web of corruption involving construction companies and politicians from Lula's Workers' Party (PT) and its allies. Comperj was scaled back to a single refinery, whose completion date was repeatedly postponed, to 2020 at the earliest. In 2016, Pedro Parente, the new chief executive of

Petrobras, said he did not know whether the company would ever recover the $13 billion it had by then invested in the complex.[18] Itaboraí felt the chill. Luis Fernando Guimarães, a municipal official, reckoned there were 4,000 empty offices in the town in 2015. The municipal government laid off 10 per cent of its workforce and slashed the salaries of the remainder by 20 per cent. Itaboraí set out to remarket itself as a logistics centre. But its big advantage, its location where a new motorway around Guanabara Bay meets the main coastal highway, was scotched when that 'darned Dona Dilma' as Guimarães called the president, reneged on a promise to build the last stretch to the town.

Comperj was a symbol of Lula's grand vision for Brazil, of a rebirth of state-led national industrialisation. That vision was impregnated with hubris; it was shattered by the demise of the commodity boom, economic mismanagement and a political implosion. Brazil seemed to have lost its way, at least temporarily, after two decades in which its democracy had delivered unprecedented socio-economic and political progress in Latin America's largest country.

Reform through democracy

After a decade of false starts, with the Real Plan of 1993–94 Brazil finally began to stabilise its economy and embarked on modernising reforms of the kind adopted earlier elsewhere in the region. Reform in Brazil was slow and incremental, democratic and consensual. It involved bottom-up institution-building rather than top-down dictation.[19] There were several reasons why reform came late to Brazil and took this form. Unlike, say, Argentina, Brazil enjoyed rapid and almost uninterrupted economic growth for three decades until 1980. And unlike Argentina, Brazil had found ways of living with inflation, chiefly by generalised indexation, in which prices were adjusted automatically. It was an effective but insidious system, which aggravated inequality. 'Inflation gave to many people (but not to the great mass of poor Brazilians) the illusion of abundance', noted Fernando Henrique Cardoso, who would eventually end it.[20]

Another delaying factor was that the 1982 debt crisis and the economy's subsequent stutters coincided with a protracted – and accident-prone – transition from dictatorship to democracy. The generals allowed free elections for state governors in 1982, but then snubbed a popular campaign for a direct election for president three years later. That ensured that the first civilian federal government in two decades would be weak. Tragically, it was weakened further when Tancredo Neves, the leader of the opposition Party of the Brazilian Democratic Movement (PMDB) and the man chosen as president by the Congress, died before he could take office. His vice-president, José Sarney, took over, but as a longstanding supporter of the military regime who had switched sides at the last moment, he lacked Neves's legitimacy. The election in 1989 of Fernando Collor de Mello, a young telegenic politician from the backward north-eastern state of Alagoas, proved to be another false start. His technically flawed anti-inflation plan failed. His high-handed treatment of Congress backfired: facing impeachment for corruption by the Senate, he resigned at the last minute. His only lasting achievements were to have slashed import tariffs and begun to privatise the state's vast holdings. He was replaced by his vice-president, Itamar Franco, an obscure PMDB politician from Minas Gerais.

A third factor was that reform in a federal democracy is inevitably slow and complex. Brazil is simply too large and diverse to be a 'delegative democracy', in which the president can decree far-reaching change from the top. With the brief exception of Vargas's *Estado Novo*, Brazil has always resisted absolutism: it was not coincidental that its monarchy was a constitutional one, and that its dictatorship of 1964–85 chose to purge, but not shut down, the Congress, and limited its military presidents to fixed six-year terms.

Brazil's fledgling democracy equipped itself with a new constitution in 1988 which proved to be a double-edged sword. On the one hand, it added to the difficulties of economic reform by entrenching the failing economic model of statist nationalism and corporatist privilege just when this was going out of fashion across the world. It imposed heavy fiscal costs. With the federal executive weak, state governors and mayors secured widespread devolution of power and money; subsequent federal governments partially duplicated devolved service-provision. In reaction to the dictatorship's shackles on political parties, the constitution-writers in Brasília rejected any rules that might impose party discipline on legislators. But on the other hand, the constitution provided a cornerstone for democratic progress in Brazil, in a belated effort to reverse the social backwardness that was in large part a legacy of slavery. In 1980, the country's indicators of social wellbeing were still unusually poor, in relation both to its level of income per person and to the rest of Latin America. In that year, a third of Brazilian children were not at school. The constitution turned education, health and social assistance into universal rights, laying the foundations for a less unequal country. And it increased the powers and independence of public prosecutors, which would have important consequences.[21]

For a dozen years after the debt crisis broke in 1982, no government managed to tame inflation for more than a few months. Yet just when Brazil appeared ungovernable in democracy, matters were in fact beginning to change.[22] In 1993, Itamar Franco, the eccentric interim president, switched his foreign minister, Fernando Henrique Cardoso, to the finance ministry. The job was a poisoned chalice: inflation would top 2,700 per cent that year. Nevertheless, his acceptance of it would lead to Cardoso, a brilliant and cosmopolitan sociology professor who lacked the common touch, being elected president of Brazil for two successive terms. He assembled a team of talented liberal economists, who came up with the Real Plan, a clever mix of budget cuts, a new currency and a mechanism to break price indexation and inflationary expectations. According to Cardoso, 'the root cause of inflation in Brazil was really very simple. The government spent more than it earned.'[23] The forecast federal deficit in 1994 was $20 billion of a total budget of $90 billion. Yet dealing with the problem was not simple at all. As Cardoso noted, 'the budget was a work of fiction. The accounts of the Central Bank and the Treasury were mixed together and nobody knew much about either of them.'[24] Apart from budget reform, the groundwork also included putting an end to federal 'loans' to state governments, which were rarely repaid, and renegotiating the foreign debt. Cardoso's team correctly perceived that Brazilians were fed up with inflation and would support almost any measures to end it. They secured congressional approval in 1993 for cuts in spending, and in constitutionally mandated transfers to states and municipalities. But unlike previous failed stabilisation plans, the Real Plan did not involve either wage or price freezes. Its centrepiece was a 'virtual' currency, known as the Unit of Real Value, which operated alongside the devalued *cruzeiro* for several months. This allowed relative prices to adjust, and persuaded Brazilians that the new currency – the *real*, launched on 1 July 1994 – would preserve its value. It worked: annual inflation fell to two digits by 1995 and to under 2 per cent by 1998. Unlike many other countries in the region, Brazil vanquished inflation without a recession. The increase in the real value of wages sparked a consumption boom. Bringing inflation under control in itself caused the poverty rate to drop by a fifth.[25]

Only weeks before the launch of the *real*, it had seemed inevitable that Lula, narrowly defeated by Collor in 1989, would win the 1994 presidential election. The success of the Real Plan turned the race upside down. According to Cardoso, 'the *real* rescued hope and trust, not just in the currency and economic stabilisation, but in the country'.[26] While Lula, because of his personal journey from poverty to leadership, was a symbol in himself, Cardoso was not, and needed the symbol of the *real* to win. Lula, the PT and the rest of the left made the mistake of opposing the Real Plan. Its success meant that Cardoso won the election outright with 54 per cent of the vote. Yet achieving the new president's ambitious goals of consolidating economic stability, integrating Brazil's economy with the world, modernising the state and tackling social problems would involve a lengthy – and still unfinished – political battle.

Cardoso's battle to modernise Brazil

Cardoso was the leader of the Party of Brazilian Social Democracy (PSDB), which in 1988 had broken away from the amorphous PMDB. The PSDB, with strong support in São Paulo, Minas Gerais and Ceará in particular, was a mainly middle-class party of professionals and technocrats. Cardoso defined the PSDB as 'a centre-left coalition of committed democrats . . . we advocated a blend of free-market reform and social responsibility' in the mould of Felipe González in Spain, Bill Clinton in the United States and Tony Blair in Britain.[27] The PSDB formed an electoral coalition with the conservative Liberal Front Party, and with the smaller Brazilian Labour Party (PTB). In office, Cardoso invited the PMDB to join the government. In theory, his administration enjoyed the support of 70 per cent of the Congress, making constitutional reform easy. Yet in practice, changing the constitution was a Herculean task. Many nominal supporters of the government regularly voted against it when public spending or corporatist privileges were at stake. Nevertheless, in eight years Cardoso's two administrations secured the approval of 30 constitutional amendments, most aimed at freeing the economy from its corporatist shackles and creating a modern social-democratic state, and all tenaciously opposed by the PT. Yet despite these successes, Cardoso's governments were dogged by the difficulty of mobilising political support for fiscal reform in the teeth of myriad special interests.

After the initial squeeze at the start of the Real Plan, the budget deficit steadily rose again. The end of inflation exposed a number of 'fiscal skeletons', as they were called. The government absorbed some of the debts of the states, and bailed out the state-owned Banco do Brasil, the country's largest bank, to the tune of $8 billion. Interviewed in his wood-panelled office in Brasília's Planalto Palace in March 1999, when his government was reeling from a forced devaluation, Cardoso admitted ruefully that if he had had his first term again, 'I would be much more severe in controlling federal spending and in encouraging state governors to do the same.'[28] The price of loose fiscal policy was that the economic team headed by Pedro Malan, the shy, pipe-smoking finance minister from 1995 to 2001, came to rely on an overvalued currency and high interest rates to consolidate its victory over inflation. To make matters worse, throughout Cardoso's two terms, Brazil was hit by periodic bouts of international financial instability, in which the price of shares and bonds would plunge, and vast sums of money would leave the country. The origins of these episodes were usually external. But they affected Brazil badly, because of its fiscal vulnerability (which they aggravated) and because of its pegged exchange rate. By 1997, many economists reckoned that the *real* was overvalued by about 20 per cent, and Brazil's current account deficit had climbed to 4.2 per cent of GDP.

In January 1999, days after Cardoso had begun his second term, his government was finally forced to float the *real*. After a few anxious weeks, financial order was restored, with the help of a loan from the IMF and a skilful new Central Bank president, Arminio Fraga, who had previously worked on Wall Street for an investment fund operated by George Soros. In the wake of the floating of the currency, the government adopted inflation targeting and strict fiscal targets. These were underpinned by the approval in 1999 of a Fiscal Responsibility Law, which codified all the public-finance reforms of the Cardoso era, placing limits on the indebtedness of all levels of government. Critics charged Cardoso with deliberately delaying an inevitable devaluation while he secured a constitutional amendment allowing a second consecutive presidential term, which he went on to win in October 1998. His rebuttal was that the economic team was divided over whether or not to devalue; that he was waiting for a period of calm in the international financial markets (which never came); and that he was worried that inflationary habits could easily return.[29] Certainly, the devaluation carried a high political cost. Cardoso lost much of his previous popularity and his government lost the initiative in Congress amid infighting among some of his key supporters. A promising economic recovery was derailed in 2001, partly by a drought-induced energy shortage and partly by the knock-on effect of Argentina's troubles.

In headline terms, the Cardoso government's economic record was disappointing: the economy grew at an annual average rate of just 2.3 per cent between 1995 and 2002, while unemployment rose from 4.4 per cent to 7.5 per cent over the same period (or to 11.2 per cent using the new, more realistic methodology adopted in 2001). Yet conquering inflation was a historic achievement, and dealing with its aftermath was a long and messy job. Unlike in many other Latin American countries, devaluation was not followed by a banking crisis. That was in large part thanks to a well-executed programme, known as PROER, which cleaned up the banking system without bailing out miscreant or irresponsible bank shareholders, at a net cost of just 3 per cent of GDP.[30] Officials argued plausibly that behind the disappointing growth figures lay a process of structural change in the economy that would bear fruit in the medium term. Having abandoned its past introversion, Brazil was becoming much more integrated with the world. More than $170 billion in foreign direct investment poured in, much of it attracted by a large-scale privatisation programme. The reduction in trade protectionism forced Brazilian firms to become more efficient. Productivity, which was negative in the 1980s, rose at an annual average rate of 1.1 per cent in the decade after 1994.[31] The devaluation triggered an export boom: Brazil's exports rocketed from $51 billion in 1998 to $214 billion in 2005, as industries as diverse as cars and agriculture modernised.

Much to his annoyance, Cardoso's opponents in the PT sneeringly dubbed him a 'neoliberal'. In his memoirs, he went to great lengths to rebut this, insisting that 'if we did anything in the ten years that I was minister or president, it was to rebuild the administrative machine, give greater consistency to public policies, in summary to remake the state'.[32] What characterised the Cardoso government's reforms was pragmatism, in which the freeing of markets was combined with measures aimed at creating a modernised, regulatory state. Cardoso also put much stress on reforming social policies. He won approval for a constitutional amendment which obliged state and municipal governments to boost teachers' salaries and classroom equipment in the poorest areas. Primary-school enrolment increased to 97 per cent of the relevant age group, while secondary enrolment increased by 70 per cent. The number of family health teams carrying out preventive medicine in the community expanded fiftyfold.[33] The government also began targeted anti-poverty programmes, and a large-scale agrarian reform that saw 80,000 families a year receive land. Social spending rose to 19.1 per cent of GDP by 2002, up from 17.6 per cent a decade earlier.[34] Yet the economic disappointments and intermittent financial turmoil of the second term meant that Cardoso was unable to see his chosen successor, José Serra, his health minister, elected. In October 2002, at the fourth attempt, Lula won the presidency with 53 million votes to Serra's 33 million in a run-off ballot.

Lulismo: continuity, change and corruption

For Brazilian democracy, Lula's was a historic victory. In the country of social injustice, his life story was a saga of triumph over adversity worthy of a *telenovela*. He was the seventh child of a dirt-poor family from the north-east. Aged seven, he made the boneshaking journey in a *pau de arara* (an open-bed truck known as a 'parrot's perch' because passengers must cling to an overhead rail) to join his father, who had migrated to the port of Santos, in São Paulo state. Lula went to work selling oranges and peanuts on the wharves, while becoming the first in his family to complete primary school. His formal schooling went no further. He entered a government training scheme, becoming a lathe operator at a metal-bashing firm. He first came to public notice as the leader of the metalworkers' strikes during the later years of the military dictatorship. Out of those strikes would eventually come the Workers' Party (PT), in which trade unionists were joined by community activists nurtured by Catholic liberation theology, and leftist academics. Though never formally a Marxist party, for two decades or more after its foundation in 1979 the PT adopted far-left policies, such as debt default, nationalisation of the banks and wholesale redistribution of wealth. But successive electoral defeats persuaded Lula and his key ally in the party, José Dirceu, the PT's president, to move to the centre and seek alliances. That process suddenly gathered pace during the 2002 campaign. Weeks before the vote, Lula met Cardoso and signalled his assent to an IMF loan which committed the next government to stick to responsible fiscal and monetary policies.[35] 'I changed. Brazil changed', Lula repeated during the campaign. His television commercials, made by a professional marketing man, projected the soft-focus message of 'Lula, peace and love'. It was a return to the pragmatism of his days as a trade-union leader – except that the candidate had donned Armani suits. That union background marked Lula out from Latin America's many more doctrinaire leftists. José Sarney, the conservative former president who would become his ally, said of Lula that he was 'a man who knows the value of 3 per cent'.[36] Lula was affable and spoke to ordinary Brazilians in homespun metaphors. He had extraordinarily sharp political instincts. He was by nature a negotiator rather than an ideologue, a reformist not a revolutionary. 'Each day, even if we advance a centimetre, we are going forward – without any miracles, without breaking away from our international commitments, simply doing what needs to be done', he said in 2004.[37] Lula's own personal history allowed him to stake a claim to be much more than just an ordinary politician. He was one of the few leaders who could speak both to the world's plutocrats at the World Economic Forum in Davos and to discontented anti-globalisers at the World Social Forum, which originated in his own party's stronghold of Porto Alegre.[38]

On the night of his electoral victory, Lula claimed before ecstatic supporters thronging São Paulo's Avenida Paulista, that Brazil had rejected 'the current economic model, based on dependence, in favour of a new model of development'. But in practice, for several years Lula would maintain the main thrust of Cardoso's economic policies. In the weeks preceding his victory, Brazil's financial markets had yet again suffered a panic attack: the *real* lost around 40 per cent of its value in the six months before the election, sending inflation and the public debt (much of which was denominated in dollars) spiralling upwards. Lula moved quickly to calm the markets' nerves. Antonio Palocci, the new finance minister, was a former Trotskyist turned pragmatist. He immediately announced a tightening of fiscal policy. To head the Central Bank, Lula named Henrique Meirelles, a former chief executive of BankBoston, who was a member of the PSDB. The Central Bank nipped inflation in the bud by yanking up interest rates yet again. Lula's calculation was plain: a year of pain followed by three years of gain. He also knew that debt default would be disastrous for Brazil: most of the public debt was held by Brazilian banks and pension funds, not foreign investors. 'It is infantile to blame the IMF for these measures. We are taking them because they are in Brazil's interest', Palocci told a packed meeting of financiers at the Bank of England.[39] The government's economic orthodoxy brought anguished disillusion to the PT's left: half a dozen of its legislators left to set up a splinter party. But it paid off. Helped by rising world prices for Brazil's exports of iron ore and soya beans and cheap money in rich countries, the economy began to grow strongly, the currency and the public finances strengthened, and foreign investors looked favourably on the country. Palocci pushed through important reforms of the bankruptcy law and credit markets, which helped to unleash a consumer boom. In 2009, Brazil achieved a coveted investment-grade credit rating, which had the effect of lowering the interest rates on its government and corporate bonds.

In the 2002 election campaign, Lula had pledged himself to eliminating hunger, and the PT prided itself on its commitment to social policy. Yet in this area, his government got off to an oddly unconvincing start. After a year of fumbling, it finally recognised the value of its predecessor's anti-poverty programmes. It consolidated five of these into *Bolsa Família* (Family Fund), a cash transfer programme for poor families. By 2006, this was reaching 8.7 million families, or roughly a fifth of the population, making it 'the most important income-transfer programme in the world', according to Lula.[40] (By 2013 it had been extended to 13.8 million families.) His government also increased the real value of the minimum wage by 25 per cent. 'How many countries have achieved what we have: fiscal responsibility and a strong social policy at the same time? Never in the economic history of Brazil have we had the solid fundamentals we have now', he claimed, with a hyperbole which became characteristic, arguing that the country was now ready for 'a leap in quality'.[41]

Lula was less skilful than Cardoso in building a solid governing coalition. The PT had done less well than the president in the 2002 election, winning only 91 of the 513 seats in the lower house of Congress. He kept nearly all the important ministries in the hands of the PT and he could count on the support of a handful of small left-wing parties: José Dirceu, his chief of staff, struck deals with several rent-a-parties. But in 2005, the government was rocked by revelations about those deals. After the head of one of the parties was implicated in a bribery scam at the federal postal service, he retaliated with claims that the PT was paying a monthly stipend, dubbed the *mensalão*, to dozens of members of Congress from allied parties, in return for their votes. The scandal forced the resignations of Dirceu, a dozen other senior officials and the entire top leadership of the ruling party.[42] It dented the PT's sanctimonious claim to hold a monopoly on political ethics, and was a warning to the party (which went unheeded).

Lula insisted that he knew nothing of the *mensalão*. Many Brazilians, especially poorer ones, appeared either to give him the benefit of the doubt, or to conclude that his party was no worse than any of the others. Much of Brazil's press took a different view and became implacably hostile to Lula. The scandal damaged the PT's standing among the middle class. But economic growth and *Bolsa Família*, together with the affection that many poorer Brazilians felt for their president, won Lula a second term at an election in October 2006, in which he secured 61 per cent of the vote in a run-off ballot. Whereas in 2002, Lula had polled heavily in Brazil's more developed south and south-east, this time he owed victory to the votes of the poorer, more backward north and north-east.

Surfing the commodity boom, basking in popular acclaim and carried away by Petrobras's discovery of vast new oilfields, in his second term Lula drifted away from modern social democracy and back towards the corporatist 'national developmentalism' of Kubitschek and Ernesto Geisel, the most powerful and nationalistic of the military presidents. One restraint had gone when Palocci resigned as finance minister in 2006, over corruption claims stemming from his period as mayor of Ribeirão Preto, a city in São Paulo state.[43] He had wanted to use the commodity boom to eliminate the fiscal deficit and to improve the quality of public spending. His plan was quashed by Dilma Rousseff, who replaced Dirceu as Lula's chief of staff. The new finance minister, Guido Mantega, was more pliant than Palocci. Lula dropped his earlier talk of reforms to Vargas's labour code or the tax system. He put Dilma (as Brazilians called her) in charge of a big public-works programme, and groomed her as his successor. When the world financial crisis broke, Brazil suffered brief tremors, but the government was able to ramp up spending and subsidised loans from the BNDES, the National Development Bank. The economy roared back, growing at an annualised rate of 8 per cent in the 15 months to mid-2010. In the presidential

1 Simón Bolívar: the great Liberator left an ambiguous political legacy.

2 Francisco de Paula Santander, the forgotten liberal.

3 Francisco Laso's *Three Races or Equality before the Law*, an early denunciation of racism by a liberal Peruvian painter and writer.

4 Revolutionaries at Tampico: Mexico's revolution of 1910–17 created a corporate state.

5 Ernesto 'Che' Guevara (left) and Fidel Castro led a revolution in Cuba, but failed elsewhere.

6 In 1992 Hugo Chávez staged a failed coup against an elected government – something he would later suffer when in power.

7 Successful reformers: Fernando Henrique Cardoso of Brazil and Ricardo Lagos of Chile.

8 Luiz Inácio Lula da Silva (right) made Brazil less unequal but his reputation was tarnished by corruption scandals and the impeachment of his inept successor, Dilma Rousseff (left).

9 Vicente Fox and Felipe Calderón: democracy finally arrived in Mexico in 2000.

10 A new, emerging middle class: proud first-time homeowners at a housing project in Mexico.

11 & 12 The changing face of Lima's shanty towns: Huáscar, San Juan de Lurigancho, 1985, and the Megaplaza shopping centre in the Cono Norte, 2004.

13 Bolivia's 'water wars': a protest in El Alto against water privatisation.

14 Child labour in the coca industry.

15 Chile's students demand free university education.

16 Climate change is melting glaciers and disrupting livelihoods in the Peruvian Andes.

17 Evangelical Protestantism – the new religion of Latin America's poor.

18 The Rio de Janeiro *favelas*: a failure of policing.

19 São Paulo: getting around by helicopter in Brazil's global city.

election, Dilma beat the PSDB's José Serra by 56 per cent to 44 per cent in a run-off, thus becoming Brazil's first woman president. Lula had presided over faster economic growth combined with income redistribution and social inclusion, an unprecedented combination for Brazil. Unlike Chávez in Venezuela, he hadn't harassed business. His popular appeal went far wider than that of the PT. He left office with an approval rating of over 80 per cent. André Singer, a political scientist who had worked for him, talked of *lulismo*, which he defined as a moderate reformism that had reduced extreme poverty without confronting the established economic order. He saw it as having generated a lasting political realignment in Brazil.[44]

Nemesis for Dilma and the PT

Dilma had never before held elected office. Lula had picked her out because he thought she was an efficient bureaucrat. From a comfortable middle-class background in Belo Horizonte, Dilma had been a member of a Marxist urban-guerrilla group during the early years of the dictatorship. She was arrested and was tortured during 21 days (she did not give away her address, where arms were stored, though she never used them). She spent almost three years in jail in São Paulo. On her release, she completed an economics degree. She made her political career in Brizola's Democratic Labour Party (PDT) in Rio Grande do Sul, only joining the PT in 2000.[45] Dilma was a strong and tough woman of feminist convictions, respected for her grasp of detail and personal honesty, but feared for her harshness and temper. She was a 'manager-president', according to Luciano Coutinho, the president of the BNDES.[46] But she was also more ideological and less flexible than Lula. In her inaugural speech, she stressed the importance of tax and political reform and of improving the quality of public services and public spending, though she would achieve little of this. In addition, she promised zero tolerance of corruption and waste. On that, she seemed to make good: in her first year, she sacked seven ministers from her ramshackle coalition, in all but one case because they faced allegations of graft.

Although she failed to withdraw what should have been the temporary fiscal stimulus of 2010, the economy cooled under her stewardship as the commodity boom receded. Just as in the 1970s, Brazil was too slow to adjust to a change in external conditions. Although the government was aware of the 'Brazil cost', as business people called the country's lack of competitiveness, it failed to grapple with its main elements: a lack of transport infrastructure; a labyrinthine tax system; archaic and costly labour laws; and mountains of red tape. Instead, Dilma favoured a kind of soft state capitalism, with a bewildering range of subsidies, tax breaks and selective tariff increases to favour some sectors and companies at the expense of others.

Then, suddenly, in June 2013, Brazil was shaken by weeks of mass protests over poor public services, which began in São Paulo and quickly spread across the country, bringing up to 1.5 million people onto the streets at their height. Discontent was crystallised by a bus-fare rise just when the preparations for the 2014 football World Cup revealed scandalous waste and corruption. The budget for the 12 stadiums (eight would have sufficed) climbed to around $3.6 billion, three times more than South Africa had spent on hosting the previous tournament. Big new stadiums were built in Manaus, Cuiabá, Natal and Brasília, whose local clubs never attracted more than a few thousand fans. Nevertheless, Dilma bounced back to win a second term the following year, but only narrowly, beating Aécio Neves of the PSDB in a run-off by 51.6 per cent to 48.4 per cent. She won for two reasons. First, she was the beneficiary of public gratitude at full employment, rising wages, the exit of some 40 million Brazilians from poverty since 2002 and the PT's social programmes – a low-cost housing scheme, as well as *Bolsa Família*, student grants, scores of new technical colleges and irrigation and rural electricity projects in the *sertão*, the arid interior of the north-east. Income inequality had fallen steadily. Secondly, as investment dried up and commodity prices plunged, she spent her way to a second term: the fiscal deficit doubled in 2014, to 6.75 per cent of GDP (and even this figure did not include some held-over payments). For the first time since the Fiscal Responsibility Law of 1999, the government did not post a primary fiscal surplus (i.e. before interest payments).

Even before the election, a cloud of scandal had begun to form. In March 2014, the federal police arrested Paulo Roberto Costa, the head of Petrobras's procurement division from 2004 to 2012. Prosecutors discovered an elaborate scheme of bribes and kickbacks on Petrobras contracts dating back to 2004. They dubbed their investigations Operation *Lava Jato* (Car Wash) because they began with the discovery that a money-transfer service at a petrol station opposite the Hotel

Meliã in Brasília was being used to launder cash from kickbacks. In March 2015, Rodrigo Janot, the public prosecutor, filed with the Supreme Court a list of 49 politicians for investigation. All but one were from the ruling coalition: eight were from the PT and seven from the PMDB.[47] From that date on, *Lava Jato* dominated the news in Brazil.

Early one morning in June 2015 a squad of federal police turned up at a spacious mansion in Morumbi, an opulent São Paulo neighbourhood, and arrested its owner, Marcelo Odebrecht, the third-generation boss of a family conglomerate that had become Latin America's largest multinational construction company, with interests in petrochemicals and infrastructure management.[48] Under Marcelo's stewardship since 2008, Odebrecht had tripled its revenues, to $45.8 billion, and almost doubled the number of its employees, to 170,000. *Forbes* magazine reckoned that he was the eighth-richest person in Brazil in 2014, worth $6 billion. On the order of Sérgio Moro, a young federal judge in Curitiba who was leading the judicial end of the *Lava Jato* investigation, Marcelo Odebrecht was held in a federal police lock-up for months. Such treatment of the powerful was unprecedented in Brazil. His lawyers complained of an abuse of human rights.[49] Months later, the police raided the house in Salvador (the home city of Odebrecht) of Maria Lúcia Tavares, who had worked for the company for almost 40 years as a secretary. They found a bulging file containing details of payments made to hundreds of code-named recipients. As Tavares and then Marcelo Odebrecht sought plea bargains, and with Odebrecht's revenues and reputation bleeding, the full details of what was probably the world's most elaborate scheme of bribery and corruption emerged. In an agreement reached with authorities in Brazil, the United States (where the shares of a subsidiary were listed) and Switzerland, Odebrecht and a subsidiary agreed to pay a minimum of $3.5 billion in fines, the biggest anti-corruption settlement in history. The investigators found that, over 15 years, Odebrecht had paid nearly $800 million in bribes, related to more than 100 projects in 12 countries (ten in Latin America and two in Africa), from which it derived $3.34 billion in 'benefits' (i.e. excess revenues for overcharging on contracts), according to the US Department of Justice. Odebrecht had set up a special 'bribes department', called the Division of Structured Operations, and even bought a bank in Antigua through which to funnel corrupt payments. In March 2016, Marcelo Odebrecht was sentenced to 19 years in jail.[50]

Odebrecht was the biggest offender, but not the only one. Other Brazilian construction firms admitted to having joined it in a cartel, handing over bribes in return for padded contracts from Petrobras and other public entities.[51] The politicians accused of profiting had the right to trial by the Supreme Court, which took longer, but few doubted that many would be found guilty. The courts had already jailed the PT's treasurer and one of its senators, who had been the government leader in the upper house, as well as managers at Petrobras and the construction firms. In all, by January 2017, 260 people had been charged and 25 sentenced in lower courts as a result of the *Lava Jato* investigation; 68 faced accusations in the Supreme Court. At that point, 13 senators and 22 congressmen were under investigation. Prosecutors found evidence of bribes totalling 6.4 billion *reais* (more than $2 billion at the current exchange rate, but more at the time the payments were made).[52] In April, the Supreme Court authorised a second wave of investigations into eight ministers, and more than 60 politicians, this time including many from the PMDB and a number from the PSDB. This followed plea-bargain testimony from 78 former Odebrecht managers.

The *Lava Jato* investigation lapped ever closer to Lula himself. Prosecutors filed several charges against him, including accepting a beachside apartment and a country retreat as gifts from construction companies. Lula insisted that the properties were not owned by him, and that he was the victim of legal harassment and political persecution. Two years of investigations had found 'not an undeclared cent in my accounts, no shell companies, no secret accounts', he retorted. He pointed out that the PT governments had empowered the federal police and prosecutors and passed new anti-corruption legislation, allowing plea bargains.[53] Like many former heads of government, after leaving office Lula became an ambassador for his country's businesses, giving paid conferences. At the least, he showed poor judgement in drawing so close to the construction magnates. To clear his name, Lula threatened to run for the presidency again in 2018. In early 2017, he remained one of Brazil's more popular politicians. But his reputation was tarnished: polls suggested he would find it hard to win the presidency. Barring an extraordinary twist of fate, his active political career looked to be over. But his memory lived on among millions of poorer Brazilians.

Critics accused Moro and the prosecutors of conducting a political witch-hunt, and of abusing his powers of 'preventive prison' to force confessions from suspects and to induce plea bargains. André Singer, Lula's former adviser, wrote of the emergence of a 'Party of Justice', with strong allies in the media, and with an anti-PT agenda.[54] Certainly, Moro occasionally overplayed his hand: he was reprimanded by the Supreme Court when he authorised the leaking of telephone calls by Lula, including one to President Rousseff. He and other Brazilian judges developed a taste for making public statements outside their courtrooms, which risked a politicisation of justice. Yet the *Lava Jato* investigation was closely supervised by the Supreme Court, a majority of whose justices had been chosen by Lula and Dilma. The judges could claim that the use of plea-bargaining and preventive detention and the rallying of public opinion were necessary if the long tradition of impunity for the powerful in Brazil was to be broken.

Lessons from the fall

Less than two years into her second term, in August 2016, Dilma was impeached, by 61 votes to 20 in the Senate. She was accused of fiddling the public finances by spending without congressional authorisation – the independent audit tribunal had rejected the government's accounts for 2014, an unprecedented step. She claimed she was the victim of 'a coup' which installed a centre-right government headed by Michel Temer, her vice-president and the leader of the PMDB, the PT's main ally since 2006. Dilma pointed out that she had not been accused of corruption, unlike many of accusers in the Congress, and had no Swiss bank accounts or Panamanian offshore companies – unlike Eduardo Cunha, the PMDB speaker of the lower house, who was the driving force behind the impeachment. (Cunha would be successively stripped of his post and his role as a member of the lower house of Congress, before being jailed while facing trial at the Supreme Court on charges, as part of *Lava Jato*, that he accepted some $40 million in bribes and attempted to obstruct justice.) It was true that Dilma was impeached over a legal technicality. At least some of her former supporters in Congress turned against her because, to her credit, she refused to intervene to halt the *Lava Jato* investigation (she probably couldn't have done so anyway). But the process was not a coup: it took place over nine months, giving her ample time both to defend herself and to mobilise congressional support; it followed strict constitutional procedures; and it was supervised by the Supreme Court. Most Brazilians did not think Dilma's departure was a coup: in municipal elections six weeks after the impeachment, the PT suffered a drubbing, while the main parties in Temer's administration did well.

There were three factors behind the impeachment. The first was that Dilma's mismanagement of the economy in her first term quickly caught up with her, tipping Brazil into deep recession and forcing her immediately to renege on her mendacious campaign promises. She had won by claiming, in highly effective TV commercials produced by João Santana, the PT's new campaign guru, that the PSDB's 'neoliberalism' was the only threat to Brazil's economic and social progress. With Brazil facing the imminent loss of its investment-grade credit rating, immediately after the election she reversed course. She appointed as finance minster Joaquim Levy, an economic liberal and fiscal hawk, with instructions to cut spending. The problem was that Dilma's reckless disregard, in her first term, of the macroeconomic tripod of inflation targeting, a floating exchange rate and fiscal prudence left her government with no policy tools to offset the fall in commodity prices and the inevitable fiscal squeeze. With inflation rising sharply, the Central Bank could not loosen monetary policy; and with public debt soaring, the government had to rein in credit from the state banks. To make matters worse, at critical moments Dilma failed to back Levy.

Dilma and the PT insisted that Brazil was simply a victim of the commodity crash. Yet other Latin American commodity exporters, such as Peru, Chile and Colombia, continued to register economic growth, albeit at a slower rate. Brazilians faced a much harsher fate. After stagnating in 2014, GDP contracted by 3.9 per cent in 2015 and by 3.6 per cent in 2016. Inflation reached 10.7 per cent in 2015 and 8.5 per cent the following year. Almost 3 million formal-sector jobs were wiped out, as unemployment climbed to 12 per cent (from 4.3 per cent in December 2014), and the real value of wages fell. Some 3 million Brazilians fell back into poverty, and income inequality began to rise again.[55]

The second factor was the hydra-headed *Lava Jato* investigation. There was no evidence that Dilma was personally involved in acts of corruption. But they happened on her watch: before becoming president, she had chaired the board of Petrobras from 2003 to 2010. Some of the company's transactions should have invited her suspicion. A refinery in Pernambuco budgeted at $2.3 billion ended up costing

$20.1 billion. In 2012, Petrobras completed the purchase of another refinery, at Pasadena in California, for $1.2 billion, for which its previous owner had paid $42.4 million in 2005. Petrobras lost $792 million on the transaction, according to Brazil's audit court.[56]

The deteriorating economy fused with public anger at corruption to destroy Dilma's public standing: by August 2015, her approval rating had fallen to just 8 per cent. She lost control of Congress at the outset of her second term, when Cunha, who had his own agenda focused on staying out of jail, was elected as speaker; and then she lost control of her coalition, when the PMDB quit in early 2016. Even so, when Cunha accepted an impeachment motion for debate in December 2015, few political analysts expected it to prosper. But public opinion was squarely behind impeachment, as manifested in several huge demonstrations, as well as in opinion polls.

The third factor in Dilma's downfall was her own lack of leadership and elementary political skill. A Brazilian president has huge powers of persuasion; that she failed to secure the support of even the 172 deputies (a third of the total) she needed to halt impeachment was a damning indictment.

From the outset of her second term, Dilma was in office but not in power. Brazil suffered a costly breakdown in governance, which destroyed business confidence and thus prevented economic recovery. Nevertheless, impeachment was the most divisive way of overcoming this power vacuum. It would have been better had Dilma resigned; but she repeatedly refused to do so. Another way out would have been for the electoral tribunal to annul the 2014 election, since there was plenty of evidence that money from Petrobras kickbacks had helped to finance her campaign. Had it done so before January 2017, that would have triggered the fresh election that Brazil needed.

For the PT, ejection from government after more than 13 years was a stunning reverse and a political failure. Its claim to be a new kind of Brazilian political organisation, standing for radical democracy, helped it become Latin America's biggest left-wing party. But instead of evolving towards Latin American social democracy, it veered towards a polarising populism, in which it claimed to stand for 'the people' and 'the poor', even as it allied with some of the most backward sectors of Brazilian politics in order to stay in power. In both the *mensalão* and the Petrobras scandals, the PT sacrificed its ethical values to that end.

According to Paulo Delgado, a former PT congressman, the party made the mistake of thinking that 'a just cause would legitimate a lack of principles'.[57] *Lulismo* had expanded social provision for poorer Brazilians, but it had also revived the corporate state, with its handouts and privileges for the better-off. That was fiscally unsustainable.

Brazil at an impasse

Lava Jato exposed a profound rottenness at the heart of Brazil's political system. The country was grappling not just with a costly economic slump and social regress, but also with the discrediting of its whole political class and, potentially, of democracy itself.

After two decades of progress, Brazilian democracy had reached an impasse.[58] The country had fallen off a fiscal cliff, as the recession slashed tax revenues. Business confidence had collapsed. The middle class, new and old, was anxious about its status. Though there were signs that the economy would recover in 2017, the political malaise will be harder to fix. Political reform had been notionally on the policy agenda for more than two decades, but foundered on the difficulty of achieving a consensus for change among the beneficiaries of the status quo. It had become urgent.

The failure of the writers of the 1988 constitution to draw tighter rules for the formation of political parties led to their proliferation. By 2016, there were 36 legally registered parties, 27 of which were represented in Congress. With the exception of the PT and the PSDB and a handful of others, the rest were organisations of professional politicians without discernible ideologies, whose sole interest was in pork and patronage – to get a slice of the federal budget and of the federal payroll for themselves and their followers. To manage this fragmented legislature, Cardoso and Lula adopted a practice that came to be called 'coalitional presidentialism' – the formation of broad legislative coalitions drawing on these parties for hire, while reserving key jobs for their own parties. The system worked reasonably well, for a while. But as parties multiplied, so its costs rose. One consequence was that Lula and Dilma formed vast cabinets, of up to 39 ministers. The number of plum jobs in the president's gift swelled to almost 25,000. And the political pressure for wasteful public spending was enormous.

A second problem was that the electoral system impeded the accountability of politicians to voters and encouraged corruption.[59] The

Congress was elected under proportional representation, but each state constituted a single electoral district. In addition, deputies were chosen under an 'open list' system: they were elected according to the share of the total vote in the state of each party or alliance, but who won from each party list depended on their individual vote. Many voters did not know who their congressman was; the way to win was to represent organised interest groups; and campaigning was hugely expensive. Much of the money came from corporate donations; illicit undeclared donations were so common that they had a name, *caixa dois* (the second till). For some commentators, the Petrobras scandal was simply a magnified example of political business as usual, of *caixa dois* with extra dollops into back pockets, and of an incestuous relationship between construction companies and government whose roots went back to the dictatorship. For others, it was far more sinister: an attempt by the PT to rig the system in order to remain in power indefinitely.

Had the two decades of progress been a deceptive interlude, and not the bright new future many had imagined? There were some reasons for hope. Chief among them was that the institutions were working and the rule of law was being applied, with unprecedented rigour, by a new generation of prosecutors and judges. Many Brazilians had come to see corruption and poor public services as intolerable – just as they had inflation in the early 1990s. That provided an opportunity for change. Temer had many flaws: he was a consummate political insider; he picked a cabinet composed purely of white men, five of whom had to resign in the first six months because of corruption allegations; and he himself might yet fall victim to *Lava Jato*. Yet he also seemed to sense what had to be done, and had a grip on the Congress.

Secondly, Temer attempted to grapple with some underlying problems. Public spending (excluding debt service) had risen inexorably, from 22 per cent of GDP in 1991 to 37 per cent in 2014. That was a far higher level than average for middle-income countries. Some of that increase went on making Brazil a less unequal society, on education, health and social programmes. But despite the huge increase in spending, Brazil continued to suffer from shoddy infrastructure and an underfunded health service. Half of Brazilians lacked a proper sewerage connection, the murder rate was 25 per 100,000 people in 2015 (almost five times that of Argentina), and the country's prisons were a deadly disgrace. The state's fiscal incontinence was the main reason for Brazil's chronically high interest rates, which raised the cost of credit for house-holds and businesses. The problem was that the state spent too much on vested interests and the relatively well-off – for example, on the public-sector payroll, pensions and credit subsidies. Indeed, according to the World Bank, government subsidies to business exceeded 5 per cent of GDP and cost almost twice as much as social assistance programmes for the poor. Much spending was marred by inefficiency, as well as corruption.[60] Creating new municipalities and stuffing their payrolls with retainers was a growth industry for politicians.

The collapse in revenues hit some state governments hard. One example was Rio de Janeiro, where police and state workers demon-strated both before and after the Olympics over non-payment of wages. The state government had received a windfall from oil royalties. It spent it unwisely: the state's payroll more than doubled between 2009 and 2014, to more than 450,000, more than half of whom were receiving retirement pensions.[61] The state's governor in that period, Sérgio Cabral, was arrested in November 2016, accused of taking $65 million in bribes on contracts for infrastructure related to the World Cup and the Olympics.

This was the background to a controversial constitutional amend-ment secured by Temer's government, under which federal spending will increase at no more than the rate of inflation for 20 years. Far from being the heartless 'neoliberal' measure its critics claimed, this is essen-tial to restore viability to Brazilian public finance and allow the economy to return to growth, thus staunching social regress. The amendment should encourage an open political debate about spending priorities, and make clear the cost of wasteful spending. Temer proposed a reform of pensions: this was aimed at raising the average retirement age from the mid-50s to 65, hardly a regressive measure.

Temer's government also backed another proposed reform, one that would have the effect of limiting the number of parties in Congress. In early 2017, it was an open question whether or not the political system would be able to cleanse itself. Brazilians often compared *Lava Jato* with Italy's *mani pulite* (clean hands) offensive by judges and prosecutors against political corruption in 1992–93, whose unintended consequence was the rise to power of Silvio Berlusconi. There was a similar risk of Brazilians turning to a populist 'anti-politician'. But there were also signs of political renewal in the country. And *Lava Jato* may yet prove to have been a fatal blow to Brazil's long tradition of patrimonialism and clientelism. For all Brazil's problems, they seemed more manageable than those of Latin America's other giant, Mexico.

Mexico: reform, democracy and misgovernment

A couple of kilometres to the north of the Zócalo, Mexico City's historic main square, lie the ruins of Tlatelolco. In Aztec times, it was the twin city of Tenochtitlán, the site of what was at the time the largest market anywhere in the Americas and the scene of the final act in the Spanish conquest of the capital.[62] All that is left are the depleted bases of a dozen or more temple platforms set in a sunken garden. The site is overlooked by the monastery church of Santiago Tlatelolco, its austere baroque bulk fashioned by the Spaniards from the reddish-black volcanic stone of the ruined temples. Beyond the church rises the ugly early-1960s concrete tower that housed the Mexican foreign ministry until 2006. On the other three sides stand the apartment blocks of a government housing project from the same era. The raised open space of concrete flagstones between the buildings is called the Plaza de las Tres Culturas or the Square of the Three Cultures – indigenous, Spanish colonial and republican *mestizo*. In the ideology of the Institutional Revolutionary Party (PRI) these fused more harmoniously than in the architectural clashes of the square. At least so claims the stone plaque overlooking the garden: 'On 13 August 1521, heroically defended by Cuauhtémoc, Tlatelolco fell into the power of Hernán Cortés. It was neither a triumph nor a defeat. It was the painful birth of the *mestizo* people that is Mexico today.'

More recently the square was the site of another act of bloodshed, one that in retrospect would also come to be seen as marking another painful birth – that of Mexican democracy. In 1968, the student protests that began in Paris and swept campuses across the world from Berkeley to Berlin found an echo in Mexico. The president at the time, Gustavo Díaz Ordaz, was a narrow-minded authoritarian. Even as the student movement was fizzling out, he saw in it a threat to Mexico's image in the world: the Olympic Games were due to open in Mexico City in mid-October. On the evening of 2 October, a march by a few thousand students reached the square at Tlatelolco. As the marchers prepared to listen to speeches, watched over by an army detachment, members of a government-organised plain-clothes paramilitary squad, acting as agents provocateurs, fired on the crowd from a balcony in one of the apartment blocks, wounding the army general in charge. That prompted the army to rake the square with fire from armoured cars, bazookas and machine guns, as well as small arms. The exact death toll is still not known. The student movement put the figure at 150 civilians and 40 members of the security forces killed.[63] After the massacre, the regime's characteristic response was denial, captured by Rosario Castellanos, a poet, in lines carved into a second stone monument in the square, this one unveiled on a rainy evening in October 1993, on the twenty-fifth anniversary of the massacre:

> *¿Quién? ¿Quiénes? Nadie. Al día siguiente, nadie.*
> *La plaza amaneció barrida; los periódicos*
> *dieron como noticia principal*
> *el estado del tiempo.*
> *Y en la televisión, en el radio, en el cine*
> *no hubo ningún cambio de programa,*
> *ningún anuncio intercalado ni un*
> *minuto de silencio en el banquete.*
> *(Pues prosiguió el banquete.)*

> [Who? Whom? Nobody. The next day, nobody.
> The square awoke swept clean; the newspapers
> gave as the main news the state of the weather.
> And on the television, on the radio, in the cinema
> there was no change in the programme,
> no special announcement, nor a
> minute of silence at the banquet
> (For the banquet indeed continued).][64]

Nevertheless, the massacre of Tlatelolco would prove to be a profound shock to the PRI system. It punctured the official myth of consensual political order. It alienated the middle class, who had been the system's greatest beneficiaries. It would cause future governments to react in ways that eventually would further destabilise the system. As Enrique Krauze, a historian, put it: 'There had been a profound loss of legitimacy on that dark night of Tlatelolco ... Though the deep-seated cult of authoritarian government in Mexico would not recognize the fact, 1968 was both its highest point of authoritarian power and the real beginning of its collapse.[65]

In the decades after the Second World War, Mexico had enjoyed rapid economic growth under an economic policy called 'stabilising development', in which the exchange rate was fixed at 12.5 pesos to the dollar, the public debt was low and the budget in balance.[66] The policy was jettisoned by Luis Echeverría, who succeeded Díaz Ordaz as president in 1970. As interior minister in 1968, Echeverría was complicit in the massacre of Tlatelolco and the repression of the student movement. As president, he appeared to embrace some of the ideas of the student leaders. He posed as a champion of the third world, and launched rhetorical attacks on businessmen (whose investment slowed as a result). He redoubled efforts to co-opt the universities and the middle class, by throwing public money at them. The total number of public-sector jobs expanded by a staggering amount, from 600,000 in 1970 to 2.2 million in 1976.[67] He paid for the breakneck expansion of the state by printing and borrowing money. Over his term, foreign debt increased sixfold, while the real value of wages halved as inflation took off. José López Portillo, Echeverría's successor, initially seemed to promise more moderate government. But the discovery of a huge offshore oilfield in the Gulf of Campeche allowed López Portillo to resume the policies of Echeverría, until falling oil prices and rising interest rates caused the public finances to collapse like a house of cards.

If Tlatelolco had damaged the PRI's political legitimacy, the devaluation, debt default and bank nationalisation of 1982 undermined its claim to economic competence. Yet the PRI's retreat from power, and the transition to democracy in Mexico, would be extremely gradual and would occupy almost two more decades. They formally began with a political reform in 1978, which legalised the Communist Party and other left-wing groups. The opposition was allowed to win a quarter of the seats in the Chamber of Deputies the following year. But the established order did not lightly surrender power. Miguel de la Madrid, who inherited the wreckage left by López Portillo, began to return the economy to the policies of 'stabilising development'. But he did little to reform politics. The government's response to a devastating earthquake in the centre of Mexico City in 1985 showed a characteristic mixture of denial and incompetence. Among some 370 buildings that collapsed was one of the blocks of flats at Tlatelolco, killing 700 people. In all,

20,000 people were killed and another 180,000 were left homeless. In many cases, it was left to unofficial volunteers to rescue survivors from the rubble and care for the homeless. Out of this tragedy came a powerful grassroots movement for urban renewal, a rarity in a country where the state left little room for independent civic organisations.[68]

De la Madrid exercised the traditional presidential prerogative of choosing his successor, Carlos Salinas. That prompted the most serious split in the PRI for almost half a century. Cuauhtémoc Cárdenas, a former governor of Michoacán and the son of Mexico's most revered president, had rallied the PRI's left wing against de la Madrid's liberal economic policies. He opted to run against Salinas as the candidate of a collection of small left-wing parties. The election marked another milestone in the PRI's steady loss of credibility. Salinas was declared the winner, with 50.4 per cent to 31 per cent for Cárdenas, but only after the interior ministry's computers tallying the count had shut down for several hours.[69] Massive demonstrations against electoral fraud took place across the country. Cárdenas probably spared Mexico a bloodbath when he urged his supporters to channel their anger into forming a new Party of the Democratic Revolution (PRD).

Salinas: *perestroika* without *glasnost*

Salinas made a determined attempt to rebuild the PRI system by restoring its lost reputation for economic competence, while updating its mechanisms of political control. Though his father had been industry minister in the 1960s, Salinas seemed to be a new kind of PRI politician. He had a doctorate in political economy from Harvard. Although prematurely bald, he was aged just 40 when he became president. He spoke softly, but always with a hint of steel. He liked to describe himself as a consensus-builder and negotiator.[70] But he was ruthless and hyperactive. He surrounded himself with a clutch of liberal economists with doctorates from American universities. The finance minister, Pedro Aspe, brought inflation down and renegotiated the foreign debt. Salinas boldly challenged several political taboos: he put aside the PRI's history of anti-clericalism by restoring relations with the Vatican, and ordered an end to six decades of land reform, instead granting members of *ejidos* (communal farms) the right to obtain individual title to their plots. For these reforms, he secured the support of the National Action Party

(PAN), the conservative opposition. In the most iconoclastic move of all, he challenged the deep-rooted anti-Americanism of Mexico's political leadership by opening negotiations for NAFTA, a free-trade agreement with the United States and Canada.

This whirlwind of economic modernisation attracted much praise abroad. But the reform programme was less liberal (let alone 'neoliberal') than it seemed. Salinas left intact the state monopolies of oil and electricity. He excluded energy and many services from NAFTA. Telmex, the telecoms company, was transformed from a public monopoly into a private one. Foreign banks were barred from the bank privatisation. The president relied on many of the institutions, levers of power and clientelistic networks of Mexico's corporate state. Private business was especially loyal. At a dinner in 1993 that would become infamous, Salinas sat down with two dozen of Mexico's richest businessmen, most of them beneficiaries of privatisations or other favours. He asked for $500 million for the PRI to fight the 1994 election. Most were happy to stump up their allotted $25 million.[71] Inflation was reduced partly through the *pacto*, an incomes policy negotiated with business and with Fidel Velázquez, the general secretary of the Confederation of Mexican Workers (CTM), the main trade union. Under this arrangement, real wages halved in the decade to 1992.[72] In deference to Don Fidel, who in that year was re-elected for an eighth consecutive six-year term at the age of 91, Salinas did not touch the restrictive labour laws.

Salinas did make a few gestures towards political modernisation. For the first time, the PRI surrendered its monopoly of state governorships, PAN victories being accepted in Baja California and Chihuahua. In many other cases, Salinas would wait to see the strength of opposition protests. He sometimes intervened not to recognise an opposition victory, but to force the 'winning' PRI candidate to resign, to be replaced by a presidential appointee. In all, he removed 17 governors in 14 of Mexico's 31 states.[73] Salinas felt obliged to enact an electoral reform. This created a Federal Electoral Institute (IFE). Although nominally independent, it was still controlled by the interior minister, who chaired its general council.[74] The president could count on pliant media, dependent on government money. Those he could not co-opt, Salinas coerced. Early on, he imprisoned the powerful leader of the oil workers' union, ostensibly for corruption, but in reality for having favoured Cárdenas. The PRD complained that 250 of its activists were killed during Salinas's term. Referring to the parallel between the government's economic reforms and the contemporaneous dismantling of communism in the Soviet Union, a senior aide said candidly: 'The Soviet Union shows that it is not easy to do *perestroika* [economic reform] and *glasnost* [political liberalisation] at the same time. The worst of all worlds would be to be left with neither, and without a government or society that functions.'[75]

Salinas also tried to rebuild the PRI's support among the poor. Migration to the cities and the growth of the informal economy meant that millions of Mexicans had slipped through the ruling party's corporatist net of peasant, trade union and professional organisations. To reach them, Salinas created the National Solidarity Programme (Pronasol). Over his six-year term, this swallowed $18 billion, or around 40 per cent of total public investment. It handed out money for building health clinics, school classrooms, rural roads and community development projects. The programme was closely identified with Salinas himself. Under its auspices, almost every week he would leave Los Pinos, the presidential compound, and criss-cross the country. In elaborately choreographed trips by plane, helicopter and convoys of 4x4s, he would whisk to half a dozen events in a day, opening drinking-water schemes or clinics in dusty villages and handing out property titles in urban shanty towns. Poverty experts criticised the programme for not reaching the poorest and for its lack of co-ordination – the new clinics might lack doctors, for example. But above all it was designed to be politically effective. It made Salinas popular and helped the PRI to win comfortably a mid-term election in 1991.[76]

In the end, Salinas overreached himself. Even before the end of his term, his attempt to rebuild the PRI and its regime began to unravel. Some of his advisers talked of turning the PRI into the Solidarity Party. Together with his choice of Luis Donaldo Colosio, a gentle and loyal associate, as the presidential candidate for 1994, this stirred fears that Salinas would seek to remain in charge, breaking an unwritten rule of the system. Undercurrents of corruption eddied around the presidential family. All this exploded into the open with three (still-unresolved) murders. The elderly cardinal-archbishop of Guadalajara was killed by drug traffickers as he arrived at the city's airport. Then Colosio himself was shot dead by a lone gunman at a campaign rally in Tijuana – a political assassination of a gravity unmatched in Mexico since the murder of Álvaro Obregón by a Catholic fanatic in 1928. Months later, Francisco Ruiz Massieu, the PRI's general secretary and former husband of Salinas's sister, was the victim of a contract killing in the centre of Mexico City.

These murders were not the only violent challenge to political order. On 1 January 1994, the date that NAFTA came into effect, several hundred indigenous guerrillas seized the colonial town of San Cristóbal de las Casas in the southern state of Chiapas in the name of the previously unknown Zapatista Army of National Liberation (EZLN). As Carlos Fuentes, the novelist, put it, just when Mexico was moving closer to North America its rulers were forcibly reminded that parts of their country still belonged to Central America. Chiapas had never known democracy – the PRI regularly won elections there with more than 90 per cent of the vote. Unlike in the rest of Mexico, the state's ranchers and coffee *hacendados* had successfully resisted land reform, and now Salinas had ended any chance of it. Militarily, the Zapatista uprising would be brief. After more than 100 people were killed as the army drove the rebels out of San Cristóbal and other towns, Salinas quickly declared a unilateral ceasefire. Far from shoring up authoritarianism, as some of its critics feared, NAFTA constrained the regime's ability to unleash repression, because it focused the outside world's attention on Mexico. Initially, at least, the Zapatistas attracted widespread sympathy, thanks in part to the communication skills of their leader, a ski-masked former university teacher of Marxist philosophy who styled himself Sub-Comandante Marcos.[77] They would gradually be rendered irrelevant, in large part because of Marcos's inability to adapt to the arrival of democracy.

Days after Ernesto Zedillo took over as president on 1 December 1994, the cracked edifice of *salinismo* came tumbling down. The political turmoil of an electoral year had caused Salinas and Aspe to abandon their previous macroeconomic prudence. The government began to finance itself with short-term dollar debt. The political violence gave investors the jitters: money flew out of the country. Once again, as it had at the end of each presidential term since 1976, political handover coincided with economic turmoil, pointing to the regime's post-Tlatelolco instability. Three weeks after Zedillo took office, his government was forced to let the currency float. After weeks of drift, with the help of big loans from the United States Treasury and the IMF, the government managed to stabilise the economy and recovery quickly followed. The cost was heavy: GDP contracted by 6 per cent in 1995, but domestic demand fell by 14 per cent and would not recover its level of 1994 for three years. To make matters worse, many of the newly privatised banks faced collapse. Having benefited from lax regulation under Salinas, they received generous treatment from Zedillo when they got into difficulties. In essence, they were allowed to pass to the government their non-performing loans, some of which were to their own directors. The government offered unlimited deposit insurance. The Zedillo administration did belatedly tighten supervision and accounting standards, and lifted the ban on foreign commercial banks. By 2006, foreign banks accounted for more than four-fifths of the system. In all, the bank bailout cost the taxpayer around 20 per cent of GDP.[78]

The terms of the bailout reflected the government's weakness. The new president lacked Salinas's political flair. But he had some important qualities: he was honest and decent, he believed in economic reform, and he was a democrat. Right from the outset, he said that he preferred the rule of law to the unwritten rules of presidential supremacy, that he would maintain a 'healthy distance' from the PRI and that he would not choose his successor.[79] This amounted to a voluntary abdication of authoritarianism. Zedillo took two other crucial steps towards democracy. A judicial reform created an independent and powerful Supreme Court. In 1996, by consensus among the three main parties, the IFE was reformed to become wholly independent of government. The government also pushed through a reform granting independence to the Central Bank.

Zedillo could restore Mexico's fortunes, but not those of the PRI. If the 1982 debt crisis damaged its reputation for economic competence, this was destroyed by the 1994–95 debacle. As most Mexicans saw their living standards plummet, they were angered by the bailout of the billionaire bankers and by the revelations of corruption at the top. In the mid-term election of 1997, for the first time the PRI lost its majority in the lower house of Congress. In 2000, after 72 years in power, the PRI would finally lose the presidency.

Political change, and gridlock

Vicente Fox was ideally equipped to end the rule of the PRI. A farmer who had been the manager of Coca-Cola's Mexican operations, Fox came late to politics. In 1991, he was denied victory in an election for governor of the central state of Guanajuato by fraud; he won four years later and almost immediately launched a presidential campaign. His popularity obliged the PAN, a party of conservative Catholic lawyers, to choose this rough-edged businessman as its candidate. He was thick-skinned, determined and a natural media performer. His campaign was simple but devastatingly effective: he promised *el cambio* (the change), but not adventurism. He appealed to democrats across the political spectrum.

On the face of things, Fox's victory seemed to set the seal on Mexico's transition from authoritarian politics and an inward-looking state-dominated economy to an outward-looking, globalised liberal democracy. But in many ways he turned out to be a disappointing president, partly because that transition was both more complicated and less complete than it appeared.[80] Fox's biggest achievement was that during his presidency Mexico enjoyed greater political freedom than perhaps at any other time in its history. But the PAN lacked a legislative majority, and the president lacked the political skills to fashion consensus. Not only did Fox choose to live and let live with the PRI's authoritarian legacy, but he also failed to put in place the new rules – for law enforcement and federalism, for example – that Mexico's fledgling democracy needed. The president sent reforms of energy, taxes and labour laws to Congress, but they got nowhere. Just as Fox was moving into Los Pinos, Mexico's economy was hit by two blows from outside. In the United States, the dotcom bubble burst, slowing industrial production on both sides of the border. At the same time, China joined the World Trade Organization, marking the arrival of a powerful competitor to Mexico for footloose manufacturing plants. These twin blows caused three years of economic stagnation and the loss of some 700,000 jobs, most of them in the *maquiladora* (assembly) plants producing goods for export. Nevertheless, Mexico continued to attract investment in higher-value goods, such as cars and electronics. Growth picked up in the second half of Fox's term, and at least economic and financial stability was maintained.

The presidential election of 2006 reflected the fine balance in Mexico between progress and frustration. The campaign was dominated by Andrés Manuel López Obrador, the candidate of the centre-left PRD. As governor of the Federal District, he kept himself constantly in the public eye, with new roads, non-contributory pensions for the elderly and a daily early-morning press conference at which he set the political agenda. He combined this practical action with lacerating populist criticism of Fox and of the rich and powerful in Mexico. He promised to govern for the poor, and railed against the bankers and businessmen who had benefited from crony capitalism. He slammed the economic policy of the past two decades as 'a failure'. He said he would maintain fiscal balance ('you can't have deficits'), but implausibly said he would finance a big increase in public investment merely by cutting bureaucratic waste.[81]

For many months, as López Obrador led the opinion polls, the only question in Mexican political circles was whether he would be a second Hugo Chávez or a second Lula. In reality, the answer was neither. He resembled Argentina's Néstor Kirchner in his profound lack of interest in the world beyond his own country; he took pride in not having a passport. His political mentor was Echeverría. López Obrador had spent his formative political years in the PRI, leaving to join Cárdenas in 1988. His detractors saw in López Obrador a throwback to the PRI's authoritarian populism of the 1970s. In a country where politics was long dominated by backroom deals, López Obrador was a politician of the public plaza in the tradition of South America, rather than Mexico. He sometimes showed scant regard for the law, and two of his senior aides were implicated in corruption. For all his political skills, he was a polarising figure who scared middle-of-the-road democrats. Many of them switched their support to Felipe Calderón, the PAN's candidate. Fairly or not, he portrayed López Obrador as a 'danger to Mexico', a second Chávez.

Calderón won by a whisker, with 35.9 per cent of the vote against 35.3 per cent for López Obrador (PRD), a margin of just 233,831 votes out of 42 million. The PRI polled a meagre 22.2 per cent. López Obrador immediately cried fraud, though he never produced any plausible evidence. He launched a campaign of 'civil resistance'. For seven weeks, his followers camped out in the Zócalo and along Reforma, Mexico City's grandest avenue. The electoral tribunal ordered a recount of 9 per cent of the ballot boxes – those in which López Obrador's campaign claimed that most irregularities had occurred. But this only shaved 10,000 votes from Calderón's margin of victory.[82] Even so, López Obrador refused to concede defeat. 'To hell with your institutions', he cried, calling Fox 'a traitor to democracy' and Calderón a usurper. He proclaimed himself Mexico's legitimate president.

By then, most Mexicans had stopped listening to him. There was much irony and little truth in his claim that the 2006 election was a repeat of 1988. The truth was that Mexico's independent electoral authorities passed a severe test in 2006, with only a few glitches. The irony was that many of López Obrador's closest aides were, like him, former PRI officials who had been complicit in the fraudulent campaigns of the past. In the view of Héctor Aguilar Camín, a historian, the protests of 2006 were those that the PRI didn't stage when it lost power in 2000. 'Alternation in power had happened very cheaply for us. It's the first protest against this young democracy, done by the ex-priistas of the PRD.'[83]

The narrowness and disputed nature of his mandate meant that Calderón faced a difficult task in governing Mexico, let alone changing it. But he had certain advantages. Unlike Fox, Calderón was a party man through and through and a devout Catholic. Aged only 44 in 2006, he had much political experience, having headed the PAN's congressional caucus. A lawyer, he also had technocratic credentials, having studied economics and, at Harvard, public administration. He faced a more favourable economic situation than Fox had inherited. The world financial crisis tipped Mexico into a deep but brief recession in 2009, aggravated by an outbreak of swine flu. It recovered swiftly, in part because the government was able to apply counter-cyclical stimulus. The main tasks that appeared to confront Calderón were to create a more dynamic economy by demolishing the remaining vestiges of the corporate state and to help to fashion more effective democratic institutions. On these, he made little progress, beyond shutting down the state-owned electricity company in Mexico City, which was a fief of a trade-union mafia. The president's priorities lay elsewhere.

Democracy without the rule of law

'Organised crime is out of control', Calderón declared on taking office. Perhaps because he felt a need to establish his authority owing to the narrowness of his mandate, Calderón declared war on Mexico's drug gangs. These had grown steadily more powerful over the previous dozen years. When cocaine consumption first took off in the United States in the 1970s and 1980s, the main smuggling route involved island-hopping across the Caribbean from Colombia in light aircraft. It was the success of the US drug warriors in shutting down this route that brought big-time organised crime to Mexico, as the Colombians began to send drugs that way. Relatively small gangs, most based on extended-family networks in the villages of the inaccessible mountains of the Sierra Madre, where the states of Sinaloa, Durango and Chihuahua meet, had long run heroin and marijuana across the border. Aggregated in a loose confederation known as the Sinaloa 'cartel', they moved into cocaine.

Two things helped them grow. The first was proximity to the United States. They gained control of retail distribution in many American cities, allowing them to dictate terms to the Colombians. And they armed themselves with ease in American gunshops and laundered their profits in American banks. The second factor was the flaws of the Mexican state. One of the PRI's historic achievements was to get the army out of politics, but in return it ran its own affairs and was wildly oversized for the country's security needs. Under the PRI regime the job of the police was to impose political order, not solve or prevent crime. The police were corrupt, badly paid and ill-trained, and mistrusted: a survey in 2007 found that seven out of ten crimes were not reported.[84] The federal government only began to build a professional police force in the 1990s. State governors were happy to tolerate – or profit from – drug traffickers on their patch, provided they kept a low profile. Partly because the Colombians at first paid their partners in product, the Mexican gangs began to push cocaine at home. In some areas, especially in northern Mexico, they acquired de facto control. The Sinaloa mob was challenged by the Zetas, a murderous outfit of former army special-forces soldiers, and other rival crime syndicates.

Weeks before Calderón took office, a mob called La Família had chucked seven severed heads onto a dance floor in a town in his home state of Michoacán, in a declaration of defiance. The new president's response was to send 7,000 army troops to the state. That was the prelude to a broader crackdown that would see more than 50,000 soldiers deployed on the streets. This was supposed to be a temporary expedient, while he overhauled policing. He expanded the federal police (from 9,000 in 2006 to 30,000 by the end of his term), and pushed through a constitutional reform intended to create a single, reformed public-security system spanning the 32 state and more than 1,600 municipal police forces. Brushing aside nationalist scruples, the government accepted $1.4 billion in aid from the United States and stepped up northward extradition of drug traffickers. According to Eduardo Medina Mora, Calderón's attorney general, the aim of the government's crackdown was not to end drug trafficking 'because that is unachievable', but rather 'to take back from organised criminal groups the economic power and armament they've established in the past 20 years, to take away their capacity to undermine institutions and to contest the state's monopoly of force'. In response, the gangs staged beheadings, torture and ghoulish episodes of terror, mainly against rivals, that both horrified and numbed Mexicans. As the body count mounted, Medina Mora insisted that this was a sign of progress, a sign that the gangs were feeling the pressure and turning on each other.[85] Nevertheless, as the murder rate surged from 8 per 100,000 in 2007 to almost 22 per 100,000 in 2010, public opinion began to turn against the 'drug war' and Calderón became unpopular.

In a bitter political defeat, his presidency was followed by the PRI's return to power, in the person of Enrique Peña Nieto. An immaculately coiffed, telegenic figure, married to a well-known *telenovela* starlet, with a team of bright technocrats from the world's best universities, Peña Nieto had been governor of the state of Mexico, which surrounds the capital, and was a scion of the PRI's most retrograde political machine. His implicit promise was that only the PRI could restore order to Mexico. He won, with just 38.2 per cent of the vote, mainly by default, against López Obrador (31.6 per cent) and a weak PAN candidate. He proved to be an effective political tactician. He forged a legislative 'Pact for Mexico' with the PAN and PRD: in his first two years, he pushed through many of the reforms that, by technocratic consensus, Mexico needed. Their common denominator was the weakening of monopolies, both public and private. An education reform was aimed at breaking the control of the powerful teachers' union (whose leader Peña arrested) over appointments and salaries. Telmex was subjected to more effective competition. His historic achievement was to break the state monopoly on energy, and open all parts of the energy industry up to private, including foreign, investment. Undoing Cárdenas's nationalisation was overdue. Pemex, the state oil company, was bloated, debt-ridden and corrupt, and oil production was falling sharply. Industry had to pay almost twice as much as rivals in the United States for electricity.[86] But no previous president had dared break this nationalist taboo. Foreign companies bid for deep-water exploration blocks and rushed to connect up Mexico and Texas with gas pipelines.

Just when Peña Nieto was basking in praise for his reforming zeal, his presidency began to unravel. In September 2014, 43 students from a teacher-training college at Ayotzinapa in the southern state of Guerrero disappeared, after buses they were travelling on were intercepted by municipal police in the town of Iguala. With the collusion of the mayor of Iguala and his wife, the police handed the students over to a drug gang, but exactly what happened to them next – and where their bodies were – remained unclear more than two years later. The incident shocked and outraged Mexicans, because of the graphic way in which it dramatised the penetration of local politics by organised crime. It also exposed Peña Nieto's limits as a politician. The government seemed paralysed: it took the president a month to meet the grieving families of the victims (and 17 months to visit Iguala).[87] Weeks later, the government abruptly cancelled a $3.7 billion contract for a high-speed train when it emerged that Grupo Higa, one of the construction firms involved, was the owner of a $7 million palatial mansion (dubbed the 'white house') used by Peña Nieto and his wife as their private home.

Peña Nieto had originally tried to play down the issues of crime and corruption. He no longer could. But he struggled to respond effectively. He had a promising plan to set up a new paramilitary police force, called the Gendarmería to control roads and rural areas (in the mould of Spain's Civil Guard or Porfirio Díaz's *rurales*), to be staffed with 40,000 soldiers retrained as policemen. But the army blocked the change and the finance ministry baulked at the cost. Only 5,000 made the switch. A similarly promising crime-prevention plan was poorly executed. And so was another initiative that would have created a single security command in every state. After falling in the first three years of Peña Nieto's government, the murder rate rose again in 2016 almost to its peak under Calderón. Between 2007 and 2016, the authorities took out nearly all of the gang leaders. But others replaced them. The violence was feeding on itself. In half a dozen of Mexico's 32 states, violence and disorder were becoming chronic. More than 100,000 Mexicans had died, around 30,000 were reported to have disappeared, and some 35,000 were displaced from their homes. Ten years after Calderón launched his 'war on drugs', more than 50,000 soldiers were still being used for policing. Abuses by the security forces were common, and were rarely punished. 'This cannot be settled by bullets', General Salvador Cienfuegos, the army minister, said in a rare public comment. 'We would be delighted if the police did the job it's there for.'

Ayotzinapa and the 'white house' were fatal blows to Peña Nieto's credibility and popularity. His weakened government faced an additional problem in Donald Trump, with his insults against Mexicans, his plan to build a border wall ('and make Mexico pay for it') and his tirades against NAFTA. At the urging of Luis Videgaray, the finance minister (who had also accepted a house from Grupo Higa), and against the advice of the foreign minister, two months before the US election Peña Nieto invited Candidate Trump to Los Pinos. Mexicans were appalled when their president did not publicly demand an apology from Trump. In the aftermath of the visit, Peña Nieto's approval rating fell to 12 per cent, the lowest ever recorded for a Mexican president. No Mexican government would have found it easy to handle Trump. Nevertheless, Peña Nieto and his small coterie of advisers had been exposed as limited provincial politicians with little grasp of the requirements of the presidency, let alone the demands of the world stage. In a column in *The Economist*, I quoted a former official who said of Peña Nieto 'he doesn't get that he doesn't get it'. It was a comment that was widely repeated in Mexico and seemed to sum up the president.

The Mexican conundrum

Almost two decades after the achievement of electoral democracy, and more than a quarter of a century after the Salinas economic reforms, Mexico presented a paradox. On the one hand, the lives of many Mexicans had improved. They had better housing and access to cheaper consumer goods, whose prices fell dramatically with the opening of the economy. The middle class grew and poverty fell more than was captured in the official statistics, which used a much higher poverty line than in the rest of Latin America. Some Mexican states, mainly in the centre and north of the country, posted economic growth of 6 per cent a year. Mexico had become one of the world's 15 biggest manufacturing economies, and one of its five biggest car producers. And some parts of the country were largely free of violence.

On the other hand, economic growth in Mexico as a whole averaged just 2.4 per cent a year since NAFTA was approved in 1994 (despite

Trump's claim that Mexico had 'taken advantage' of the US). Many of Mexico's poorer and more indigenous southern states were sunk in stagnation. While part of Mexico appeared to have successfully embraced globalisation, more than 40 per cent of the workforce was trapped in unproductive small businesses, often family-based and informal. The McKinsey Global Institute, a think-tank, found that while the productivity of Mexico's large firms rose by 5.8 per cent a year between 1999 and 2009, the productivity of small businesses fell by 6.5 per cent a year over the same period. Some 7 million young Mexicans were so-called 'ni-nis' – neither in work nor in study – and were thus potential recruits for the drug gangs. What made this dualism surprising was that Mexico had several big economic advantages (at least until Trump came along). It is next door to the world's biggest market, to which NAFTA gave it easy access; it has a large and sophisticated industrial base; and its macroeconomic management was sound. It has free-trade agreements with 44 countries.[88]

What Mexico showed was that free trade, sound macroeconomic management and electoral democracy were not enough. Missing were both the rule of law and accountable and effective government, and without them Mexico was at the mercy of crime and corruption and could not become a developed country. The end of the PRI system was followed by the fragmentation of power: no president has enjoyed a majority in Congress since 1996. Because Mexico's constitution does not allow for a run-off election, the next president, to be elected in 2018, might win with only around 30 per cent of the vote. Mexican federalism, a fiction under the old PRI regime, has degenerated into a racket: the federal government transfers to the states around $25 billion a year, with no controls on how it is spent. States and municipalities collect only 16 per cent of their revenues.[89] As in Brazil, the cost of election campaigns has risen dramatically.

Corruption costs Mexico as much as 10 per cent of GDP, according to IMCO, a think-tank. Between 2000 and 2013, 41 state governors were implicated in corruption scandals, but only two were jailed. Crime was out of control, partly because some local governments, no longer beholden to the centre, allied with it, rather than fought it.[90] Murder was a state, not federal, felony in Mexico. With the exception of the Supreme Court, the judiciary was deeply corrupt. The legal system did not work, either to enforce contracts or to serve citizens. That deterred investment by small or medium companies, local or foreign. And it encouraged violence. In a telling passage in his memoir on Mexico, Alfredo Corchado, a longstanding correspondent there, quotes his driver as saying: 'They threaten you for everything and anything. Fear works better than taking someone to court, or calling an attorney. Corruption always gets in the way – when you try to do it the right way, you come out without a peso.'[91]

Neither the courts, nor the federal nor the state legislatures operated as effective checks on executive power in Mexico. The political parties were accountable only to their own leaders. As Luis Rubio, a political analyst, put it, 'most of the legal, regulatory and political structure in Mexico comes from the "old regime" . . . just because it collapsed doesn't mean that it ever actually vanished.'[92] But the old, worm-eaten political structure is increasingly incapable of providing governance. For example, Peña Nieto's much-vaunted education reform was not implemented in some states, because of the power of a dissident teachers' union. 'What Mexico has today is a system of government that works for itself, and not for the public or for the country's progress', Rubio concludes. There is one cause for hope. Civil society in Mexico has become more powerful and vocal than ever before. Because of pressure from society, Peña Nieto's government has pushed through laws against corruption and making the attorney general's office independent. Civic groups have mobilised to try to make sure that these changes take root in practice. That is just one example of the way that Latin American societies have changed.

CHAPTER NINE

Changing Societies

Walk down the side of the presidential palace in Lima, cross the River Rímac on a stone bridge built in 1610, turn right past the colonial-era bullring at Acho and you are transported from the remnants of vice-regal splendour into the grubby, dynamic chaos of twenty-first-century urban Latin America. Hundreds of brightly painted minibuses, taxis and moto-taxis (tuk-tuks) vie to take you to San Juan de Lurigancho, a broad desert valley surrounded by grey Andean foothills that stretches north-eastwards for miles. Settlement only began there in the 1960s. By 1980, the municipal district of San Juan de Lurigancho was home to 260,000 people; in 2011, that figure exceeded a million, or more than a tenth of the population of metropolitan Lima. It was only the largest of a score of 'shanty town' districts grouped in three *conos* (cones) that project into the desert to the north, east and south of Lima.

The foundation of these squatter settlements was graphically described by Norman Lewis, a British travel writer, who visited Peru in 1972:

> The new arrivals, urban slum-dwellers who could no longer afford to pay their rent, or Indians to whom conditions in places like these were sybaritic compared to the destitution of the Altiplano, simply marked out their claims, knocked four stakes into the ground and nailed straw-matting to them to make an enclosure ... Dust covered everything, including the repellent strips of *charqui* (dried meat) and the blackened slices of cow's heart on the food stalls. Everything was squalid and makeshift. There was filth and foraging pigs in the streets, water stored in oil drums and bought at racket-eering prices, and all the sicknesses one would expect to find in such a place. And yet hope was not absent. The government had given these people nothing whatever, but they had come together and turned themselves into a smoothly working community.[1]

In the 1980s, wave after wave of families fleeing the 'dirty war' between the Maoist terrorists of Sendero Luminoso ('Shining Path') and the army erected their *esteras* (huts of straw-matting), moving further up the valley and the hillsides. A study of Huáscar, a neighbourhood of San Juan de Lurigancho, by Emma Raffo, a Peruvian anthropologist, recorded that in 1984, eight years after its foundation, most houses were barely half-built and the streets were unpaved. There was electricity, the installation of which was paid for in part by the inhabitants themselves, but no drinking water or sewerage. Nobody had property titles.[2]

These were difficult years in Lima. The terrorist insurgency of Sendero Luminoso coincided with, and aggravated, an economic maelstrom of depression and hyperinflation. In 1992, income per head in Peru was some 30 per cent lower than its 1981 peak, and two thirds of Peruvians lived in poverty.[3] Government services broke down. Sendero Luminoso's attacks on the power grid meant that for several years *Limeños* only received electricity one day in two if they were lucky. Rubbish accumulated by the roadside, the few parks in the city were reduced to dusty waste ground and public health deteriorated. This collapse of basic state services was dramatised in 1991, when Peru suffered an outbreak of cholera, a disease that had been eradicated from the Americas in the 1920s and whose causes are poverty and poor sanitation.

Peru regressed further than almost anywhere else in the region. Yet from the early 1990s its economy embarked on a remarkable growth spurt. Income per person rose at an annual average rate of 3 per cent between 1990 and 2013 (compared with 1.7 per cent for Latin America as a whole). By 2014, only 21.8 per cent of Peruvians were still living below the poverty line.[4] Several factors contributed to this renaissance. They included free-market economic policies, which were underpinned by a broad socio-political consensus; a boom in mining investment; the exploitation of a natural gas field which lowered energy costs; and an agricultural revolution, in which the top-down co-operatives imposed by the agrarian reform of General Juan Velasco in the 1970s were split up into family plots by spontaneous decision of the co-op members, creating commercial farms which grew asparagus, mangoes, grapes and other fruit and vegetables for export. The policy consensus survived the election in 2011 of Ollanta Humala, a former army officer who ran as a populist nationalist, but governed as a centrist. In 2016, he was succeeded by Pedro-Pablo Kuczynski, a 77-year-old former investment banker, who narrowly defeated Keiko Fujimori, whose father had governed Peru as an elected autocrat in the 1990s and was serving a jail sentence for corruption and human-rights abuses. Both candidates broadly subscribed to the free-market economic model.

The migrants who streamed into Lima and other coastal cities were leaving behind conditions of servitude, misery and isolation in the Andes. Their presence in the cities, and that of their descendants, has democratised the country from the bottom up. Peru still bears the traces of a caste society with a racist white elite. But the march of *mestizaje* is unstoppable, the elite is less white and less homogeneous than it was in the 1970s, and there is more social mobility. *Mestizaje* is above all a cultural process. The *conos* of Lima have become 'melting pots that fuse the distinct regional traditions' and 'the powerful centre of a new *mestizaje* of predominantly Andean colour, generating cultural styles, economic options, organisational systems and creating the bases of a new institutionality', argued José Matos Mar, an anthropologist of Andean Indian descent, in an influential book originally published in Peru in 1984.[5] Matos Mar was a man of the left, but his view of the informal economy as an emerging and alternative legal order was similar to that which Hernando de Soto would express in *The Other Path* two years later.[6]

The *conos* of Lima reflected Peru's recent progress. The city's northern suburbs, the oldest-established of the *conos* with a population of 2.2 million, were home to some 20 per cent of Lima's middle class, according to one estimate.[7] Megaplaza, a modern shopping mall, opened there in 2002, after an investment of $50 million. Its 45,000 square metres of retail space include two department stores, a multiplex cinema and restaurants.[8] Since then, half a dozen other malls have opened in the *conos*. In San Juan de Lurigancho, where work was due to start on a mall in 2017, the main avenues are asphalted right to the end of the valley, with trim grass in the central reservations. An overground metro line connects the district with the centre of Lima, running for 34 kilometres to Villa El Salvador in the Southern Cone. There are hypermarkets, banks, chain stores and restaurants, as well as private clinics, private schools advertising English lessons, gymnasiums and technical education institutes. There is a profusion of evangelical Protestant churches and two Mormon temples. Most houses have electricity, water and sewerage; the smell of excrement no longer pervades the district. On the distant hillsides, there are still *esteras* and huts of wood or brick belonging to the poorest or the most recently arrived. But in Huáscar, all the streets are paved and the neighbourhood is dotted with small parks. Most of the houses are of brick and concrete and comprise two or three storeys; some are finished and faced with whitewashed cement. Most families have fully equipped kitchens and bathrooms, large colour television sets and many have computers.[9]

This progress has been achieved through a dose of collective action and much individual initiative. Obtaining public services involved a long fight by neighbourhood associations. The women in Huáscar organised *comedores populares* (community kitchens), receiving support from NGOs, the Church and eventually the government. San Juan de Lurigancho is home to thousands of textile, furniture and footwear businesses, many of which are informal, but some of which are successful exporters. In follow-up fieldwork in 2006, Emma Raffo found that the vast majority of families she had known in 1984 had improved their circumstances.[10] For all of them, their house was their most important asset. Though they had property titles, none would contemplate offering the house as a guarantee for a loan.[11] In some cases, rooms were rented out or used for small businesses. In others, married children set up home on the second or third floor. The second generation was better off than their parents had been at the same stage of their lives. They were also better educated than their parents: while few had achieved the dreams of their parents that they would become doctors or lawyers, nearly all had finished secondary school, many had some tertiary technical education and some had university degrees. The younger generation was less deferential, and conscious of their rights as citizens of a democracy. This relative success was based on decades of unremitting hard work, the construction of their houses, and a shift from the nuclear family to a multi-generational domestic group, whose members collaborated to finance education and look after older members, for example. But some families remained poor, especially those which had suffered from break-up, domestic violence and alcohol or drug addiction.

Setting a floor of citizenship

Peru currently offers the most dramatic example of social progress in Latin America, but the trend is similar across the region. Latin American societies are less poor, less unequal, more middle class, healthier, less badly educated and better informed and connected than ever before. Poverty in the region as a whole fell from 48.4 per cent in 1990 and 43.9 per cent in 2002 to 28.1 per cent in 2013, according to calculations by CEPAL, based on household surveys and national poverty lines (which usually involve an income sufficient to cover basic needs).[12] Between 2002 and 2008 alone, around 40 million Latin Americans left poverty (see Chart 4). Extreme poverty, defined as having insufficient income to cover basic food needs, fell too, from 19.3 per cent in 2002 to 11.3 per cent in 2012. Income inequality also diminished (see Chart 5). Data from household surveys for the first decade of the twenty-first century showed the Gini coefficient, the standard measure of inequality, falling on average in Latin America from around 0.55 at the turn of the millennium to around 0.49 by 2010.[13] Welcome though this tendency was, Latin America remained

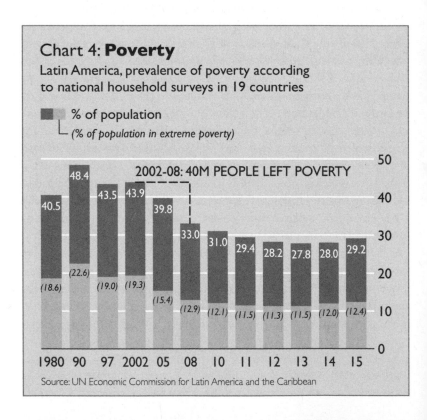

Chart 4: **Poverty**

Latin America, prevalence of poverty according to national household surveys in 19 countries

■ % of population
└ (% of population in extreme poverty)

2002-08: 40M PEOPLE LEFT POVERTY

| 1980 | 90 | 97 | 2002 | 05 | 08 | 10 | 11 | 12 | 13 | 14 | 15 |

40.5 · 48.4 · 43.5 · 43.9 · 39.8 · 33.0 · 31.0 · 29.4 · 28.2 · 27.8 · 28.0 · 29.2

(18.6) · (22.6) · (19.0) · (19.3) · (15.4) · (12.9) · (12.1) · (11.5) · (11.3) · (11.5) · (12.0) · (12.4)

Source: UN Economic Commission for Latin America and the Caribbean

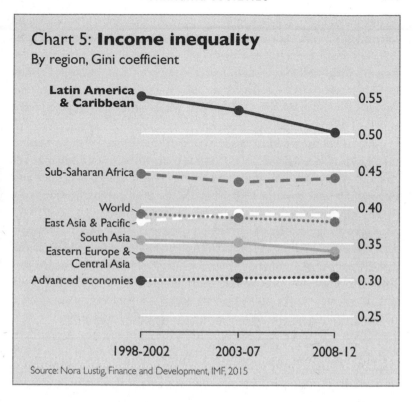

Chart 5: **Income inequality**
By region, Gini coefficient

Latin America & Caribbean — 0.55 — 0.50

Sub-Saharan Africa — 0.45

World — 0.40
East Asia & Pacific
South Asia — 0.35
Eastern Europe & Central Asia
Advanced economies — 0.30

0.25

1998-2002   2003-07   2008-12

Source: Nora Lustig, Finance and Development, IMF, 2015

highly unequal: the Gini coefficient for the United States, China and Russia was between 0.41 and 0.42.[14]

The flip side of the fall in poverty was a swelling of the middle class. This was the subject of some triumphalism, with claims that Latin America had become predominantly middle class. That was not true: common sense suggested that many of those who had emerged from poverty were more accurately described as lower middle class or the working poor and their situation remained fragile. What it means to be middle class is a matter of definition and debate. For sociologists, education, occupational status and ownership of assets are all relevant factors, and so is perception of one's relative place in the social order.[15] Economists tend to look just at income, which is more easily measurable. In a study in 2012, the World Bank nodded in the direction of the sociologists by applying a criterion of economic security: to have no more than a 10 per cent chance of falling back into poverty over a five-year period required an income of $10 to $50 per person per day, it reckoned. By that measure, the middle class in Latin America had expanded by 50 per cent between 2003 and 2009, from 103 million people to 152 million. By 2012, for the first time, the middle class outnumbered the poor. But the largest group, at 37 per cent of the population in 2012, was what the bank called 'the vulnerable', with an income of $4 to $10 per day: they had emerged from poverty but could easily return to it.[16]

The rise of the middle class raises many questions. What lay behind it and can it be sustained? Why, despite everything, are a large number of Latin Americans still poor and do inequalities of race, gender and opportunity still remain? And what are the political implications of a bigger middle class?

Three things lay behind the fall in poverty. The first and most important was economic growth, which brought higher wages and near full employment to many Latin American countries. There were also two new factors at work, which eased income inequality and which showed that democracy was bringing positive social change to Latin America: a new approach to social assistance, and the spread of education.

The first of these was palpable in the state of Oaxaca in southern Mexico, a corrugated land of forested mountains scored by brown, serpentine rivers. Such are its geographical contortions and ethnic diversity that its 3.4 million people are divided into 570 separate municipalities, more than twice as many as in any other Mexican state. One of them is Santiago Tlazoyaltepec, reached by a drive of a little less than two hours from the state capital up a precipitous dirt road flanked by cool forests of pine and evergreen oak. Like many of the settlements established by the Mixtecs (whose name means 'people of the clouds' in their own language), Tlazoyaltepec straggles along the tops of sinuous mountain ridges. Rather than a town, it is a clutch of separate ribbon villages with a total population of some 10,000 people. The world owes the domestication of the turkey to the Mixtecs. But today, they scratch a living from small *milpas* (maize fields). In 2006, when I visited and asked how things were going, the answer was a repetitive lament: '*no hay trabajo*' ('there's no work').[17]

Even so, people were living a little better, conceded Panfilo Santiago, the municipal councillor in charge of education – a short, thick-set man, whose Spanish was delivered in a strong Mixtec accent. One reason was that many of the younger people had gone north, to the United States or to the tomato fields of Baja California. They either returned richer, or sent money back home. The relative prosperity of families where someone had gone to *el norte* (the north) was displayed in the status symbols of the Mixtec highlands: a big Ford or Chevrolet pick-up parked outside the door and, increasingly, a two-storey concrete house in place of a wooden hovel. The second reason was that some 70 per cent of the people who remained in Tlazoyaltepec were enrolled in an anti-poverty programme begun under the name of *Progresa* by the government of Ernesto Zedillo, expanded and renamed *Oportunidades* by Vicente Fox and retained by Enrique Peña Nieto as *Prospera*. In 2006, the scheme was paying mothers a modest monthly allowance, provided they kept their children at school and took them for regular health check-ups. The payments were small, but rose with the age of the children. In Tlazoyaltepec, María Elena Velasco had two young children that she was bringing up on her own because her husband was working in Baja California. She received 360 pesos (about $35) every two months from *Oportunidades*. 'It helps a bit', she said. 'We'd like it to be more, but it helps.'

Though similar schemes were pioneered by some local governments in Brazil in the 1990s, *Progresa*, designed by Santiago Levy, a Mexican liberal economist, was the first large-scale example of what have come to be known in the jargon of development as 'conditional cash transfer' programmes or CCTs. It was matched in Brazil under Lula by *Bolsa Família*, which was the brainchild of another liberal economist, Ricardo Paes de Barros. By 2010, similar schemes had spread to a total of 18 Latin American countries, covering some 25 million families or 113 million people (around a fifth of the total population).[18] Indeed, they spread to many other developing countries around the world, becoming a successful Latin American public-policy export.

CCTs had some clear advantages. They often replaced a hotchpotch of wasteful and ill-directed subsidies on food or other items; they were generally well targeted at those most in need; and they were cost-effective. Their total cost in Latin America in 2010 was just 0.4 per cent of GDP. Their aim was not just to alleviate extreme poverty in this generation, but also to prevent it in the next, by ensuring that young Latin Americans were healthier and better educated than they would otherwise be. They overcame the limitations of established social security systems, which left out the large numbers of Latin Americans not in formal-sector jobs. The details of the schemes varied, with some putting more emphasis on providing a minimum income and others on strict conditionality. Though the results were uneven, on the whole the evidence was that CCTs did help to improve nutrition and school attendance and raised women's self-esteem, especially in the larger and less poor countries of the region, such as Brazil, Colombia and Mexico.[19] They also became a means by which governments could react to recessions, by expanding coverage or raising payments, for example.

Some governments attempted to link CCTs to skills training. *Chile Solidario* used social workers to try to reach those who suffered from 'multi-dimensional' extreme poverty and slipped through social safety-nets. As well as offering cash transfers, it aimed to ensure that the poorest benefited from existing housing and education programmes. A typical beneficiary was Olga Durán, a 35-year-old single mother in Peñalolén, a suburb on Santiago's eastern fringe. Sprawling up the slopes towards the snow-capped Andean cordillera, Peñalolén was a mix of lower middle-class respectability and enclaves of poverty, with new housing estates adjoining older, single-storey dwellings. Ms Durán lived in a two-room wooden hut behind one of those single-storey houses, which was occupied by her mother. She moved there after being stabbed by her husband, from whom she was separated. Through *Chile Solidario*, she studied baking and won a grant to set up a small food stall. Her eldest son was able to stay at school, where he did well, winning a scholarship to study electronics.[20] Under Dilma Rousseff, Brazil introduced a scheme that had some similarities to *Chile Solidario*.

In many countries in 2017, CCTs had survived changes of government: they had become an enduring part of the political landscape and a floor, albeit a low one, of democratic citizenship. But useful as they were, that did not mean they offered a complete answer to Latin America's social needs and inequalities. And as other benefits, such as minimum pensions, came to be attached to CCTs, Levy worried that Latin America was creating an incentive to remain in the informal sector by erecting a non-contributory system of social protection in parallel with a contributory one.[21]

The classroom battles

The second factor behind the decline in income inequality has been the swift spread of education in Latin America. In the 1990s, the region achieved near-universal primary education. Nine out of ten children now go on to start secondary schooling. In 2012, almost three-quarters of the relevant age group were in secondary school, up from 59 per cent in 1999. Pre-school education for 3–5-year-olds has expanded greatly in this century, from 54 per cent to 74 per cent of the age cohort.[22] This big expansion in educational coverage seems to have played an important role in making income distribution less unequal, by reducing the wage premium commanded by those with higher levels of education.[23] But there are signs that this effect has diminished. (In another view, the fall in income inequality is chiefly because the faster growth induced by the commodity boom increased the demand for unskilled labour in services, but only temporarily.[24])

The problem is that the poor quality of schooling means it does not redress inequality of opportunity. Children whose parents had fewer-than-average years of schooling tend to lag, too. Poorer students fare worse than average in school tests, as do rural schoolchildren. Though there have been signs that this lack of social mobility is starting to diminish, they are tentative.[25] For all these reasons, a broad consensus has emerged that Latin America must improve the quality of education and make a bigger effort to upgrade the skills of the existing labour force.

In the PISA standardised international tests of the reading, maths and science abilities of 15-year-olds, Latin America is in the bottom third of the world class. In the 2015 tests, involving 72 countries or cities, the region showed both wide variation and some overall improvement in educational performance. Chile, Uruguay and Costa Rica, along with the city of Buenos Aires, were the region's best performers; Peru and Colombia had improved significantly compared with 2012; Brazil, having improved in the past, had stagnated, as had Mexico.[26] Several Asian and Eastern European countries of similar income levels to Latin America performed much better. What this meant was that in 2015, 15-year-olds in Chile, Uruguay and Costa Rica were on average two years behind their peers in the OECD; and in Brazil, Colombia, Mexico and Peru, they were three years behind. Bottom of the class was the Dominican Republic, which was five years behind. And that was on average: worryingly, half the Latin American students who participated in the tests lacked basic reading, scientific and mathematical skills. Only Peru managed to cut the percentage of low-performing students in all three subjects. Sadly, days after the results came out, Jaime Saavedra, the country's outstanding education minister since 2013, was rewarded for his efforts by being impeached on spurious grounds by the *fujimorista* opposition in Peru's Congress.[27]

The expansion in higher education in the region has been impressively swift. Between 1995 and 2010, the number of students tripled, to comprise about four young people in ten aged 20–24. The private sector has provided the means for such a rapid expansion: nine out of ten new universities in Chile and Peru are private, as are eight out of ten in Brazil. Yet the quality of these new private universities varies widely, and on average is poor. According to one ranking, in 2011 only nine Latin American universities figured in the top 500 in the world.[28]

What prevents Latin American children from learning more? Traditionally, the region's school systems were centralised and under-funded. They were staffed by poorly motivated teachers organised in powerful trade unions. A lack of school buildings meant that the school day was often short, to accommodate two shifts. Visit a typical public school in Latin America, and a number of teachers would be absent, while those who were present would be teaching by rote – writing on the blackboard, their backs turned to a classroom of noisily chattering children.

Many of these weaknesses have started to be addressed. Take Peru, where spending on education had been low since the economic slump of the 1970s and 1980s. Under Humala's government, it rose from 2.9 per cent of GDP in 2010 to 3.6 per cent in 2015.[29] Saavedra used the extra money to begin a crash programme of repairing dilapidated school buildings and to phase out the shift system, extending the school day. He generalised a previous pilot plan to link teachers' pay to performance, rather than just to years of service.

Or take, for example, the Liceo Bicentenario San Pedro, a secondary school in Puente Alto, a gritty district on the southern fringes of Santiago, Chile's capital. Opened in 2012, the school nestled amid the vestiges of a shanty town, where urban sprawl met the vineyards of the Maipo valley. Most of its pupils were drawn from families classed as 'vulnerable'. Yet in national tests it ranked fourth among municipal (i.e. public) schools in Chile. Alejandro Hidalgo, the young headteacher, said he had the freedom to hire motivated young teachers in sufficient numbers that they had time to prepare their classes properly. When I visited the school in 2014, the noise level in the classrooms was moderate and the teachers were visibly commanding the attention of their pupils.

Over the past 20 years, public spending on schooling has increased in most countries of the region, to an average of 4.8 per cent of GDP – the same percentage as in the OECD countries. Some countries have decentralised school administration – Minas Gerais, which has the best educational results of any Brazilian state, was a pioneer. Many governments have set up national evaluation systems. There are two key pending assignments. The first is to improve the quality of teachers and teaching. Traditionally, Latin America turned out large numbers of teachers recruited from less-bright school leavers. It trained and paid them badly (salaries were between 10 per cent and 50 per cent less than those of other professionals). And so they taught badly. That was borne out in a study by the World Bank, in which researchers made unannounced visits to 15,000 classrooms in more than 3,000 public schools (both primary and secondary) in several Latin American countries between 2009 and 2013.[30] They found that the teachers spent less than 65 per cent of their time in class actually teaching, compared with a benchmark of good practice in schools in the United States of 85 per cent. The rest of the time was spent on administration or simply wasted. That is the equivalent of a day's schooling lost per week. The observers also found that teachers relied overwhelmingly on the blackboard. Boosting student learning demands far-reaching changes in the way that teachers are recruited, trained and rewarded. Reforming an entire profession is complex, especially in the face of the power of teachers' unions. But some countries have made a start. Chile and Peru offer scholarships to bright students who train as teachers. Chile, Ecuador, Mexico, Peru and the city of Rio de Janeiro have approved laws to link pay and promotion to performance, rather than years of service. The big test will be whether teachers who repeatedly fail evaluations are ejected from the profession. That requires political courage: implementation of Mexico's education reform was blocked in several of the country's poorest states, such as Oaxaca and Guerrero, where it was most needed, by a dissident branch of the teachers' union. It was determined to retain the existing system under which it was the union that decided on the hiring and (very rarely) firing of teachers and school principals.

A second test is early-years provision. Inequality of opportunity starts at birth. Much research from around the world finds that children who are poorly nourished and poorly parented in their earliest years will learn less at school and be less successful as adults. In Miraflores, a prosperous district of Lima, the Humpty Dumpty private nursery offers 32 hours of training in 'early stimulation' for parents and their babies, for around $100. Many of its alumni will doubtless go on to private schools and lucrative careers. In San Juan de Lurigancho, day care often means grandmother, at best. Latin American governments have made an effort to expand day-care provision, mainly with the laudable aim of helping mothers to work outside the home. Brazil and Chile doubled the proportion of children in day nurseries in the decade to 2015, while in Ecuador the figure increased sixfold. But much of the provision was in big centres, accommodating up to 300 infants, where staff were few, ill-trained and poorly paid, and the quality of care was so 'dismal' that it 'may harm – rather than help – the children who use it', according to a study by the IDB. The evidence suggested that home visits and child minders might offer a better and cheaper service.[31]

Towards universal health care

At least Latin American children are much healthier than their parents. Infant mortality in the region fell from 54 deaths per thousand births in 1990 to 17 in 2015, a swifter fall than in any other part of the world in the same period.[32] Average life expectancy at birth has risen steadily, to 75 years. Babies are better fed than in the past (or than in other developing regions). That is in line with a general improvement in health indicators in the region.[33] This is in part the consequence of an impressive, though still incomplete, commitment by the region's democracies to offer health care to all their citizens. And it entails new challenges, as the region has undergone an epidemiological transition: Latin Americans are increasingly suffering from the rich-world ailments of heart disease, cancer, diabetes and obesity, which require more expensive treatments.

Many of the constitutions of the 1980s and 1990s proclaimed a right to health care. But the democratic governments inherited profoundly unequal and defective health services. Typically, there were three tiers. The rich and the middle class had private insurance and went to private clinics and hospitals. Some of these, such as the Albert Einstein or the Sírio-Libanês hospitals in São Paulo, were world-class; others offered status, but indifferent care. Formal-sector workers were enrolled in contributory social security systems, which in Latin America – almost uniquely in the world – owned and operated hospitals. And the poor traditionally had to rely on poor-quality public hospitals, where patients had to pay for medicines, and sometimes for syringes and sheets.

Since 1995, total spending on health care has risen everywhere in Latin America (except in Uruguay, where it was already high), averaging around 7 per cent of GDP in 2010.[34] That was not so far from the figure for the OECD countries (9 per cent), though in some Latin American countries the private component of spending was higher (in Brazil it was 45 per cent).[35] Many governments moved towards creating universal health care, by linking up the social security and health ministry systems. The boldest move was in Brazil, where the 1988 constitution merged the two into the taxpayer-funded Sistema Único de Saúde (SUS). This comprised primary health care and teams of family doctors, as well as hospitals. Partly because of the weight of private health insurance in Brazil, the government found it hard to provide sufficient funds for the SUS or to provide enough doctors in poor and remote areas. This prompted Dilma Rousseff to import some 15,000 doctors from Cuba, a controversial measure, but one that was popular and justified.

Colombia's 1991 constitution created a universal and decentralised insurance-based system. Its framers expected two-thirds of the population to be covered by contributory insurance schemes. In practice, half are in the government insurance scheme, to which they pay little or nothing. The Constitutional Court ruled in 2008 that the benefit plans offered by each system had to be the same, even though the government scheme had less money. The constitution also separated health-care purchasers from providers, in an effort to encourage efficiency and transparency. By 2012, many health management companies were bankrupt, because local governments, which had to underwrite the state insurance scheme, failed to reimburse them fully. Costs rose because drug companies got the courts to mandate prescription of expensive pills. President Juan Manuel Santos brought in Alejandro Gaviria, an economist, to sort out the mess. He defined benefit plans more tightly, requiring more payments by patients who could afford them. He also set up an equivalent of Britain's National Institute for Health and Care Excellence to decide which drugs offered value for money and would be covered. There were still a lot of inequities, he acknowledged, but he argued that a poorer Colombian living in a big city gets better health care than their peers anywhere else in Latin America.[36]

Peru adopted a more gradual approach to the same end of universal coverage. The administration of Alejandro Toledo launched the Seguro Integral de Salud (SIS), a government insurance scheme which covered an expanding range of basic treatments and drugs and involved low contributions. Though it operated alongside the traditional social security health system (called EsSALUD), the gap between the two systems in terms of spending per patient, access and quality was 'very close to disappearing', according to Daniel Cotlear, a health specialist at the World Bank.[37] Patients in Huáscar interviewed by Emma Raffo in 2015 expressed appreciation for the SIS, and many said health services had improved. But they complained that the SIS didn't always cover the cost of their medicine; that meant relying on the resources of a family member. Many complained that to get an appointment, they had to get up at 4.00 a.m. and queue, and that hospital bureaucrats treated them disrespectfully. Some used the private doctors in the area for an initial consultation, in part because these doctors used their contacts to get appointments for tests and such like. There was a lingering stigma attached to the SIS and a subjective belief that care in EsSALUD was superior.

In Huáscar, the small health centre from the 1980s had become a small hospital by 2006, with 76 beds and one ambulance. It was the only hospital in the whole of San Juan de Lurigancho. The 54 doctors worked in the mornings; in the afternoons they crossed the road and practised privately in modest consulting rooms. According to Dr Mario Ruiz, the hospital's director, the district had the highest rate of tuberculosis in Peru. But a planned TB ward was unfinished.[38] By 2015, the hospital had expanded further and looked much smarter. It was no longer the sole facility in San Juan de Lurigancho: there was a large EsSALUD hospital nearby, and a number of health centres, as well as private clinics. The mayor wanted a 500-bed district hospital and had set aside land for this.

The demographic challenge

Until the 1970s, Latin American women married early and bore many children. Earlier improvements in public health and life expectancy meant that the population was growing explosively. But since then, the region has undergone a remarkably swift demographic transition. The spread of education among girls, and of contraception, meant that women began to marry later and to have progressively fewer children. The fertility rate (i.e. the number of births per woman) fell from almost 6 in 1960 to 2.2 in 2010. That is only just above the rate required to keep the population stable. As always, the picture varies across the region: in Brazil and Chile, the fertility rate is already below this replacement rate, though in some other countries, such as Bolivia and parts of Central America, for example, it is much higher.[39]

Several far-reaching changes have flowed from this. Until about 1995, the absolute number of children in Latin America continued to grow – requiring big investments in extra school places. There is currently a 'bulge' of young adults seeking employment, while the numbers of 'dependants' (under-15s and over-65s) is relatively low. This constitutes a 'demographic dividend' – the adding of workers to the labour force boosts economic growth and makes it easier to pay for the pensions of the old. But this dividend is fast running out as the population ages. While in the 1990s the active workforce expanded at 3 per cent a year, by 2016 that figure had fallen to 1.6 per cent, despite an increase in women working outside the home.[40] Unless even more women and more older people work, the labour force will probably stop growing sometime in the 2020s. This 'demographic transition' happened very gradually over many decades in Europe. In Latin America it is happening much faster.

There is one potential bright spot in this: the reduction in the number of young men will probably reduce crime rates. Nevertheless, the demographic transition represents a twofold challenge. First, according to Ruchir Sharma, experience around the world shows that a percentage-point decline in the size of the labour force will shave around a percentage point off economic growth.[41] That underlines the importance of rectifying the region's lamentable lack of productivity growth. Second, Latin America will not be able to afford to pay its pensioners, unless its pension schemes are reformed.

These schemes suffer from several flaws. Only 45 per cent of workers in the region contribute to any kind of scheme at all. Some of them are absurdly generous, partly because retirement ages have not been raised in line with rising life expectancy. In Brazil, the average retirement age is 54 and the average pension is equal to 70 per cent of final salary. Only 11 per cent of Brazilians were over 65 in 2013, and yet pensions commanded almost as big a slice of national income as in Greece, where the elderly make up 29 per cent of the population.[42] Spending so relatively much on pensioners is unfair to young people: Latin American governments typically spend six times more per person on the over-65s than on the under-6s.[43]

In the 1990s, several governments privatised pension schemes, partly for fiscal reasons. State-operated pay-as-you-go pension systems were generally poorly managed, and many had been raided by governments for other purposes. Chile and several others switched to individual capitalised accounts managed by private funds (known as AFPs). This did help to reduce the fiscal burden and to develop local capital markets. But the AFPs charged high fees, especially at the start. Typically, workers were required to contribute 10 per cent of salary, which many found too much. The result was that many failed to make contributions. And even those that did found that their pensions were modest. 'The AFPs have failed', according to Santiago Levy of the IDB. He favours a small universal pension, funded by an earmarked consumption tax, augmented by voluntary schemes.[44] In the boom years, several governments (such as Mexico, Peru and Bolivia) introduced small non-contributory pensions. The problem was that they didn't link these to the contributory system, thus undermining the incentive to join it.

Risk of regress

Until 2015, Danuza Rocha da Paixão worked as an office cleaner in São Paulo. But with Brazil's economy falling into recession, the business closed and she had to look for another cleaning job. 'I used to earn much more than I do today, although I do the same thing', she said. She had to postpone buying clothes, in order to buy food. 'I have to calculate everything carefully, or I'll end up with nothing.' She moved to a cheaper rented house, but could not afford to buy all the furniture she needed.[45]

As Latin America's economies slowed after 2011, so did social progress – in some places going into reverse. By 2015, poverty had edged up again in the region as a whole, to 29.2 per cent, and extreme poverty to 12.4 per cent. Perhaps the biggest short-term challenge was how to prevent social regress. A study by UNDP in 2015 estimated that 2.8 million Latin Americans had fallen back into poverty, and that a further 25–30 million 'ultra-vulnerable' people were at risk of doing so, mainly because of their lack of assets, savings and social protection (such as health insurance).[46]

The medium-term challenge was how to eliminate poverty. There were reasons to think that slower growth was not the only factor in the levelling off in its reduction. There was a large core of some 130 million Latin Americans in chronic poverty who hadn't benefited much from growth.[47] In Colombia, perhaps partly because of its internal armed conflict, these people made up close to 40 per cent of the population, and in Guatemala 50 per cent. They lacked the skills, motivation or contacts to get employment or make the most of social programmes. There was a growing acceptance among researchers and policymakers that poverty was not just about income, but rather it was 'multi-dimensional'. The chronically poor were less likely than those who escaped poverty to have basic services, such as clean water and sewerage. They often lived in poor housing conditions, and their children were more likely to drop out of school. And they were more likely to be of indigenous or African descent, to be women and to live in rural areas. This highlighted some continuing structural inequalities in the region and, until recently at least, the lack of political will to reduce them.

That was clear in Cotacachi, a small, pleasant town in a verdant valley between two towering volcanoes, a couple of hours' drive north of Ecuador's capital, Quito. Between 1996 and 2009, its mayor was Auki Tituaña, an economist who wears the traditional pigtail, white felt hat and poncho of the Quichua-speaking Indians of the Ecuadorean Andes. Aged 39 when interviewed in 2004, he recalled that when he was a child, his mother would drag him into the street to let a *mestizo* pass on the pavement. When Indians came down from their plots in the hills to the market, town officials would confiscate their ponchos and hats as a means of press-ganging them to sweep the streets without pay. Such discrimination has been challenged by new organisations of Latin Americans of indigenous and African descent. There is less racism than there was, but those who suffer it are more conscious and less tolerant of it. 'The *mestizo* has begun to look on us with greater respect, but they still don't see us as equal partners', Mr Tituaña said.[48]

From the Mexican Revolution onwards, governments in several countries recognised the cultural legacy of indigenous people and made paternalistic efforts to improve their lot. The aim was assimilation. Indian peoples, it was tacitly thought, would disappear under the twin processes of *mestizaje* and urbanisation. They did not. According to censuses, there were around 42 million Latin Americans who defined themselves as indigenous people in 2010, or nearly 7.8 per cent of the total population. More than 85 per cent of them were in just six countries: Mexico (16.8 million), Peru (7.6 million), Guatemala (5.9 million), Bolivia (4.1 million), Colombia (1.5 million) and Ecuador (1 million).[49] They comprised more than 800 separate peoples; they ranged from sophisticated urban traders, as in Cotacachi, Cusco and La Paz, to small groups living in voluntary isolation in the Amazon rainforest.

The numbers of indigenous people living in poverty has declined in this century. There have been other improvements. Whereas it took the United States half a century (from 1935 to 1985) to cut infant mortality among African-Americans from 80 to 25 per 1,000 live births, Peru managed the same reduction for its Amerindian population in less than 15 years, from 1995 to 2008.[50] Nevertheless, indigenous people are still more than twice as likely to be poor and almost three times as likely to be extremely poor than the population as a whole. And they have less education, poorer health and worse living conditions than the rest of the population. Indigenous girls are less likely than boys to go to school. In both Guatemala and Peru, indigenous people make up the bulk of victims of past 'dirty wars' involving left-wing guerrillas and the security forces. Yet they retain a powerful cultural identity.

That identity has tended to be rooted in their traditional rural lifestyles. One response to their plight has been migration to the cities: around half of those who self-identify as indigenous live in urban areas. These urban indigenous people are less badly off than those in the countryside, but worse off than the rest of the urban population. In Lima, for example, many mothers whose children work on the streets are first-generation migrants, whose first language is Quechua.[51] Adapting successfully to the city may take a generation. But many in the second generation tend to merge into *mestizo* culture (as the assimilation approach forecast). Even in Bolivia, the move from countryside to city has provided opportunities. Take Felipe Copaja, a man of Aymara descent, who owns a small workshop in a side-street in El Alto. He was born in an Indian village on the Altiplano. His parents were *campesinos* (peasant farmers). 'Because of poverty, they came to work in El Alto', he said. 'But they continued to go back and forth. They sold weavings and handcrafts.'[52] When he was ten, Felipe came to El Alto, where he completed secondary school, trained as a mechanic and set up his own business. Though dissatisfied with corruption and what he called 'impunity' (i.e. the lack of the rule of law), speaking in 2004 he said that racial discrimination was less pervasive than in the past. 'I've done quite well', he declared. His daughter was due to start studying medicine at La Paz's San Andrés University, the city's oldest seat of higher education. His son hoped to follow her to university.

But there has also been a second response: collective mobilisation. Until recently, indigenous people rarely organised politically along ethnic lines; if they did at all, it was as *campesinos*. The first sign of that changing came in Ecuador in 1990, when a newly formed confederation grouping Indian peoples from the Amazon and the Andes staged a national 'uprising', blocking roads and obliging the government to negotiate. The Zapatista rising, though led by a white former university professor, drew worldwide attention to the grievances of Mayan Indians.

Democracy gave indigenous people political rights, often for the first time. In the 1970s, Catholic bishops and priests played an important role in training indigenous leaders in several countries. Then globalisation kicked in. The quincentenary of Columbus's 'discovery' of the Americas focused attention on the continent's original inhabitants. An international network of activists and NGOs provided financial and other support to indigenous organisations, their leaders and their protests. The Indian cause was given legal force by Convention 169 of the International Labour Organization (ILO). Most Latin American governments signed it, committing themselves to guarantee indigenous people equal rights, as well as to respect their lands and traditions.[53] Some scholars argue that 'neoliberalism' was another factor in the rise of ethnic militancy, both through the dismantling of the corporate state and its replacement by a liberal philosophy of individual rights, and through the opening up to investment in mining and oil by multinationals, often on indigenous lands (see the next chapter).[54] But the corporate state had rarely done much for indigenous people, and state-owned mining and oil companies were rarely sensitive to their land claims. Rather, liberal democracy has offered Indian groups the chance to participate in politics more effectively. They formed political parties in Bolivia and Ecuador. Their advent is part of a broader eclipse of class politics by the politics of identity. In Bolivia, Evo Morales came to power claiming to represent Bolivia's indigenous peoples, and in many ways he did (see Chapter 11). Two decades earlier, however, he would have described himself as a *mestizo*, which he was.

In a round of constitution writing in the 1990s, the ILO's provisions were incorporated in ten countries, including Bolivia, Ecuador and Peru. Governments, long committed to the aim of racial integration, came to recognise that they rule multicultural societies. The basic, and justified, demand of many movements of the indigenous was for equal treatment. Calls for local autonomy and collective rights were potentially more complicated. Some of these demands were met by democratic local government, as in Cotacachi. The appeal to collective rights was in part a defence mechanism, and the expression of a desire to maintain a traditional way of life and all its rich cultural legacy. It also harked back to the *República de Indios*, the caste society of the colonial period. The risk was that it would become a way to entrench modern-day *curacas* and would become a cover for the suppression of individual rights (such as in forced marriages). One way or another, in this century indigenous Latin Americans have succeeded in making themselves visible to the centres of power, and have participated vigorously in democracy. But they are still struggling to be treated as full and equal citizens.

That applies also to the descendants of African slaves, who by one count make up some 30 per cent of Latin Americans.[55] Like indigenous peoples, blacks are more likely to be poor. In Brazil, for example, according to data published in 2008, they earned on average less than half as much as whites.[56] Yet until recently, it was widely believed in Brazil that blacks were poorer because of their class, not their race. '*O dinheiro branqueia*' ('money whitens'), the Brazilian saying went. Centuries of miscegenation – and the absence of any official colour bar – meant that Brazilians are a multi-hued rainbow nation. Traditionally, Brazilians' self-image is that they are whiter than others might see them. In the 2000 census, 54 per cent described themselves as white, 38.4 per cent as *pardos* or *mulatos* (i.e. mixed) and only 6 per cent as *negros* (blacks). That self-image was paralleled in the notion of 'racial democracy', officially adopted by republican governments. Getúlio Vargas encouraged expressions of African culture both in music (*samba*) and religion (*candomblé* and *umbanda*), and these became an integral part of Brazilian national culture.[57] *Feijoada*, a stew of beans and cheap cuts of pork that is Brazil's national dish, has its origins in the slave quarters.

Discrimination might not have been officially encouraged, but it existed, expressed in job advertisements that required 'good appearance' or in the ubiquitous second, service lift in middle-class apartment blocks to which servants were relegated. A study in São Paulo in 1995 found that blacks were twice as likely to die a violent death as whites.[58] Around the same time, the city's justice secretary, who was black, complained that he had been stopped four times in a year by police, who suspected him of having stolen his official car.[59]

Since the return of democracy, race finally made it onto the political agenda in Brazil, pushed there by small, mainly middle-class groups of black activists.[60] In the 1990s, the government began to implement what Cardoso called 'an eclectic mix of affirmative action policies'.[61] Ministries began to introduce racial quotas for jobs. Affirmative action gathered momentum under Lula. For the first time, a black judge was appointed to the Supreme Court. From 2001 onwards, more than 70 public universities introduced racial admissions quotas. These were controversial: opponents argued that importing US-style affirmative action policies risked dividing Brazilians along colour lines. But in 2012, the Supreme Court unanimously upheld the legality of quotas. Shortly afterwards, Dilma Rousseff signed a law giving federal universities four years to ensure that half their intake of students came from public schools, and that the racial make-up of these students reflected that of the state where they were located. While its implementation in a country where race is a spectrum – not binary – was likely to be messy, this marked an important attempt to try, belatedly, to redress the legacy of slavery.[62]

In Colombia, a large population of African descent suffered poverty, neglect and discrimination, and were disproportionately affected by the armed conflict in the country. Take the Pacific coast, home to a million people, 90 per cent of whom were Afro-Colombians. In Quibdó, the capital of Chocó department, 'you might think you're in Haiti', said Paula Moreno, a former culture minister and activist. Unemployment in the city was 70 per cent. In Brazil, Colombia and Peru, racial discrimination was illegal. That was sometimes enforced: an upmarket discotheque in Lima was fined after it refused entry to a dark-skinned Peruvian. Economic growth and the loosening of class divisions meant that it was not uncommon to see *mestizos* as customers, as well as waiters, in the city's famed restaurants. Yet the elites in Latin America tended to remain socially distant from the *mestizo* masses. Changing that would take time and determination.

Ni Una Menos

Those elites are also overwhelmingly male. Latin American *machismo* has started to be questioned, but not yet much weakened, by modernity. A quarter of all families in the region are headed by women.[63] Men often come and go. Women increasingly work outside the home. On average, in 2012, they were paid only 84 per cent as much as men for the same work, but that represented an increase of 12 percentage points since 1994.[64] Although there has been some progress in women's representation in politics, partly through laws which set quotas, they still occupied only 29 per cent of seats in legislatures in 2014.[65] But the most pressing gender issues in Latin America concerned violence and sexual and reproductive health.

On 8 October 2016, Lucía Pérez, a 16-year-old girl, was drugged, raped and murdered by impalement in Mar del Plata, a seaside resort in Argentina. Her horrific death did not go unremarked: thousands of demonstrators, mainly women dressed in black, marched through Buenos Aires and other cities to demand that the government do more to end violence against women. It was the third march by *Ni Una Menos* (Not One Less), a campaign against 'femicide' (the murder of a woman because of her sex) since a founding demonstration mobilised hundreds of thousands in Argentina, Chile and Uruguay in 2015. That year, an estimated 235 women in Argentina were victims of femicide. Even so, that was far fewer than in some other countries of the region, such as in Central America. Ciudad Juárez in Mexico became notorious for femicide: some 450 women and girls were killed there between 1993 and 2006.[66] Their beaten or mutilated bodies were often found dumped on waste ground. Some of the deaths were the result of domestic violence. But many others appeared to be linked to the trafficking of women for prostitution or sexual abuse by drug mafias and their allied youth gangs. 'They kill them because they are women and because they are poor', said Esther Chávez, a feminist accountant who set up Casa Amiga, a counselling centre and women's refuge in the city.[67]

Many governments have raised the penalties for the crime, but do not prosecute it with sufficient energy. In Argentina, 70 per cent of murders of women are within the home, committed by their partners, and these are often not taken seriously by the police, according to Sabina Cartabia, a lawyer involved in *Ni Una Menos*. Under public pressure, the government of Mauricio Macri has promised to build 36 women's refuges and increase electronic tagging of violent men.[68]

Studies suggest that around a third of Latin American adult women suffer domestic or sexual violence. Bolivia's ombudsman reported that in 2014, 34 per cent of girls there suffered sexual abuse before the age of 18. Partly as a result, teenage pregnancy is extraordinarily common. In Latin America, 69 in every thousand girls aged 15–19 gave birth in 2012, according to the UN – a rate that is exceeded only in sub-Saharan Africa. Only a fifth of adolescent pregnancies in Latin America are intentional, compared with 67 per cent in Africa.[69] In theory, most governments in the region provide contraceptives and sex education to young people. But not in practice. In Argentina, for example, imparting sex education and contraception are the responsibility of provincial governments, and most do not.

Child abuse and unintentional teen pregnancy intersect cruelly with Latin America's rigid restrictions on abortion. It is legal in Uruguay and Mexico City; it is allowed in some cases, such as rape, foetal malformation or threat to life, in Argentina and Colombia. But the Catholic Church often presses doctors not to practise abortion even when it is legal. The consequence is that 4.2 million Latin American women have clandestine abortions every year, and around a million are hospitalised as a result of complications, according to the Guttmacher Institute, an NGO. The fight to separate Church and state in Latin America began in the nineteenth century, waged by Juárez and others. It is not over.

A revolution in prayer

But the Church itself has faced change, both within and without. In the 1960s, liberation theology shook the Church out of its lethargy. It became more or less official doctrine when a conference of Latin American bishops held in Medellín in 1968 declared that the region was in a state of 'structural sin' and 'institutionalised violence', and that the task of the Church was to pursue an 'option for the poor'. Liberation theology was heavily influenced by dependency theory; it would have its most visible political impact in Central America, among Nicaragua's Sandinistas and El Salvador's FMLN; it also shaped many outsiders' view of Latin America and its problems.[70] Across the region, the liberation theologians worked through Christian base groups and trained a generation of community leaders. They were influential in the founding of many left-wing social movements. Revolutionary priests can still be found in Latin America. But liberation theology failed in its effort to create a mass 'popular' Church that would pursue socialism, as its promoters wanted. That was partly because Pope John Paul II and the Vatican hierarchy successfully isolated the liberation theologians through the preferment of conservatives (some of them ultra-reactionaries) as bishops. But it was mainly because ordinary Latin Americans were resistant to the 'popular' Church.[71]

In the *favelas* and shanty towns from São Paulo to Lima and in the highland villages of Mexico and Guatemala, it is evangelical Protestantism, not 'popular' Catholicism, that has won converts and changed social attitudes among the region's poor. According to the Pew Research Center, a think-tank, only 69 per cent of Latin Americans now consider themselves to be Catholic, down from 92 per cent in 1970. Protestants now account for 19 per cent, up from 4 per cent. Over the same period, the share of those with no religious affiliation grew to 8 per cent. In parts of Central America, barely half the population is Catholic, and in Brazil only 61 per cent.

There are thousands of different evangelical churches and sects. Some are originally imports from the United States, but many, especially in Brazil, are of home-grown inspiration. The politics of these churches are varied, but are nearly always directed rather narrowly at promoting their own interests. What they have in common is a stress on teeto-talism, hard work and progress through individual effort, without neglecting charity for the less fortunate. Whereas the liberation theologians and their base communities focused on trying to change society, the evangelical Protestants offer counselling and succour to individuals with the concrete problems of their everyday lives. These churches well express the driving ambition of the lower middle class. They have acquired a mass audience among the poor, among black Brazilians and indigenous Guatemalans, and also among women. They preach the importance of the family as a stable unit, in which men should assume their responsibilities; they are less tolerant than Catholics of male infi-delity, as well as of alcoholism. In some ways, the Pentecostals have been agents of modernisation in Latin America, preaching individual initia-tive, hard work and entrepreneurialism. They also celebrate material success: Fraternidad Cristiana, a home-grown Protestant Church, opened a temple that was said to be the largest building in Central America, complete with a 'Burger King drive', seating for over 12,000 and parking for more than 3,500 cars, all at a cost of $20 million.[72] At the same time, they have obvious flaws: they have had their share of fraudsters, and many of their religious practices – speaking in tongues, miracles and the like – seem medieval. They are intolerant of homosexuality and gay rights. But in ways that have often been overlooked, they have changed Latin America, and especially some of its poorer places. So much for the contention that the Counter-Reformation still dominates the lives of the Spanish-speaking peoples, as Claudio Véliz argued as recently as 1994.[73]

The main response of the Catholic Church to the advance of Protestantism has been the charismatic revival movement, founded in the United States in the 1960s. Like many of the evangelical churches, it is a Pentecostal movement that emphasises the spontaneous experience of the Holy Spirit and the opportunity for individuals to change their lives. Like evangelical Protestants, the charismatics offer support to the upwardly mobile. In places like São Paulo, they draw hundreds of thousands to open-air masses. Another response was the election of the first Latin American pope in Jorge Bergoglio, the former archbishop of Buenos Aires. In office as Pope Francis, he has offered Latin America a theological version of Peronism: he has been less doctrinaire than his predecessors on questions of personal morality, and openly sympathetic to populist governments and social movements in the region. But there is little reason to imagine that this will stem the Church's slow decline in the region.

Connected citizens

Predominantly rural until the mid-twentieth century, in a matter of a few decades Latin American societies have swiftly become overwhelmingly urban. In 1940, more than 60 per cent of the population lived in the countryside. Today, according to a possibly exaggerated definition by the United Nations, 80 per cent live in cities, making Latin America among the world's most urbanised regions.[74] That partly reflects the failure of efforts at agrarian reform to redress the region's uniquely unequal pattern of landholding. But migration is above all a search for opportunity, an expression of choice. Urban life offers far more possibilities of receiving modern services than the peasant farming that many migrants (or their parents) have left behind. Latin America's swelling megacities are theatres of social inequality, but also cauldrons that have forged citizenship. In the region's cities in 2014, almost everyone had access to electricity, nine out of ten had piped water and two-thirds were connected to a sewerage system. In rural areas, these figures were lower.[75] Access to basic public services has transformed the lives of many Latin American families over the past few decades.

The countryside is not condemned to decline. In Peru, for example, a burst of rural roadbuilding and the spread of mobile phones are transforming some of the poorer parts of the Andes. Rural incomes rose by an annual average of 7.2 per cent in real terms between 1994 and 2011, according to a study by Richard Webb, a former president of the Central Bank.[76] Many countries have enjoyed agricultural revolutions in the past two decades, applying technology to commercial export farming. That can benefit smaller-scale farmers, as well as agribusiness. And Latin America's swollen megacities have their own problems. In this century, the rate of economic growth in many of the big Latin American cities began to lag behind that of smaller towns and cities, having outpaced it in the previous half-century.[77] Congestion, housing shortages, deficient public transport, pollution and lack of urban planning are hobbling the big cities. That is an opportunity for mid-sized cities, many of which are growing strongly; but it is a problem, too.

Nevertheless, urbanisation, together with the fall in poverty and spread of education, has brought changed attitudes and higher expectations. The demographic transition means that the region has a large number of young people: in 2016, some 156 million of them, or 26 per cent of the total population, were 'millennials' (aged 15–29).[78] These millennials have led the communications revolution, as Latin Americans swiftly take to the internet and social media. By 2016, 62 per cent used the internet (compared with a world average of 50 per cent), while more than 320 million used Facebook.[79] There were more than 200 million smartphones by December 2015, a figure the industry expects to more than double by 2020.[80]

Class divisions have become much less rigid. At the bottom, a greatly expanded urban working class is no longer predominantly made up of unionised factory workers: in most Latin American countries, the informal sector of small unregistered businesses makes up 40–50 per cent of the workforce. In the past, many members of Latin America's small middle class were public employees. Fernando Henrique Cardoso, a sociologist as well as politician, has noted that the new middle-class groups are linked to the market, rather than the state. They include managers and owners of small businesses, and many professionals in the media, entertainment, leisure and financial industries; many have risen from families of lower status.[81]

The masses of young, connected, urban Latin Americans are organised in different ways than they were in the past. In most countries, trade unions are much weaker than they were in the 1970s. Left-wing social movements, from landless workers to regional groups, which flourished in the 1990s and 2000s, are less prominent than they were. In their place there is a myriad of campaign and community groups, NGOs and more or less spontaneous movements arranged through social media. 'Civil society' – this tapestry of social movements, voluntary associations and pressure groups – is vocal, robust and lively in many countries. That, too, is relatively new: had Alexis de Tocqueville strayed south during his celebrated investigation of 'Democracy in America' in 1831, he would have found few of the voluntary organisations that so impressed him in the early United States.

On paper, a more middle-class society offers the prospect of more stable democratic politics in Latin America, more resistant to the appeals of populism. After all, the middle class has more to lose, and has an interest in respect for property rights and accountable government. Studies have shown that the political values of middle-class people differ from those of the poor. They value democracy and individual freedom more, and are generally more tolerant. They are more hostile to corruption and clientelism.[82] On the other hand, as Francis Fukuyama has pointed out, the middle class can turn to revolutionary politics if its expectations are disappointed. And when it still constitutes only a small segment of the population, it may ally with elites against democracy, if it fears that its status is threatened by the access of the poor to the system. Some analysts have detected such sentiments in the hostility of Brazil's traditional middle class to the PT governments. Some among the middle classes have opted out of state provision, in education and health. Others have made new demands on government, for better public services and less corruption. Those demands began before the economic downturn, but were amplified by it. They pointed to the weaknesses of the state in Latin America.

CHAPTER TEN

The Defective State

Attached to the Texan city of El Paso, but a long way from anywhere else, Ciudad Juárez has attracted hundreds of thousands of Mexicans to its export assembly plants. Here the Rio Grande, which divides the two cities, is for much of the year a shallow stream, its broad bed encased in concrete levees. On its north bank rises the tall metal fence, backed every few hundred metres by a green Border Patrol 4x4, that – long before Trump's threatened wall – interrupted the northward flow of people, but not of goods. Cross the bi-national bridge from El Paso to the east of the city centre and not much visibly changes as you head south. The highway that circles around Juárez is lined with dozens of large modern factories, all built since NAFTA came into force. Trucks leave with blades for wind turbines, car parts and consumer electronics. But follow the fleets of white-painted works buses that leave the *maquiladora* plants when the shift changes in the late afternoon, and the contrast is sharper. They deliver the workers to their homes in the poor, western *colonias* that sprawl over the hills and gulches of the Chihuahua desert. Though the winding road that hugs the south bank of the Rio Grande was asphalted a dozen years ago and has become a dual carriageway, it passes small concrete huts of one or two rooms built on foundations of old tyres, as well as unpaved streets running with sewage. Across the river, the rush-hour traffic roars along Interstate 10.[1]

The biggest difference between the two sides of the river is less immediately tangible than the gap in public infrastructure or in living standards: it is in the degree to which the rule of law is applied. Between 2008 and 2011, Juárez descended into hell. It was an important export route for drugs. Under the impact of Felipe Calderón's offensive against the drug mobs, it became notorious as the world's most violent city. With a population of 1.4 million, it suffered 300 murders a month. 'Here the war on drugs was a massacre', said Nohemi Almada, an activist. 'We all grew used to seeing bound corpses in the street.' The nadir came in

January 2010, when gunmen slaughtered 15 students at a birthday party. A chastened Calderón went to Juárez and promised help. The federal government poured money into the city, some of it for upgrading the local police. Representatives of business and professional associations formed a security round-table, which held the authorities accountable for meeting targets and pressed them to co-ordinate, explained Arturo Valenzuela, a surgeon and member of the group. Murders fell steeply, to 311 in the whole of 2015. Bars and restaurants were full again. But the turnaround was fragile. Murders began rising again in 2016. In April 2017, *El Norte*, a newspaper which had played an important role in rallying the community, announced that it would cease publication after one of its journalists was murdered.[2] One factor behind the resurgence of violence seemed to be the turf wars unleashed by the fall of Joaquín 'El Chapo' Guzmán, the leader of the Sinaloa 'cartel', who had twice escaped from supposedly high-security jails. After being recaptured in 2016, Guzmán was held in a federal prison just outside Juárez, on the edge of the Chihuahua desert. Its turreted low bulk was guarded by a dozen vehicles from Mexico's army, many with guns mounted, as well as by the federal police. Yet Guzmán was too hot for the Mexican state to handle: in January 2017, he was extradited to the United States.

The limping leviathan

In its inability to provide security to its citizens, the state in Mexico, as in many other Latin American countries, is failing in its most basic function. That is symptomatic of a broader weakness of the state in the region. But it may seem surprising: after all, prior to the liberal reforms of the past quarter-century, the Latin American state seemed both sprawlingly large and almost omnipotent, both economically and politically. Yet this leviathan had rotting entrails and feet of clay. 'The state is useless', was the withering verdict of Fernando de la Rúa, Argentina's president in 1999–2001, after he took office.[3] Rather than an ideological statement, this was a factual description.

As previously noted, the relative absence of wars in independent Latin America removed what was a main driver of state formation in Europe (see Chapter 2). Nevertheless, in the period from the mid-nineteenth century to the 1930s, most Latin American countries achieved a stable administration that exercised at least a degree of control over much of the national territory. That process was uneven: states were relatively sophisticated in the Southern Cone, but weaker than average in Central America and some of the Andean countries. These fledgling states normally had to overcome local or regional rebellions. According to one account, state-building efforts were more effective in countries with a dominant capital city, and where the central government deployed officials in the provinces, rather than delegate those functions to local potentates.[4] Until the advent of air travel, geography was often a challenge to extending the writ of the state across the national territory. Laurence Whitehead cites an 'extreme' but illustrative case in the 1920s, of a Bolivian official appointed to administer his country's rubber-producing provinces in the Amazon lowlands. This official would leave La Paz for the Chilean coast, take a ship through the Panama Canal to England and then a return boat to Manaus, and proceed upriver to his post, to find that the local currency there was sterling rather than the Bolivian peso.[5]

From the Second World War onwards, the nation-builders and the populists greatly expanded the state apparatus. Governments assumed responsibility for education, health and social security for the first time. The state grappled with the national security demands of the Cold War and the developmentalist project of controlling the national economy. Public employment grew. But for all its vaunting ambition, the Latin American corporate state suffered from two basic weaknesses. The first was that a professional, technical approach to public administration often lost out to 'patrimonialism' (the capture of public institutions by private interests) and/or clientelism (the use of public resources, or award of public employment, to sustain a political following).[6] The result was inefficiency and corruption.

The second, related weakness was the inability of these states to command sufficient tax-raising capability. Direct taxes on income and property were often resisted, or evaded, by the wealthy. Instead, states came to rely on inflationary financing and debt. More and more tasks were placed upon the state, but without the resources required to carry them out. By 1980, Latin America suffered 'over-extended, inflexible, unresponsive, voracious and over-political bureaucracies', as Whitehead put it.[7] A surfeit of public employment went hand in hand with a growing deficit in the provision of public services, such as education and health care, and deterioration in their quality.

Democracy and economic reform required a different kind of state – one that was regulatory, rather than proprietorial; less ambitious, but more service-oriented, efficient and inclusive. Since the 1980s, some progress has been made in this direction. But state bureaucracies have faced a moving target. More middle-class, educated and connected societies were no longer satisfied with isolated public works, but wanted more sophisticated public goods, such as high-quality health services, university education and public transport. The state did not modernise as fast as the economy or the society.

Even so, reform was sufficiently wide-ranging as to merit the description of a 'silent revolution', according to a study in 2006 by researchers at the Inter-American Development Bank.[8] Democratisation prompted the reform of electoral authorities. It also brought decentralisation: in 2004, local and regional governments carried out 19.3 per cent of public spending, up from 13.1 per cent in 1985. The Washington Consensus stimulated the reform of economic policymaking bodies, the area where most progress was made. Many countries reformed their budgetary institutions, and a dozen imposed legal restrictions on the fiscal deficit. Several set up counter-cyclical stabilisation funds in which to save part of any windfall from commodity prices. A dozen countries gave greater legal or operational independence to their central banks in the conduct of monetary policy. Many central banks and finance ministries became centres of technocratic excellence.

Tax systems were reformed, with the aim of simplifying them and reducing evasion. These reforms typically saw a reduction in the top rates of corporate and personal income taxes, as well as the introduction of (or increase in) VAT. These changes made tax systems less of a drag on economic efficiency. But by relying on indirect taxes, they did nothing to make them more progressive (i.e. to use taxes as a means of making the distribution of income more equal). Overall, most tax systems in the region had little direct impact on income distribution.[9] And as exemptions and modifications accumulated over time, they became a complicated burden on business. Tax evasion is significantly higher than in developed countries, and enjoys considerable social legitimacy.[10]

In this century, faster economic growth and the advent of left-wing governments led to the growth of tax revenues. Taking into account social security contributions and income from royalties and transfers (e.g. from oil companies), total government revenues grew from an average of 18.6 per cent of GDP in the early 1990s to 23.2 per cent (of a bigger GDP) in the second half of the 2010s. But the range is huge: from 33.4 per cent of GDP in Brazil to 12.6 per cent in Guatemala. The regional average is a dozen percentage points lower than in the OECD countries.[11] That is not surprising: the share of the economy accounted for by government tends to rise with income and economic development. But even so, some Latin American countries, especially in Central America, still do not gather enough taxes to finance a modern state able to provide basic services for all.

The rise in revenues was mirrored by an increase in social spending. Broadly defined (to include housing and environmental protection, as well as education, health and pensions), this rose from an average of 12.6 per cent of GDP in the early 1990s to around 19.5 per cent in 2014.[12] In a third wave of state reform, in several countries management of the social ministries became more professional. Peru was one example. In 2011, Humala set up a new social development ministry under Carolina Trivelli, an economist. She shut down a food subsidy programme because it was 'clientelist and corrupt'. With the support of the economy ministry, she brought in well-qualified young professionals to manage her ministry, paying them salaries of up to $8,000 a month. They drew up a national strategy for social inclusion which aimed to tackle the various dimensions of poverty (including malnutrition, housing conditions and health) with performance targets. Most of the targets were met.[13] Yet overall, social spending in the region was not necessarily well targeted. Taken together, the impact of taxes and social benefits reduced the Gini coefficient by only 2.8 percentage points on average in Latin America, compared with 17.8 points in the OECD countries.[14] That was partly because of the bias of pension and social security systems towards the relatively better-off.

Some governments had scope to increase taxes. But for many, the main challenge in the next few years will be to make public spending and the state far more effective and efficient. The main obstacles are the lack of high-quality staff and poor organisation. All too often, the basic administrative functions of the state, from registering businesses to implementing government policy, are carried out inefficiently. Governments often find it easier to create new agencies, rather than reform existing ones. But that has led to duplication. Islands of technocratic excellence often operate in a sea of mediocrity. The IDB has evaluated government bureaucracies in the region and has found a modest improvement in their effectiveness and sophistication in this century, but also widespread variation. Chile, Brazil and Costa Rica stand out as the most effective.[15]

Civil services continue to suffer from four big flaws. The first is an obsession with procedures and hierarchies and a disdain for service and outcomes. This is aggravated by the habit of governments of churning out endless new decrees and regulations. Many civil servants have to follow thick procedural codes, but are not made accountable through performance targets. Organs of control have failed to prevent corruption, but have instilled a terror of initiative. For example, Trivelli told me she was subjected to a time-consuming investigation because she had authorised publication of a pamphlet which included data whose release required a formal ministerial resolution.

Corrupt officials exploited procedural mania in ways that perversely fostered the informal sector. A Mexican economist told me the story of his family's short-lived textile factory, set up in 1997 in a town 40 kilometres from Puebla to export T-shirts to the United States. At its peak, it had 200 workers, all formally employed and enrolled in the Mexican Social Security Institute (IMSS). 'We were very visible', he said. When the firm refused the mayor's request to pay for the paving of some streets, he arranged for the bus companies to stop picking up its workers. As well as local taxes and social security contributions, the firm had to pay for its own bus service and its own doctor, because the nearest hospital was in Puebla and the IMSS was slow to arrange medical appointments. These costs contributed to the company's inability to withstand Chinese competition, and it shut down in 2000. The Mexican government acts in a manner akin to a 'stationary bandit', in Mancur Olson's definition of the origins of the state.[16] As Luis de la Calle, another Mexican economist, put it, formal companies are subject to 'multiple windows' of extortion – by unions, municipal officials, labour inspectors, IMSS inspectors, the tax office, the police and the Zetas, none of which are in practice subjected to legal restraint. Stay informal, and 'you benefit from a "single window" of extortion: you pay the Zetas and they protect you', he noted.[17]

The second flaw concerns staffing, in which a legacy of politicisation often overcomes meritocracy. Too often the civil service is stuffed with political hangers-on. That perhaps explains why public-sector salaries tend to be higher than those in the private sector for low-level jobs, but lower for senior grades, according to a study by CAF, a regional development bank.[18] And public employees tend to enjoy especially generous pension benefits. As Miguel Ángel Centeno points out, 'the result is a public administration that functions more as a system to maintain employment privileges for some members of the middle class than to provide key services to citizens'.[19] Typically, civil services lack clear career structures. For populist reasons, presidents sometimes cap the pay of senior officials, encouraging corruption and making it hard to recruit capable, honest people. There have been some improvements. In 2003, Chile approved a law, with bipartisan support, which created an elite corps of senior public-sector managers, who were supposed to be chosen in open competition, subjected to performance targets and paid well. In practice, many Chilean ministers have sidestepped the law, using temporary contracts. Peru tried to set up a similar corps of public-sector managers and in 2013 passed a law to create a unified professional civil service, replacing 150 separate labour contracts. But four years later it had still not been implemented.

A third problem is that many countries have decentralised responsibility for broad swathes of government, such as education and health, without taking steps to create capable bureaucracies at the local level. With the exception of Brazil, regional and local governments have raised very little of their own revenue (though there was scope for them to impose higher property taxes, for example). Decentralisation has been a chequered experience, with examples of both excellence and misgovernment. One of the best known of the former is the Brazilian state of Ceará. When Tasso Jereissati, a young reformist from the PSDB, was elected governor in 1987, he broke with the corrupt, clientelistic pattern of government in Brazil's poor north-east.[20] He eliminated 40,000 jobs (out of a total payroll of 146,000) which were held by non-existent 'ghost' workers. At the same time, the state government launched a far-reaching community health programme and a successful drive for universal schooling. On the other hand, in Brazil the multiplication of municipalities has exercised a voracious claim on public finances. Since the 1988 constitution, more than a thousand new municipalities have been created, as local government became a growth industry. In Peru, many mayors have spent on bullrings or other ostentatious public works, but they have also invested in rural roads.

Improvements have often depended on individuals. In Colombia, first Bogotá and then Medellín became well known for effective municipal government. But Bogotá has declined in this century, under one corrupt and two ineffective mayors. Effective mayors come in many different guises. Take Guayaquil, Ecuador's largest city, a steamy port and, in the 1980s, a crime-ridden place, where the poor lived in huts built on mangrove swamps. It was transformed by the stewardship of Jaime Nebot. A fleshy, moustachioed man who was the political boss of the powerful Syrian-Lebanese community, he wore a large gold chain beneath his *guayabera* shirt. In 2015, he received visitors in the grand, marbled and frescoed municipal palace on the waterfront which dated from a cacao boom in the 1920s and which he had had restored. 'When I came into office it was falling down, used by vultures and [he said euphemistically] as a *garçonnière*.'[21] In his fourth term as mayor, he put his success down to efficient administration and responding to popular demands. He tarted up the waterfront, built new parks and a bus rapid-transit system, and replaced the slums in the swamps with housing developments for which the town hall offered mortgage subsidies. Having twice lost presidential elections, Nebot concentrated on being a city boss. Even those on the left, who originally saw him as corrupt and authoritarian, were positive about his recent record.

The fourth big problem is that government agencies are accustomed to operating in separate, vertical silos. Yet many of the most pressing policy tasks require different state agencies at all levels of government to act in a co-ordinated manner.

Sometimes all these flaws combine, as in the difficulty some governments have had in getting long-announced infrastructure projects moving on the ground. Three other failures of co-ordination are worth examining in detail: security and the rule of law; environmental management and the mitigation of climate change; and conflicts over extractive industries.

Legalism and lawlessness

Latin American societies have long suffered a paradox. From Iberian colonialism, they inherited a formalistic legalism. Yet this coexisted with widespread lawlessness. One manifestation of this paradox was the size of the informal economy. Another was that crime – and especially violent crime – became an epidemic in the region. Between 1995 and 2012, the annual murder rate oscillated between 20 and 25 per 100,000 people. Despite economic growth and social progress, it ended the period at 24.[22] In 2013, eight of the ten most violent countries in the world, and 42 of the 50 most violent cities, were in the region. Latin America and the Caribbean accounted for only 9 per cent of the world's population but 33 per cent of its murders. In the decade to 2010, more than a million Latin Americans died as a result of criminal violence, according to the UNDP. Robberies trebled in the 25 years to 2010; and six out of ten involved violence. Kidnapping was widespread in some countries. Extortion was a plague, preying on small businesses and preventing or deterring them from growing. A 2012 poll found that nearly two-thirds of respondents avoided going out at night for fear of crime, and one in eight had moved house in order to feel safer. The picture was not uniformly dark. Chileans were less likely to be murdered than inhabitants of the United States. Murder rates in different parts of Brazil varied as widely as they did in the region as a whole. But murders soared in Central America, Venezuela and Mexico, and increased from a low base in Peru.

No wonder polls showed that crime had replaced the economy as the main public concern. As well as forcing many people to change their habits and inflicting immeasurable human suffering, crime is a development problem. According to the IDB, the direct price of crime – income forgone by victims and prisoners, and private and public spending on security – costs the region 3.6 per cent of GDP per year: twice as much as in developed countries.[23] Above all, the crime epidemic represents a colossal failure of the state and of public policy.

There are several factors behind this. They include the pace of urbanisation and the economic dislocations of the 1980s and 1990s, and the bulge of young men in the population, as well as low wages and family breakdown. It was a troubling indictment of the schooling and vocational training systems that in 2015 more than 20 million young people (aged 15–24) were neither in education nor in work – they were known as *ni-nis*, for *ni estudia ni trabaja*.[24] The ubiquity of firearms meant that crime was often violent. A big factor was the rise of organised crime, much of it related to the drug trade. All of this interacted with the pervasive weakness and inefficiencies of the police, the prosecutors, the courts and the prisons. In other words, crime was so prevalent because those committing it knew they were unlikely to be apprehended. In 2011, the global rate for homicide convictions was 43 for every 100 murders; in Latin America it was close to 20.[25]

The police forces that democracy inherited in Latin America had in many cases historically been a subordinate branch of the armed forces.[26] In Brazil, for example, the main police force is known as the *polícia militar* (military police); though administered by the state governments, it is an auxiliary branch of the army, regulated by the defence ministry. This military connection meant that the police tended to use (sometimes lethal) force all too readily, and made reform more difficult.[27] In the past, the main job of police forces was to preserve political control and public order, rather than to prevent and detect crime. They served government rather than the public. Their professional status and salaries were low, training was inadequate, and corruption was common. In many countries, the police were feared and mistrusted: fewer than four out of ten respondents to Latinobarómetro, a regionwide poll, expressed any confidence in them.[28] As a result, many crimes were neither reported nor investigated. This mistrust was often justified. The police themselves were sometimes responsible for violent crime, or worked in complicity with criminals (the disappearance of the student teachers from Ayotzinapa in Mexico in 2014 was a notorious case). Reports by groups such as Human Rights Watch and Amnesty International regularly charted the use of deadly violence by police against civilians.

The instinctive response of many politicians and of public opinion to the rise in crime was *mano duro* (iron fist) policies. El Salvador, for example, made it an offence merely to belong to a gang, and incarcerated thousands of youths in overcrowded and out-of-control prisons. The murder rate soared, interrupted only by a brief gang truce, turning El Salvador into the world's most violent country.

Some citizens sought private solutions. The rich sometimes retreated to gated communities. Private security guards often rivalled the police in numbers. In Brazil, a proposal to ban the sale of guns and ammunition was defeated in a referendum in 2005. According to one estimate, there were perhaps 17 million guns in Brazil at that time, around half of them unregistered.[29] The poor sometimes took justice into their own hands: lynchings were not uncommon in Guatemala, rural Peru and Bolivia. Residents in some poor districts of Lima erected their own gates across their streets.

Vigilantism has a long history in the region. In Peru, peasant farmers formed vigilante patrols known as *rondas campesinas*. Originally a defence against rustlers, in the war against Sendero Luminoso in the 1980s and 1990s they were promoted by the armed forces as part of a successful counter-insurgency strategy. The most notorious example of vigilantism was the paramilitary armies in Colombia. Vigilantes appeared in Michoacán, in Mexico, in 2013, as farmers battled a drug mafia. By 2016, these 'self-defence' groups had spread to 20 of Mexico's 32 states, according to Eduardo Guerrero, a former security official.[30] The problem is that once such groups acquire armed power, they end up using it for private ends. Police, on or off duty, sometimes doubled as vigilantes. In Rio de Janeiro, militias of serving and former police and firemen controlled some *favelas*, preying on residents.

At the other extreme, Chile's *carabineros* were almost incorruptible. A Spaniard was arrested in February 2017 in Santiago for attempting to bribe a policeman who gave him a ticket for using his mobile phone while driving.

The region has seen many attempts at police reform. These have often involved a mixture of community policing, better wages and incentives, use of technology (such as the mapping of crime or closed-circuit cameras) and a focus on solving serious crimes, such as murders. In São Paulo city, such methods helped to cut the murder rate from 69 per 100,000 people in 1999 to 12 per 100,000 in 2011 (though it later edged up again). Improvement in Rio de Janeiro began later, with a 'pacification' policy for the *favelas*. This involved special forces evicting gang leaders, and then the setting up of community police stations, called Pacifying Police Units (UPPs) and staffed with newly recruited and specially trained police. Between 2008 and 2012, murders fell by 75 per cent in the pacified *favelas*. Sadly, the state government, beset by mismanagement and falling revenues, was unable to sustain the progress.

Like education, police reform was a long-term project and required high-level political commitment. There were enough successful experiments to indicate that it could be done. But success depended, too, on more effective prosecutors, courts and prisons. In Peru, for example, the attorney general was sacked in 2015 and investigated over allegations that he had colluded with an organised-crime ring that had gained control of a regional government and local prosecutors. Under pressure from aid donors, Guatemala in 2006 took the extraordinary step of outsourcing the investigation and prosecution of serious crime to a UN-backed body, the International Commission against Impunity in Guatemala (CICIG). It played a big role in the arrest of two former presidents, but its success will ultimately turn on whether it can make Guatemala's own institutions more effective.

Judiciaries tend to be archaic, venal and slow. Since the 1980s, nearly every Latin America country has attempted some kind of judicial reform. The aims have included increasing the independence and efficiency of the judiciary, modernising the legal system, widening access to the law and improving respect for human rights. Yet these aims sometimes involved trade-offs: a more independent judiciary may be less efficient and more corrupt, for example. Reform was most effective at the top: supreme courts in countries such as Argentina, Brazil and Mexico became more independent and more professional, dealing with fewer, more important cases than in the past. In Colombia, a Constitutional Court created under a new constitution in 1991 developed sweeping powers of judicial review. Access to justice in the region was broadened by mechanisms such as *defensorías del pueblo* (ombudsman's offices), which were set up in 15 countries. Several countries, including Mexico, replaced the Napoleonic system of written evidence with oral, adversarial trials. Much was claimed for this change, but it is not clear whether in itself it will improve the quality of justice.

The last and most degraded link in the criminal justice chain was Latin America's notoriously brutal and overcrowded prison system. In 2012, the murder rate in the region's prisons was three times higher than among the general population.[31] Brazil's prisons were perhaps the worst of all: in 2011 its jails held 515,000 inmates, around two-thirds more than their nominal capacity. In Brazil, as in several other countries, around half of prisoners have not been convicted of any offence. Many jails are in practice run by criminal gangs; unsurprisingly, recidivism rates are high. Yet there have been attempts at prison reform. The most promising was in the Dominican Republic. There, more than half the country's jails have been turned into Correctional and Rehabilitation Centres, which focus on educating and rehabilitating their charges. It works: in 2013, the reoffending rate of former inmates was just 2.6 per cent, extremely low by international standards.[32]

But if there is one country that stands out for having gone furthest towards imposing the rule of law in the face of enormous obstacles, it is Colombia.

'Lead or silver'

Enrique Low Murtra wanted nothing more than to leave his job as Colombia's justice minister to open a law office and return to his previous career as a university teacher. 'I would like to imagine that vengeance is not eternal. To be exiled, like Scipio, from one's own country seems to me to be an injustice', he said.[33] A gentle, avuncular man who had once been a Supreme Court judge, he was still only 49. He spoke softly as the rain pattered down outside his office in a colonial mansion in Bogotá in March 1988. But he would indeed suffer exile – and worse. Two months earlier, on the instruction of Colombia's president, Virgilio Barco, Low Murtra had signed warrants for the arrest and extradition to the United States on drugs charges of the five leading members of the Medellín 'cartel'.[34] They included Pablo Escobar, perhaps the world's most ruthless and notorious drug baron. Faced with constant death threats, the minister sent his daughter out of the country. 'Even going for a haircut has become a problem', he said. So intense did the threats become that in July 1988, Barco sent Low Murtra to Switzerland as ambassador. That did not save him. In 1991, he was back in Colombia, working – as he had hoped – as a law professor at the University of La Salle. No longer in government service, he had no bodyguards. He was gunned down at the entrance to the university.[35]

Drug violence hit Colombia earlier and harder than anywhere else, interacting with political violence to the point that the survival of the democratic state seemed imperilled. The drug trade had begun quietly in the 1970s, with marijuana and then cocaine (derived from the leaves of coca, a hardy shrub long grown in the Andes). Few people in Colombia bothered much until the traffickers began to use their cocaine wealth to go into politics. Pablo Escobar, who had begun life as a car thief and small-time hoodlum, became the alternate to a Liberal congressman. A reformist faction of the Liberal Party, led by Luis Carlos Galán, denounced the infiltration of 'hot money' into politics. When Rodrigo Lara Bonilla, a member of Galán's group, was appointed justice minister in 1983, he started cracking down on the drug trade, with enthusiastic support from the US embassy. He denounced Escobar by name in a session of Congress. Weeks later, Lara Bonilla was shot dead by a hired assassin on a motorbike, as he was being driven in his ministerial car in Bogotá.[36]

This was the start of ten years of warfare of terrifying intensity by the Medellín drug mob against the Colombian state and others they saw as a threat to their business. The victims included judges, politicians and journalists, as well as hundreds of policemen and ordinary Colombians. The carnage reached a crescendo in 1989, when three presidential candidates (including Galán, the likely winner) were murdered and an Avianca jet with more than a hundred passengers on board was blown up in mid-flight between Bogotá and Cali. The country's politicians had had enough: the Constituent Assembly, called into being to reform Colombia's constitution, voted to ban extradition – the fate most feared by the traffickers. The new government of César Gaviria negotiated the surrender of Escobar and his henchmen. But after 13 months in comfortable confinement near Medellín, Escobar escaped hours before he was to be moved to a maximum-security jail. After a desperate manhunt lasting 16 months and involving half a dozen different US government agencies, Escobar was finally cornered and killed in Medellín in December 1993.

Escobar famously offered those who stood in his way the choice of *plomo o plata* (lead or silver), a bullet or a bribe. Either way, the rule of law was the loser. The drug trade enveloped Colombian democracy in violence and corruption. To defeat Escobar, the Colombian state recruited some dubious allies. These included not just his foes in the Cali drug mob, who were less flamboyant and more businesslike than their counterparts in Medellín. They also encompassed a criminal gang called *Los Pepes* (short for 'people persecuted' by Pablo Escobar), whose leaders included the brothers Fidel and Carlos Castaño, who would become leaders of the United Self-Defence Forces of Colombia (AUC), as the umbrella group of right-wing paramilitaries was known.[37]

The demand for illegal drugs, and especially cocaine, in the United States – and later in Europe and elsewhere – brought into being vast and powerful organised crime networks. Drugs began to be sold and consumed within Latin America as well. Brazil became the world's second-largest consumer of cocaine, after the United States; Argentina was a big consumer, too. Drug traffickers began to pay their local foot soldiers in product, which stimulated local consumption markets. Many of those recruits were drawn from the army of *ni-nis*. They followed the logic of a Mexican saying: 'Better five years living like a king than 50 years like an ox.' Cocaine was at the heart of an illegal drug business in the Americas worth perhaps as much as $150 billion a year – half as much again as the size of the economy of Ecuador.[38] Production of heroin and of synthetic drugs, such as methamphetamines, became increasingly important, especially in Mexico.

Richard Nixon was the first American president to declare a 'war on drugs'. But this only got serious under George H.W. Bush, after an explosive increase in the use of crack cocaine in the United States.[39] In 1989, in a televised speech to the nation, he singled out cocaine as 'our most serious problem'. He committed the US armed forces, whose commanders were seeking a new role after the end of the Cold War, to this new battle. He offered unprecedented amounts of aid to the Andean countries. And he urged upon them a three-pronged strategy of the eradication of coca fields; the use of the security forces to interdict processing facilities and trafficking routes; and 'alternative development' of legal crops in or near drug-producing areas.

Almost three decades and several billions of dollars later, the drug warriors could point to a series of tactical victories, in particular places at particular times. But the flow of cocaine was never seriously interrupted, and its street price in the United States, having fallen in the 1980s and early 1990s, has remained more or less constant since.[40] That is partly because of productivity improvements in coca growing (such as high-density planting) and refining.

The prohibition of cocaine and other drugs has meant that their retail price is determined by risk, rather than by the cost of production. Most of the mark-up occurs once the cocaine enters the United States or Europe – because law enforcement is tighter and the risk is thus greater. So even if repression in the producer countries succeeds in increasing coca leaf prices, this has little effect on cocaine prices. The effect of prohibition on the price means that drugs generate superprofits, which are accumulated by mafias. To defend those profits, they deploy armed power, which challenges the monopoly of force, which should be a hallmark of the state. And they seek to corrupt the agents of the state. They have been aided by the ease with which they can purchase semi-automatic weapons legally in US gun shops. Secondly, repression of the drug trade has had the effect of spreading it, in what analysts call 'the balloon effect'.

Both the drug trade and the American-sponsored 'war' against it have been very costly for Latin America. American aid has been feeble in relation to the scale of the problem. Involving the armed forces and the police in fighting the drug trade has sometimes corrupted them. It has also drawn resources away from other priorities, such as citizen security. Democratic governments have used heavy-handed repression of peasants, who have been trying to earn a better living by growing coca. Such repression has sometimes produced a nationalist reaction: the rise of Evo Morales to Bolivia's presidency owed much to the American insistence on eradicating coca.

As the balloon effect took hold, so local factors became accelerators for organised crime. In Central America, for example, in the aftermath of the civil wars of the 1970s and 1980s, both guns and unemployed young males were plentiful. In addition, youth gangs (known as *maras*) emerged in the 1980s among the children of Central Americans who had migrated to Los Angeles to escape war and poverty at home.[41] In the 1990s, some of these youths began to return to Central America. They took the gangs with them – to El Salvador, Guatemala and Honduras, in particular. Though they began as small, neighbourhood outfits, they gradually merged with organised crime. As territorial control became central to the modus operandi of the drug mafias, the *maras* became their partners and agents.

The damage to the social fabric wrought by the drug traffickers and the gangs was immense. Take Eduardo (not his real name), a young Guatemalan whose family returned from the United States when he was eight. His father's tattoos marked out his *mara* past; a rival gang killed him outside their home. To avenge his death, Eduardo joined his father's gang as a *sicario* (hitman) and killed the murderer. Interviewed in 2011, he carried the scar of a bullet on his chest and his beaten right arm hung limply by his side. He was trying to make a life, studying computing. His prospects were uncertain.[42]

Or take Rosario, which has become Argentina's drug entrepôt, as well as its agribusiness capital. Traffickers bring Bolivian and Peruvian cocaine down the Paraná river from Paraguay to export it from Rosario's wharves to Europe. Surrounding the city are the *villas*, the poor districts that are home to tens of thousands of migrants from Argentina's poor northern provinces. Interviewed in 2015, Gabriel Chumpitaz, a local councillor for Mauricio Macri's PRO party, reckoned that in the *villas* some 80,000 residents had become consumers of *paco* (cheap, semi-processed cocaine), many of them 9–15-year-olds. In 7 de Septiembre, a *villa* of one-storey houses and huts, Debora Ledesma, a tall 18-year-old school drop-out training to be a football referee, complained that the *bunker* (as drug sales points were called) on her street functioned 24 hours a day, offering 'home delivery'. A fortnight before, 'they killed a boy two blocks from my home at 6.00 p.m.', she said. Buses had stopped going to the area in the evenings. Rosario had the highest murder rate in Argentina. In a traditionally well-governed province, organised crime penetrated the police. In 2013, in an incident that shocked the country, hitmen fired a dozen gunshots at the home of the provincial governor. 'Rosarinos have changed their habits. They stay at home. They've lost their freedom', said Chumpitaz.[43]

Some Latin Americans (though not Macri) began to call for the legalisation of drugs. The pioneers were three former presidents: Fernando Henrique Cardoso of Brazil, Ernesto Zedillo of Mexico and Colombia's César Gaviria. They were joined by two sitting presidents, Juan Manuel Santos of Colombia and Otto Pérez Molina of Guatemala (though he later resigned over corruption charges). José Mujica of Uruguay went a step further, pushing through a law which legalised and regulated the production and consumption of marijuana. Its legalisation in several US states meant Mexico might follow. But hard drugs were where most of the money was, and drug gangs had anyway diversified into extortion and other illegal businesses. And the profits to be had from cocaine provided a ready source of cash for illegal armed groups.

Democratic security in Colombia

At first glance, San Vicente del Caguán looked like any other small cattle town on the fringes of the Amazon basin. On its stiflingly hot, bustling streets, lined with half-finished houses of concrete and brick, Japanese pick-ups and motorbikes jostled with horse-drawn carts. From early afternoon, Mexican *rancheras* blared out from the loudspeakers of the numerous brothels. What made San Vicente unusual in 2001 was the presence in the main square of a small office of the FARC – the Revolutionary Armed Forces of Colombia, the largest and longest-lasting leftist guerrilla army in Latin America.[44] For three years, the government of Andrés Pastrana allowed the FARC to control a Switzerland-sized swathe of mountains, jungle and grassland around San Vicente. The FARC had demanded this 'demilitarised zone' as a condition for getting peace talks going. But the talks made little progress. The FARC used them for propaganda purposes. They held public hearings on how to reduce unemployment, while carrying on their war with increasing savagery.

That war began in the 1960s, but underwent several changes in character. The FARC's origins lay in peasant self-defence groups organised by the pro-Moscow Communist Party during the conflict between Liberals and Conservatives in the 1950s, known as *la violencia*. Even in 2001, most of the FARC's guerrillas were of peasant origin, according to Alfonso Cano, who was in charge of political affairs in its ruling secretariat.[45] The FARC combined peasant stubbornness with narrow, provincial dogmatism. Its longstanding leader, Manuel Marulanda (known as '*Tirofijo*' or 'Sureshot'), who died in 2008, was not known to have visited any city larger than Neiva (population: 250,000) in southern Colombia. Though the FARC was nominally the military wing of the Colombian Communist Party, it quickly came to dominate the party: it imposed its doctrines of 'prolonged popular war' (learned from the Vietnamese) and the 'combination of all forms of struggle' (i.e. military action plus legal politics) on the party, which has shrivelled into insignificance. As it recruited in the cities, the FARC also began to espouse 'Bolivarianism', a gaseous populist nationalism copied from Hugo Chávez.

The FARC's original justifications for its armed struggle were land and opposition to the power-sharing pact between Liberals and Conservatives known as the National Front, which ended *la violencia*. Yet Colombia had long been mainly urban; the power-sharing pact ended formally in 1974 (and in practice in 1986); and the country's democracy was the subject of almost continuous political reform. Peace agreements saw three small guerrilla groups lay down their arms in 1990–91 – but not the FARC or the ELN, its smaller rival of originally Guevarist inspiration. A new constitution followed in 1991, designed to open up politics to new parties and to decentralise power. The FARC had taken part in peace talks launched by President Belisario Betancur (1982–86) and set up a political party called the Unión Patriótica. This won 4.5 per cent of the vote in the 1986 presidential election. But over the next five years, more than a thousand of its members were murdered, including two of its presidential candidates. Most were killed by the right-wing paramilitaries, who at the time had close links with some army commanders. The FARC cited this as proof that it was excluded from democracy. But its opponents noted that, while appearing to accept democracy, it had held a clandestine congress, at which it had agreed to build up its army during the truce under Betancur, with the aim of seizing power militarily.[46] For that reason, some army commanders opposed Betancur's orders for a ceasefire and the release of guerrilla prisoners, and began to work with the paramilitaries. The FARC also got into the drug business in a big way, as well as into extortion and kidnapping. By 2001, the best estimates were that it was making $250–300 million a year from drugs (while its paramilitary foes were making perhaps $200 million).[47] In a lengthy interview with the author, Cano admitted that the FARC received money from *retenciones* (i.e. kidnappings). When asked about drug income, he said this was 'everywhere in the world economy'.[48]

By the 1990s, the FARC's actions had much more to do with plunder and a self-sustaining militarism than with social grievances. Drug money helped the FARC to expand greatly, from perhaps 5,000 fighters in the early 1980s to a peak of around 20,000 in 2002. In the mid-1990s, the FARC began to operate in larger units. It inflicted several humiliating defeats on the armed forces, in which small detachments were overrun by forces of several hundred guerrillas, and some 500 police and troops were taken prisoner. The guerrillas also launched devastatingly inaccurate and bloody home-made mortar attacks on small towns, as well as frequent sabotage attacks against infrastructure. They would erect roadblocks on main highways, abducting motorists for ransom. The armed forces were far too small and too immobile to respond effectively.

The growth of the FARC was possible because of the weakness of the security forces and of the state – the flip side of Colombia's aversion to militarism and its tradition of civilian government. The relative impotence of the army prompted an expansion in the guerrillas' polar opposite, the AUC paramilitaries. 'The AUC exists because [the] armed forces have not done their institutional duty of guaranteeing lives, property and honour', Carlos Castaño, one of its leaders, told the *Washington Post*.[49] The paramilitaries proceeded to act with even greater savagery than the FARC. They used terror to control territory, massacring groups of villagers whom they held to be collaborating with the guerrillas. Trade-union leaders were targeted, partly because of the past enthusiasm of some of them for armed struggle.[50] So were human-rights workers. Journalists and social scientists were the targets of both the AUC and the FARC. By the late 1990s, the government's writ extended over only about half of rural Colombia. Insecurity began to affect the hitherto vigorous economy: combined with the new constitution's fiscal liberality, that triggered a sharp recession in 1999, and unemployment climbed to 20 per cent. A million or so Colombians moved abroad in the late 1990s. There were widespread fears that Colombia was on the way to becoming a failed state.

When Pastrana, a personable former television news anchor from a prominent Conservative family, was elected president in 1998, he took two important decisions. One was to open peace talks with the FARC. The other was to seek a strategic alliance with the United States. He was more successful in the second of these. Under Plan Colombia, drawn up jointly by Colombian and American officials, the United States granted Colombia about $10 billion in mainly military aid between 1999 and 2015. Most of this went on some 70 helicopters and the training and equipping of new army battalions. The aim was to fight the guerrillas (and the paramilitaries) by fighting drugs, and so squeeze their finances.

While the state was strengthening its defences, so was the FARC. Its politics were remarkably intransigent. Not for it the compromises with democracy made by the Central American guerrillas of the 1970s and 1980s. 'Our struggle is to do away with the state as it now exists in Colombia, preferably by political means, but if they don't let us then we have to carry on shooting', Cano told me in 2001. The FARC would not demobilise in return for 'houses, cars and scholarships' or a few seats in Congress. 'This country will be saved when we have the chance to run the state', he claimed.[51] To that end, even as it supposedly talked peace, the FARC carried on its war, recruiting and staging brazen kidnappings. Colombians became disillusioned with a 'peace process' that wasn't. In 2002, with an election looming, Pastrana called off the talks and sent the army back to San Vicente and its environs. The talks had served only one purpose. They 'allowed the country and the world to see the government's willingness to seek a negotiated settlement, and the opposition to democracy of the insurgents', as General Fernando Tapias, the armed forces commander, put it.[52]

The presidential election saw a crushing victory for Álvaro Uribe Vélez. A lawyer and Liberal former governor of Antioquia, the economically important area around Medellín, Uribe was an austere, intense figure. His father, a cattle farmer, had been kidnapped and murdered by the FARC. He seemed to believe that he was a man of destiny: he promised that he would be 'the first soldier of Colombia' and would double the size of the security forces. In normal times, this uncompromising message would have been electorally unattractive in Colombia, a country whose mainstream politics were moderate, consensual and mistrustful of a powerful state. But these were not normal times. Uribe, running as an independent, captured the national mood. He would govern for eight years.

Uribe's 'democratic security' policy involved a big military build-up, financed in part by a new wealth tax. The armed forces expanded steadily, from some 150,000 to 270,000 by 2015. Uribe continued the job Pastrana had begun of turning a conscript army into a salaried, professional force. The government bought its own large fleet of Blackhawk helicopters and Brazilian-made Super Tucano ground-attack aircraft, equipped with US-supplied laser-guided bombs. Uribe placed permanent police detachments in 150 municipalities (of a total of 1,100) which had lacked them. He created a force of some 20,000 part-time 'peasant soldiers' (later renamed 'popular soldiers') for local guard duties. He also turned the army into an offensive force, creating nine new mobile brigades and six new mountain battalions, which occupied the high Andean massifs that had served as transit corridors and strategic refuges for the FARC. All this was micro-managed by the president himself. He recounted with glee to visitors that his Friday-night relaxation was to stay at his desk until 2.00 a.m., ringing police and army commanders across the country to quiz them about security in their areas.[53] Each weekend he would set off to remote towns or villages and hold public meetings to discuss local problems.

The army build-up changed the strategic balance of the war. The FARC were driven from much of central Colombia, forced back to remote jungles and to operating in smaller groups. Several thousand guerrillas deserted, individually or in small groups. According to intelligence estimates, the FARC's total strength, including lightly armed support militia, fell from 40,000 in 2000 to fewer than 18,000 by 2013. In 2000, more than half of Colombia's municipalities suffered terrorist actions and/or the presence of illegal armed groups. By 2012, only 11 per cent of municipalities were affected.[54] For the first time, the army tracked down and killed senior FARC commanders, including Cano in 2011. Three years earlier, the armed forces had bombed a camp just over the border in Ecuador, killing Raúl Reyes, Marulanda's secretary, and seized his laptop computer. In response, Ecuador's Rafael Correa and Venezuela's Hugo Chávez, broke off diplomatic relations (they were restored in 2010). Files on the laptop confirmed that the FARC enjoyed close and co-operative relations with Chávez's government in Venezuela.[55]

The weakening of the FARC enabled Uribe's government to persuade the paramilitaries to demobilise. The terms on which they did so were controversial. Under the Justice and Peace Law approved in 2005, those of their leaders who were accused of crimes against humanity were required to give an account of their actions and, if convicted in the courts, would face a reduced sentence of no more than eight years' confinement in a special facility (perhaps a prison farm). The government also had a powerful lever over those of the AUC leaders who were wanted on drugs charges in the United States: it would suspend extradition only while they co-operated. Officials argued that the law was a reasonable compromise between peace and justice, given that the paramilitaries had not been militarily defeated. Uribe insisted that the AUC chiefs would not be able to get away with intentional omissions in their statements, because the government 'has made visible those involved in atrocities'.[56] But human-rights groups complained that the law was too lenient in not requiring a binding confession and in not ensuring that the paramilitaries dismantled their criminal networks. Colombia's Constitutional Court agreed: it put more teeth into the law, requiring full confessions on pain of forfeiting reduced sentences. Whatever its imperfections, the process quickly appeared to acquire momentum. In late 2006, 57 paramilitary leaders were jailed pending court hearings.

Uribe took the same tough approach to the drug issue as he did to security. With American support, he unleashed a massive programme of aerial spraying of coca fields with glyphosate, a weedkiller. According to measurements by the United Nations Office on Drugs and Crime, by 2004 the area under coca had fallen to half its 1999 peak (before drifting up again thereafter). The spraying was controversial; in 2006, the government switched tactics, and put more emphasis on manual eradication and on the development of alternative economic activities.

Predictably, Plan Colombia had proved to be far more effective as a counter-insurgency plan than as an anti-drug plan, though it had been sold to the American public as the latter.

Uribe's democratic security policy certainly made Colombia a safer place. The murder rate fell steadily, as did kidnappings. The main roads became safe to travel again. Greater security brought a boom in investment and economic growth. His supporters saw Uribe as the saviour of his country. Most Colombians tended to that view: in opinion polls, respondents regularly gave the president an approval rating of 60–75 per cent. His popularity and political success allowed him to persuade Congress to change the constitution to allow him to stand for a second consecutive term. In a country that had historically been deeply suspicious of an over-mighty executive, that was perhaps his most surprising achievement. In 2006, he was duly elected with a thumping 62 per cent of the vote.

But there was a dark side to Uribe's achievements. His obsessive insistence on eliminating the FARC led his army commanders to reward units for their 'kill rate'. Some responded by rounding up unemployed youths, murdering them and passing their corpses off as dead guerrillas, in cases known as 'false positives'. Several hundred army officers and troops would, in due course, be found guilty of these crimes in civilian courts. 'It's a matter that's difficult to understand', admitted Luis Carlos Villegas, who was appointed as defence minister in 2015. He said it was 'unacceptable', and attributed it to the rapid expansion in the security forces and the pressure for results.[57] During Uribe's presidency, investigations by journalists and prosecutors began to lay bare the penetration of politics and of state institutions by the paramilitaries. The former head of the civilian intelligence agency from 2002 to 2005 was found guilty of collaborating with the AUC. The Supreme Court would eventually convict more than 30 politicians of collusion with the paramilitaries. Nearly all were allies of Uribe; one, Mario Uribe, was the president's cousin. Investigations revealed that in some areas of the Caribbean coast, in particular, the paramilitaries had seized control of local politics, murdering, intimidating or bribing those who stood in their way. They used that control to extort commissions from public contracts. They also controlled much of the drug trade in the area. Contrary to the claims of the left, there was no evidence that the president was personally linked to the paramilitaries. However, he was sometimes guilty of poor judgement in his choice of friends and collaborators. Uribe insisted that the scandals were only coming out because of the climate of greater security and because of the demobilisation of the paramilitaries, and the investigations under the Justice and Peace Law. There was some truth in that.

The man of destiny had strengthened the authority of the democratic state. But by seeking a second term, he had vested that authority in himself. He tried to get a third term, but his government had alienated the judiciary by spying on judges. This time the Constitutional Court baulked. Uribe gave grudging support in the 2010 election to Juan Manuel Santos, a Liberal grandee who had been his defence minister between 2006 and 2009.

Peace, at a controversial price

Elected on a platform of consolidating Uribe's security achievements and placing more stress on jobs, in office Santos dedicated himself to seeking a peace agreement with the FARC. Behind that lay a double judgement: that the FARC was sufficiently weakened that it would accept democracy, but that it was still sufficiently strong that a military solution to the conflict implied many more years of fighting and more deaths and destruction. From the outset, the new talks were very different from those Pastrana had held. There was no ceasefire, no 'demilitarised zone'. Negotiations took place in Havana, in private sessions and following a tight six-point agenda drawn up in secret preliminary talks, whose sole aim was a 'final agreement for the end of the conflict'.[58] The FARC had abandoned Cano's vision of taking power and imposing communism.

Fairly swiftly, the two sides reached agreement on rural development, including measures to broaden access to land and to issue legal title to all rural properties. This, said Santos, was 'what the countryside needs; we have to do this with or without the FARC'.[59] Both sides agreed to a joint effort to tackle drug-trafficking, as well as a voluntary, community-based programme for replacing coca with legal alternatives, backed up by manual eradication. In 2015, Santos suspended aerial spraying of coca, after the World Health Organization issued a (disputed) ruling classifying glyphosate as a possible carcinogen. The government also set in train an elaborate scheme to compensate the victims of the conflict with cash payments and other help. It flew groups of them to Havana, where in emotional scenes they confronted the FARC.

The talks got bogged down for more than a year over the most difficult issues: whether the FARC's leaders would face punishment of some kind, and on what terms they would give up their weapons and become a political party. The government negotiators pushed hard for at least some of the FARC commanders to accept confinement in a facility resembling a prison. There were two reasons for their insistence. First, Colombia was a signatory to the Rome Statute, which set up the International Criminal Court and international law no longer accepts blanket amnesties (of the kind Colombia had offered the M-19 and others in the 1980s). Secondly, public opinion was deeply hostile to and suspicious of the FARC, because of their terrorist bombings, kidnappings and appalling treatment of their hostages, some of whom spent years chained to trees in jungle camps.

In the end, a compromise was struck. Guerrilla commanders accused of crimes against humanity would have to appear before a special peace tribunal. Provided they confessed to their crimes at the outset, they would receive five to eight years of community service, with 'effective restrictions on liberty' but nothing resembling a jail. Similar terms would apply to military officers accused of war crimes. Another part of the agreement set aside five seats in each house of Congress for the FARC's future political party for the next two elections. It also created 16 additional seats in areas battered by the conflict, where only locals would be able to run.

Opponents led by Uribe denounced the agreement as granting the FARC immunity for their crimes and a free pass to Congress. The former president accused Santos of handing the country over to '*castrochavismo*'. The government's peace negotiators replied that the FARC were being held to account in a court of law, and that the agreement marked a new international benchmark for trying to reconcile the contradictory demands of peace and justice in conflict resolution. Many victims' organisations accepted this argument. Uribe's Justice and Peace Law had granted similar terms to the paramilitaries. But the agreement exposed a misunderstanding. Many Colombians believed the talks were, in essence, about the FARC's surrender. The guerrillas had other ideas: their commanders repeatedly pointed out that no guerrilla army had negotiated peace only for its leaders to go straight to jail. 'This is the best agreement that was possible', Santos insisted.[60]

Both the government, in organising a lavish peace ceremony, and the FARC, in its triumphalist statements claiming political victory, misjudged public opinion. Bucking the opinion polls, the agreement was narrowly defeated in a referendum in October 2016. It didn't help that a hurricane cut turnout on the Caribbean coast, which mainly voted 'Yes'. Those areas still suffering armed conflict backed the agreement. Yet – as with the UK's Brexit four months previously – voters used a referendum to express their contempt for a political elite which they saw as out of touch with their concerns. Santos, who was awarded the Nobel Peace Prize days after the referendum, hastily convened further talks with the opposition and the FARC. Six weeks later, he came up with a tweaked agreement. The most important changes were that the FARC's political party would get less public money and could not contest the 16 conflict-area congressional seats; the peace tribunal would be composed purely of Colombian, and not foreign, judges; and only provisions regarding international humanitarian law, and not the whole agreement, would be written into the constitution. Many of the other changes spelled out matters implied in the original accord, such as that the tribunal would define the place where convicted FARC leaders would be confined, and that this would not be much bigger than a village. The 'No' vote thus served to improve the agreement.

Santos did not risk another referendum. Over the protests of the *uribistas*, the revised agreement was approved by Colombia's Congress. That set the stage for the FARC fighters to gather in 23 designated areas, under UN supervision, where they were due to hand over their weapons and begin civilian life in the course of 2017. The real test of the effectiveness of the peace agreement will be on the ground, in a Colombia that is a world away from the niceties of Bogotá. As Sergio Jaramillo, Santos's peace commissioner, had warned during the talks: 'These negotiations are extraordinarily difficult, but not remotely as difficult as implementation will be.'[61]

From 'three Colombias' to one

Tumaco must once have been a kind of paradise. Built on two small islands in the glaucous shallows of a large bay on the Pacific, its beaches are watched over by frigate birds and pelicans. Today, its population of 115,000, mostly Afro-Colombians, lives in some of the most deprived conditions in Colombia. Yet bottles of Royal Salute 21-year-old whisky, priced at 500,000 pesos ($172) 'sell like water', according to a sales assistant in one of the town's liquor stores. The reason is to be found an hour's drive east, and a further hour's ride in a fast launch up the River Mira, past emerald-green coca fields on the southern bank. In September 2016, the ensign of the FARC – the national flag with an additional image of two AK-47 rifles crossed over a map of Colombia – was fluttering from a tall pole at the waterside when I visited El Playón, a clutch of huts and bars blasting out lilting *vallenato* music. For most of this century, the slice of land between the river and Ecuador was FARC territory. Under their aegis, coca cultivation surged in the Tumaco area from 1,800 hectares in 2000 to 16,900 hectares in 2015, or 17.5 per cent of the national total. Not only did the cocaine trade generate the demand for expensive whisky in Tumaco, but it drove a big increase in violence, as the FARC's militias in the town degenerated into *sicarios*. In 2015, they were in the process of switching their loyalty to the *Urabeños*, a criminal gang.[62]

Critics saw Santos's suspension of aerial spraying of coca as a concession to the FARC, and the peace agreement's commitment to paying compensation for coca eradication as an incentive to plant (the latter was true, though the depreciation of the peso in 2015 also stimulated what was mainly an export industry). Officials saw the agreement as a chance at last to crack down on the drug industry for good, by enlisting rural communities in that effort. In any event, since the suspension of spraying, coca cultivation had surged, occupying a record 188,000 hectares in 2016, according to surveys by the US government.[63] Santos's administration set an ambitious target of trying to wipe out more than half of the crop in 2017, with half of the reduction to come from voluntary agreements. Achieving this target depended on how quickly the government could start to meet its commitment to improve rural infrastructure and governance. It would not be easy.

There were 'three Colombias', according to the National Planning Department.[64] One, in the main cities, was a sophisticated place, with rapid economic growth and first-world social indicators. A second Colombia had seen social improvements, but lacked good jobs. The third, made up of 3 million people in places like Tumaco and its hinterland, lacked even basic services. Not coincidentally, this third Colombia was where the conflict had persisted. The task facing the Colombian state was to bring peace, justice, services and economic opportunity to these areas.

The conflict between the FARC, the state and the paramilitaries had imposed an enormous cost on the country. According to the National Centre for Historical Memory, a public body set up by Santos, around 220,000 people were killed as a result of it between 1958 and 2012. Four out of five were civilians. Violence, or the fear of it, helped to dislodge more than 6 million Colombians from their homes, mainly in the countryside. The conflict reinforced inequalities. The peace agreement with the FARC did not quite end it: the ELN remained an irritant, while the *Urabeños* and two other drug gangs that were heirs to the paramilitaries comprised perhaps 5,000 people, 2,000 of them armed.[65] The immediate task for the security forces was to prevent them from moving into the vacuum left by the FARC's demobilisation, and then to subject them to the rule of law.

Since the dark days of Escobar, Colombia had become a much safer country. The murder rate dropped steadily, from 78 per 100,000 people in 1991 to 24.4 per 100,000 in 2016. The figures in Medellín over the same period showed an even more dramatic improvement – from 386 per 100,000 to 18 per 100,000 (in 2014). As well as the security build-up, better policing had much to do with that. Óscar Naranjo, an outstanding police commander, introduced a national community policing plan. In Medellín, the national trend was reinforced when Sergio Fajardo, a mathematician, was elected mayor in 2003 and invested in urban projects designed to bridge the city's socio-economic divide, such as cable cars connecting shanty towns to the metro and new public libraries and day nurseries in poorer areas. One of his successors, Aníbal Gaviria, worked with the police and prosecutors to create well-equipped specialist task forces to investigate murders.

Yet there were still worries. Colombia was able to tackle many of the threats it had faced because it enjoyed political consensus and relatively strong institutions. The feud between Uribe and Santos ruptured the consensus and prompted a poisonous polarisation. And allegations of politicisation undermined the credibility of the judiciary, while claims of corruption weakened the standing of politicians. Much thus depends on the new government, to be elected in 2018. Apart from peace, other issues will claim its attention. One was tragically highlighted when flooding and mudslides killed more than 300 people in Mocoa, the capital of Putumayo department, in March 2017. Santos blamed the disaster on erratic weather caused by climate change. That is a challenge that faces many Latin American governments.

Rivers of doubt

In December 2014, 11,000 delegates and activists descended on a tent city erected in the grounds of Peru's defence ministry in Lima for the twentieth round of UN climate negotiations. In two weeks of talking, they agreed the framework for what, a year later in Paris, would become the first global agreement to restrict greenhouse gas emissions, in a bid to limit the rise in temperatures to no more than 2 degrees above pre-industrial levels by 2050. The Paris agreement depends on voluntary, but peer-pressured, national commitments; it is backed by a UN Green Climate Fund aimed at helping poor countries mitigate the effects of climate change. There has been widespread scepticism, both as to whether the Paris agreement is enough, and whether it will be complied with (it has not helped that Donald Trump quickly disavowed US commitments and moved to dismantle clean energy policies). Nevertheless, over the past few years Latin America has emerged as an important protagonist in the global talks.

That is partly because the region is acutely vulnerable to climate change. The combination of deforestation, warming and less rainfall poses a risk that parts of the Amazon rainforest could dry out, becoming vulnerable to fire and dieback and turning into savannah. Rapid melting of glaciers in the Andes increases the risk of both drought and flooding, since they act as natural regulators of water flow, as well as affecting hydroelectric generation. Low-lying areas in the Caribbean basin are vulnerable to rising sea levels. Since the 1990s, stronger storms and other weather-related natural disasters have become more frequent. All this has an impact on human lives and livelihoods, as well as on economic growth.[66] In the early months of 2017 alone, in addition to the Mocoa disaster, Chile endured its worst-ever forest fires. And Peru suffered a 'coastal El Niño' weather event, prompted by intense localised warming of the ocean: in weeks of heavy rains and mudslides, 113 people were killed, 180,000 homes were rendered uninhabitable, and 242 bridges and more than 2,500 kilometres of highway were damaged.[67] Perhaps not surprisingly, Latin Americans show more awareness of climate change than people anywhere else. In polling by the Pew Research Center, 77 per cent of respondents in Latin America believed that climate change is already harming the world, compared with 60 per cent in Europe and 41 per cent in the United States.[68]

Latin America contributes around 9.5 per cent of global emissions, slightly more than its proportion of the world's population. The lion's share of this comes from deforestation and land-use changes. The region stands out as being the first part of the developing world to have accepted responsibility for contributing to reducing emissions. In 2008, Peru was the first developing country to promise a voluntary cut, pledging to stop deforestation (net of new planting) by 2021; Brazil promised to cut emissions by 36 per cent below their trend by 2020; Mexico passed a law aimed at reducing emissions by 30 per cent by 2020; and at the Lima summit, the countries of the Pacific Alliance, a trade group comprising Chile, Colombia, Mexico and Peru, made a donation to the Green Climate Fund.

Not all the region is behind this effort. Venezuela, Bolivia and Cuba regard the job of slowing climate change as the responsibility of developed countries. But they have become increasingly isolated. Not for nothing have two Latin American women in succession – Christiana Figueres of Costa Rica and Patricia Espinosa of Mexico – been charged with leading the world's efforts, as executive directors of the UN Framework Convention on Climate Change.[69]

Promises are one thing; their implementation is another. The Amazon is the world's largest 'carbon sink', absorbing greenhouse gases. For most of the past century, it has been seen by Brazil and its neighbours as a resource to be developed and plundered. But as Brazilians have become city dwellers, so more of them have come to value environmental conservation. Over the past quarter-century, the country has put in place the tools to preserve the rainforest. Brazil has the capacity to monitor deforestation in real time, using satellites and aerial reconnaissance. It has designated 42 per cent of the forest as protected areas, either as indigenous reserves or natural parks. As Lula's environment minister between 2003 and 2008, Marina Silva, the child of Amazonian rubber-tappers, oversaw tougher enforcement of the law against deforestation. Government agencies and NGOs promoted sustainable management of the forest and its resources. But it was a constant battle: deforestation fell sharply from the mid-1990s to 2013, but then edged up again, partly because of the knock-on effect of recession. Governments in the other Amazonian countries have been far less effective than Brazil in managing their segments of forest. Landowners and their political allies have fought attempts to protect the environment. According to one count, more than half of the 185 killings of environmental activists worldwide in 2015 took place in Latin America.[70]

The outlook is more promising for clean energy. Mainly because of the weight of hydroelectricity in the matrix, in 2014 Latin America produced 53 per cent of its electricity from renewable sources, compared with a world average of 22 per cent. For almost seven months in 2016, Costa Rica ran purely on renewable power, putting it on track to meet its target of zero net emissions by 2021. Uruguay came close to that, too.

Alternative energy, such as wind, solar and geothermal, accounts for only around 2 per cent of total generation (compared with a world average of 6 per cent), but the figure is growing fast. Countries such as Chile, Brazil, Mexico and Argentina have tweaked their regulations to encourage alternative energy without offering subsidies. Nature has endowed Latin America with much sun and wind. It is starting to make the most of it. El Romero, the largest solar-energy plant in the region and one of the dozen biggest in the world, began generation in 2016. Its 775,000 grey solar panels stretch across the undulating plateau of the Atacama desert in northern Chile, benefiting from an average of 320 days of sunshine a year.[71]

While trying to limit future emissions, governments have had to deal with the reality of a changing climate. It is a task for which they are not well equipped. For example, Peru's government set aside $1 billion to invest in strengthening roads, bridges and river defences ahead of an expected El Niño in 2015–16. When the event did not occur, much of the money was diverted to other uses, or regional governments failed to carry out projects. Replacing the roads and bridges damaged in 2017 will cost $2.6 billion, according to the government.[72] Many of the homes lost were built illegally in river valleys, which are usually dry but are subject to occasional flooding.

By employing strict enforcement of building codes, Chile has managed to reduce deaths from earthquakes. The rest of the region needs to do the same with regard to enforcing planning restrictions in flood plains. In Peru, scientists predict that climate change will lead to more rainfall on the north coast (a desert) and more drought further south. Ecological conditions are changing (not always for the worse): potatoes are growing at ever-higher altitudes; coffee cultivation is likely to move northwards; plagues and crop losses will increase. One duty of government is to provide information to farmers. Another is to mitigate the impact of changes in rainfall patterns on the fragile ecology of the Andes.

The retreat of glaciers is a visible symbol of climate change. Peru is the site of 70 per cent of the world's tropical glaciers, but it has lost a third since the 1980s. However, high-altitude lakes and wetlands (known as *bofedales*) are more important for the regularity of water flow, and thus for farming. Sustaining those requires an integrated approach to water use and management. Take the valley of the River Cañete, which reaches the Pacific 150 kilometres south of Lima. Its broad lower reaches are given over to irrigated commercial farming – of maize, avocados, asparagus, artichokes and grapes. In its middle course, the river flows past Lunahuaná, an attractive grape-growing town whose tourist attractions include freshwater crayfish and white-water rafting. Above the town, the road narrows to a single lane, clinging to ledges on steep mountainsides or threading its way through canyons where telluric forces have assembled jumbles of boulders. By kilometre 150, the road has climbed to 3,500 metres above sea level and reaches the village of Laraos, with its dramatic sweep of agricultural terracing built by the Wari civilisation more than a thousand years ago, and still used for growing potatoes. The finger lakes and springs above the village have less water, reports Laraos's mayor, Abel Beltrán.[73] The *bofedales* are being weakened by over-grazing, as locals gradually switch from farming to rearing cattle and sheep. All this threatens the water flow in the valley as a whole. In 2014, the environment ministry was promoting a plan, by which farmers in the lower valley would pay higher water charges, in order to finance projects in which the *campesinos* in places like Laraos would conserve and strengthen water sources and the *bofedales*. The legal framework existed, and so did a seed fund of $1 million in aid money. The missing element was that the regional government and the national water authority had to form a council of stakeholders from the whole valley; by 2015 they still had not done so. This kind of consultation and co-ordination among diverse stakeholders is required, too, for another pressing task in many Latin American countries: to win community consent for mining and other large projects.

Mining discontent

A thousand kilometres further south from Cañete, the Pan-American Highway drops down from the high desert of the La Joya plain and enters the green braid of the valley of the River Tambo. The river burbles past fields of rice, potatoes and sugar cane. It is a tranquil, bucolic scene. In April 2016, it was the site of several weeks of pitched battles between police and hooded protestors hurling stones from catapults; three people (one a policeman) were killed and 200 were injured. The protest was over a plan by Southern Peru Copper Corporation, a Mexican company, for a $1.4 billion copper and gold mine, called Tía María, on the desert bluffs above the valley. Southern (as Peruvians call the firm) said the mine would generate 650 well-paid permanent jobs and add $500 million a year to Peru's exports. Local farmers insisted that it would kill their livelihoods by polluting the river (which the company denied). Ten months later, nearly all the houses in the valley were adorned with flags: 'Farming Yes, No to the Mine'.[74]

Humala's government approved the project, but it was unable to create social and political consent to it. That was not unusual: Peru has lost some $8.5 billion in investment in mining projects blocked by conflict since 2000.[75] Battles over the exploitation of natural resources are common across the region: by one count, in 2014 there were 215 such conflicts, in 19 countries of Latin America.[76]

In 2013, Chile's Supreme Court suspended Pascua-Lama, a huge gold-mining operation straddling the border with Argentina, over fears that it would pollute rivers, after Barrick Gold, a Canadian firm, had already spent $5 billion on the project. Colombia's Constitutional Court has blocked some mining ventures; El Salvador has followed Costa Rica in banning mining altogether; in Brazil, the future of hydroelectric dams in the Amazon basin has been cast into doubt by the refusal of Ibama, the environmental agency, to license a proposed dam on the River Tapajós; and in Ecuador, Correa's government at first banned oil exploration in Yasuní, a national park in the Amazon, only to do a U-turn.

Behind these disputes there often lies a lack of trust, as well as asymmetries of power and sometimes the intervention of anti-capitalist political groups. Mines tend to be in remote areas, characterised by poverty and lack of public services (though this was not true of the Tía

María project). Modern mining is capital intensive. It generates relatively few jobs, and these often require skills that local people lack. (The same goes for oil and gas projects.) But even after the commodity bust, it provided a vital source of foreign exchange. And in countries such as Chile and Peru, industries have sprung up to supply mines with equipment and services. The problem is that most of the benefits have accrued to the nation as a whole, while many of the costs, such as pollution and disruption, have been borne locally. In democratic Latin America, big extractive projects can no longer simply be imposed, as they were in the past (often by state companies). Fourteen countries of the region are among only 22 worldwide to have signed the International Labour Organization's Convention 169 on the rights of indigenous and tribal peoples. This requires governments to consult these people about projects or laws that affect them. Chile, Colombia and Peru have all written this into law. And governments require increasingly professional environmental impact assessments before approving projects. Most multinational mining companies nowadays know that they have to act responsibly. On the other hand, activists have been slow to recognise that widespread illegal and informal mining causes far more environmental damage: illegal gold miners have deforested swathes of rainforest in Peru and have polluted rivers with mercury.

In big projects, disputes can arise over land purchases, relocation of villages and compensation payments. Apart from a deep attachment to the land, behind protests over feared pollution often lies the consciousness – or illusion – among local communities that approval of a mine or other project offers a now-or-never opportunity to rise out of poverty and/or to get schools, hospitals and other public services. Mining companies find themselves forced to provide services that should come from the state. Some mining bosses complain that prior consultation and environmental regulation have become a means of extorting money from them.

Done properly, the consultation process can prevent conflict and lend legitimacy to mining, and many multinational companies have grasped that. One is Gold Fields, a South African company that has developed a medium-sized gold mine in Hualgayoc in Cajamarca, an area in northern Peru where several large projects had been blocked by protests. Gold Fields began by holding several meetings with local people, at which managers explained the project and listened carefully to concerns. The company promised to employ some locals and to provide training to others in using the money that they received from the sale of their land to set up service businesses to supply the mine. It brought in an NGO to work with herders to improve pastures, dairy cattle farming and cheese production. It worked with local mayors to install electricity and drinking water.[77]

But governments cannot assume that mining companies will voluntarily make the effort required to win local consent in this way. They need to play a more proactive role themselves.

CHAPTER ELEVEN

The Stubborn Resilience of Flawed Democracies

Like many Latin American airports, that of El Alto – which serves Bolivia's capital, La Paz – has in the decades since its construction been enveloped by urban sprawl. It is now surrounded by bustling streets lined with houses of concrete and brick in varying stages of completion. The airport shares its name with a satellite city that in 1980 had barely a third of its current population of 850,000. In those days, the airport bordered pasture dotted with small adobe farmhouses. The passenger would step out, breathless, onto the tarmac of what, at 4,000 metres above sea level, is the world's highest commercial airport, to be greeted by an uninterrupted view of the Cordillera Real, a line of majestic snowy peaks that march away north-westwards towards Lake Titicaca. (Since 1980, two-fifths of the glaciers have disappeared.)[1]

To the south stretched the infinite bleakness of the Altiplano, the high-altitude plain that covers much of western Bolivia. La Paz, sprawling over the flanks of a vast volcanic crater that plunges down from El Alto, is the world's largest Andean Indian city. Many of its streets were – and still are – used as markets. The vendors were nearly all Aymara-speaking women, dressed in bowler hats and knee-length flounced skirts known as *polleras* – the costume of seventeenth-century Spanish peasants, imposed upon them by the viceroys and long since adopted as a symbol of cultural identity. Some would sit cross-legged in the street in the fierce midday sun, minding a sheet of blue polythene on which were laid out only a few neat mounds of mandarins – half a dozen for a few pesos. At the other extreme of al fresco retailing, on the lower reaches of Avenida Buenos Aires, tightly packed stalls groaned under the weight of cassette players and televisions, smuggled in defiance of import restrictions.

In March 1980, La Paz was tense.[2] After 15 years of military rule, the armed forces had turned over power to a rickety, interim civilian government. The city was abuzz with rumour. The previous November, a coup attempt had failed, but only after 200 people had been killed and 125 more had 'disappeared'. Another coup was in the air: a prominent local journalist who denounced this had just been murdered. In July 1980, the coup duly came, just weeks after a centre-left coalition had won a clear mandate in an election. Once again, a window of opportunity for democracy seemed to have slammed shut. But it was to be the last successful military coup against a civilian government in Latin America – or at least the last one that installed a military dictatorship. Though brutal and corrupt, the junta proved short-lived, partly because its links to the cocaine trade aroused the hostility of the United States. In 1982, it collapsed, allowing the elected centre-left government to take office. The new president, Hernán Siles Zuazo, was a leader of the 1952 revolution and had held office in the 1950s. This time he presided over chaos. Like the rest of the region, Bolivia was bankrupt. The government resorted to printing money on a massive scale. In 1985, inflation peaked at an annual rate of 25,000 per cent. In return for a five-dollar bill, the visitor would receive long, tightly packed bundles of greasy and tattered banknotes, bound together with string or rubber bands. As well as moneychangers, the streets were thronged with almost daily demonstrations by miners and other workers demanding wage increases to compensate for inflation. In an obscure office in the Central Bank, a concrete and glass skyscraper that soared incongruously over the low, whitewashed buildings of the city centre, sat a representative of the International Monetary Fund, an urbane German. He was happy to pass the time of day with a visiting freelance journalist, doubtless because nobody else would listen to him.

Against this unpromising background, an unlikely experiment began. An early election in 1985 brought to power for the third time Víctor Paz Estenssoro, the leader of the 1952 revolution, who was by then aged 78. Advised by a young American economist called Jeffrey Sachs, his government swiftly ended hyperinflation by raising petrol prices and closing the fiscal deficit.[3] Paz Estenssoro went on to dismantle many of the economic institutions he had erected a generation earlier. He liquidated chronically loss-making state-owned industries and, after the world tin market collapsed, also Comibol, the state mining firm, laying off thousands of workers. Subsidies, import controls and protective tariffs were all slashed or abolished. Government authority was restored: when the militant miners marched on La Paz, they were stopped halfway by a state of emergency and army tanks. Bolivia thus followed Chile in using free-market reforms to conquer hyperinflation, but it was the first country in the region to do so as a democracy.

In all this, Paz Estenssoro's lieutenant was the planning minister, Gonzalo ('Goni') Sánchez de Lozada, a wisecracking, cigar-smoking mining magnate. Goni had been brought up in the United States and spoke Spanish with a curious mixture of soft Andean throatiness and an American drawl. In 1993, he was elected president. To attract foreign investment, he devised a variant of privatisation that he called 'capitalisation', in which private companies injected capital investment into state-owned firms, in return for a 50 per cent shareholding and management control. Foreigners took over not just the telecoms company, the railways, the national airline and electricity companies, but also the oil and gas industry, a nationalist totem.

Overriding 60 years of mercantilist xenophobia, he signed an agreement with Brazil to build a pipeline to export Bolivian gas to São Paulo. As he prepared to leave office in 1997, Goni was ebullient. Having created a new natural-gas industry, he forecast that Bolivia would soon enjoy 'Asian rates' of economic growth.[4] He spoke proudly of his social reforms, too. The state's shares in 'capitalised' companies were used to endow a new private pension system and to make an annual payment (of $248 in 1997) to all Bolivians aged over 65. He decentralised power and money to local government. His vice-president, an Amerindian intellectual, promoted bilingual education, so that indigenous children would receive some of their initial schooling in their first language.

Not only had Bolivia become an unexpected advertisement for the Washington Consensus, but as power alternated after each election between coalitions of centre-left and centre-right, democracy seemed to take root. A country that had so long been the continent's unstable, suffering heart seemed to have become a success story. Yet that appearance proved deceptive. In the 1990s, the economy grew at only half the 8 per cent a year Goni had promised. That was not enough: in 2001, annual income per head was under $950, and 63 per cent of Bolivians were poor, according to the World Bank. Then growth petered out, as the economy was hit by Argentina's collapse and by a US-backed campaign to eradicate all illegal coca. Coca had long been grown in the Yungas, close to La Paz, for such traditional uses as chewing (the mild narcotic effect is a welcome antidote to the cold) and coca tea (which helps tourists adapt to high altitude). In the late 1970s, coca spread to the Chapare region near Cochabamba, where it was sold for the drug trade. The American eradication campaign was supplemented by modest aid to develop alternative crops in the Chapare, such as bananas, palm hearts and pepper. But these only paid a third as much as coca, and employed fewer people.[5]

In 2002, Goni was again elected president. But this time he had a slender mandate, and the country was in a surly mood. The best hope of kickstarting faster economic growth lay in vast deposits of natural gas. These had been discovered since privatisation, just as Goni had forecast. He pressed ahead with a project, promoted by a consortium of foreign companies, to export the gas via a Chilean port to Mexico and the United States. This made economic sense, but it touched both the electrodes of Bolivian nationalism: hostility to Chile (dating from the War of the Pacific) and resentment at the exploitation of the country's natural resources by foreigners (dating from the colonial silver mine at Potosí.) The result would be an explosive political short-circuit. To make matters worse, the government had to try to reduce a huge budget deficit. According to Goni, the drug 'war' cost Bolivia 5 per cent of GDP; the transitional cost of the pension reform to the government amounted to another 5 per cent. The president went to Washington for help. 'I said to Bush that I needed $150 million, otherwise I was going to be seeking political asylum in the coming year. They gave $10 million', he recalled later.[6] In October 2003, crowds of stone-throwing demonstrators, organised by far-left groups opposed to the gas-export plan, blockaded the roads through El Alto for a fortnight, cutting La Paz off from the airport and the rest of the country. When the government ordered the army to open the roads, 59 people were killed in the resulting clashes. Abandoned by Congress, Goni was forced to step down. He was taken by helicopter to the airport, and to a life of exile in the suburbs of Washington, DC – just as he had warned Bush might happen.

Constitutional forms were preserved: power passed to the vice-president, Carlos Mesa, an articulate historian, who had previously hosted a popular television programme. But in June 2005, he suffered the same fate as Goni. After three weeks of roadblocks in El Alto and elsewhere, organised by the same leftist groups who now wanted nationalisation of the gas industry, Mesa resigned. The president of the Supreme Court took over as Bolivia's third president in as many years, and called an early election for December 2005.

That election was won emphatically by Evo Morales, the most widely supported of the protestors' leaders. Of Aymaran descent, he led both the coca-workers' unions in the Chapare and a left-wing party called the Movement to Socialism (MAS). Morales secured 54 per cent of the vote in an election in which 80 per cent of those registered turned out – by far the largest mandate since democracy was restored in 1983. He ran on a platform of nationalisation of oil and gas, a constituent assembly to entrench indigenous rights, and an end to coca eradication. He was, he said, the United States' 'worst nightmare'. Ironically, Morales was in part a creation of the United States and its 'war on drugs'. When he launched his first presidential campaign, in 2002, he was a relatively minor figure. But he received an unexpected boost when Manuel Rocha, the American ambassador, said that if Morales won, his government would cancel all aid to Bolivia (which averaged $100 million a year). Bolivians saw this as a crude intervention in their democracy and gave Morales 22 per cent of the vote. Morales is often referred to as Bolivia's first indigenous president. Yet he left his Andean village as a young man and headed for the coca fields of the Chapare. In the 1980s, the Chapare was booming, pulling in Bolivians from all over the country, and was a melting pot of *mestizaje*, comparable to Potosí in the early seventeenth century.[7]

Morales is culturally a *mestizo*, as are most Bolivians, and his politics were derived from Bolivia's tradition of radical syndicalism, though he was less lettered than the miners' leaders of the past, many of whom had read Marx and Trotsky. His political home was the headquarters in Cochabamba, Bolivia's third city, of the Federación del Trópico, as the coca-workers' union calls itself. In January 2004, this occupied part of an unfinished six-storey office block of raw concrete opposite a scruffy park near the centre of the city. Shortly after 8.00 a.m. on a weekday morning, supplicants began arriving at the office. By the time Morales turned up two hours later, a couple of dozen were lined up waiting for a word with the leader. Several women sought scholarships for their sons; a group of teachers came to discuss a strike. Like most urbanised men of Amerindian descent, Morales wore ordinary western clothes. He cut an unsmiling, but not unattractive figure, with a boyish shock of black hair. Morales's political ideas were a vague blend of dependency theory, utopian socialism, anti-globalisation rhetoric, indigenous rights and the pragmatism of a trade-union leader.

What he was seeking, he said, was 'a refoundation' of Bolivia through a constituent assembly, to create 'a new country, without discrimination or exploitation, where indigenous, *mestizos* and *blancoides* [whitish people] live together'.[8] Bolivia was rich, but it was impoverished because its wealth was in the hands of multinational corporations, he claimed. He said he wanted 'a mixed economy'. Foreign companies would no longer hold oil and gas deposits in concession. These would pass to Yacimientos Petrolíferos Fiscales Bolivianos (YPFB), the state hydrocarbons company. But multinationals would be encouraged to sign service contracts with YPFB to operate the fields. Morales insisted he was a democrat, though one who favoured 'participatory democracy'. He said he admired Fidel Castro and Hugo Chávez – he was a frequent visitor to Caracas – but also Lula ('how he combines the mixed economy is very intelligent').

In office, he was true to those words – with all their contradictions. He appointed to his cabinet activists from social movements with little experience of governing. In April 2006, he travelled to Havana, where he formalised an alliance with Chávez and Castro. On his return home, with Chávez at his side he led army troops into a gas field operated by Brazil's Petrobras and declared the nationalisation of the oil and gas industry – provoking a furious reaction in Brazil. Yet his management of the economy would be pragmatic. He signed new contracts with Petrobras and other multinationals which recognised YPFB's formal control over the gas and increased the royalties the government received. He reversed earlier privatisations, but went no further. Thanks to the commodity boom, he enjoyed a big increase in revenues from gas and mining, but was more responsible than Chávez in using them. These revenues financed an increase in public employment and credit and a consumer boom, but also the building of hospitals, schools and roads in the Altiplano. Poverty fell steeply, though no faster than in free-market Peru. Álvaro García Linera, a white Marxist intellectual who was Morales's vice-president, argued that creating socialism in a country like Bolivia first required the state to build capitalism.[9]

Morales did take some leaves out of Chávez's book. He pushed through a new constitution, which enhanced the rights of indigenous people, put his own supporters in the judiciary, and was ruthless in neutralising opponents. Faced with a rebellion by conservative provincial governors in the east of the country, he jailed one and negotiated with others. He threw out the American ambassador and the Drug Enforcement Administration. Morales was popular. He was twice re-elected, winning more than 60 per cent of the vote each time. But in

2016, he narrowly lost a referendum to change the constitution to allow him to run for a fourth term in 2019. He faced slowly growing dissent from former supporters.

Evo Morales represents one face of Latin American democracy today. It is an ambivalent face. On the one hand, the movement of which he is a leader bundled two presidents from office without regard for the constitution or democratic political procedures. In office, he showed little respect for the separation of powers. Whether he would allow himself to be freely voted out was unclear. On the other hand, the election of Morales underlined that democracy in Bolivia, and in Latin America, no longer excluded those who claimed to stand for radical change and to represent the poor majority and indigenous people. Like many Bolivians, Morales saw his country's democracy as having been hijacked by corrupt and self-serving traditional parties. Like the populist leaders of the past, he pursued a road which combined electoral politics with popular mobilisation. Like them, he espoused 'resource nationalism'. With his base in social movements of trade unions, peasant farmers and urban migrants, he had a stronger claim than the other hard-left Latin American regimes to be leading a genuine social revolution.

Elsewhere in Latin America, democracy is far more robust and has plenty of less ambivalent leaders. Social inclusion and liberal democracy do not have to be mutually exclusive alternatives, as countries such as Brazil and Chile have shown. Bolivia is an extreme case, not the mean. But many other countries share – to some degree at least – some of Bolivia's weaknesses, past and present, including political fragmentation, the weakness of political parties and institutions, a populist challenge to liberal democracy, the irruption of powerful social movements and the temptation to abolish term limits. The region's democracies must also grapple with corruption and the discredit of traditional politicians.

The pendulum stops

At its simplest, democracy involves 'a competitive struggle for the people's vote', as Joseph Schumpeter put it.[10] Yet democracy also involves the way in which government is exercised, not just chosen. At its heart are restraints on the state and on executive power, in order to hold them accountable to citizens and to guard against despotism. Since Montesquieu, the separation of the legislative and judicial functions of government from the executive has been seen as the best way to achieve such restraints on power. The everyday practice of democracy involves the gradual accretion of rules, habits and institutions, including freedom of expression and association and inclusive citizenship.[11] It is no coincidence that established democracies all have market economies, since a command economy involves a concentration of power that is inimical to political pluralism and competition. In addition, market capitalism tends to produce a large middle class of property owners who have an interest in education, freedom, participation and the rule of law. When Chávez told the BBC that 'democracy is impossible under capitalism', he was precisely wrong.[12] But on the other hand, the close association between democracy and market capitalism conceals a paradox, in that market economies generate inequalities in political influence which are undemocratic.[13] The undue influence of the rich and powerful poses a special challenge to democracy in egregiously unequal societies such as those of Latin America.

Getting from the mere replacement of dictatorship with an elected government to this full institutional panoply of rule-bound political pluralism has often been envisaged as a transition – a journey whose destination political scientists have called 'consolidated democracy'. Arrival means not just that democracy should be stable, but that its citizens enjoy the rule of law, backed by an effective state capable of regulating the market and providing public goods (e.g. security and clean air).[14] In the formulation of Juan Linz and Alfred Stepan, consolidation is reached when democracy becomes 'the only game in town'. Political science has tended to see the achievement of consolidated democracy as irreversible. But the recent rise of populism in the United States and Europe, and cases of 'deconsolidation', such as in Venezuela and Poland, throw that into question.[15]

Looked at comparatively, Latin American democracy has held up surprisingly well. Only in Venezuela and Nicaragua was there clear regress to dictatorship, although in the first case this was vigorously contested. In other parts of the world, the democratic wave of the 1970s and 1980s has been interrupted. Since 2005, political freedom globally has, on balance, retreated each year, according to Freedom House, an NGO which tracks this.[16] Populism and autocracy threatened liberal democracy in several Eastern European countries. Surveys showed that faith in, and satisfaction with, democracy was declining even in Europe and the United States, especially among younger voters.

Latin America's democracies have been subjected to stress tests over the past three decades. The 'lost half-decade' of economic hardship of 1998–2002 saw a rise in political instability. Eight presidents were ousted before the end of their term between 1998 and 2005. But half that number came from just two countries (Bolivia and Ecuador), and two more were of doubtful legitimacy, having won rigged elections (Alberto Fujimori in Peru in 2000 and Jean-Bertrand Aristide in Haiti). Public support for democracy wavered. The Latinobarómetro poll found in 2004 that some 55 per cent of respondents 'would not mind a non-democratic government if it could solve economic problems'.[17] In the same poll, 71 per cent of respondents thought that 'the country is governed for the benefit of a few powerful interests'.

Economic recovery and the alternation of power through elections brought a recovery in support for democracy. But this saw a slight decline, as economies stagnated after the commodity boom. In 2016, the Latinobarómetro poll found support for democracy at 54 per cent, down from a peak of 61 per cent in 2010, but more or less in line with the long-term average. Three out of four respondents agreed with the statement 'democracy may have problems, but it is the best system of government'. But only one in three was satisfied with the way the democracy worked in practice. Many democratic institutions were held in relatively low esteem. Only one in four respondents expressed any confidence in the judiciary or the Congress.[18]

These opinions pointed both to the underlying resilience of democracy in Latin America and to the continuing potential for discontent to be capitalised upon by populist leaders. There were big variations from country to country. On many indicators, Uruguay and Costa Rica stood out as consolidated democracies. Chile and Colombia were candidates, too. These four countries had two characteristics in common. One is that their population is ethnically more or less homogeneous – they lack the racial divide of Brazil or Peru. Another is that they had gone furthest towards establishing democracy a century ago. They had long experience of 'oligarchical democracy', to employ that helpful oxymoron.[19] In other words, these countries succeeded in institutionalising rules for political competition early on, although important social groups, especially the rural poor, were more or less excluded. Only when these rules were more or less established, and when economies were developing, was the whole population brought into the system. Uruguay was a pioneer in establishing universal suffrage and a welfare state. These were achieved in Costa Rica through a revolution in 1948. To preserve the tradition of peaceful political competition which they believed had been threatened, the victors of the revolution, José Figueres and his social-democratic National Liberation Party, abolished the country's small army. That helped to ensure that in Costa Rica, unlike Uruguay and Chile, democracy was not overthrown in the 1970s. Yet whatever the shortcomings in the quality of democracy elsewhere in the region, in many countries it had 'put down roots', as Fernando Henrique Cardoso, Brazil's former president, put it.[20]

The current democratic period in Latin America is qualitatively different from those that went before, in three ways: the pendulum between dictatorship and democracy has stopped; universal, effective suffrage has at last been achieved; and decentralisation has deepened democracy.

The fact that democracy has survived nearly everywhere is often taken for granted. It should not be. Given that tanks on the streets were such a dominant motif in Latin America for much of the twentieth century, the almost complete absence of military coups was noteworthy. In only three cases were presidents ousted by military interventions. One was in Haiti in 2004, when the United States and France arranged for Aristide to be flown out, as a rebel band advanced on Port-au-Prince – a move he later denounced as a coup. The second was in Ecuador in January 2000, when the army high command ordered Jamil Mahuad to resign, installing his vice-president in his place, after several junior officers had joined an uprising by indigenous Ecuadoreans who occupied the Congress building. The third was in Honduras in 2009, when the army ousted the president, Manuel Zelaya, who had fallen under the sway of Chávez and fallen out with his country's Congress and judiciary. When Zelaya called an 'informal' referendum on convoking a constituent assembly, the army obeyed an order from the Supreme Court to eject him, hustling him onto a plane out of the country. Roberto Micheletti, the speaker of the Congress, took over as interim president.

There were a few other military interventions in politics. In 1992, Alberto Fujimori, Peru's elected president, used army tanks to shut down the country's Congress and its courts in an *autogolpe* (self-coup).[21] There were several attempts at a coup in Paraguay in the 1990s, all of which failed. In Venezuela, Chávez and his supporters staged two coups against the elected government of Carlos Andrés Pérez, in 1992 and 1993. They helped to create a climate in which Pérez was impeached for corruption a year before the end of his term. Chávez himself was briefly toppled by a coup in April 2002, before being restored to power by loyal troops (see Chapter 7). Zelaya in Honduras apart, since the mid-2000s only three presidents have failed to complete their term. Dilma Rousseff was impeached; and Otto Pérez Molina in Guatemala resigned before being imprisoned for corruption. A more problematic case was that of Fernando Lugo, a left-wing former bishop elected in Paraguay in 2008. In 2012, he suffered a lightning impeachment, being bundled out of office in two days in denial of due process. It was, in narrow terms, constitutional, but not democratic.

Since 1990, no military officer on active duty has served as president of a Latin American country.[22] In most countries, coups have not been attempted even in circumstances of social breakdown that would certainly have prompted military intervention in the past. That goes for Argentina during its economic collapse of 2001/02, when middle-class savers and unemployed workers temporarily joined in protests whose slogan was: '*que se vayan todos*' – 'kick all the politicians out'. That message might once have been taken as a green light by ambitious generals. Bolivia is a similarly striking case. In May 2005, when protestors forced Carlos Mesa to resign, the country's politicians were divided as to who should replace him. In the past, that kind of chaotic power vacuum would inevitably have triggered a military coup. On this occasion, however, the armed forces quietly but firmly threw their weight behind the selection by Congress of the head of the Supreme Court as interim president with a mandate to call an early election. In the power vacuum that led up to Dilma Rousseff's impeachment, Cardoso noted that 'twenty years ago we would have been discussing the names of generals. Today nobody knows the names of any generals. We talk of the names of judges.'[23]

This absence of open challenge to democracy is partly because the external climate has changed. Ever since George H.W. Bush decided that democratisation was the best policy for managing the conflicts of the final years of the Cold War in Latin America, the United States has opposed military coups against elected governments. An egregious exception to this record was the short-lived coup against Chávez in Venezuela, which the United States failed to denounce and appeared to support (though this was vehemently denied).[24] Aristide's overthrow in

Haiti was another exception. Regional forces have played a role, too. Brazil and Argentina, for example, acted in concert with the United States to prevent a coup in Paraguay in 1996. Coups thus faced international opprobrium. In the aftermath of the would-be putsch in Paraguay, the Mercosur trade group, of which Paraguay was a member (along with Brazil, Argentina and Uruguay), adopted a 'democracy clause' which called for the suspension of a member country in the event of any interruption of constitutional rule. In 2001, the Organization of American States adopted a Democratic Charter, which included similar provisions.

Yet the main reasons for the relative security of democracy are internal. In most countries, memories of the economic failure and repressive rule of most of the military governments of the 1970s appear to have inoculated the body politic against any early repetition. This is particularly true in Argentina, where more than anywhere else the armed forces were discredited by their record when in power. The generals themselves seem to have lost the appetite for trying to run the government. Democratic governments have established control over the armed forces, though this has been a gradual, uneven and contested process. Across the region, unified defence ministries have replaced separate self-governing ministries for each service. Most defence ministers nowadays are civilians (in Colombia, Chile, Argentina and Ecuador, recent ministers have included women). Progress has been made in settling border disputes, often despite reservations from the military. Democratic governments in Brazil and Argentina have scrapped incipient nuclear weapons programmes and agreed to joint inspection of nuclear facilities. Peru's Fujimori was a questionable democrat, but he did settle his country's border dispute with Ecuador, which had thrice been a motive for skirmishes of varying severity. Some governments have given their armies new roles in UN peacekeeping, as well as in responding to natural disasters. In only two countries do the armed forces still play an important political role: Cuba and Venezuela. In relation to the size of their economies, Latin American countries spend less on defence than those in any other region of the world. In 2015, defence spending accounted for just 1.2 per cent of GDP, down from 1.77 per cent in 1995.[25] Even so, in many cases that is higher than need be. Defence spending is rarely subject to rigorous, threat-based assessments. Rather than have armies fight the 'war on drugs', it would be better to shift resources to police forces.

The issue of holding the soldiers to account for the crimes of the dictatorships has been difficult, but progress has been made in some countries, especially Chile. Under the Kirchners, Argentina sent scores of elderly generals to jail, but did nothing against the surviving Montoneros, whose violence did much to trigger the 1976 military coup (and several of whom served in the Kirchners' governments). In Brazil, a Truth Commission to investigate the military dictatorship of 1964–85 was not set up until 2012. Uruguayans have twice voted in referendums to uphold an amnesty law covering the crimes of the dictators and their guerrilla opponents. 'Museums of memory' have opened across South America. Cristina Fernández turned what was the Navy Mechanical Institute, the most notorious of the torture centres of the 1976–83 dictatorship, into a 'Space of Memory and Human Rights', run by several far-left groups. Their proponents argue that recalling the crimes of the past is essential to prevent their recurrence.

But there are dangers, too, in the region's fashion for 'historical memory'. Memory is subjective and selective. It cannot take the place of history. Memory, in the form of human-rights groups, repeated the figure of '30,000 victims of state terrorism' in Argentina, as a sign at the Memory Park in Buenos Aires puts it. History, in the shape of an independent commission, could identify only 8,960 (though that is horrific enough). Had many more people disappeared, it is reasonable to assume that their families would have denounced their disappearance during the 35 years since the dictatorship ended. The Argentine armed forces gave unverified estimates ranging from 15,000 to 22,000 to Chilean and US intelligence agents.[26] Whatever the number, there is no doubt that the repression was horrific and went far wider than the armed left-wing groups. The barbarity of Pinochet and the Argentine and Uruguayan juntas was inexcusable. But 'historical memory' shows that although the right may bloodily have won the Cold War in Latin America, the left has won the peace and is busy rewriting history. One consequence of that is that the region has been quick to condemn anything that smacks of a coup against an elected president, but has been complacent in the face of abuses of power, democracy and human rights by governments such as those in Venezuela and Cuba.

A second reason for the relative stability of democracy in the current period is that it has become more representative. The region has had a liberal constitutional tradition for almost two centuries, as we have seen, even if this has often been honoured in the breach. But in the nineteenth century, voting was typically limited by property and other qualifications to no more than 10 per cent of the population. In 1912, Argentina became the first country to introduce universal male suffrage (though it excluded immigrants). Women gained the vote between 1932 (Uruguay) and 1967 (Ecuador). But property and literacy requirements were retained in several countries, in effect denying the vote to many of the poor.[27] Since the 1980s, for the first time, elections involving universal suffrage have become routine. Suffrage is not only universal, it is also more effective than in the past. Electoral fraud has now become the exception rather than the norm. The combination of universal suffrage and the removal of the military veto over politics has not only ended the pendulum swings between dictatorship and democracy that marked Latin America in the mid-twentieth century, but has also allowed the left to take and hold power through the ballot box. For the first time, everyone can vote and anyone can be elected to office, not just the traditional political elite.

As well as becoming more diverse, democracy has been deepened through decentralisation. The Spanish and Portuguese monarchies had imposed a centralised system of government. In the Spanish colonies, there were municipalities, and their *cabildos* (councils) were often elected from among the local whites. But, at least until the Bourbon reforms, they had little power or money. Despite the rhetoric of nineteenth-century Liberals, power remained fairly centralised in the republican era. Only Brazil and Argentina were genuinely federal republics. Under the PRI, Mexican federalism was an elaborate fiction. Across the region, the biggest change was at municipal level. In 1980, only three countries in the region chose their mayors by direct election. By 2005, 17 did so, while in six others they were chosen from among directly elected local councillors.[28]

Latin American democracy has also become more participatory. Many of the new constitutions that almost all Latin American countries drew up in their transition to democracy partook of that spirit. Referendums have become a regular feature of political life. Parties have taken to choosing their presidential candidates in open primaries, in which any citizen can vote. At the local level, the 'participatory budgeting' espoused by the Workers' Party (PT) mayors of Porto Alegre in Brazil has been widely imitated across the region. Despite all these advances, Latin American democracies also suffer from some deep-rooted flaws.

Presidentialism and its problems

Nowadays political scientists tend to care more about the quality of democratic institutions than about 'consolidation'.[29] In Latin America, democratic institutions were often poorly designed, political parties relatively weak, and pre- or anti-democratic forms of political behaviour survived. Recent debate has homed in on whether or not democracy in the region is generating accountable government, and in particular on the issue of presidential powers.

Latin America is a land of presidents. But many countries lack the stable two-party system that in the United States has allowed presidentialism to function fairly smoothly. That two-party system is the result of the US having adopted a British style, first-past-the-post electoral system of single-member districts. Uniquely, Latin America combines presidentialism with legislatures elected by proportional representation (PR). In continental Europe, where PR is common, it is associated with parliamentary regimes in which multi-party coalition governments are the norm. Latin America's awkward mix of presidentialism and PR has contributed to a pattern in which presidents lack legislative majorities, stimulating conflict between the executive and legislatures that do not face the threat of dissolution that breaks gridlock in parliamentary systems.

Some political scientists have argued that this pattern was a factor behind the democratic breakdowns of the 1960s and 1970s, a nd have called for Latin America to adopt parliamentarism. This prompted a lively academic debate in the early years of restored democracy – one with a few faint practical echoes.[30] The debate was liveliest in Brazil, which had parliamentary government under its constitutional monarchy in the nineteenth century, and briefly from 1961 to 1963. Brazil's Constituent Congress of 1987–88 discussed adopting a parliamentary regime. The matter was put to a referendum in 1993, when another option was to return to constitutional monarchy. But presidentialism won easily (with 55 per cent of the vote against 25 per cent for parliamentarism).[31]

The fact is that presidentialism fits naturally with Latin America's cultural tradition of personal leadership, from Aztec *tlatoani* to Spanish viceroy to republican *caudillo*. In the past, Latin America's awkward hybrid – of presidentialism plus proportional representation and multi-party systems – tended to produce gridlock. Whatever their constitutional strength, the reality was often that of presidents castrated by political fragmentation. A review of 71 South American presidents elected in relatively fair contests from 1930 to 1990 found that in an 'overwhelming majority' of cases, their parties lacked a legislative majority.[32] In some countries, this dispersal of power has continued in the current democratic period.

A study in 2005 of the previous two elections in 18 countries found that the president's party had a majority in the lower house of Congress in only three cases (Chile, Honduras and Nicaragua), though in a further six, the president's party had 40 per cent or more of the seats (Argentina, Costa Rica, the Dominican Republic, Guatemala, Peru and Uruguay).[33] In Mexico, since 1997 no president has enjoyed a congressional majority. Peña Nieto's legislative pact was a successful but temporary effort to overcome this. Brazil's 'coalitional presidentialism' was an initially successful response to political fragmentation, but at a rising cost (see Chapter 8).

One response to this was the crude assertion of presidential power, riding roughshod over the legislature and judiciary – a tradition begun by Bolívar. As long ago as 1994, Guillermo O'Donnell, the Argentine political scientist, warned of 'delegative' democracies in which 'whoever wins the presidential election is authorised to govern as they see fit, restricted only by the crude reality of existing power relations and by the constitutional term-limit on their mandate'.[34] He had in mind Carlos Menem in Argentina, Fernando Collor in Brazil and Fujimori in Peru. Menem made frequent use of decree powers and packed the Supreme Court with cronies (as every previous Argentine president since Perón had done, with the notable exception of Raúl Alfonsín). Collor froze Brazilians' savings by decree.

Fujimori's use of army tanks to shut down Peru's Congress in 1992 brought international condemnation, but local acclaim. He maintained that the politicians were blocking anti-terrorist legislation and his economic programme. He also declared the judiciary in permanent 'reorganisation', filling it with stooges. Fujimori faced exceptional circumstances. These included the hyperinflationary economic chaos bequeathed by Alan García, and the vicious insurgency of Sendero Luminoso (Shining Path), a fundamentalist Maoist group, which brought the loss of some 70,000 lives in a 'dirty war' with the security forces from

1980 to 1993. Fujimori's heavy-handed methods worked – but only for a while and at a long-term cost to Peru's democracy. He crushed the Shining Path, stabilised the economy, and built many schools and health clinics in Andean villages. He legitimised his *autogolpe* with a new constitution approved by referendum, which concentrated powers in the presidency and allowed him to stand for (and easily win) a second term. He was ever the elected autocrat. In an interview in 1995, when he was about to start his second term, I pressed him on whether the way to make permanent the transformation in Peru's circumstances he had wrought was to devolve power to new democratic institutions. Three times he dodged the question.[35] He claimed that he governed according to 'technical' rather than 'political' criteria – an answer reminiscent of Porfirio Díaz's motto of 'little politics, much administration'. If Fujimori was the archetype of 'delegative democracy', the term also fit the regimes of Hugo Chávez, Evo Morales and Rafael Correa.

A second response to political fragmentation was to change the rules. Latin American democracies fiddled compulsively: one study of 18 countries found 220 reforms of electoral and party systems between 1978 and 2005. These tended to boost presidential power, on the one hand, and to ensure that previously excluded groups, such as indigenous people, were better represented.[36] Since the 1980s, constituent assemblies drew up new constitutions in ten countries; in addition, between 1978 and 2008 there was an average of ten constitutional amendments a year in the region as a whole.[37] These constitutional changes often involved a relaxation of presidential term limits. At the outset of their transition to democracy, 16 out of 18 countries banned their presidents from seeking a second consecutive term (though 12 allowed non-consecutive re-election). In 2016, five countries allowed this; seven permitted non-consecutive re-election; and three countries – Nicaragua, Venezuela and Honduras – had abolished term limits altogether (and Ecuador has approved doing so from 2021). In 2017, Paraguay's president was attempting to overturn his country's ban on consecutive re-election. Only Mexico, Guatemala and Colombia (which changed back after allowing Uribe and Santos two terms each) restricted their presidents to a single term.

In some cases, allowing consecutive re-election has involved negotiation with the opposition, and has been combined with a shortening of the presidential term or moves to make the president more accountable, as in Argentina in 1994. More often, it has strengthened presidents. In practice, incumbents have a big advantage in Latin American elections. Of the 19 incumbent presidents who have run for re-election in the region since the 1980s, only two have lost (Daniel Ortega in Nicaragua in 1990, after a war, and Hipólito Mejía in the Dominican Republic in 2002, after a financial crisis). That is partly because incumbent presidents have access to the resources and powers of the state. One study found that a 1 per cent increase in public spending in an election year widens the incumbent's margin of victory by 1.3 per cent.[38] If that is the case, it suggests that Dilma Rousseff did indeed buy her way to a second term. The big push to relax term limits coincided with the commodity boom. As revenues flooded in, so presidents enjoyed the luxury of being able to fulfil campaign promises. Many were popular, enjoying approval ratings of above 50 per cent.

Yet presidents have not had it all their own way everywhere. Legislatures in Latin America have often been written off as rubber stamps. But they have often enjoyed more influence than has met the eye.[39] In some countries, they have played a fairly effective role both in scrutinising governments and in crafting legislation. That was true of Brazil, Chile, Colombia and Uruguay in particular, according to a study by the Inter-American Development Bank.[40] It also applied to post-Fujimori Peru. And there are signs that impeachment has replaced the role of coups in arbitrating in situations of conflict or power vacuums. In some countries, however, legislatures have been weakened by high turnover among their members. In the United States, around 90 per cent of members of Congress win re-election. In Latin America, according to the IDB's study, only in Chile and Uruguay did at least half of congressional deputies win immediate re-election; and in Argentina and Peru, the figure was less than 20 per cent.[41] Judiciaries, too, restrained executive power in countries such as Brazil, Chile and Colombia.

As the boom gave way to economic stagnation, presidents once again tended to be unpopular and political fragmentation again loomed as a risk to the effectiveness of democracy. Yet Peru is an interesting case in this respect: since the post-Fujimori restoration of democracy, presidents have lacked congressional majorities and have suffered declining popularity, yet they have managed to reach the end of their terms. Survival is one thing; the ability to get reforms through is another.

Parties in flux

The difficulties in assembling effective governing coalitions threw the spotlight on the shortcomings of political parties. Political scientists have long seen parties as the bedrock of democracy, both expressing and channelling interests. In Latin America, they are flourishing in quantity, but not necessarily in quality. The standard academic study of party systems in the region, edited by Scott Mainwaring and Timothy Scully and published in 1995, found striking differences in the degree to which these were institutionalised. By 'institutionalisation', the authors meant four things: that patterns of party competition show some regularity, that parties have stable roots in society, that parties and elections are widely seen as legitimate, and that parties have an independent organisation and are not merely personal vehicles for political leaders.[42] On these criteria, Costa Rica, Chile, Uruguay, Venezuela and Colombia all had institutionalised party systems, while Peru, Brazil, Ecuador and Bolivia did not. Yet this finding was in some ways misleading. A decade later, the party system in Venezuela and, to a lesser extent, Colombia, looked much less institutionalised and Brazil's rather more so. Two decades later, Venezuelan parties had coalesced into two hostile coalitions, while Brazil's party system had become the most fragmented anywhere in the democratic world.

The weakening of political parties has been a worldwide trend in this century, reflecting the post-modern blurring of class and ideological divisions. Latin America has been no exception. In many countries, party systems have evolved in ways that reflect social changes, such as the preponderance of the informal economy or the inclusion of indigenous peoples. In some cases, party evolution seems to have weakened the prospects for effective democratic government, but in others it reflects adaptation to changed socio-economic and political realities. New parties have emerged. Some are based on ethnic-identity politics, such as Bolivia's MAS. Others have found a niche. In Colombia, a new moderate left party, the Polo Democrático Alternativo, which rejected guerrilla violence, emerged on the scene by winning the mayoralty of Bogotá in 2004 – a feat it twice repeated.

Voters were merciless in punishing parties that they held to have failed in their management of the economy. The Radical Party, part of Argentine political history since the 1890s, was severely weakened by being in power during the 2001/02 economic collapse. That is ironic, since it had inherited the policies that brought Argentina to disaster from the Peronist administration of Carlos Menem. The Radicals returned to power only as the junior partner in a coalition with Mauricio Macri's PRO, a new party of the centre-right, which defined itself as 'modernising' rather than conservative. In Mexico, the debt crisis of 1982 and the bungled devaluation of the peso of 1994 were central to the decline and fall from power of the PRI. Peru's ruling Acción Popular, the moderate, reformist party of Fernando Belaúnde, the president in 1963–68 and 1980–85, won just 6 per cent of the vote in the 1985 election. Bolivian voters in 2005 punished the Movimiento Nacionalista Revolucionario, the previously hegemonic party that led the 1952 revolution, for what they saw as the failure of Goni's 'neoliberalism'. The same applied to Acción Democrática in Venezuela in 1993. Colombia's Conservative Party paid the price for presiding over the country's first recession in half a century in 1999–2000, even if much of the blame lay with the preceding administration of Ernesto Samper, a Liberal. Voters were more lenient with presidents who, having campaigned against applying 'shock therapy' to inflation, proceeded to implement drastic economic stabilisation plans – provided these worked. Thus, Menem in Argentina and Fujimori in Peru were re-elected.

Only a handful of countries preserved in the twentieth century the two-party systems (usually of Liberals and Conservatives, albeit sometimes under different names) that were characteristic of the nineteenth-century republics. They included some of the more solid democracies: Uruguay, Costa Rica and Colombia. In Colombia and Uruguay, party allegiance ran deep, being passed from generation to generation within families as a badge of identity, as if it were support for a football team. Yet in the twenty-first century, two-party hegemony has collapsed or is under strain in all of those countries. In Uruguay, the left-wing Frente Amplio (Broad Front) coalition won the presidency in 2004, breaking a duopoly of the Colorado ('Red' or Liberal) and Blanco ('White' or Conservative) parties that dated back more than a century. In Costa Rica, corruption scandals that implicated three former presidents shook public trust in the two main parties. In Colombia, the Conservative and Liberal parties survived, but were diminished and faction-ridden.

In Chile, something close to a two-party system evolved after the Pinochet dictatorship. Chile was unique in having developed a

European-style multi-party system by the mid-twentieth century, with strong socialist, communist and Christian democrat parties. The electoral system bequeathed by the dictatorship, which discriminated against third parties, and the memory of tragic consequences of political division in 1973, encouraged the socialists and the Christian democrats to join with others to form a single centre-left coalition, the Concertación. The two main parties of the right joined up in an alliance. But in the past few years, splinter parties have formed across the political spectrum. It remains to be seen whether Bachelet's electoral reform, which has introduced larger, multi-member constituencies, can engender a multi-party system. In Mexico, the relatively stable three-party system that emerged in the 1990s was shaken up when López Obrador formed a new personalist party, Morena.

Brazil in the 1990s was an 'exceptional case of party weakness', as Mainwaring put it.[43] Legislators switched from one to another of the score or more of parties in the Chamber of Deputies. Their main loyalties were to their home state, where most politicians built their political careers, and to powerful cross-party sectoral lobbies, such as the *ruralistas* (farmers), the *muncipalistas* (ex-mayors or town councillors), the bench of evangelical Protestants or even the football caucus. Yet parties did matter. The PT and Cardoso's Party of Brazilian Social Democracy retained fairly cohesive identities and anchored coalitions. But with scores of politicians accused of extracting corrupt or illicit campaign donations, it was not clear how public discredit would reshape the party system.

Peru was another extreme case, one of a 'democracy without parties'.[44] Fujimori was contemptuous of political parties and sought to undermine them. Of the four parties that dominated politics in the 1980s, only APRA and Acción Popular lived on, and only as rumps. Ironically, the strongest party in the 2010s was Fuerza Popular (Popular Force), the *fujimorista* party run by Alberto's children, Keiko and Kenji. Otherwise, politics was practised by a series of ephemeral personalist parties and shifting coalitions of independents, though the left showed signs of revival in the 2016 election. The party of Pedro-Pablo Kuczynski, who was narrowly elected president in 2016, won only 18 of the 130 seats in Peru's Congress, where Fuerza Popular held a majority. In countries such as Peru, where parties were so weak, the mass media played a disproportionately preponderant political role in sustaining democracy.

Mixed messages from the media

In the early 1990s, as Salinas was propelling his country into the North American Free Trade Agreement, finding out what was happening in Mexico was about as easy as it was in the Soviet Union. Televisa, a private company, had acquired a near monopoly on television, with four national channels, in return for its loyalty to the regime. Its evening news programme was the mouthpiece of Los Pinos, the presidential office. It offered upbeat daily reports of the president's doings. The opposition, especially its leader, Cuauhtémoc Cárdenas, was simply ignored, except for occasional smear reports alleging that he was linked to violence. In those days, Mexico City had a dozen daily newspapers. All had small circulations, and all were kept alive by government payments. *Proceso*, a newsweekly, was more independent, but survived by being impenetrably dull. In other countries in the region, many powerful media groups emerged timidly into the era of democracy, with an innate conservative and establishment bias.

Much has changed in the past three decades. On the one hand, in many countries the media have become much freer and more professional. Investigative journalists have bravely exposed abuses and corruption. For example, an investigation in 2013 by *La Nación*, an Argentine newspaper, revealed that companies owned by Lázaro Báez, a construction magnate, had made year-round block bookings for dozens of rooms in a luxury hotel in Patagonia owned by the Kirchners. Báez, a former bank clerk, was the largest single beneficiary of public-works contracts in Patagonia in the decade in which the Kirchners ruled Argentina. The paper found no evidence that the hotel rooms were ever occupied. Earlier, an investigation by a newspaper in Costa Rica, also called *La Nación*, turned up evidence that three of the country's former presidents had received bribes. Some media outlets played an important role in putting issues such as education on the public agenda and in giving civil-society groups a voice. In some countries, the media has become more even-handed politically. One study found that news coverage of recent elections in Brazil, Chile and Mexico was largely unbiased among the main candidates.[45] In Brazil, Globo, the most important television network, tried hard to be scrupulously fair in its treatment of Lula's governments in news bulletins, and much of its programming output was of good quality.

There were several blemishes. The first was that in several countries media freedom had been radically curtailed. That obviously applied to Cuba, where 29 independent journalists were arrested in 2003 and given prison terms averaging 27 years, after summary trials. Independent journalists continued to face official harassment under Raúl Castro. In Venezuela, opposition-supporting media outlets were harassed into near extinction. Several were bought up by business people close to the regime. That happened in Bolivia, too. In Ecuador, Rafael Correa bullied the media into self-censorship, filing several cases for criminal libel against journalists who had offended him and fining media outlets whose coverage he disliked. In these cases of polarisation, opposition media outlets had often taken on an overtly political role, campaigning against far-left governments in ways that were more appropriate for political parties.

A second problem was the violence meted out to journalists in the region, especially by organised crime. According to the Committee to Protect Journalists, Colombia, Brazil and Mexico are among the 11 most dangerous countries in the world to be a journalist, with a total of 124 reporters killed because of their work since 1992.[46] Third, in several countries, such as Peru, media ownership is highly concentrated. Nevertheless, overall the media has been both an important watchdog and an essential ingredient in the emergence of open societies in Latin America.

Corruption and campaign finance

The spectre of corruption hangs ever more threateningly over democratic politics in the region. Corruption has long been endemic. Voters tolerate politicians who 'steal but get things done' (an epithet first applied to a populist governor of São Paulo in the 1940s). That tradition has lived on in some places. Campaigning to be mayor of the small town of San Blas on Mexico's Pacific coast, Hilario Ramírez Villanueva admitted at a rally in 2014 that in a previous term of office: 'I did steal. But only a little . . . it was only a little shaving. And what I took with this hand I gave back with the other hand to the poor.' Ramírez, who also groped a young woman in public and was accused of links with drug traffickers, was elected with 40 per cent of the vote. He celebrated his victory by throwing banknotes at the crowd. In 2017, he attempted to register his candidacy for governor of Nayarit state.[47]

Chile and Uruguay are among the world's 25 cleanest countries, according to the ranking of perceptions of corruption compiled by Transparency International, a Berlin-based watchdog. Worldwide, corruption tends to diminish with income per head. Yet two-thirds of Latin American nations are in the bottom half of the ranking, even though the region's income is above the global median.[48] The commodity boom brought unprecedented wealth to governments, so there was more money to steal. But overall, even if the amounts involved became eye-wateringly large, it was not clear that corruption became more pervasive. Polls reported that slightly fewer respondents said they had to pay bribes. Corruption came in many varieties, from petty gouging by low-level officials to the grand larceny of Venezuela or Mexican state governors.

Before the boom, an egregious case involved Alberto Fujimori in Peru. His closest aide, Vladimiro Montesinos, the sinister intelligence chief, spun a vast web of bribery and extortion, and manipulated the media in an attempt to win an unconstitutional third term for Fujimori. Both men are serving jail sentences for corruption and human-rights abuses. The corrupt activities of Odebrecht, the Brazilian construction firm, were unique in their continental scope. In its settlement with the US Department of Justice, Odebrecht admitted paying $388 million in bribes to political leaders and their associates in nine other Latin American countries, as well as Brazil (and Angola and Mozambique). In the wake of this revelation, scandal ricocheted across the region. In Peru, a prosecutor charged Alejandro Toledo, a former president, with receiving $20 million in bribes. Prosecutors in half a dozen other countries were investigating suspected bribes.

What is clear is that corruption has become more visible, because of the scrutiny of the media and civil-society groups, and that public tolerance of it has diminished. That is partly because of the economic slowdown. The combination of austerity and corruption is politically toxic. This helped Chávez to come to power in Venezuela. There is a risk that the discrediting of the political system by corruption scandals might again lead to the search for saviours in the form of populist outsiders. But the best antidote to corruption is transparency and the rule of law. On that there is some progress.

In Mexico, civil-society groups pushed hard to try to ensure that Peña Nieto's proposed 'anti-corruption system' had teeth. 'We are in an era in which public opinion is playing a fundamental role' in fighting corruption in Latin America, according to José Ugaz, a Peruvian lawyer who was the special prosecutor who sent Fujimori and Montesinos to jail and who, in 2015, was chosen as the head of Transparency International.[49] Many countries adopted international conventions against bribery, and toughened their own laws. Brazil's *Lava Jato* investigation was only the most prominent example. Missing, still, was greater transparency around public contracting, as the Odebrecht case highlighted.

In particular, while public–private partnerships (PPPs) have been a useful way to raise financing for big infrastructure projects, their complexity has invited gouging, with contractors making low bids and then corruptly securing big increases in costs through addenda. José Luis Guasch, formerly at the World Bank, found that 78 per cent of all transport PPPs in Latin America were renegotiated, with an average of four addenda per contract and a cost increase of $30 million per addendum. Thus, the cost of a road linking Brazil and Peru rose from $800 million to $2.3 billion through 22 addenda.[50]

In many cases, as in the Petrobras scandal in Brazil, corruption was at least partially related to the financing of political campaigns, even if some money from illicit donations probably ended up in the pockets of those involved. Odebrecht admitted to buying influence by making campaign donations in Peru, Colombia and Venezuela. Latin American elections were increasingly expensive, and that carried dangers. Although there are few precise figures, Brazil's general election in 2006 may have cost a colossal $2.6 billion, despite a large public subsidy in the form of free television advertising slots in the final weeks of the campaign.[51] In some cases, the electoral system serves to magnify the cost: in Brazil's 'open list' system, voters choose individual candidates for Congress from party slates. Even in the era of social media, candidates in many countries use the expensive, old-fashioned campaign tools of outdoor advertising and open-air rallies. Corporate donations, especially when they are under the table, sometimes lead to the private capture of slices of government. In Chile, for example, big fishing companies have financed politicians who should have regulated them, but instead allowed them unrestricted rights to plunder the depleted seas in perpetuity.[52]

Governments have long sought to regulate campaign finance, but often ineffectually. Uruguay was the first country in the world to give public subsidy to political parties, in 1928. Now most Latin American democracies do. In Mexico and Argentina, subsidies serve to breed small, parasitic parties which feed off the taxpayer. But in most countries they are small. Whatever the rules, the reality is that a small coterie of private businesses stump up most of the cash for campaigns almost everywhere, except perhaps in Uruguay and Costa Rica. In the wake of scandals, steps have been taken to tighten the rules. Chile's parliament approved a law which restricted outdoor advertising, increased public subsidies, banned corporate donations and regulated those from individuals. Brazil's electoral tribunal banned corporate donations and shortened the duration of the official campaign. In Brazil, there is some evidence that these measures may have helped incumbent mayors win re-election in the municipal elections of 2016.[53] But campaign finance is fraught with such trade-offs. The imperative is to clean up politics by cutting the cost of campaigns.

Stasis and renewal

Corruption was all the more politically damaging because, fairly or not, the traditional political parties were widely seen as self-serving, out of touch and unaccountable. Many of the region's political leaders were Duracell politicians, with the *caudillo*'s habit of dying with their boots on. 'All political careers end in failure', observed Enoch Powell, a British politician. But in Latin America, some seemed never to end at all. José Sarney, whose political career began in the 1950s and who was Brazil's president in 1985–90, went on to spend 24 years as a senator. Although he stepped down in 2015, he still exercised influence through his son, who was a federal deputy and twice the environment minister. Raúl Alfonsín clung to leadership of Argentina's moribund Radicals into his 80s; Leonel Brizola, a political disciple of Getúlio Vargas, was planning yet another failed presidential campaign when he died in 2005 aged 82.

Some were inspired by the example of Salvador Allende, who won the presidency at the third attempt, or Lula who won after three successive defeats. Pedro-Pablo Kuczynski won Peru's presidency at the second attempt, aged 77. Ricardo Lagos, a former president who had seemingly retreated to the role of respected elder statesman, tried but failed to become the candidate of Chile's Socialist Party in 2017 at the age of 79. Certainly, increased life expectancy and better health have been a factor in prolonging political careers. But so has been the move to allow re-election. As Daniel Zovatto, an Argentine political scientist and electoral specialist, has observed, non-consecutive re-election exercised a bigger brake on political renewal than two recurrent terms, since 'it sends presidents not into retirement but to the substitutes' bench, from where [as in basketball, rather than football] they expect to return'.[54]

As well as old politicians, Latin America continued to see old-style politics in the form of clientelism (although the former were not necessarily its practitioners). By one definition, clientelism is the 'individualised, contingent exchange of goods or services for political support or votes'.[55] What this often means is that social benefits which ought to be – and maybe are – a right are awarded as favours. Clientelistic practices have a long history in Latin America, and have taken many forms. At their crudest, they involve paying for votes in cash or kind. In a more sophisticated way, organised clientelism was at the root of the appeal of populist parties. The Kirchners funnelled benefits to the unemployed through activist groups that formed part of their political clientele, for example. There have been some signs that clientelism has grown weaker with the spread of education. As noted, voters tend to punish governments that they think have let them down, and that applies at the local as well as the national level. A study of clientelism in local government in Argentina, found that it tends to disappear where there are high levels of political competition and a large middle class.[56]

One way in which Latin American voters have sought political renewal is by supporting 'outsiders' – a habit they developed long before Donald Trump or Italy's Five Star Movement. This phenomenon is especially prevalent in the Andean countries, but is not confined to them. Alberto Fujimori was the archetype. A university rector with no previous political experience, he formed an ad hoc party and rose from nowhere in the opinion polls just a month before the election of 1990. He capitalised on popular disillusion with a political establishment that had failed to defeat either inflation or terrorism. Similarly, Alejandro Toledo managed to become the vehicle of opposition to Fujimori while lacking a serious party.

There was an echo of the outsider in Álvaro Uribe's crusade for the presidency against his party's official candidate. But Uribe was an experienced professional politician. That was not true of Venezuela's Hugo Chávez or Lucio Gutiérrez, an army colonel involved in the 2000 coup against Mahuad and elected as Ecuador's president in 2002. Ollanta Humala, a nationalist former lieutenant-colonel with an ad hoc party, won Peru's presidency at the second attempt in 2011. The main claim to fame of Mauricio Macri, before he was elected as a congressman in 2005 and then mayor of Buenos Aires two years later, was that he was president of Boca Juniors, Argentina's most popular football club. Macri belonged to a sub-group of businessmen, who were thus outsiders only in a political sense. Álvaro Noboa, an Ecuadorean banana magnate, came close to winning his country's presidency in 2002 and again in 2006. Sebastián Piñera, one of Chile's wealthiest businessmen, was elected president in 2010. Ricardo Martinelli, a supermarket owner, won Panama's presidency. Piñera put his assets into a blind trust. Others have been less scrupulous.

The rebellion against the political establishment took other forms, too. Many of the left-wing social movements and campaigning groups that emerged in the 1990s and 2000s were 'anti-party', and some sought direct political representation. Some political scientists are worried that O'Donnell might have exaggerated the lack of 'horizontal accountability' exercised by legislatures and judiciaries, but that he overlooked the extent to which a breach has opened up in 'vertical accountability' – in the extent to which institutions manage to channel the interests and concerns of voters.[57]

The voters' sense of disconnection and the demand for political renewal could see more populist leaders elected in the future. Until poverty and inequality diminish, some voters will continue to be tempted both by the clientelistic promise of votes for favours and by the miracle preachings of populists. The Venezuelan disaster acted as a vaccine against the radical populism of the left. But it is not guaranteed to be effective. There is a clear risk that fossilised political structures may not be able to respond to the demands of more dynamic and connected societies.

CHAPTER TWELVE

The Loneliness of Latin America

The small state of Tlaxcala, in the highlands east of Mexico City, was home to the people who were Hernán Cortés's most important allies in his assault on the Aztec capital of Tenochtitlán.[1] More recently, Tlaxcalans had to respond to a different sort of invasion, one of cheap Asian textiles. That this involved painful change was clear from a visit to the state in 1992, five years after Mexico's government had begun to open the economy to international trade, and just when it was negotiating the North American Free Trade Agreement with the United States and Canada:

> Only birdsong disturbs the silence inside the La Josefina textile factory . . . Yards of cotton cloth still hang from its lines of looms, stopped in mid-weave when the factory shut a year ago and its 100 workers were laid off. The nameplates on the machines explain what happened. They are from a bygone Lancashire: the cast iron looms were made more than a century ago by John M. Summer of Manchester, J. Dugdale & Sons of Blackburn and G. Keighly of Burnley. The spinning machines came from Dobson & Barlow Ltd, Bolton, in 1912, and the carding equipment from Platt Bros of Oldham in 1920. Since 1881, La Josefina had made yarn and cotton cloth for the Mexican market. It closed because its machines, though still in perfect working order, could not compete with modern, electronically controlled rivals . . . 'Yarn came in from India, Korea and Taiwan at half the price we sold at', Valentín Rangel, La Josefina's administrator, says. 'We were caught out, technologically backward and without the capital to renew our machinery.'[2]

A dozen years later, Tlaxcala had moved on. The state's main roads were studded with new factories. Some supplied the expanding Volkswagen plant nearby at Puebla, the German car giant's main production site for North America. Turn off into the hills, and there was evidence of improvement in what was long a poor area, dependent on peasant farming and textiles. In villages, two- and three-storey houses of brick and concrete had replaced the small huts of a decade before, though – as elsewhere in rural Mexico – the *Oportunidades/Prospera* conditional cash transfer programme and remittances from migrants had both played their part. Tlaxcala did not get rich, however. In the presidential elections of 2006 and 2012, Andrés Manuel López Obrador was the most-voted candidate there, as in most states in Mexico's poorer centre and south. López Obrador did not call openly for a return to the statist protectionism of the past. But he did call for a renegotiation of NAFTA to suspend the requirement on Mexico to lift the remaining tariff on the import of maize and beans.

Many Latin Americans, just like people elsewhere, are ambivalent towards globalisation. For some of them, the past 35 years have brought more pain than gain. Hundreds of thousands of workers lost their jobs in factories like La Josefina. Baroque labour laws offered no protection against economic realities, and nor did they provide unemployment insurance to ease economic adjustment. In the end, many more new jobs were created in the region; but that took time, and they often went to younger and better-qualified workers. Yet on balance, globalisation has served Latin America well. This certainly applies in Mexico, which – thanks to NAFTA – is one of the most globalised countries in Latin America.

For much of its life, even before Donald Trump trashed it as 'the worst trade deal maybe ever signed anywhere', NAFTA had a bad reputation on both sides of the Rio Grande.[3] In the popular mind in Mexico, NAFTA came to be associated with the peso collapse and recession of 1994–95, which were not directly related to it. Mexicans were encouraged to believe that the trade agreement would deliver instant prosperity, just as voters in the United States were told that it would end Mexican migration. Its achievements were inevitably more modest, and its history was somewhat chequered. Rapid initial growth in cross-border trade and investment then slowed. The terrorist attacks on 11 September 2001 brought time-consuming border security checks. In the same year, China joined the World Trade Organization. That prompted manufacturing plants to leave Mexico in search of cheaper labour, though others later replaced them. Both the US and the Mexican governments dragged their feet on upgrading border infrastructure. Nevertheless, trade between the two countries increased fivefold between 1994 and 2014, and NAFTA brought into being seamless cross-border supply chains, especially for industries such as cars, aerospace and electronics.

Although Mexico had a trade surplus of about $60 billion with the United States, some 40 per cent of its northbound exports embodied US-made components. Without NAFTA, the United States would have lost many more manufacturing jobs to China. And Mexico would not have become an advanced manufacturing country. Thanks to the trade agreement, oil accounted for just 13 per cent of Mexico's total exports by 2005, down from 80 per cent in 1980. In negotiating NAFTA, Salinas had insisted on keeping energy off the table (the US did the same for the movement of labour). In unilaterally opening Mexico's oil, gas and electricity industries to foreign investment, Peña Nieto boosted energy integration between the two countries, prompting a growing network of gas pipelines. NAFTA's most visible impact on Mexico was in places like Monterrey, the industrial hub in the north-east of the country, which transformed itself into a handsome city of swirling freeways, glass office blocks, innovative universities and frequent international conferences. Its benefits gradually spread out to many places in the north and centre of the country. If they did not reach the poorer south, that was hardly the fault of the trade agreement, but rather because of poor government and lack of transport infrastructure.

Torments in the name of freedom

For Mexico, Trump represented a nightmare. NAFTA had been a bold political bet by Salinas, setting aside generations of nationalist opposition to closer collaboration with the United States. Trump seemed to call this bet into question. He began his campaign for the Republican nomination in Las Vegas in June 2015 by accusing Mexico of sending drugs and 'rapists' across the border. He repeatedly pledged to build a 'Great Wall' along the border and have Mexico 'pay for it', as well as to deport 11 million undocumented migrants (half of them Mexicans), stop American companies building factories there, and tear up NAFTA and impose tariffs of 35 per cent on Mexico's exports. It was humiliating, insulting and unremittingly hostile behaviour towards a country that had chosen to become a US ally. And it came when Mexico was at a low ebb, grappling with crime and corruption and with a weak and discredited government. Not surprisingly, opinion polls showed a rise in support for López Obrador, like Trump a populist nationalist, for the 2018 presidential election. In office, Trump quickly signed an executive order to build the 'wall', but his administration showed signs of understanding that NAFTA had advantages for the United States. A tough negotiation was in store, in which Mexico had some cards. It could seek to re-route its purchases of US farm goods to South America, as well as to diversify its export markets, and it could dally with China. But in the end, geography is economic destiny for Mexico.

For Latin America, there was a sad irony in the arrival of a protectionist, populist nationalist in the White House. It came after relations with the United States had improved under Barack Obama and just when much of the region was turning its back on populism. Some Latin American countries, especially those on the Pacific seaboard had never lost interest in free trade. Mexico, Chile and Peru were all signatories of the Trans-Pacific Partnership (TPP), the trade deal that Obama negotiated and which also included a number of Asian countries. They planned to go ahead with the TPP anyway, even though Trump said the US would not ratify it.

But others had turned against trade. At the turn of the century, parts of Latin America suffered the kind of backlash against globalisation that now affects the United State and Europe. It took the guise of 'antiimperialism' and reached its peak at the fourth Summit of the Americas at Mar del Plata in 2005. There, 29 countries – including Mexico, Colombia, Peru and Chile, as well as the United States and Canada – affirmed their commitment to 'reactivate' negotiations for the Free Trade Area of the Americas (FTAA), a plan to extend NAFTA to the whole of the hemisphere, launched at the first such summit in Miami in 1994. But Venezuela, Brazil and Argentina said that 'the necessary conditions' for the FTAA were lacking.

Outside the conference hall, Chávez spoke for two and a half hours to a rally of some 25,000 people organised by aides of Néstor Kirchner, and attended by Diego Maradona, a footballer made rich by globalisation. The Venezuelan president said he had come 'to bury' the FTAA and 'to take part in a birth, that of ALBA', as he called his anti-American alliance (see later in this chapter). Back at the conference, Mexico's

Vicente Fox gave Chávez a public dressing down. George Bush flew on from Mar del Plata to Brasília, where Lula entertained him to a barbecue. Brazil 'doesn't want to bury the FTAA but to build it on a realistic basis', Celso Amorim, the foreign minister, felt obliged to make clear.[4] Brazil had its own view of globalisation, which focused on multilateral diplomacy and 'south–south' ties in a 'multipolar' world.

The United States was partly to blame for the failure of the FTAA. Like Brazil, it had always been ambivalent about it. Several things conspired to doom the agreement. The most important was the stalling of the Doha Round of world trade talks that were supposed to free trade in agriculture – a vital cause for Brazil, Argentina and other South American countries. The United States insisted that it could only eliminate subsidies to its farmers in the context of a global, not regional, deal on agriculture. A less ambitious FTAA might still have been possible, but neither Brazil nor the United States was prepared to push hard for it. As the FTAA talks became moribund, both sought to build their own trading webs in the region.

The US concluded bilateral trade agreements with Chile, Central America and the Dominican Republic, and then with Peru, Colombia and Panama. They were called 'free-trade agreements' (FTAs), but they were in reality preferential deals; and for the Latin American signatories they were a third-best option. They were less beneficial than a global trade deal; a united Latin America would have had more bargaining power in the FTAA negotiations than individual countries could exercise in bilateral deals. For example, Florida farmers excluded free trade in sugar from the Dominican Republic–Central American FTA; for no good reason, to please Wall Street investment banks, the United States insisted that the trade agreements should bar the imposition of selective controls on capital inflows of the kind Chile had successfully used in the 1980s and 1990s to stabilise its economy. Yet even with these limitations, many Latin American governments concluded that a third-best deal with the US was better than none at all. One motivation for Peru and Colombia was to render permanent those preferences granted temporarily to non-commodity exports from the five Andean countries by a 1991 law as part of the 'war on drugs'. But the main Latin American interest in these agreements was that they would encourage foreign investment. They had the effect of 'locking in' some of the free-market reforms – which is why they were so bitterly opposed by the far left – and the commitment to economic stability. But they fell well short of the kind of external sponsorship of development that the European Union offered to countries on its southern and eastern periphery.

Bolívar had presciently observed that the United States seemed 'destined by Providence to plague America with torments in the name of freedom'.[5] His comment nicely summed up his own mixed feelings of admiration for and distrust of the United States, as well as its combination of idealism and heavy-handedness in its dealings with its southern neighbours. The latter-day 'Boliviarians' had a cruder view. Chávez and his followers peddled the grossly exaggerated notion that Latin America as a whole had been forever under the thumb of the United States. In fact, the US never paid much attention to South America. The larger countries of Latin America showed as much diplomatic independence towards the United States as do those of Europe. That was not to ignore the fact that US intervention had had a significant – and often negative – impact in the countries of the Caribbean rim, with Cuba and Guatemala being the clearest examples. The asymmetries of power between the two Americas generated a certain arrogance in US behaviour and corresponding resentment in Latin America. Behind such attitudes lay not just history, but a mutual lack of knowledge and comprehension.

Latin American attitudes towards the United States are inevitably complex. On the one hand, ordinary Latin Americans admire the prosperity, freedoms and security of their northern neighbour – and yearn to migrate there. On the other, Latin American elites, justifiably or not, often see the US as a threat. They fear cultural invasion, political interference and economic domination.[6] But in practice, for most Latin American governments the United States is a fact of life to be managed, and an opportunity to be made the best of. For many, it is their main export market, especially for higher value-added manufactures; and for some it is their main source of aid.

While in the past they had condemned *Yanqui* interventionism, many Latin American politicians came to lament what they saw as a lack of US engagement with the region. As a presidential candidate in 2000, George W. Bush had gone to Miami to deliver a campaign speech, in which he promised to take Latin America seriously. As an adopted Texan with a Mexican sister-in-law and a smattering of bad Spanish, Bush seemed to have a genuine personal interest in the region. In September 2001, he invited Vicente Fox to the White House and, amidst the panoply and junketing of a state visit, said that the United States had 'no more important relationship' than that with its southern neighbour. Days later, the terrorist attacks against the United States changed Bush's priorities. Latin Americans, having suffered 'pre-emptive unilateralism' from the United States in the past, were unsympathetic to the war in Iraq. The Bush administration, in turn, felt betrayed by Chile and (especially) Mexico, which as temporary members of the UN Security Council hewed to an anti-war line.

Plan Colombia, and the democratic imperatives behind it, was ill understood in the rest of Latin America. More visible was the constant low-level bullying of the 'war on drugs'. Rightly or wrongly, the Bush administration was accused of being unhelpful when Argentina's economy collapsed in 2001 (though it came smartly to the rescue when Uruguay and Brazil wobbled the following year). Frustration was fuelled by the perception during Bush's first administration that nobody very senior in Washington was in charge of policy towards the region   a perception heightened by the apparent US endorsement of the failed coup against Hugo Chávez in Venezuela in 2002, and the failure to come to the aid of Goni in Bolivia the following year. To make matters worse, on the two issues that mattered most to many Latin American governments – trade and migration – policy was largely determined on Capitol Hill by the US Congress, rather than by the White House.

In Bush's second term, policy towards the region became much more pragmatic. The administration sought to reduce Chávez's influence in the region through quiet diplomacy, rather than the rhetorical aggression that had marked much of Bush's first term. In a five-country week-long tour of the region early in 2007, Bush talked of poverty and social injustice, and invoked the memory of Kennedy's Alliance for Progress. He established a good personal relationship with Lula. Thomas Shannon, a career diplomat who became the State Department's top official for the region in 2005, insisted that the United States would try to work with left-wing leaders who were democratically elected.[7] Missing was a clearer commitment that those countries that stuck to the path of democratic reform would reap the benefits of a close alliance, especially in the form of more equitable trade deals and, for the poorer ones, greater development aid.

Barack Obama arrived in the White House facing pressing issues at home, in the shape of the financial crisis and the continuing wars in Iraq and Afghanistan. Not surprisingly, he showed little initial interest in Latin America, but he did show an appreciation of the history of intervention in the region and a preference for multilateral diplomacy. In April 2009, just three months after he took office, he travelled to Trinidad and Tobago for the sixth Summit of the Americas, where he told Latin America's leaders that he wanted to begin 'a new chapter of engagement' and an 'equal partnership . . . based on mutual respect and shared values'. Most dramatically, he pledged to seek 'a new beginning with Cuba'. Six years later, at the seventh Summit in Panama, Obama declared that he had met those commitments. In the wake of their historic agreement to restore diplomatic relations, Obama and Raúl Castro talked for an hour in Panama, the first face-to-face meeting between leaders from the two countries since Vice-President Richard Nixon met Fidel Castro in 1959. The rapprochement was welcomed by Latin American presidents of all political stripes, who had long seen the US embargo against Cuba and its exclusion from hemispheric institutions as counterproductive.[8]

The Obama administration faced a Latin America that was both more self-confident and independent minded, thanks to the commodity boom and rapidly growing trade with China, and more internally divided than in the past, as the Mar del Plata summit had dramatised. In his first term, Obama took a largely reactive approach to the region, which resulted in some fumbles. The first test came in Honduras, when the army ousted Manuel Zelaya. The administration fell in with the demand of Brazil and other Latin American countries that Zelaya be unconditionally reinstated. But the interim president, Roberto Micheletti, lobbied congressional Republicans and proved immune to pressure. Eventually, US officials brokered a deal involving a fresh election, but Brazil and other left-wing governments in the region waited up to a year before recognising the result. Further frictions with Brazil followed, over Lula's failed attempt to broker a nuclear deal with Iran, over his country's quest for a permanent seat on the UN Security Council and then over revelations by Edward Snowden, the former National Security Agency (NSA) contractor, that the NSA had tapped Dilma Rousseff's phone.

In his second term, Obama took a closer interest in Latin America, naming Joseph Biden, the vice-president, as his special envoy to the region. They developed some modest but useful policy initiatives, such as an aid programme targeted at reducing drug-related violence in Central America and a plan to tackle energy shortages in the Caribbean. The administration gave diplomatic support to Colombia's peace process. It downplayed the 'war on drugs'. His critics saw Obama's Cuba policy as giving the Castros' regime a free pass. They charged him with doing little or nothing either to prevent Venezuela's slide to dictatorship, beyond approving sanctions against a few individuals, or to slow the rise of Chinese influence in Latin America. But it was not clear that the United States possessed effective tools to prevent these developments. And Obama was right that change would only come to Cuba from within.

The defining paradox of relations between the two parts of the Americas is that while no region commands less attention in the foreign policy of the United States than Latin America, no region is more important to the daily lives of (North) Americans. Ties of trade, investment, tourism, family, migration, remittances and culture bind the two together. Whatever Trump might do, many of those ties are likely to survive. But the United States is not the only outside player in Latin America. Indeed it never has been.

It has long been true that the further south you go in the Americas, the less powerful is US influence. For Brazil and Argentina, the European Union is a more important trade partner and source of investment than the United States. Many Latin Americans yearn for Europe to act more generally as a counterweight to the United States in the region.

A generation of politicians and writers who sojourned in Paris's *Quartier Latin* during the 1960s and 1970s argued that Latin America had more in common with the social-democratic values of Europe than with hard-driving Anglo-Saxon individualism. That was debatable. But it was true that on many issues, ranging from policies towards Cuba and drugs to support for the UN and multilateralism, many Latin American governments tended to be closer to European positions than to those of the United States. There was much bonhomie expressed at EU–Latin American summits, which began at Rio de Janeiro in 1999 with the oxymoronic declaration of '55 priorities' for this transcontinental partnership. In practice, relations have been low-key. Europe has been too distracted by problems closer to home, from the euro crisis to Brexit, to show much interest. Spain has been the main exception. Its banks and utility and construction companies began to invest heavily in the region in the late 1990s. Through the Iberoamerican summits, which began in Guadalajara, Mexico, in 1993, it tried to position itself as the main point of contact of Latin America with Europe, though that was never the case for Brazil.

The Chinese chequebook

One of the gleaming office towers around Puerto Madero, a glitzed-up former timber wharf in Buenos Aires, is emblazoned with the initials of the Industrial and Commercial Bank of China. In 2011, via a tie-up with Standard Bank of South Africa, it bought a network of more than a hundred bank branches in Argentina that formerly belonged to BankBoston. Over the past decade, Chinese cut-price supermarkets have multiplied across Argentina; Chinese-built trains now ply the suburban lines built by the British more than a century ago; Chinese companies have won contracts to build hydroelectric plants and to refurbish the Belgrano Norte freight railway, which will carry soya beans to ports around Rosario for export to China.

In the twenty-first century, with great speed, China has become a significant economic partner for Latin America. Its appetite for Andean copper, Brazilian iron ore, Venezuelan oil and Argentine and Brazilian soya beans drove up their price and created a new trading relationship. From almost nothing in 2000, total trade between China and Latin America soared to almost $300 billion in 2013. But then it began to decline, as commodity prices fell and China's growth slowed. As cheap Chinese manufactures continued to flood into Latin America, the trade balance moved heavily against the region. China became a big investor, too. Initially these investments were almost exclusively in mines and oilfields, but they broadened to include infrastructure and manufacturing. Chinese companies have snapped up Brazilian electricity and construction companies, as well as an investment bank. Between 2005 and 2016, the China Development Bank and China Export-Import Bank extended credits to Latin American governments totalling $141 billion – more than the World Bank and the IDB combined. The vast majority went to just four countries: Venezuela, Brazil, Argentina and Ecuador.[9]

The left-wing governments in Latin America seemed to see China as a kind of anti-imperialist free lunch. Both sides shared a view of the existing international economic order as unfair to them. China was happy to lend without political or economic policy strings. Unlike Africa, Latin America did not allow the Chinese to buy up farmland or bring in their own labour for projects (except in some Caribbean islands). But snags soon arose. Trade with China served to increase the weight of commodities in Latin America's exports, and contributed to de-industrialisation in the region.[10]

Much of Mexico's textile industry, Brazilian shoemaking and toy manufacturing was wiped out, or moved to China, for example.[11] The rise of China served to depress Latin America's manufactured exports, especially those of Mexico and Central America, which had grown fast in the 1990s. The World Bank found that for Latin America, a 1 per cent increase in trade with countries of 'the north' was associated with a 1.6 per cent rise in economic growth; while a similar increase in the region's trade with 'the south' (defined to include Asia) brought only 0.3 per cent in extra growth.[12] That was partly because of 'Dutch disease' – the tendency of commodity booms to go hand in hand with a stronger currency, an effect augmented by Latin America's low savings rate and import of investment capital. More recently, the rise in Chinese wages and the depreciation of Latin American currencies has offered some relief.

Chinese officials have insisted that they want good relations with all governments in the region, whatever their political colour. They have concluded trade agreements with Chile, Costa Rica and Peru. They were reportedly worried that their Venezuelan ally would default on its loans. Chinese experts on Latin America insisted that the country's interest in Latin America did not involve a search for influence in what some in the United States used to consider its 'backyard'. 'We're not seeking special influence. We have reiterated [to the United States] that our relations with Latin America aren't a threat to anyone', Qui Xiaoqi, China's ambassador in Brasília, told me in 2009. But the idea of having friends in the Americas to begin to match the US's alliances in East Asia was surely attractive.

Certainly, Xi Jinping, China's president, paid attention to Latin America, launching an annual summit with the region's leaders and paying a visit each year after he became China's president in 2013. In 2015, his government announced plans to double trade with the region over ten years and to more than double the stock of investment. That may prove hard. But China was clearly in Latin America to stay. And it was down to Latin American governments to negotiate better deals with it. As Susana Malcorra, Argentina's foreign minister, told me: 'They will fill all the space you let them have. The onus is on us.'[13]

Less forgotten

China was not the only new outside player in the region. Two decades after the end of the Cold War, Russia started to show renewed interest in Latin America. It began with Cuba and Venezuela. Chávez bought weapons worth $4.4 billion from Russia, including Sukhoi fighter jets. In 2008, Russia sent a small naval flotilla to the Caribbean for joint exercises with Cuba and Venezuela. In 2014, Vladimir Putin visited Latin America, stopping off in Brazil and Argentina, as well as in Cuba and Nicaragua. He saw the region as a market for Russian nuclear technology, as well as arms. Russia became the financier of last resort for Maduro's regime in Venezuela, gaining stakes in oilfields in return for cash. Unlike China, Russia's interest in the region seemed opportunistic and marginal.

Much was made by conservatives in Washington of Iran's activities in Latin America. Chávez went out of his way to court Mahmoud Ahmadinejad, Iran's president from 2005 to 2013, who offered credits for industrial ventures in Venezuela, none of which produced lasting results. Ahmadinejad made two visits to Latin America, on both occasions taking in Bolivia, Ecuador and Nicaragua, as well as Venezuela. These efforts appeared aimed at securing diplomatic allies in international bodies, while irritating the United States. Some analysts saw a more sinister dimension. An Argentine judge, initially with government backing, issued arrest warrants for seven Iranian officials in connection with the bombing of the Israeli embassy in Buenos Aires in 1992 and of a Jewish community centre in the city two years later that between them killed 114 people and injured more than 500. But there was no firm evidence of a continuing and active Iranian-inspired terrorist presence in the region.

Brazil saw itself as an important player in what some called the 'rise of the South' and the evolution of a 'multipolar world'. Lula and Celso Amorim, his foreign minister, put particular emphasis on IBSA, a grouping they set up that linked Brazil with India and South Africa, three big multiracial developing-world democracies. They participated enthusiastically in the annual summits of the BRICS countries, which began in Russia in 2008, and in the development bank that the group set up. Brazil also joined China's Asian Infrastructure Investment Bank. Under Lula, Brazil opened 33 new embassies, 14 of them in Africa and many of the rest in the Caribbean. Africa was the main focus of Brazil's small but growing foreign-aid programme. Embrapa, the country's admired agricultural research agency, set up a research station to provide technical help with cotton-growing in West Africa. Brazil became a significant player in global trade and environmental diplomacy. But critics at home complained of little concrete return from a foreign policy which they saw as driven by ideological preference, rather than underlying national interest. Brazil's considerable soft power was damaged by its economic slump, political implosion and the evidence that Odebrecht and other construction companies had paid bribes across Latin America and in Africa. And Brazil's vision of itself as the leading actor in a united South America met opposition, both from Hugo Chávez and from the free-trading countries of the Pacific seaboard.

The rhetoric and disappointing reality of regional integration

The Uruguayan town of Fray Bentos, on the broad River Uruguay marking the border with Argentina, harks back to the first era of globalisation. In 1865, an Anglo-Belgian company set up a factory there to make meat extract, using the formula developed by Justus von Liebig, a German chemist. It developed into a vast enterprise, employing 1,500 workers by 1911, and exporting corned beef, Oxo cubes and other meat products to Europe. Fray Bentos became a company town. It still boasts a barrio of neat workers' housing and a town centre of trim parks, with theatres and public buildings embellished with the architectural flourishes of the *belle époque*. The meat factory, by then owned by Britain's Vestey family, shut down in 1967, and is now an industrial museum, receiving tourists from Montevideo. Part of it has been turned into a campus for a new technological university, with Chinese-equipped electrical engineering laboratories. Across town, on the riverbank not far from the border bridge, stands a large new factory, a $1.2 billion pulp mill built by Metsä-Botnia, a Finnish company.

For three years until 2010, the bridge, the shortest land route between Montevideo and Buenos Aires, was blocked by Argentine demonstrators, encouraged by the Kirchners. They complained that the paper mill would pollute the river, although they had no such concerns about several older, much dirtier, Argentine pulp mills on the River Paraná bordering Paraguay. The dispute went all the way to the International Court of Justice, which found no evidence of pollution, though it said Uruguay should have consulted Argentina about the plant. What made the closure of the bridge extraordinary was that not only did both countries have left-wing governments at the time, but both are also members of Mercosur, a putative common market. The paper-mill dispute marked the nadir of regional integration in Latin America, whose history is one of much soaring rhetoric and disappointingly little achievement.

The dream of Latin American unity goes back to Bolívar. He believed that the newly independent republics had to stick together as a matter of survival. He set up a short-lived union of Gran Colombia, which dissolved when Venezuela and Ecuador left. He convoked a Congress of America in Panama in 1826, though in the end it was attended only by delegates from Mexico, Central America, Colombia and Peru, together with an invited British observer (Bolívar himself observed the proceedings from Lima). His aim seems to have been to establish a kind of confederation, though he quickly resiled from this as an impossibility. Right from the start, there was a tension between the unity of a region with a shared experience of independence and the nationalism that had brought that about.[14] It is a tension that persists to this day.

For much of Latin America's history, regional integration was neither a priority nor a realistic possibility. Many countries spent the nineteenth century and much of the twentieth occupied in the most basic task of nation-state building, of controlling vast territories of broken geography. For example, it was only with the march of coast-hugging Brazilians to Amazonia and the centre-west, beginning in the 1970s, that Brazil felt any great need to engage with its Spanish-speaking neighbours.[15] Until 1985, apart from a couple of border encounters, only three Brazilian presidents had ever visited Argentina (and only two Argentine rulers had made the trip the other way). In the 1960s, schemes such as the Latin American Free Trade Association increased trade, especially in manufactures, through selective preferences. But the intention was only to widen markets that were still protected from the outside world, in a doomed effort to make import substitution work better. The Central American Common Market made fitful progress in linking five small economies, while the five-nation Andean Pact (later renamed Andean Community) could rarely agree to a set of policies and stick to them.

Mercosur, formed in 1991 by Argentina, Brazil, Paraguay and Uruguay, promised to be different. It involved two of Latin America's three largest economies. It was formed by democratic governments that were committed to trade liberalisation and sound macroeconomic policies. Its philosophy was 'open regionalism', not the building of a protectionist fortress. It set out to create not just a free-trade area, but an EU-style customs union, with a common external tariff and a common foreign trade policy, under a strict timetable and a clear set of rules. The idea was that companies could set up anywhere in the four countries and gain seamless access to a market of $1 trillion, achieving the economies of scale that are so often elusive in Latin America. At first, all went well. Trade among the four countries grew swiftly, to $20.3 billion in 1998, when it amounted to a quarter of their total exports; local companies and multinationals reorganised their activities on a regional basis. Outsiders began to take note of what touted itself as the world's fourth-largest integrated market, after NAFTA, the EU and Japan.[16] Chile and Bolivia joined the free-trade area as associate members of Mercosur. In 1999, Mercosur began talks with the EU on a free-trade agreement to parallel the FTAA.

Then things began to go wrong, as first Brazil devalued and later Argentina's economy collapsed. By 2002, trade among Mercosur's four full members had fallen to half its 1998 level; it would not surpass that level until 2005, but by then intra-Mercosur exports represented only around one-eighth of the four's total exports.[17] Far from pressing ahead with implementing the agreed rules, more and more ad hoc exceptions were punched in both the free-trade area and the putative customs union. These were blessed by presidential diplomacy, which papered over rising disenchantment. A dispute-settlement tribunal was eventually set up, along with a small permanent secretariat in Montevideo.

But there were several underlying tensions. Paraguay and Uruguay felt permanently snubbed, as Brazil and Argentina tended to do bilateral deals. Brazil's disproportionate size meant that this arrangement was not as effective as the 'Franco-German axis' of co-equal giants that long drove the EU. For Brazil, Mercosur was more a geopolitical project of Itamaraty, the powerful foreign ministry, than a priority for the private sector of São Paulo, let alone that of the north-east. Itamaraty gave priority to widening Mercosur, whereas the other three founding members had more to gain from its deepening. In practice, all of them were reluctant to make the sacrifices of sovereignty required to make a common market work – even on such relatively minor matters as establishing a common customs code and sharing customs revenue.

Under Lula and Argentina's Néstor Kirchner, presumed political affinity replaced 'open regionalism' as the guiding philosophy of Mercosur. Several experienced diplomats in both Brazil and Argentina lamented the short-sightedness of this approach.[18] Chávez pulled Venezuela out of the Andean Community in protest at the negotiation by Peru and Colombia of trade agreements with the United States. Although Colombia, not Brazil, was the most important market for Venezuelan industry, he applied to join Mercosur. With unwise alacrity, Mercosur accepted Venezuela as a full member, although Chávez was hardly a man known for his commitment to sharing sovereignty and accepting rules. Then came the blockade of the bridge at Fray Bentos, a violation of Article 1 of Mercosur's founding treaty, which required the free circulation of goods between the four member states. Kirchner had earlier unilaterally and without notice reduced exports of natural gas to Chile and halted the export of electricity to Uruguay.[19] At the same time, the Mercosur presidents entertained an absurd scheme promoted by Chávez to build an 8,000-kilometre pipeline to take natural gas from Venezuela to Buenos Aires, at a probable cost of $20 billion. Needless to say, it never happened.

As its twice-yearly summits became back-slapping expressions of political solidarity, Mercosur became increasingly protectionist. The Kirchners instituted managed trade, imposing non-automatic import licences for trade within the bloc. The only bit of it that more or less functioned was a bilateral agreement between Brazil and Argentina on cars. While other countries opened up to the world, Mercosur managed only two extra-regional trade accords, with Israel and the Palestinian Authority. Only in 2016 did Mercosur begin serious talks with the EU on a trade agreement first mooted in 1999.

The result was that Mercosur excluded itself from the global and regional value chains which, in the twenty-first century, are at the heart of world trade. The group's original ambition to create a single market receded. A customs union is supposed to have no internal borders. Yet even after the bridge at Fray Bentos reopened, crossing the frontier was an arduous exercise for lorries. Both Uruguay and Argentina maintained border posts. Customs checks, sanitary inspections and other paperwork meant that trucks were delayed for up to 24 hours in early 2017, according to Oscar Terzaghi, the mayor of Fray Bentos.

The divided states of Latin America

Bolívar's name means little outside the northern Andes, let alone in Brazil or Mexico.[20] Yet Hugo Chávez conceived of the Bolivarian revolution as a Latin American, not just Venezuelan, project. In an effort to win allies and neutralise diplomatic pressure from the United States, Chávez used part of his oil windfall to buy influence abroad. This began with a strategic alliance with Cuba, under which Venezuela supplied the island with 90,000 barrels per day of oil at subsidised prices, and agreed to invest up to $1 billion to revamp and supply an unfinished Soviet-era oil refinery at Cienfuegos in Cuba.[21] This alliance was formalised as the 'Bolivarian Alternative for the Americas' (or ALBA, meaning 'dawn' in Spanish). Chávez presented this as a rival continental project to the FTAA (whose initials were ALCA in Spanish). The goals of ALBA were to fight poverty and social exclusion through government-managed trade, Venezuelan oil wealth and Cuban know-how in public health and political organisation. But above all, it was conceived by Chávez as a political alliance against the United States. It was joined by Bolivia, Nicaragua and Haiti, as well as six small English-speaking Caribbean island states. Venezuela offered a dozen Caribbean countries cheap credit for oil imports in a scheme known as Petrocaribe, assuring Venezuela's government of a clientele of votes on international bodies such as the Organization of American States.

For all his talk of regional unity, Chávez was a factor of discord. Partly under his influence, Latin America looked more divided than it had been for a generation. Chávez posed a particular problem for Brazil, whose diplomatic priority was to lead a South American bloc. Lula had a unique talent for being all things to all men. Brazil was not interested in joining Chávez's anti-American front, and it maintained good relations with both the United States and Venezuela. But Lula's friendly relations with Chávez went down well with his Workers' Party. And they helped to guarantee lucrative contracts in Venezuela for Brazilian construction firms. This stance also brought some embarrassments: Evo Morales's nationalisation of Petrobras's natural-gas assets in Bolivia, with Chávez by his side, was a humiliation for Lula. Brazilian diplomats claimed that their quiet diplomacy was a moderating influence on Chávez. But it was hard to see much evidence of that.

At Brazil's instigation, Mercosur and the Andean countries joined forces in the South American Community in 2004, which four years later became the South American Union (UNASUR). Rafael Correa, Ecuador's president, dipped into his oil revenues and paid $66 million to endow the new organisation with a striking building in the form of a U, its cantilevered wings clad in silver and black glass, just metres south of the line of the Equator outside Quito. The more or less explicit aim was to displace the Organization of American States, whose members include the United States and whose headquarters are in Washington.

It set up ministerial councils on issues such as defence and health. It facilitated talks between government and opposition in Bolivia in 2008. It did the same in failed negotiations between Venezuela's government and the opposition in 2016. Ernesto Samper, a former Colombian president who was UNASUR's secretary general from 2014 to 2016, claimed that the group reflected 'a political scenario' in which most South American leaders are 'socialist, left or progressive'. He saw the organisation's 'democratic clause' as linked to 'the real validity of social rights' rather than respect for the separation of powers.[22] As the political pendulum swung in South America, UNASUR's future, as well as its utility, was unclear.

Yet another regional organisation, the Community of Latin American and Caribbean States, came into being in Caracas in 2011, bringing together all the countries in the Americas, except the United States and Canada. It became the counterpart organisation for summits with the EU, China and other regional groups.

The most consequential new body is the Pacific Alliance, formed by Chile, Colombia, Mexico and Peru. The declaration of Lima of 2011 stood out from the verbose annals of Latin American integration for its rare combination of brevity and impact. Its aims were to promote the 'deep integration' of the member economies through the free movement of goods, services, capital and labour, and to strengthen their ties with the world and especially with the Asia-Pacific region. The four members moved swiftly. They abolished tariffs on 92 per cent of their merchandise trade, with the remainder to be freed by 2020. They scrapped tourist visa requirements for each other's citizens, and opened some shared embassies abroad. The stock markets in the four countries agreed to link up in a regional bourse called MILA. The Alliance attracted considerable outside interest, signing up 49 countries as observers by 2016. It is a great diplomatic brand. But the economic reality is that the four countries are separated by great distances, and have few economic links.

In its commitment to free markets, free trade and democracy, the Alliance was a tacit snub both to ALBA and to Mercosur. Latin America appeared to have divided itself into two rival blocs: the free-trading, free-market Pacific Alliance and the more statist and protectionist Mercosur. Some Latin Americans invoked the spectre of a new 'Treaty of Tordesillas' that had separated Spanish and Portuguese settlement in the region. The formation of the Alliance underlined that in its project for South American unity, Brazil had failed to offer enough to its partners. Although it negotiated trade agreements with most of them, in practice its vast domestic market remained relatively protected and difficult to penetrate. Brazil's critics in the Pacific countries complained that instead of supplying regional 'public goods', such as open markets and dispute-resolution mechanisms, it helped elect political allies by supplying campaign gurus and donations, in order to gain corrupt contracts for its construction companies.[23]

While the politicians strut and squabble, the private sector has got on with the job of integration. Scores of Latin American companies have internationalised, often at first moving into neighbouring countries and then venturing into the United States, Europe or Asia. In 2016, the Boston Consulting Group included 23 firms from Latin America on its list of top emerging-market companies, and it saw another five as established 'global leaders'. Most were from Brazil and Mexico, but some were from Chile and Peru, and there was one each from Argentina and Colombia.[24] The Brazilian contingent included the likes of Vale, one of the world's largest mining companies; Gerdau, a steelmaker; and two food giants, JBS and BRF. From Mexico, there was América Móvil (Carlos Slim's telecoms firm); Cemex, the world's second-biggest cement

firm; and Grupo Bimbo, a bakery giant. Many Latin American manufacturers that survived the changes of the previous two decades were
'leaner and meaner' and became suppliers to rich-world multinationals,
as one study has argued.[25] The number of Latin American companies
with annual sales of over \$1 billion increased from 170 in 1999 to 500
by 2010.[26] Although some of the *multilatinas*, as they were called, saw
their revenues fall as economies decelerated, they were a resilient bunch.

The rise of the *multilatinas* could not disguise the sluggish state of
intra-regional trade. Despite all the talk of integration and a big increase
in trade agreements among Latin American countries this century, the
share of their exports that stayed within the region has remained stubbornly at around 20 per cent. That is low, compared with Canada and
the United States (35 per cent), East Asia (50 per cent) and the European
Union (60 per cent). There are several reasons for this: many Latin
American economies are fairly small; they produce similar things; and
they are separated by huge distances. All these are factors that tend to
discourage trade.

A world made at home or in China

The end of the commodity boom meant that Latin America was casting
around for new sources of economic growth and new exports. The rise
of protectionism in the world economy made that harder. It meant that
regional integration became even more important. The centre-right
governments that came to power in Argentina and Brazil were keen to
get Mercosur working again. They drew up a list of bureaucratic obstacles to trade which they planned to sweep away. There was much talk of
'convergence' between Mercosur and the Pacific Alliance. The two
groups had different rules and philosophies, and merging them was a
technical and political impossibility. But there was scope for them to
co-operate more.

For the past half-century, Latin American policymakers have more
or less consciously tried to imitate the European Union. That has been
a mistake. The region lacks the disastrous history of inter-state wars and
the compact geography that made European integration politically
imperative and economically feasible. Indeed, the whole of the
28-member European Union would fit comfortably within the boundaries of Brazil.

The rhetoric of Latin American integration masked both the nationalism of many politicians (especially on the left) and the often shameless protectionism of business lobbies. To redress that was a political task. It also called for a much more practical approach, in which improving transport links and harmonising norms and standards were priorities. Venezuela's slide into dictatorship and its humanitarian disaster posed a different kind of test for the region. For years, Latin America stood by in silence, its historical instinct for non-intervention in internal affairs outweighing the 'democracy clauses' that all regional organisations possessed. That began to change in 2016, as the situation in Venezuela deteriorated and as centre-right governments came to power. But whether the region had the stomach for more energetic diplomacy was unclear.

Most of Latin America has bet on economic openness and democracy. This book has argued that the reasons for this are mainly internal to the region. Even so, external influences matter. If the United States and the European Union continue to turn their backs on the region, some Latin Americans may reconsider, especially if China starts to offer a serious alternative.

CHAPTER THIRTEEN

So Near and Yet So Far

By stages since the 1960s, the Pan-American Highway heading south from Lima has become a gradually lengthening motorway. In 2011, it reached Chincha, a bustling, chaotic town 195 kilometres south of the capital, which could take an hour to traverse in a maelstrom of articulated lorries and marauding moto-taxis.

In 2005, the government had signed a contract to extend the motorway for a further 35 kilometres, bypassing Chincha. But because successive administrations failed to complete the compulsory purchase of the required land, the new stretch only opened in December 2016. Still missing are the last 65 kilometres to Ica, the capital of a rich farming region of irrigated desert, which over the past quarter-century has prospered by exporting asparagus, grapes, pisco and other agricultural products. Ica enjoys full employment, and has drawn in many migrant labourers from the Andean highlands. In a low building at the entrance to the town, amid vineyards, stands the Centre for Agroindustrial Technological Innovation, known as CITE-Vid. Founded by the government in 2000, with Spanish aid and the support of private business, it has helped to raise productivity in Peru's grape, wine and pisco industries. It advises farmers, for a fee, and offers them the services of a small research laboratory and a model distillery. Between 2000 and 2014, the output of grapes per hectare more than doubled. Peru became the world's third-biggest exporter of table grapes to China, and annual production of pisco, a grappa-style brandy, rose from 1.8 million litres to 7.8 million litres.[1] Pisco, an ancient product, is starting to gain an international name.

Peru has achieved impressive economic growth and poverty reduction in this century. But the momentum is slowing. Peru still has a sound macroeconomic framework and market-friendly policies. Yet something is missing, exemplified by that 11-year wait for the Chincha bypass: a public sector that is able to provide public goods and co-ordination.

To take another example, a second runway for Lima's successful but congested airport was similarly delayed for a dozen years by the government's tardiness in purchasing the earmarked land and building a one-kilometre tunnel for a highway underneath it, as well as by regulatory disagreements with the airport's private operators.[2]

Infrastructure is not the only bottleneck. There have been discontinuities or lacunae in public policies. One example was the sacking by Congress in 2016 of Jaime Saavedra, the successful education minister, in a country where 54 per cent of 15-year-olds cannot understand what they read. Seven out of ten Peruvians work in the informal sector. The country's judiciary is slow and corrupt. Partly because of the weakness of its political parties, Peru's governments failed to take advantage of the commodity boom to construct the more effective state and stronger institutions needed to sustain economic growth and spread its benefits. In that, it was not alone.

Stuck in the middle-income trap

After a decade or more of socio-economic progress and the gradual reinforcement of democracy, Latin America risks getting stuck in what some economists call 'the middle-income trap'. In recent decades, only a relatively small number of developing countries, all in Europe and East Asia, have made it to the coveted status of 'developed' nations, and of these only Poland and South Korea had more than 20 million people. Definitions of developed status vary. In 2012, the UN listed 36 countries as developed, by which it meant they had an annual income per person of more than $12,615 in nominal terms.[3] The IMF assigned 'advanced economy' status in 2010 to 39 nations or territories with an income per person of $22,000 in purchasing-power parity terms (i.e. taking into account the cost of living); this also took account of their degree of export diversification and financial integration with the world. In 2012, Argentina, Chile, Panama and Uruguay were all close to this benchmark, while another group of countries, including Mexico, Brazil, Colombia, Costa Rica and Peru were not all that far behind.

Why is it so hard to achieve development? In synthesis, because as they get less poor and their populations grow more slowly, so countries must rely for economic growth on productivity and what economists call 'human capital' (better health, education and skills), rather than cheap labour and an expanding workforce. As well as a growth slow-down because of an inability to make this switch to continuous improvement in competitiveness, productivity and human capital, Alejandro Foxley, a former finance and foreign minister of Chile, highlights two other factors behind the middle-income trap. These are the weaknesses of social protection and of institutions. Overcoming the middle-income trap is thus essentially a political process.[4]

As we have seen, over the past two or three decades Latin America has forged a broad consensus in favour of democracy, macroeconomic stability, economic openness and social inclusion (the importance of eliminating poverty and reducing inequality). Those countries that have strayed from this consensus have, to varying degrees, foundered. *Chavismo* showed itself to be a blind alley, a formula for conflict, authoritarianism and misery. Brazil paid a high economic price for Dilma Rousseff's disdain for the rigours of macroeconomic stability and economic openness, and her embrace of a milder repetition of the state intervention and protectionism of the past.

One task facing the region is thus to stay the course. Another is to forge new consensus on three basic things. The first is to improve the rule of law and tackle more effectively the scourge of violent crime and citizen insecurity. The second is to entrench and extend the still tentative progress in education and health and to move beyond conditional cash transfers to improve skills training, and also to work out what kind of welfare state Latin America needs and can afford. And the third issue is that of productivity itself, of encouraging more efficient and diversified economies. Some of these tasks require more tax revenue. But all of them require a different kind of state and the forging of broad political consensus.

On tackling crime and violence, Colombia offers some lessons. Chief among these is the importance both of territorial control by the security forces and of the professionalisation of the police. And the police need to work in close co-ordination with prosecutors and the courts. Above all, tackling crime demands political will from the top. No country has solved the problem of judicial reform. Ways have to be found of making the judiciary accountable to society. And Latin America needs to rethink its prisons policy.

As Foxley argues, the main obstacle to consolidating the new middle class is the poor quality of education, which acts as a brake on its aspirations and opportunities. Many Latin American countries are at a potential turning point. Unless they improve the quality of public provision, a large segment of the new middle classes will seek private alternatives. But that is not necessarily a recipe for improvement. Many parents are going into debt to pay for a poor-quality university education, from which their children then have to drop out.[5] Much the same goes for health. There is a role for private provision in both education and health, so long as it is well regulated and providers are required to offer full information to users. But if Latin America is to start to offer equality of opportunity to its citizens, public provision – or at least financing – of quality education and health is essential. On the supply side, that means reinforcing the incipient attempts to offer a new deal to teachers, involving better and more practical training, better salaries and a proper career structure, in return for rigorous evaluation and the ejection from the profession of those who repeatedly fail.

Conditional cash transfers (CCTs) have formed a basic safety net which the region long lacked. But as Santiago Levy has argued 'CCTs are not meant to be permanent welfare, but temporary investments in the human capital of the poor'. They filled a yawning gap left by the region's Bismarckian contributory social security systems, which are based on contributions deducted from formal-sector payrolls. At their peak in 1981, these systems covered only 61 per cent of the population.[6] Nowadays around half of Latin American workers labour in the informal economy, and most of them are therefore outside the systems. Clearly social protection in the region needs to be comprehensively rethought. Instead, governments have seen political opportunity in adding non-contributory benefits to CCTs, such as minimum pensions and health policies, in parallel with formal social security systems. As Levy has pointed out, despite their good intentions, governments that adopt this dual approach are imposing a tax on formal employment and granting a subsidy to informal employment. That is doubly damaging: on the one hand, the resulting hotch-potch of social protection falls well short of a universal approach; and on the other, the entrenchment of informality undermines productivity, since informal workers are less productive than formal ones.[7] Latin America thus needs a debate on how to move to universal systems of health care, pensions and social protection that are not linked to its dual labour market. One alternative would be to finance such a system out of general taxation; another would be an insurance-based system, with the state helping only those who are too poor (rather than too informal) to contribute. Needless to say, neither is politically simple. The ageing of the population, with the extra health-care and pension costs this implies, makes this debate urgent, as well as important.

The imperative of innovation

The end of the commodity boom has served to dramatise the imperative of boosting productivity, innovation and economic diversification in Latin America. What economists call 'total factor productivity'[8] in the seven biggest Latin American economies grew by just 0.2 per cent a year between 1961 and 2008, while in seven East Asian countries over the same period it rose by 2.2 per cent (and in China by 2.3 per cent), according to Augusto de la Torre.[9] As already noted in Chapter 6, boosting productivity requires many changes, from improving education and skills to the regulation of business.

Several things stand out. One is the weight of the informal economy and small businesses in Latin America. Visit almost any city in Latin America and the central districts will be clogged with street vendors, peddling anything from clothes to pirate DVDs to health remedies or construction materials. They are just the most visible segment of a massive informal economy of unregistered businesses. According to the International Labour Organization, the informal sector accounted for 47 per cent of total non-agricultural employment in Latin America in 2015.[10] Why was the informal sector so big, even before the distortions that recent social policies might have introduced? That is a matter of much debate. One school of thought blames over-rigid labour laws that make it expensive to hire and fire workers. Another highlights the failings of the legal and regulatory systems (see Chapter 10). Another way to view the informal sector is as the consequence of Latin America's past failure to invest in human capital on the one hand, and the low productivity of the formal sector on the other. For the unskilled, the formal sector offers little chance of a decent career. Informality is as much a social and cultural phenomenon as an economic one. There is much research that shows that many workers choose to work for themselves. They pursue the dream of running their own business, often after spending a few years picking up the rudiments of it by working in a formal job.[11]

Informal firms are a drag on productivity: they tend to lack economies of scale and up-to-date technology, and they invest little in their workers' skills. The productivity of small businesses in Latin America is only one-sixth of that of large firms, while in rich countries the difference is only 2.4 times.[12] Latin American politicians pay ritual homage to *los pymes* (small and medium enterprises). They shouldn't. In many cases these are companies that have failed to grow. The World Bank found worrying evidence that Latin American firms that are 40 years old or more are typically just half the size (measured by the number of their workers) of their peers from developed countries, and only a third as big as firms in East Asian countries, such as Indonesia, Malaysia or the Philippines.[13] Though there is much debate about the causes of informality and the stunting of business in Latin America, the region's heavy burden of regulation stands out. This is the result of an unholy alliance between conservative notaries and lawyers and leftist economic micro-management.

Even the biggest firms in Latin America – those much-feted *multilatinas* – are much less likely to innovate than their peers elsewhere.[14] That seems to be in large part because they face less competition. Latin America has too many monopolies and oligopolies. Regional integration, if pursued seriously, would serve to intensify competition. It could also stimulate economies of scale and the gradual formation of regional value or supply chains. That process lay at the heart of the rise of manufacturing in East Asia. Distances are greater in Latin America, but they are made even more so by the lack of good roads, railways and ports. Latin America invests only around 3 per cent of its GDP in infrastructure, while India manages 6 per cent, according to CAF, a development bank.[15]

Latin America lags behind both the rich countries and many in East Asia on several indicators of innovation, such as spending on research and development, scientific publication and patents. While spending on R&D in the main East Asian economies averaged 1.7 per cent of GDP in 2010, in their Latin American counterparts it was just 0.5 per cent.[16] Brazil was an exception, spending 1.2 per cent. That effort lay behind Brazil's success in agribusiness and deep-sea oil and gas production. And Brazil had some highly innovative companies, such as Embraer, the world's third-biggest aircraft maker, and Weg, one of the top three makers of electric motors, behind only Siemens and ABB.

Dilma Rousseff's Science without Borders programme, under which 100,000 Brazilian science students went abroad for a year, was a pioneering attempt to connect the country with international centres of knowledge. Only two Latin American countries, Brazil and Uruguay, had an established national innovation strategy. In several countries, there were technology start-ups of which a couple, Softtek in Mexico and Globant in Argentina, grew into large multinationals. Start-Up Chile attracted young would-be entrepreneurs from around the world by offering them space and money for a year, in the hope that their example would rub off on locals. Though Brazil had a number of private equity and venture capital funds, financing was often a missing element elsewhere. And the aura surrounding start-ups should not conceal the fact that the real challenge was to create fast-growing companies. Equally, Latin Americans still had plenty of scope to innovate by copying best practice from elsewhere, which pointed to the need for economies that were open to the import of goods, foreign investment, ideas and immigration.

Commodities will remain a core business for many Latin American countries. There is plenty of scope to add value to them, either through processing or by establishing supply chains. Agriculture is the prime example: the world will continue to demand more food. Latin America has the land, sunshine and water to produce it in abundance. Brazilian and Argentine agribusiness is technologically innovative, having pioneered 'no-till cultivation' and 'precision farming', techniques which rely on scientific research and computer-aided machinery. On the other hand, the export of fruit and vegetables is labour intensive and offers plenty of scope for innovation, as the Ica region in Peru has shown. The route to higher economic growth in the region does not involve a single formula: there is opportunity for expansion in some manufacturing industries, and in many service businesses, including tourism, in which Latin America has a winning combination of natural wonders and historic patrimony.

To grow at around 5 per cent a year, the region needs to invest about 26 per cent of GDP, rather than its current average of 21 per cent. Governments could help to boost the rate of saving and investment in the region. Latin America's reliance on foreign capital has contributed to the tendency of its currencies to appreciate in ways that have made even otherwise competitive businesses vulnerable to Chinese competition. Budget discipline and the more widespread use of sovereign wealth funds to save and invest windfall commodity gains would help in this regard. So would maintaining stable macroeconomic conditions for saving and investment.

There is a role for government, too, in fostering innovation and diversification. Industrial policy went out of fashion in the region in the 1980s – and for good reason. In Latin America, all too often it was used to lavish public subsidy, either directly or indirectly through tax breaks, to protect inefficient companies from import competition. More recently, Brazil dallied with a reprise of old-fashioned industrial policy, through protectionism, national-content rules and the subsidising of 'national champions'. In South Korea, by contrast, industrial policy was more ruthless: it involved strictly temporary help for businesses, linked to exports and innovation. Given the weaknesses of the Latin American state, a renewal of industrial policy should be approached with caution.

But there is a case for state action where the market has failed to seize upon a latent or potential opportunity. One example has been in Costa Rica, where the government investment agency has helped to develop a surgical-devices industry, by persuading a firm from the United States to set up a sterilising service in the country.[17]

Public initiatives lie behind the origins of Embraer, of Chile's salmon-farming industry, and of Ica's CITE-Vid. Piero Ghezzi, the minister for production in Humala's government in Peru, sought to build on that experience, creating a dozen round-tables for different economic sectors, aimed at sweeping away bureaucratic obstacles and providing public goods, from roads to services, where these would foster private investment. Nevertheless, Latin America would do well to keep in mind that successful national innovation programmes in East Asia have been imbued with competition: they require scientists to bid for research funds and companies to compete for seed capital. They leave decisions to experts, rather than politicians or bureaucrats. And they foster innovation networks that link universities and profit-seeking companies, keeping the state's own role to a minimum.[18]

A new kind of politics

Since at least the 1980s, Latin America has seen an ideological debate between proponents of an unfettered free market and those of state-led, protectionist economic management. That debate is sterile, passé and damaging. In a context of deeply rooted social inequalities, the libertarian conservatism of some on the right, who posed as liberals, was akin to a social Darwinism in which the winners demanded that their privileges remained untouched. On the other hand, on the left a clientelist populism, mixed with a vestigial Leninism, was inimical to growth, opportunity and the free exchange of ideas. It is clear that Latin America needs more competitive market economies and a more effective state – one that is capable of fostering economic innovation and the development of human capital, while also offering citizens greater equality and security.

To get there requires a new kind of politics. In place of the polarisation and confrontation offered by populists (and sometimes by their opponents), Latin America needs consensus-building, with the state, the private sector and civil society working together to set medium-term goals and hold governments accountable for them. Though it should be based on technical considerations, this is a political, not a technocratic task. It involves choices and trade-offs. This kind of consensus-building is not something Latin America has been good at. Its societies tend to be conflict-ridden. That may be because the promise 'to give civic and legal value to all people who live in the republic' that Juan José Arévalo made in his inaugural address as Guatemala's president in 1944 was for so long unmet in the region.[19] It is closer to being honoured today.

Similarly, ever since the days of Rivadavia and Rosas, Latin American rulers have been divided between those who looked abroad in search of modernity and those who sought inspiration within, in the interior of their own countries and their traditions. Again, that is a false dilemma. The benefits of economic openness are clear, but the politicians must ensure that they reach the hinterland. Regional integration should be a means of linking up with the world, not an alternative to it.

The tasks facing the region after the commodity boom may seem daunting. Over the past two centuries, Latin America's capacity to be knocked off course by outside events and its own shortcomings and mistakes has been legendary.

But in just 30 years, Latin America has achieved much. For better or for worse, its socio-political structures are less ossified and more flexible than those in the rich world. Democracy has not been imposed on Latin America by a conquering army. Its arrival in plenitude, if not in perfection, draws on two centuries of liberal constitutionalism and democratic experiment. Democracy is based on an increasingly vibrant, educated and demanding civil society, which will not easily surrender it.

Since the 1980s, democratic governments in Latin America have solved several big problems. They conquered inflation, though that battle was long and costly. They ended the self-imposed economic isolation of the region. In most places, they have cut the armed forces down to size and trained them in a new democratic role. And they have started to tackle the region's historic legacy of extreme inequality, widespread poverty, chaotic urbanisation and educational neglect. The tasks ahead are less onerous, but more complex.

There are lessons for the region in the catastrophic failure of *chavismo*. An accident of history – the surge in the oil price from 2001 onwards – for a while gave spurious plausibility in some quarters to an alternative course that Latin Americans seemed not so long ago to have turned their backs on. The 'Bolivarian alternative' was based on flawed premises. Its diagnosis of the region's problems was based on a mistaken reading of history. But *chavismo* was another reminder that extreme inequality provides fertile ground for populism. There was a lesson, too, for the left. It needed to recognise that the rule of law offers a far stronger guarantee of citizenship to the poor than the paternalist largesse of *caudillos*. In its enchantment with 'Bolivarianism', and renewed respect for Cuba, much of the left forgot the abiding lessons of the end of the Cold War: that central planning had failed and that communism was tyranny, not liberation.

The stumbles of Chile, Brazil and Mexico, which ten years ago seemed, in contrasting ways, to be more or less successful models of democratic reform, were less predictable than the failure of *chavismo*, and thus in some ways more disappointing. There were some grounds for hope in Brazil's robust judiciary and purge of political corruption, and in the growing strength of civil society in Mexico. Chile needed a renewal of faith in technocratic excellence and consensus-building. Whatever the arguments in Colombia about the peace agreements with the FARC, the country needed to implement them effectively and rebuild credibility and consensus among its political elites, in order to reap the dividends of peace. And, as noted in this chapter, Peru needed to equip itself with a more effective state and stronger institutions, as reinforcement for, rather than replacement of, its free-market economic model. The shackles hindering escape from the middle-income trap thus varied from country to country.

Largely overlooked by the outside world, Latin America has made much progress in the past few decades. A sense of perspective is important: three generations ago, most Latin Americans lived in semi-feudal conditions in the countryside; less than two generations ago, many were being murdered because of their political beliefs. This is not an argument for complacency in the face of Latin America's relative failures of development and the flaws of its democracies. Rather, it is to say that the relatively disappointing record of many of Latin America's democratic governments should be judged realistically against the scale of the problems that they have had to face. The problems may be more clearly visible, but progress has started to get the upper hand. Consolidating it requires incremental reform, not regressive revolution. It also requires patience, hard though that is to muster in the face of poverty. As Juan Bautista Alberdi, the Argentine liberal and constitutionalist, noted in 1837: '*las naciones, como los hombres, no tienen alas; hacen sus viajes a pie, paso por paso*'. Nations, like men, do not have wings; they make their journeys on foot, step by step.

Glossary

AD (Acción Democrática) — social-democratic party in Venezuela

ALBA (Alternativa Bolivariana para América Latina y el Caribe) — Bolivarian Alternative for Latin America and the Caribbean, an anti-US regional alliance promoted by Hugo Chávez

APRA (Alianza Popular Revolucionaria Americana) — populist movement founded by Víctor Raúl Haya de la Torre; became a Peruvian political party

AUC (Auto-Defensas Unidas de Colombia) — United Self-Defence Forces of Colombia, the umbrella group of Colombia's right-wing paramilitaries

audiencia — the supreme judicial and administrative body in Spain's American colonies

Aymara — indigenous language spoken in north-western Bolivia and in Peru around Lake Titicaca

Barrio Adentro — 'inside the neighbourhood', community health programmes organised by Venezuela's government under Hugo Chávez and mainly staffed by Cuban doctors

BNDES (Banco Nacional de Desenvolvimento Econômico e Social) — National Development Bank (Brazil)

Bolsa Família — 'Family Fund', large-scale anti-poverty programme in Brazil

BRICS — grouping formed by Brazil, Russia, India, China and later South Africa

cabildo — town council or town meeting

cacique — local political boss

caixa dois — illicit political party financing in Brazil

campesinos — peasant farmers

candomblé — religion of African origin in Brazil

Caracazo — rioting in Venezuela in protest at higher petrol prices and bus fares in 1989

caudillo — originally a regional warlord; by extension a political strongman, often of military background

CCTs — conditional cash transfer programmes, such as *Bolsa Família* and *Progresa/Oportunidades*

CEPAL (Comisión Económica para América Latina y el Caribe) — United Nations Economic Commission for Latin America and the Caribbean (ECLAC)

cepalista(s)	policies of state-led industrial protectionism promoted by CEPAL; those who supported these policies
cerrado	inland savannah (Brazil)
chavistas	supporters of Hugo Chávez, Venezuela's former president
Chile Solidario	'solidaristic Chile', a government programme aimed at eliminating extreme poverty
CIA	United States' Central Intelligence Agency
CICIG (Comisión Internacional Contra la Impunidad en Guatemala)	International Commission against Impunity in Guatemala
colonia	neighbourhood (Mexico)
Concertación	centre-left coalition that governed Chile between 1990 and 2010
conos	cones; shanty-town suburbs stretching to the north, east and south of Lima
conquistadores	conquerors
Contras	counter-revolutionary guerrilla force organised by the Reagan administration in the 1980s to fight the Sandinista regime in Nicaragua
convertibilidad	the name given locally to Argentina's currency board of 1991–2002 under which the peso was fixed by law at par to the dollar
COPEI (Comité de Organización Política Electoral Independiente)	Christian democratic party in Venezuela
CORFO (Corporación de Fomento)	state development corporation in Chile
Cortes	parliament in Spain
criollo	in the colonial and independence periods, a person of European descent born in the Americas
CTM (Confederación de Trabajadores de México)	Confederation of Mexican Workers, the main trade-union organisation under the PRI
cumbia	Colombian dance music
curacas	local Indian leaders in Peru
CVRD (Companhia Vale do Rio Doce)	Brazilian mining company now known as Vale
desarrollo para adentro	inward-looking development, the economic policies championed by CEPAL after the Second World War
descamisados	'shirtless ones', the urban poor in Argentina
ejido	communal landholding in Mexico; after the Mexican Revolution, state-sponsored peasant community
ELN (Ejército de Liberación Nacional)	National Liberation Army, the smaller of the two main Colombian guerrilla groups
Estado Novo	'New State'; Getúlio Vargas's quasi-fascist dictatorship in Brazil of 1937–45

estera	sheet of rush-matting used to build huts by squatters in Peru
EU	European Union
FARC (Fuerzas Armadas Revolucionarias de Colombia)	Revolutionary Armed Forces of Colombia, the larger of the country's two main guerrilla groups
favela	shanty town (Brazil)
fazenda	large agricultural estate (Brazil)
Fedecámaras (Federación de Cámaras y Asociaciones de Comercio y Producción de Venezuela)	Federation of Chambers of Commerce and Production of Venezuela, the country's main private-sector lobby
FMLN (Frente Farabundo Martí para la Liberación Nacional)	Farabundo Martí National Liberation Front, guerrilla coalition in El Salvador's civil war; later a left-wing political party
foco	focus; rural guerrilla group
Frente Amplio	Broad Front, left-wing coalition in Uruguay
FTAA	proposed Free Trade Area of the Americas
fuero	group or corporate rights under the Spanish colonial system
gaúcho	in Portuguese, an inhabitant of the Brazilian state of Rio Grande do Sul
GDP	Gross Domestic Product
gendarmerie	militarised police force (French)
generalísimo	supreme military commander and dictator
glasnost	the Russian term for openness, used to describe the civil and political reforms of Mikhail Gorbachev in the Soviet Union
grupúsculos	small radical left-wing factions
Guaraní	indigenous language widely spoken in Paraguay and in parts of Bolivia and Brazil
guevarista	inspired by the doctrines and example of Che Guevara
hacendado(s)	owner(s) of large estates
hacienda	large agricultural estates in Spanish America
IDB	Inter-American Development Bank
IFE (Instituto Federal Electoral)	Federal Electoral Institute (Mexico)
IMF	International Monetary Fund
indigenismo	current of thought, especially in Mexico and Peru, that promoted the importance of indigenous cultures and the integration of the Indian into the mainstream of society
junta	board or committee
junta militar	ruling military directorate
KGB	Soviet security and intelligence service
latifundio (plural: *latifundia*)	large landed estates

Lava Jato	'Car Wash'; codename of police and judicial investigation into corruption centred on Petrobras in Brazil
llaneros	cowboys or plainsmen from the Venezuelan and Colombian plains
llanos	tropical plains in southern Venezuela and south-eastern Colombia
lucha armada	armed struggle, i.e. guerrilla action
maquiladoras	export assembly plants
mara	youth gang in Central America
MAS (Movimiento al Socialismo)	Movement to Socialism; in Venezuela, a moderate social-democratic party; in Bolivia, a more radical socialist party led by Evo Morales
MBR-200 (Movimiento Bolivariano Revolucionario-200)	conspiratorial movement founded by Hugo Chávez and other military officers
mensalão	big monthly payment, as a political corruption scandal in Brazil was dubbed
Mercosur	trade bloc and putative common market founded by Argentina, Brazil, Paraguay and Uruguay
mestizaje	the process of racial and cultural mixing
mestizo(a)	person of mixed Amerindian and Caucasian descent
milpa	maize field (Mexico and Central America)
mineiros	miners; inhabitants of the Brazilian state of Minas Gerais
minifundio	small plot worked by peasant farmer (*minifundista*)
MIR (Movimiento de la Izquierda Revolucionaria)	far-left group in Chile
misiones	missions; Chávez's Cuban-designed social programmes
MNR (Movimiento Nacional Revolucionario)	corporatist-nationalist party that led Bolivia's 1952 revolution
mulato(a)	mulatto; person of mixed African and Caucasian descent
MVR (Movimiento V República)	Fifth Republic Movement, a party formed by Hugo Chávez to contest Venezuela's 1998 presidential election
NAFTA	North American Free Trade Agreement
Nahuatl	an indigenous language spoken in central Mexico and used by the Aztecs
New Majority	centre-left coalition in Chile formed by Michelle Bachelet in 2013
NGO	non-governmental organisation
ni-nis	young people who neither study nor work
OAS	Organization of American States

OECD	Organisation for Economic Co-operation and Development, a research and co-ordination body whose members are mainly developed countries
OPEC	Organization of the Petroleum Exporting Countries
Oportunidades	name assigned to *Progresa* anti-poverty programme by Vicente Fox's government in Mexico
PAN (Partido de Acción Nacional)	National Action Party, centre-right party in Mexico
pardo	mulatto; person of mixed African and Caucasian descent
PDT (Partido Democrático Trabalhista)	populist left-wing party created by Leonel Brizola in Brazil
PdVSA (Petróleos de Venezuela SA)	Venezuela's state-owned oil company
peninsulares	during the colonial period, Spanish-born residents of the Americas
perestroika	the Russian term for economic restructuring, used of Mikhail Gorbachev's reforms in the Soviet Union
Petrobras	Brazil's state-controlled oil and gas company
PISA	Programme for International Student Assessment
PMDB (Partido do Movimento Democrático Brasileiro)	Party of the Brazilian Democratic Movement, centrist party created from the official opposition to the military regime of 1964–85
poderes fácticos	de facto, rather than de jure, powers-that-be
PRC (Partido Revolucionario Cubano)	Cuban Revolutionary Party
PRD (Partido de la Revolución Democrática)	Party of the Democratic Revolution, left-of-centre party in Mexico
PRI (Partido Revolucionario Institucional)	Institutional Revolutionary Party (Mexico)
Progresa	pioneering anti-poverty programme in Mexico involving cash payments to mothers whose children attend school and health checks
pronunciamiento	declaration of military rebellion against the government
Prospera	conditional cash-transfer programme in Mexico, previously known as *Oportunidades*
PSDB (Partido da Social Democracia Brasileira)	Party of Brazilian Social Democracy, a moderate centre-left grouping
PSUV (Partido Socialista Unido de Venezuela)	United Venezuelan Socialist Party, party created by Hugo Chávez
PT (Partido dos Trabalhadores)	Workers' Party (Brazil)
puntofijismo	the pacted democracy adopted in Venezuela in 1958
Quechua (in Ecuador, Quichua)	most widely spoken indigenous language in the Andes
rancheras	Mexican popular songs that exalt rural traditions, somewhat akin to country music in the United States

ranchos	Venezuelan term for shanty towns or self-built urban slums
reconquista	the wars waged by the Christian kingdoms of Spain against the Moors
República de Indios	the legislation under which Indians in Peru and elsewhere retained considerable autonomy within their subordinate status during the Spanish colony
riesgo país	country risk, or the premium attached to emerging-market bonds
rurales	a rural paramilitary police force established by Porifio Díaz in Mexico
Sendero Luminoso	Shining Path, a fundamentalist Maoist terrorist group in Peru
telenovelas	television soap operas
tlatoani	Aztec term for ruler or king (literally, 'he who speaks' in Nahuatl)
UDN (União Democrática Nacional)	National Democratic Union, the main conservative party in Brazil from 1945 to 1964
umbanda	Brazilian religious sect drawing on African elements but of more recent origin than *candomblé*
UNDP	United Nations Development Programme
la violencia	a civil war mainly between supporters of the Liberal and Conservative parties in Colombia lasting from 1948 to 1958
Yanqui	Yankee; more broadly, pertaining to the US
YPF (Yacimientos Petrolíferos Fiscales)	Argentina's state oil company, privatised in 1991
YPFB (Yacimientos Petrolíferos Fiscales Bolivianos)	Bolivia's state oil company
zambo(s)	of mixed African and Amerindian descent

Notes

Chapter 1: The Forgotten Continent

1. Quoted in Ariel Dorfman, 'Out of fear', *Guardian*, 18 March 2006.
2. In addition to those mentioned, Nicaragua elected Daniel Ortega, a leader of the Sandinista revolution of 1979 and an old foe of the United States. In Uruguay, Tabaré Vázquez, an oncologist, achieved the first presidential victory for the Frente Amplio in 2004 and was then elected again, in succession to Mujica.
3. Interview in the *Observer*, 16 January 2011.
4. UN Economic Commission for Latin America and the Caribbean (ECLAC/CEPAL), *Social Panorama of Latin America, 2015*, Santiago de Chile, 2015, p. 10.
5. IMF, Western Hemisphere Region, Regional Economic Outlook, May 2017.
6. 'Brazil's Odebrecht to pay up to $4.5 billion to settle bribery case', *Wall Street Journal*, 21 December 2016.
7. UN Office on Drugs and Crime (UNODC), *Global Study on Homicide, 2013*, Vienna, 2014; Laura Chioda, *Stop the Violence in Latin America: A look at prevention from cradle to adulthood*, World Bank, Washington, DC, 2017.
8. 'Violent crime in Latin America: Alternatives to the iron fist', *The Economist*, 16 November 2013.
9. Mexico was something of a special case. Since 1928, it had been governed by a single party that later took the name of the Institutional Revolutionary Party (PRI). Under the PRI, Mexico enjoyed the outward trappings of liberal democracy, but not its content. In 1994, the country was still engaged in a gradual transition to genuine democracy that culminated in the defeat of the PRI in the presidential election of 2000.
10. See Chapter 6 for a discussion of the 'Washington Consensus'.
11. The term harked back to Latin America's 'lost decade' of the 1980s, triggered by Mexico's default of 1982. See Chapter 5.
12. If 'neoliberalism' means anything, it is the policies of monetarism and a minimum state espoused by Ronald Reagan and Margaret Thatcher, and better described as 'neo-conservatism' – if that term had not itself acquired a different meaning in the field of American foreign policy. In Latin America, these policies were adopted by the 'Chicago Boys', who ran Chile's economy in the early years of General Pinochet's dictatorship in the 1970s; they were echoed, in a different context, in Carlos Menem's Argentina in the 1990s. See Javier Santiso, *Latin America's Political Economy of the Possible: Beyond good revolutionaries and free marketeers*, MIT Press, Cambridge, MA, 2006.
13. In an influential essay, Jorge Castañeda, a Mexican academic and former foreign minister, talked of 'the two lefts': 'One is modern, open-minded, reformist, and internationalist, and it springs, paradoxically, from the hard-core left of the past. The other, born of the great tradition of Latin American populism, is nationalist, strident, and close-minded. The first is well aware of its past mistakes (as well as those of its erstwhile role models in Cuba and the Soviet Union) and has changed accordingly. The second, unfortunately, has not.' Jorge G. Castañeda, 'Latin America's left turn', *Foreign Affairs*, May/June 2006.
14. For a more detailed typology, see Steven Levitsky and Kenneth M. Roberts, 'Latin America's left turn: a framework for analysis', in Levitsky and Roberts (eds), *The*

Resurgence of the Latin American Left, Johns Hopkins University Press, Baltimore, MD, 2011.

15. Populism first surfaced as a political term in nineteenth-century Russia, denoting middle-class intellectuals who embraced peasant communalism as an antidote to Western liberalism. In the United States, too, populism was a rural movement, reaching its zenith in the 1896 presidential campaign of William Jennings Bryan against the gold standard. The term would later be applied to Huey Long, the governor of Louisiana from 1928 to 1932, who, in a style similar to many Latin American populists, campaigned against Standard Oil and built a ruthless political machine. In France, Pierre Poujade in the 1950s and Jean Marie Le Pen in recent times championed the 'little man', especially farmers and small shopkeepers, against big corporations, unions and foreigners. But it is in Latin America where populism has had the most enduring influence. See Michael L. Conniff (ed.), *Latin American Populism in Comparative Perspective*, University of New Mexico Press, Albuquerque, NM, 1982. Conniff in this work, and another edited collection of essays (*Populism in Latin America*, University of Alabama Press, Tuscaloosa, AL, and London, 1999), holds to the view, common among many political scientists, that populism is merely a style of political leadership with no bearing upon economic policy. Thus, he and his collaborators apply the term to leaders such as Peru's Alberto Fujimori and Argentina's Carlos Menem, whom, confusingly in my view, they see as 'neo-populist neoliberals' rather than mere conservatives. In contrast, Rudiger Dornbusch and Sebastian Edwards and their collaborators (*The Macroeconomics of Populism in Latin America*, University of Chicago Press, 1991) link populism to unsustainable redistribution. There is indeed nothing inherently left wing about populism – some of its exponents were closer to fascism than socialism. Rather, it is at heart corporatist and anti-liberal. This passage in the text also draws on 'Latin America: the return of populism', *The Economist*, 15 April 2006.

16. Interview with the author, Mexico City, 9 May 2005.

17. Richard Gillespie, *Soldiers of Perón: Argentina's Montoneros*, Oxford University Press, 1982, p. 44.

18. World Development Indicators, World Bank; IMF, *World Economic Outlook*, Washington, DC, October 2016.

19. Jorge I. Domínguez, 'Conclusion: Early twenty-first century democratic governance in Latin America', in Jorge I. Domínguez and Michael Shifter (eds), *Constructing Democratic Governance in Latin America*, 4th edition, Johns Hopkins University Press, Baltimore, MD, 2013, p. 344.

20. São Paulo Justice and Peace Commission, *São Paulo: Growth and poverty*, The Bowerdean Press in association with the Catholic Institute for International Relations, London, 1978; National Research Council, *Cities Transformed: Demographic change and its implications in the developing world*, National Academies Press, Washington, DC, 2003; Hernando de Soto, *El Otro Sendero*, Editorial El Barranco, Lima, 1986, p. 8.

21. Hernando de Soto, *The Mystery of Capital*, Black Swan Books, London, 2001, p. 30.

22. ECLAC/CEPAL, *Statistical Yearbook, 2015*, Table 1.6; David de Ferranti, Guillermo E. Perry, Francisco H.G. Ferreira and Michael Walton, *Inequality in Latin America: Breaking with history?*, World Bank, Washington, DC, 2004, Table 1, p. 2.

23. Paulo M. Saad, 'Demographic trends in Latin America and the Caribbean', ECLAC/CEPAL, Santiago de Chile, 2009.

24. Francis Fukuyama, 'The politics of Latin America's new middle class', Inter-American Dialogue, Washington, DC, 2013.

25. UNDP, *Multidimensional Progress: Well-being beyond income*, Regional Human Development Report for Latin America and the Caribbean, UNDP, New York, 2016.

26. Perhaps inevitably, the title of this book prompted several reviewers of the first edition in the United States to discuss whether their country should 'do more for Latin America'. That was not my intention; rather it was that outsiders should pay more attention to the region because of the importance of the underlying issues at stake there.

27. 'El Español: una Lengua Viva', Informe 2016, Instituto Cervantes at www.cervantes.es/imagenes/File/prensa/EspanolLenguaViva16.pdf

28. List of languages by total number of speakers (Wikipedia, accessed 22 August 2016). Wikipedia's source is the 2015 edition of *Ethnologue*, a language reference work published by SIL International, a Christian missionary group based in the United States. It adds that such estimates are hard to verify and should be treated with caution.

29. Vinod Thomas, *From Inside Brazil: Development in a land of contrasts*, Conference Edition, World Bank, Washington, DC, 2006, pp. 101–02.

30. BP, *BP Statistical Review of World Energy 2016*, Centre for Energy Economics Research and Policy, Heriot-Watt University, Edinburgh, 2016, p. 6.

31. Joseph R. Biden, Jnr, 'Building on success: Opportunities for the next administration', *Foreign Affairs*, September/October 2016.

32. Zweig, and his wife, committed suicide not long after coining his famous phrase about Brazil.

33. David Bushnell and Neill Macaulay, *The Emergence of Latin America in the Nineteenth Century*, 2nd edition, Oxford University Press, 1994, p. 3. The first known use of the term was by Michel Chevalier in the introduction to a book entitled *Lettres sur l'Amérique du Nord*, published in 1836. Chevalier's essay was translated into Spanish in 1856. See James Dunkerley, *Dreaming of Freedom in the Americas: Four minds and a name*, Institute for the Study of the Americas, London, 2004, p. 37.

34. Laurence Whitehead, 'Introduction: Latin America in comparative perspective', in *Latin America: A new interpretation*, Palgrave Macmillan, New York, 2006.

35. Sergio Ramírez, 'El Caribe somos todos', *El País*, 4 September 2001.

36. Octavio Paz, *The Labyrinth of Solitude and Other Writings*, Grove Press, New York, 1985, Chapter 2.

37. See Howard Wiarda, *The Soul of Latin America: The cultural and political tradition*, Yale University Press, New Haven, CT, and London, 2001.

38. Bushnell and Macaulay, *The Emergence of Latin America in the Nineteenth Century*, pp. 190–91.

39. Samuel P. Huntington, *The Clash of Civilizations and the Remaking of World Order*, Touchstone Books, New York, 1998, p. 46.

40. Alain Rouquié, *América Latina: Introducción al Extreme Occidente*, 4th edition (in Spanish), Siglo XXI Editores, Mexico City, 1997.

Chapter 2: The Latin American Conundrum

1. See Felipe Fernández-Armesto, *The Americas: A hemispheric history*, Random House, New York, 2003, Chapter 3.

2. Victor Bulmer-Thomas, *The Economic History of Latin America Since Independence*, Cambridge University Press, 1994, p. 27.

3. Quoted in D.C.M. Platt, *Latin America and British Trade 1806–1914*, A & C Black, London, 1972, p. 4.

4. Angus Maddison, *The World Economy: A millennial perspective*, OECD, Paris, 1998, p. 126.

5. Enrique Cárdenas, José Antonio Ocampo and Rosemary Thorp (eds), *An Economic History of Twentieth-Century Latin America*, Vol. 1: *The Export Age*, Palgrave Macmillan, Basingstoke, 2000, Chapter 1.

6. Bulmer-Thomas, *Economic History*, pp. 61–66.

7. Ibid., p. 417.

8. Jonathan Hartlyn and Arturo Valenzuela (1994), 'Democracy in Latin America since 1930', in Leslie Bethell (ed.), *The Cambridge History of Latin America*, Vol. VI, Part 2, Cambridge University Press, 1994, pp. 99–100.

9. Rosemary Thorp, *Progress, Poverty and Exclusion: An economic history of Latin America in the 20th century*, Inter-American Development Bank, Washington, DC, 1998, pp. 122–23.

10. Fernando Henrique Cardoso and Enzo Faletto, *Dependencia y Desarrollo en América Latina*, Siglo XXI, Argentina, 2003 p. 23.

11. Ibid., p. 151.

12. Fernando Henrique Cardoso, with Brian Winter, *The Accidental President of Brazil: A memoir*, PublicAffairs, New York, 2006, pp. 96–98.

13. See, for example, Andre Gunder Frank, *Capitalism and Underdevelopment in Latin America*, Penguin, Harmondsworth, 1969.

14. Thomas E. Skidmore and Peter H. Smith, *Modern Latin America*, 4th edition, Oxford University Press, 1997, p. 7.

15. Eduardo Galeano, *Open Veins of Latin America: Five centuries of the pillage of a continent*, Monthly Review Press, New York, 1997, p. 2.

16. Ibid., p. 267.

17. Ibid., p. 8.

18. To take just two of many possible examples of Galeano's questionable historical interpretations, contrast his view of the defeat in a civil war in 1891 of José Manuel Balmaceda, a Chilean president whom he portrays as an economic nationalist toppled by British intrigue, with the very different view in *The Cambridge History of Latin America* (Harold Blakemore, 'From the War of the Pacific to 1930', in Leslie Bethell (ed.), *Chile Since Independence*, Cambridge University Press, 1993, pp. 33–85). This concludes that 'Balmaceda had nothing like the clearly constructed policy on state intervention in the economy – including nitrates – ascribed to him' (p. 55). Similarly, Galeano champions the Paraguay of Dr Gaspar Rodríguez de Francia (1814–40), a sinister dictator, and his successors as 'Latin America's most progressive country'. As Paul Gootenberg, a historian of leftish sympathy, has remarked: 'the dependency rehabilitation of such freakish characters as Dr Francia of Paraguay – who are now held to offer nineteenth-century Latin America its most viable and progressive path to development – should alert us that revisionism has gone astray' (Paul Gootenberg, *Between Silver and Guano: Commercial Policy and the State in Postindependence Peru*, Princeton University Press, 1989, p. 10).

19. 'Bello: The gods that failed', *The Economist*, 14 June 2014.

20. David Bushnell, *Colombia: Una nación a pesar de sí misma*, 5th edition, Planeta, Bogotá, 2000, p. 246.

21. See Marcelo Bucheli, *Bananas and Business: The United Fruit Company in Colombia, 1899–2000*, New York University Press, 2005, Chapter 5.

22. The discrepancy in the casualty figures was acknowledged by García Márquez himself. When he realised that 'the number of deaths must have been very small', the novelist recalled, 'this was a big problem, because when I found out that it wasn't really a spectacular massacre in a novel where everything was extraordinary . . . where I wanted to fill a whole train with dead bodies, I couldn't stick to historical reality'. See Eduardo Posada-Carbó, 'La historia y los falsos recuerdos', *Revista de Occidente* (Madrid), December 2003.

23. Gabriel García Márquez, *Vivir para contarla*, Knopf, New York, 2002, p. 74. García Márquez is an incorrigible hyperbolist. In this work, the first volume of his memoirs, he narrates his experience of the riots in Bogotá in 1948 known as the *Bogotazo*. 'The deaths in the streets of Bogotá, and at the hands of the official repression in subsequent years, must have been more than a million' (p. 348). In fact, even the most pessimistic of historians put the figure at no higher than 200,000 over ten years – again, appalling enough, but not on the same scale.

24. Stephen Haber, 'Introduction: Economic growth and Latin American economic historiography', in Stephen Haber (ed.), *How Latin America Fell Behind: Essays on the economic histories of Brazil and Mexico, 1800–1914*, Stanford University Press, pp. 1–33.

25. See for example, Carlos Marichal (coordinador), *Las inversiones extranjeras en América Latina, 1850–1930*, Fondo de Cultura Económica, Mexico City, 1995; or Doug Yarrington, 'The Vestey cattle enterprise and the regime of Juan Vicente Gómez 1908–1935', *Journal of Latin American Studies*, 35:1 (2003), pp. 89–115.

26. John H. Coatsworth and Jeffrey G. Williamson, 'Always protectionist? Latin American tariffs from independence to Great Depression', *Journal of Latin American Studies*, 36:2 (2004).

27. Haber, 'Introduction', p. 12.

28. David Landes, *The Wealth and Poverty of Nations*, Little, Brown and Co., New York, 1998, p. 328 (italics in original).

29. Claudio Véliz, *The New World of the Gothic Fox: Culture and economy in English and Spanish America*, University of California Press, Berkeley, CA, 1994, p. 12. Other works in this vein include Wiarda, *Soul of Latin America*; Lawrence E. Harrison, *Underdevelopment is a State of Mind: The Latin American case*, Madison Books, Lanham, MD, 2000; and Lawrence E. Harrison, *The Pan-American Dream: Do Latin America's cultural values discourage true partnership with the United States and Canada?*, Basic Books, New York, 1997. See also Álvaro Vargas Llosa, *Liberty for Latin America*, Farrar, Straus and Giroux, New York, 2005, which mixes cultural and institutional explanations.

30. Véliz, *New World*, p. 53.

31. Wiarda, *Soul of Latin America*, Chapters 4 and 5.

32. Véliz, *New World*, p. 53.

33. José Enrique Rodó, *Ariel*, Kapelusz Editora, Buenos Aires, 1994.

34. Wiarda, *Soul of Latin America*, Chapter 5.

35. Joe Foweraker, Todd Landman and Neil Harvey, *Governing Latin America*, Polity Press, Cambridge, 2003, Chapter 3.

36. Mario Vargas Llosa, 'El Amor a Francia', *El País*, 19 March 2005.

37. Alain Rouquié, *The Military and the State in Latin America*, University of California Press, Berkeley, CA, 1987, p. 4. Alfredo Stroessner was the dictator of Paraguay from 1954 to 1989; Ernesto Geisel and Emílio Garrastazu Médici were both presidents of Brazil during its military regime of 1964–85; Gustavo Leigh was a member of the military junta headed by Augusto Pinochet which seized power in Chile in 1973.

38. Jeffrey D. Sachs, Andrew D. Mellinger and John L. Gallup, 'The geography of poverty and wealth', *Scientific American*, March 2001.

39. Cárdenas et al., *Economic History*, Vol. 1, Chapter 1.

40. Dani Rodrik, Arvind Subramanian and Francesco Trebbi, 'Institutions rule: The primacy of institutions over geography and integration in economic development', NBER Working Paper No. 9305, November 2002.

41. See de Soto, *El Otro Sendero*.

42. Francis Fukuyama, *Political Order and Political Decay*, Farrar, Straus and Giroux, New York, 2014, pp. 227–28.

43. Francis Fukuyama, *The Origins of Political Order*, Profile Books, London, 2011, Chapter 1.

44. Stanley L. Engerman and Kenneth L. Sokoloff, 'Factor endowments, institutions and differential paths of growth among New World economies', in Stephen Haber (ed.), *How Latin America Fell Behind: Essays on the economic histories of Brazil and Mexico, 1800–1914*, Stanford University Press, 1997, pp. 260–304.

45. Aníbal Quijano, 'Coloniality of power, Eurocentrism and Latin America', *Nepantla: Views from South*, 1:3 (2000), pp. 533–79.

46. Daron Acemoglu and James A. Robinson, *Why Nations Fail: The origins of power, prosperity and poverty*, Profile Books, London, 2012, p. 114.

47. Ibid., p. 18.

48. Ibid., p. 459.

49. See Francis Fukuyama, 'Conclusion', in Francis Fukuyama (ed.), *Falling Behind: Explaining the development gap between Latin America and the United States*, Oxford University Press, New York, 2008.

50. See Adam Przeworski, with Carolina Curvale, in Fukuyama (ed.), *Falling Behind*.

51. John H. Coatsworth, 'Structures, endowments, and institutions in the economic history of Latin America', *Latin American Research Review*, 40:3 (2005).

52. Bulmer-Thomas, *Economic History*, p. 88.

53. Cárdenas et al., *Economic History,* Vol. 1, p. 72.
54. See Fukuyama, *Political Order and Political Decay*, Chapter 17.
55. See Whitehead, *Latin America*, Introduction and Chapter 1; quotation on p. 42.

Chapter 3: The Seed of Democracy in the Land of the Caudillo

1. Debate still rages as to whether the M-19 was acting at the behest of drug traffickers. The files of many drug cases were among those consumed by fire during the assault.
2. Enrique Krauze, *Mexico: Biography of power – a history of modern Mexico, 1810–1996*, HarperCollins, New York, 1997, p. xiii.
3. These estimates are from Alexander von Humboldt, the great German scientist-explorer who travelled widely in Spanish America in 1799–1804. They are quoted in John Lynch, *The Spanish American Revolutions 1808–1826*, 2nd edition, W.W. Norton & Company, New York, 1986, p. 19.
4. Ibid., p. 18.
5. Raymond Carr (ed.), *Spain: A history*, Oxford University Press, 2000, p. 198.
6. Charles F. Walker, *The Tupac Amaru Rebellion*, Belknap Press/Harvard University Press, 2014 (quotation on p. 12).
7. J.H. Parry, Philip Sherlock and Anthony Maingot, *A Short History of the West Indies*, 4th edition, Macmillan, Basingstoke, 1987, p. 140.
8. France did not recognise Haiti's independence until 1825, and then only after the new state agreed to pay reparations of 150 million francs (later reduced to 60 million); Haiti did not repay the resulting debt until 1922. In January 2004, Haiti's government commemorated the bicentenary of independence. Jean-Bertrand Aristide, who was to be overthrown shortly afterwards, used the occasion to demand that France repay the reparations, which with interest, he said, amounted to $21.7 billion.
9. Lynch, *Spanish American Revolutions,* p. 24.
10. Robert Harvey, *Liberators: Latin America's struggle for independence 1810–1930*, Overlook Press, New York, 2000, Part 4; Patrick Wilcken, *Empire Adrift: The Portuguese Court in Rio 1808–1821*, Bloomsbury, London, 2004.
11. Bushnell and Macaulay, *Emergence,* p. 59.
12. Fernández-Armesto, *The Americas*, pp. 126–27.
13. Before setting sail, Columbus had watched the Catholic Monarchs, Ferdinand and Isabella, make their triumphal entry into Granada in January 1492. See J.H. Elliott, *Empires of the Atlantic World: Britain and Spain in America 1492–1830*, Yale University Press, New Haven, CT, and London, 2006, p. 19.
14. Ibid., p. 46.
15. Hugh Thomas, *Cuba or the Pursuit of Freedom*, Eyre & Spotiswoode, London, 1971, pp. 45–56.
16. See Vargas Llosa, *Liberty for Latin America*, pp. 28–29.
17. Elliott, *Empires*, p. 410.
18. Quoted in Galeano, *Open Veins*, p. 37.
19. Jorge Basadre, *Perú: Problema y posibilidad*, 5th edition, Librería Studium, Lima, 1987, p. 281.
20. Panama was a province of Colombia until 1903, when it declared independence in a rebellion inspired by the United States.
21. The author of the phrase was John L. O'Sullivan, the young editor of the *New York Morning News*. In 1845, he wrote that the US claim to the Oregon Territory was justified 'by the right of our manifest destiny to overspread and to possess the whole of the continent which Providence has given us for the development of the great experiment of liberty and federated self-government entrusted to us'.
22. Some Latin Americans had long seen the potential for river transport. 'The Mississippi is not more available for commerce than the Parana; nor do the Ohio, Illinois or Arkansas water a larger or richer territory than the Pilcomayo, Bermejo, Paraguay and

so many other great rivers', noted Domingo Faustino Sarmiento, an Argentine writer and later president, in 1845.

23. 'In the Central Andes, the majority of people traditionally resided above 2,500 m[etres], where adverse corollaries of altitude include rugged terrain, fragile topography, steep slopes, poor soils, limited farmland, short growing seasons, high winds, aridity, elevated solar radiation, erratic rainfall, precarious nutrition, cold and hypoxia. Hypoxia is the technical term for low oxygen tension due to elevational decrease in barometric pressure. It is a pervasive source of chronic stress on all life . . . cold and anoxia oblige people to eat more . . . Consequently, it costs measurably more to support life and civilization in mountains than in lowlands' (Michael E. Moseley, *The Incas and Their Ancestors*, Thames and Hudson, London, 2001, p. 27). The author is referring to pre-Conquest life, but many of these factors apply today. Tourists to Cusco or to Lake Titicaca get a brief taste of some of these deprivations.

24. Colin M. Lewis, 'Public policy and private initiative: Railway building in São Paulo 1860–89', University of London, Institute of Latin American Studies Research Papers No. 26, 1991.

25. Domingo F. Sarmiento, *Facundo: Or, civilization and barbarism*, Penguin, London, 1998, p. 9.

26. Bushnell and Macaulay, *Emergence*, p. 53.

27. Bolívar Lamounier, *Da Independência a Lula: dois séculos de política brasileira*, Augurium Editora, São Paulo, 2005, p. 80.

28. Ibid., pp. 43–68.

29. Thomas E. Skidmore, *Brazil: Five Centuries of Change*, Oxford University Press, 1999, p. 48.

30. John Lynch, *Simón Bolívar: A life*, Yale University Press, New Haven, CT, and London, 2006, p. xi.

31. Simón Bolívar, *El Libertador: Writings of Simón Bolívar*, Oxford University Press, 2003, p. xxx.

32. Simón Bolívar, 'The Jamaica Letter', in ibid., p. 23.

33. Lynch, *Bolívar*, p. 77.

34. Colombia's FARC guerrillas and Cuba's communist regime also paid rhetorical obeisance to Bolívar.

35. Ibid., p. 304.

36. John Lynch, *Argentine Caudillo: Juan Manuel de Rosas*, Rowman and Littlefield, Wilmington, DE, 2001, p. 72.

37. There were occasional exceptions. In Colombia, a Liberal constitution in 1853 included universal male suffrage and popular election of the Supreme Court. In one province, the Liberals enacted female suffrage, but this was struck down by the Court before it could be implemented (Bushnell and Macaulay, *Emergence*, p. 212). Chile abolished the property qualification (though not the literacy requirement) for voting in 1874 (ibid., p. 237).

38. See 'Bello: Relearning old lessons', *The Economist*, 1 February 2014; and Iván Jaksić, *Andrés Bello: Scholarship and nation-building in nineteenth-century Latin America*, Cambridge University Press, 2001.

39. Nicolas Shumway, *The Invention of Argentina*, University of California Press, Berkeley, CA, 1993, p. 183.

40. Thorp, *Progress, Poverty and Exclusion*, pp. 1–2.

41. See Wiarda, *Soul of Latin America*, Chapter 6.

42. Herbert S. Klein, 'Migração Internacional na História das Americas', in Boris Fausto (ed.), *Fazer a América: A Imigração em Massa para a América Latina*, Editora da Universidade de São Paulo, 1999, pp. 13–31.

43. Quoted in Krauze, *Mexico*, pp. 217 and 231.

44. Ibid., p. 219.

45. For an extraordinary account by an observer of this campaign, see Euclides da Cunha, *Os Sertoes*, translated as *Rebellion in the Backlands*, Picador, London, 1995. Mario Vargas Llosa drew heavily on da Cunha's book in his novel *War of the End of the World*. During

the Canudos campaign, the army set up a camp on Monte Favela, a hill overlooking the settlement. As a result, the word *favela* entered the Portuguese language to describe a shanty town.

46. David Rock, *Argentina 1516–1987: From Spanish colonization to Alfonsín*, University of California Press, Berkeley, CA, 1987, p. 125.

47. David Rock, 'Argentina in 1914', in Leslie Bethell (ed.), *Argentina since Independence*, Cambridge University Press, 1993, p. 117.

48. Data from Carlos Díaz Alejandro, quoted in ibid., p. 120.

49. Spiritualism is a long-forgotten doctrine identified with Victor Cousin, a French philosopher. It attempted to reconcile idealism and materialism, Catholicism and rationalist philosophy. It was highly influential in both France and among Latin America's liberal intellectual elite in the late nineteenth century, as freemasonry was to be somewhat later. See Wiarda, *Soul of Latin America*, p. 149.

50. Krauze, *Mexico*, p. 359.

51. The point is made in Alan Riding, *Distant Neighbors: A portrait of the Mexicans*, Knopf, New York, 1985, Chapter 9.

52. Alan Knight, *The Mexican Revolution*, Vol. 1: *Porfirians, Liberals and Peasants*, University of Nebraska Press, Lincoln, NE, 1990, p. 184.

53. Krauze, *Mexico*, Chapters 14 and 15.

54. Angus Maddison et al., *The Political Economy of Poverty, Equity and Growth: Brazil and Mexico*, World Bank/Oxford University Press, New York, 1992, p. 6.

55. V.R. Haya de la Torre, *El Antiimperialismo y el APRA*, 6th edition, APRA, Lima, 1985, p. 1.

56. Julio Cotler, 'Political parties and the problems of democratic consolidation in Peru', in Scott Mainwaring and Timothy R. Scully, *Building Democratic Institutions: Party systems in Latin America*, Stanford University Press, 1995, p. 328.

57. Frederick B. Pike, *The Modern History of Peru*, Praeger, Westport, CT, 1969, p. 239.

58. James Dunkerley, *Power in the Isthmus: A political history of modern Central America*, Verso, New York, 1988, p. 71.

59. Bulmer-Thomas, *Economic History*, p. 201.

60. Skidmore and Smith, *Modern Latin America*, p. 52.

61. I owe this point to Roberto Saba.

62. See Dunkerley, *Rebellion in the Veins*, Chapters 1 and 2.

63. See Leslie Bethell, 'Populism, neopopulism and the left in Brazil: From Gétulio to Lula', in Carlos de la Torre and Cynthia Arnson (eds), *Latin American Populism in the Twenty-First Century*, Johns Hopkins University Press, Baltimore, MD, 2013.

64. The figure comes from a commission of inquiry appointed by the government of Carlos Menem. Reuters, 28 September 1999.

65. In the United States and Russia in the late nineteenth century, rural populist movements arose which challenged some aspects of capitalist development. See Conniff, *Latin American Populism*, Introduction.

66. Jorge Castañeda, *Utopia Unarmed: The Latin American Left after the Cold War*, Vintage Books, New York, 1994, p. 43.

67. Paul W. Drake, 'Requiem for populism', in Conniff, *Latin American Populism*, p. 224.

68. Ibid.

69. Max Weber, *Economy and Society*, Vol. 1, University of California Press, Berkeley, CA, 1978, p. 241.

Chapter 4: Cold War and Revolution

1. This was the finding both of the Truth Commission set up under the peace accord and of the Human Rights Office of the Archbishopric of Guatemala. See Susanne Jonas, *Of Centaurs and Doves: Guatemala's peace process*, Westview Press, Boulder, CO, 2000, Chapter 1.

2. Stephen Schlesinger and Stephen Kinzer, *Bitter Fruit: The untold story of the American coup in Guatemala*, Sinclair Browne, London, 1982, p. 11.
3. Ronald Schneider, quoted in ibid., p. 227.
4. Costa Rica had few Indians and, as a result, land was distributed more evenly, rural wages were higher and there were few *haciendas*. Although the franchise was limited, Costa Rica's coffee-growing elite laid the basis of universal education and a civilian political system in the late nineteenth century.
5. Dunkerley, *Power in the Isthmus*, p. 100.
6. Leslie Bethell and Ian Roxborough, 'Introduction: The postwar conjuncture in Latin America: democracy, labor and the left', in Bethell and Roxborough (eds), *Latin America Between the Second World War and the Cold War 1944–48*, Cambridge University Press, 1992, p. 10.
7. This paragraph draws on ibid., Introduction (pp. 1–32) and Conclusion, pp. 327–34.
8. Dunkerley, *Power in the Isthmus*, p. 52.
9. Ubico granted United Fruit a second tract of land on the Pacific coast on similar terms.
10. Quoted in Stephen M. Streeter, 'Interpreting the 1954 US intervention in Guatemala: Realist, revisionist and postrevisionist perspectives', *The History Teacher*, 34:1 (2000). In 1972, United Fruit sold its remaining interests in Guatemala to Del Monte. United Fruit changed its name to Chiquita Brands in 1989. Chiquita attracted controversy for paying Colombian paramilitaries in 1997–2004; while it admitted the payments, it said they were extorted. In 2014, Chiquita was sold to a Brazilian consortium.
11. Christopher Andrew and Vasili Mitrokhin, *The Mitrokhin Archive II: The KGB and the world*, Penguin Books, 2006, p. 27.
12. The nickname derived from the Argentine usage of *che* as a frequent interjection.
13. Jorge Castañeda, *Compañero: The life and death of Che Guevara*, Bloomsbury, London, 1997, pp. 64 and 71.
14. Quoted in Schlesinger and Kinzer, *Bitter Fruit*, p. 184.
15. Quoted in Peter H. Smith, *Talons of the Eagle: Dynamics of US–Latin American relations*, Oxford University Press, 1996, p. 20.
16. Robert Freeman Smith, 'Latin America, the United States and the European powers 1830–1930', in Leslie Bethell (ed.), *Cambridge History of Latin America*, Vol. IV, Cambridge University Press, 1986, p. 85.
17. Bethell and Roxborough, *Latin America*, p. 22 footnote.
18. Smith, 'Latin America, the United States and the European powers', pp. 95–98.
19. Quoted in ibid., pp. 101–02.
20. David McCullough, *The Path Between the Seas: The creation of the Panama Canal, 1870–1914*, Simon & Schuster, New York, 1977, p. 384.
21. Quoted in Smith, *Talons of the Eagle*, p. 53.
22. Ibid., p. 63.
23. Ibid., p. 73.
24. Ibid., p. 100.
25. Smith, 'Latin America, the United States and the European powers', p. 103.
26. Thomas, *Cuba*, p. 169.
27. Ibid., p. 74.
28. 'Letter to Manuel Mercado', in José Martí, *Selected Writings*, Penguin Books, London, 2002, p. 347.
29. A treaty signed shortly after the Platt Amendment granted the United States an indefinite lease for a base for 'coaling and naval purposes' only at Guantánamo Bay. The lease can only be terminated if both countries agree. Cuba claims that it is illegal, and since 1959 has refused to cash the cheque for $4,000 in annual rent offered by the United States. See Julia Sweig, *Cuba: What everyone needs to know*, Oxford University Press, 2009.
30. Quoted in Louis A. Pérez, *Cuba Between Reform and Revolution*, Oxford University Press, 1988, p. 186.

31. Richard Gott, *Cuba: A new history*, Yale University Press, New Haven, CT, and London, 2004, Chapter 4.

32. Ibid., p. 134.

33. Tad Szulc, *Fidel: A critical portrait*, Avon Books, New York, 1986, p. 203.

34. Ibid., p. 38.

35. Ibid., p. 39.

36. Gott, *Cuba*, pp. 195–209.

37. Jorge I. Domínguez, 'US–Latin American relations during the Cold War and its aftermath', in Victor Bulmer-Thomas and James Dunkerley (eds), *The United States and Latin America: The new agenda*, Institute of Latin American Studies, University of London and David Rockefeller Center for Latin American Studies, Harvard University, 1999, p. 40.

38. Like Martí, Castro rightly saw the United States as the chief threat to the revolution. But his anti-Americanism may have been given an edge by the Eisenhower administration's support for Batista. Szulc cites a letter from Fidel to Celia Sánchez, his companion, written on 5 June 1958, shortly after a rebel position had been bombed by Batista's air force using US-supplied bombs: 'I have sworn that the Americans will pay very dearly for what they are doing. When this war has ended, a much bigger and greater war will start for me, a war I shall launch against them. I realize that this will be my true destiny' (Szulc, *Fidel*, p. 39).

39. Ibid., p. 150.

40. Jorge I. Domínguez, 'Fidel Castro's footprints', *Boston Globe*, 26 November 2016.

41. Skidmore, *Brazil*, p. 112.

42. See Gonzalo Portocarrero, *La Urgencia por Decir 'Nosotros': Los intelectuales y la idea de nación en el Perú republicano*, Fondo Editorial de la Pontificia Universidad Católica del Perú, Lima, 2015, Chapter 7; Mario Vargas Llosa, *La Utopía Arcaica: José María Arguedas y las ficciones del indigenismo*, Fondo de Cultura Económica, Mexico City, 1996, pp. 63–66.

43. José Carlos Mariátegui, *Siete Ensayos de Interpretación de la Realidad Peruana*, 13th edition, *Amauta*, Lima, 1968, pp. 44–45.

44. Quoted in Portocarrero, *La Urgencia*, p. 257.

45. See Alberto Flores Galindo, *La Agonía de Mariátegui*, Editorial Revolución, Madrid, 1991.

46. Ibid., p. 229.

47. Che Guevara, *Guerrilla Warfare*, Penguin Books, Harmondsworth, 1969, p. 13.

48. Gillespie, *Soldiers of Perón*, p. 54.

49. Stephen Moss, 'John Paul's people: a journey through the Catholic world', *Guardian*, 5 April 2005.

50. Julia Sweig, an American researcher who had access to the Castro government's archives, provides convincing evidence of this. See Julia E. Sweig, *Inside the Cuban Revolution: Fidel Castro and the urban underground*, Harvard University Press, 2002.

51. Guevara, *Guerrilla Warfare*, p. 14.

52. John Gerrasi (ed.) (1968), *Venceremos: The speeches and writings of Ernesto Che Guevara*, Weidenfeld and Nicolson, London, 1968, p. 137.

53. Andrew and Mitrokhin, *Mitrokhin Archive II*, p. 31.

54. This paragraph draws on Michael J. Kryzanek, *US–Latin American Relations*, Praeger, Westport, CT, 1996, pp. 72–76; and Smith, *Talons of the Eagle*, pp. 168–71.

55. Quoted in Andrew and Mitrokhin, *Mitrokhin Archive II*, p. 28.

56. Ibid., pp. 40–41.

57. The Mitrokhin Archive, cited in this chapter and Chapter 5, is a trove of KGB documents secretly copied over 20 years by Vasili Mitrokhin, a senior KGB archivist, and smuggled out to Britain by the Secret Intelligence Service (MI6) in 1992. Since the original documents have not been released, its contents cannot be independently verified, but they are highly plausible.

58. Castañeda, *Compañero*, pp. 58–61.

59. *Observer*, 6 November 2005.
60. Castañeda, *Compañero*, p. xiii.
61. Castañeda, *Utopia Unarmed*, p. 109.
62. Andrew and Mitrokhin, *Mitrokhin Archive II*, pp. 134–35.
63. Sergio Ramírez, *Adiós Muchachos: A memoir of the Sandinista revolution*, Duke University Press, Durham and London, 2012, p. 4.
64. 'Bello: From comrade to caudillo', *The Economist*, 17 September 2016.
65. See Raymond Bonner, *Weakness and Deceit: US policy and El Salvador*, Hamish Hamilton, London, 1985, Chapter 3; Alastair White, *El Salvador: Nation of the modern world*, Ernest Benn Ltd, London, 1973, Chapter 9.
66. John Dinges, *Our Man in Panama*, Random House, New York, 1990, pp. 299–319.
67. Frederick Kempe, *Divorcing the Dictator: America's bungled affair with Noriega*, G.P. Putnam's Sons, New York, 1990, pp. 418–25.
68. Castañeda, *Utopia Unarmed*, p. 193.
69. For a powerful account of the effectiveness of this police state a dozen years after the revolution, see Jorge Edwards, *Persona Non Grata*, Nation Books, New York, 1993. Edwards, a writer/diplomat, had been sent to Havana as chargé d'affaires by the Allende government in Chile, and was broadly sympathetic to the revolution.
70. For example, in 1992, Andres Oppenheimer, a journalist for the *Miami Herald*, concluded in a well-reported book on Cuba's travails in this period that Castro's 'final hour may stretch [for] a matter of weeks or . . . a few years'. At the time, this view was widely shared. Andres Oppenheimer, *Castro's Final Hour: The secret story behind the coming downfall of communist Cuba*, Simon & Schuster, New York, 1992, p. 9.
71. Gott, *Cuba*, p. 322.
72. 'Cuba's economy: Unappetising', *The Economist*, 23 June 2005.
73. Author's telephone interview with Oswaldo Payá, December 2005.
74. 'Cuba's budding private sector looks nervously to future', *Wall Street Journal*, 10 January 2017.
75. 'The United States and Cuba: An American invasion', *The Economist*, 26 March 2016.
76. Carmelo Mesa-Lago, *Cuba en la era de Raúl Castro: Reformas económico sociales y sus efectos*, Editorial Colibrí, Madrid, 2012, p. 63.
77. 'Cuba approves projects for development zone', Reuters, 2 November 2016.
78. The 'convertible' peso or CUC, used for foreign trade and tourism, is pegged at par to the dollar. It is not freely convertible: foreign exchange is assigned by the government. The ordinary Cuban peso, in which wages are paid and prices of most basic goods are set, is worth 4 cents. The system involves a big subsidy for imports by state companies.
79. See Michael Smith, 'Want to do business in Cuba? Prepare to partner with the general', Bloomberg, 30 September 2015.
80. Marifeli Pérez-Stabile, *The Cuban Revolution: Origins, course and legacy*, Oxford University Press, 1993, Chapter 1.
81. Carmelo Mesa-Lago and Pavel Vidal-Alejandro, 'The impact of the global crisis on Cuba's economy and social welfare', *Journal of Latin American Studies*, 42:4 (2010), p. 692.
82. The Gini coefficient is a statistical measure in which 1 means that one person holds all income and 0 means that income is shared equally among all.
83. Michael Reid, 'Cuba: Revolution in retreat', *The Economist*, 24 March 2012.
84. Ibid.

Chapter 5: Failed Reformers, Debt-Ridden Dictators

1. There is some doubt as to whether Vargas himself wrote the letter, but it was released to the press immediately after his death and accepted by the public as authentic. See Thomas E. Skidmore, *Politics in Brazil 1930–1964*, Oxford University Press, 1967, p. 142; and Boris Fausto, *Getúlio Vargas*, Companhia das Letras, São Paulo, 2006, Chapter 4.
2. Skidmore, *Brazil*, p. 14.

3. Elio Gaspari, *A Ditadura Envergonhada*, Companhia das Letras, São Paulo, 2002, p. 53.
4. Ibid., p. 92; Lincoln Gordon, *Brazil's Second Chance: En route toward the First World*, Brookings Institution Press, Washington, DC, 2001, p. 60.
5. Gordon, *Brazil's Second Chance*, p. 52.
6. Gaspari, *A Ditadura Envergonhada*, p. 102.
7. Rouquié, *The Military and the State in Latin America*, p. 139.
8. Ibid., p. 235.
9. Laurence Whitehead, 'State organization in Latin America since 1930', in Leslie Bethell (ed.), *The Cambridge History of Latin America*, Vol. VI, Part 2, Cambridge University Press, 1994, p. 37.
10. Rouquié, *The Military and the State in Latin America*, p. 248.
11. Alan Angell, 'Chile since 1958', in Bethell, *Chile Since Independence*, p. 156.
12. Ibid., p. 158.
13. Felipe Larraín and Patricio Meller, 'The Socialist-Populist Chilean experience', in Rudiger Dornbusch and Sebastian Edwards (eds), *The Macroeconomics of Populism in Latin America*, University of Chicago Press, 1991, pp. 188–89.
14. Ibid., pp. 186–87.
15. Whitehead, 'State organization', p. 38.
16. Larraín and Meller, 'The Socialist-Populist Chilean experience', pp. 198–205.
17. Andrew and Mitrokhin, *The Mitrokhin Archive II*, pp. 71–72.
18. John Dinges and Saul Landau, *Assassination on Embassy Row*, McGraw-Hill, London, 1980, pp. 38–41.
19. Andrew and Mitrokhin, *The Mitrokhin Archive II*, Chapter 4.
20. Angell, 'Chile since 1958', p. 168.
21. Rouquié, *The Military and the State in Latin America*, p. 240.
22. Carlos Prats González, *Memorias: Testimonio de un soldado*, Pehuén Editores, Santiago de Chile 1985, pp. 485–86.
23. Ibid., p. 509.
24. Ricardo Lagos, 'The legacy of a crushed dream: Never again', *International Herald Tribune*, 11 September 2003.
25. James W. McGuire, *Peronism without Perón: Unions, parties and democracy in Argentina*, Stanford University Press, 1997, p. 19.
26. Gillespie, *Soldiers of Perón*, Chapters 1 and 2.
27. Ibid., p. 71.
28. Tomás Eloy Martínez, 'El último Perón', *El País*, 1 August 2004.
29. Juan Carlos Torre and Liliana de Riz, 'Argentina since 1946', in Leslie Bethell (ed.), *Argentina since Independence*, Cambridge University Press, 1993, p. 327.
30. Gillespie, *Soldiers of Perón*, p. 223.
31. Torre and de Riz, 'Argentina since 1946', p. 328.
32. See the Commission's Report at www.nuncamas.org.
33. Quoted in 'Obituary: Augusto Pinochet', *The Economist*, 16 December 2006.
34. Cited in Rouquié, *The Military and the State in Latin America*, p. 142.
35. See Smith, *Talons of the Eagle*, pp. 199–203.
36. Guillermo O'Donnell, *Contrapuntos: Ensayos escogidos sobre autoritarismo y democratización*, Paidós, Buenos Aires, 1997, pp. 75–76.
37. See Abraham F. Lowenthal (ed.), *The Peruvian Experiment: Continuity and change under military rule*, Princeton University Press, 1975; José Matos Mar and José Manuel Mejía, *La Reforma Agraria en el Perú*, Instituto de Estudios Peruanos, Lima, 1980.
38. Bulmer-Thomas, *Economic History*, p. 283.
39. Ibid., p. 356.
40. Ibid., p. 271.
41. Ibid., p. 364.
42. See Pedro-Pablo Kuczynski, *Latin American Debt*, Johns Hopkins University Press, Baltimore, MD, 1988, pp. 45–50; Sebastian Edwards, *Crisis and Reform in Latin America: From despair to hope*, World Bank and Oxford University Press, 1995, p. 23.

43. Glen Biglaiser, *Guardians of the Nation? Economists, generals and economic reform in Latin America*, University of Notre Dame Press, Notre Dame, IN, 2002, Chapter 1.

44. And to a lesser extent Uruguay's military regime.

45. Biglaiser, *Guardians of the Nation?*, Chapters 3 and 4.

Chapter 6: From the Washington Consensus to the Commodity Boom – and Bust

1. Interview with the author, Buenos Aires, October 2001.

2. Ibid.

3. Interview with the author, reported in 'Argentina's economy: Down, and almost out, in Buenos Aires', *The Economist*, 1 November 2001.

4. 'Argentina: Between the creditors and the streets', *The Economist*, 3 January 2002.

5. *Clarín*, 1 February 2003. The official poverty line was defined as an income sufficient to satisfy basic needs.

6. Interview with Rosendo Fraga, Argentine political analyst, Buenos Aires, March 2004.

7. Duncan Green, *Silent Revolution: The rise and crisis of market economics in Latin America*, Monthly Review Press, New York/Latin American Bureau, London, 2003, p. 171.

8. Moisés Naím, 'The Washington Consensus: A damaged brand', *Financial Times*, 28 October 2002.

9. Marie-Ange Véganzones, with Carlos Winograd, *Argentina in the 20th Century: An account of long-awaited growth*, OECD Publishing, Paris, 1997, Chapter 4.

10. According to a study by Andrea Goldstein of the OECD, quoted in Michael Reid, 'Back on the pitch: A survey of business in Latin America', *The Economist*, 6 December 1997, p. 10.

11. José Carbajo and Antonio Estache, 'Public policy for the private sector', World Bank Note No. 88, September 1996. I am grateful to Andrea Goldstein for this reference.

12. Reid, 'Back on the pitch', p. 11.

13. Edwards, *Crisis and Reform*, pp. 97–98.

14. Beatriz Tountoundjian, 'La Lucha por la Sobrevivencia en la Hiperinflación Argentina', Mimeo, Fernand Braudel Institute of World Economics, São Paulo, 1990.

15. Gerardo della Paolera and Alan M. Taylor, *Straining at the Anchor: The Argentine currency board and the search for macroeconomic stability, 1880–1935*, University of Chicago Press, 2001, p. 17.

16. Paul Blustein, *And the Money Kept Rolling In (and Out): Wall Street, the IMF and the bankrupting of Argentina*, PublicAffairs, New York, 2005, pp. 26 and 35.

17. Ibid., Chapter 3.

18. Michael Mussa, *Argentina and the Fund: From triumph to tragedy*, Institute for International Economics, Washington, DC, 2002, p. 12.

19. Blustein, *And the Money Kept Rolling*, pp. 131–32.

20. Statement by President Kirchner on 15 December 2005 announcing early repayment of Argentina's debts to the IMF, at www.presidencia.gov.ar.

21. Interview with the author, Buenos Aires, March 2004.

22. Interview with the author at Inter-American Development Bank annual meeting, Lima, March 2004.

23. John Williamson, 'A short history of the Washington Consensus', paper at https://piie.com/publications/papers/williamson0904-2.pdf, p. 3.

24. Edwards, *Crisis and Reform*, p. 24.

25. Thorp, *Progress, Poverty and Exclusion*, p. 332.

26. Daniel Carbonetto et al., *El Perú Heterodoxo: un modelo económico*, Instituto Nacional de Planificación, Lima, 1987, p. 81.

27. Cited in Edwards, *Crisis and Reform*, p. 48.

28. Williamson, 'A short history of the Washington Consensus', p. 6.

29. The list, which I have summarised, was originally published by John Williamson in 'Latin American adjustment: How much has happened', Institute for International Economics, Washington, DC, 1990.

30. Williamson, 'A short history of the Washington Consensus', p. 2.

31. Brazil did not conquer inflation until the mid-1990s (see Chapter 8).
32. William Cline, 'Managing international debt: How one big battle was won', *The Economist*, 18 February 1995.
33. Cited in Sarath Rajapatirana, *Trade Policies in Latin America and the Caribbean: Priorities, progress and prospects*, International Center for Economic Growth, Santiago de Chile and San Francisco, 1997, p. 8.
34. Roberto Bouzas and Saúl Keifman, 'Making trade liberalization work', in Pedro-Pablo Kuczynski and John Williamson (eds), *After the Washington Consensus: Restarting growth and reform in Latin America*, Institute for International Economics, Washington, DC, 2003, p. 160.
35. Robert Devlin and Paolo Giordano, 'The old and new regionalism: Benefits, costs and implications for the FTAA', in Antoni Estevadeordal, Dani Rodrik, Alan M. Taylor and Andrés Velasco, *Integrating the Americas: The FTAA and beyond*, Harvard University Press, 2004, p. 145.
36. Carol Wise and Riordan Roett (eds), *Exchange Rate Politics in Latin America*, Brookings Institution Press, Washington, DC, 2000, p. 1.
37. Pedro Aspe Armilla, *El camino mexicano de la transformación económica*, Fondo de Cultura Económica, Mexico City, 1993, Chapter 10.
38. For details, see Chapter 8.
39. Private capital inflow to the seven biggest Latin American economies had totalled about 5 per cent of their combined GDP in 1997 and the first half of 1998. By mid-1998, this figure had plunged to less than 1 per cent. See Blustein, *And the Money Kept Rolling*, p. 78. The term 'sudden stop' was coined by Guillermo Calvo, then the chief economist at the Inter-American Development Bank.
40. José Antonio Ocampo, CEPAL's secretary general at the time, points out that low growth lasted for six years, from 1998 to 2003, inclusive. See José Antonio Ocampo, *Reconstruir el futuro: Globalización, desarrollo y democracia en América Latina*, Editorial Norma, Bogotá, 2004, p. 18, footnote.
41. Visit by the author, April 1980.
42. John Nellis, Rachel Menezes and Sarah Lucas, 'Privatization in Latin America', Center for Global Development and Inter-American Dialogue Policy Brief, Washington, DC, January 2004, Vol. 3, Issue 1.
43. 'Bolivia: Water, oil and the mob', *The Economist*, 20 January 2005.
44. Juan Forero, 'Bolivians find that post-multinational life has its problems', *International Herald Tribune*, 15 December 2005.
45. 'Bolivia: Evo, for ever', *The Economist*, 7 January 2017.
46. John Peet, 'Priceless: a survey of water', *The Economist*, 19 July 2003.
47. Sebastián Galiani et al., 'The benefits and costs of privatization in Argentina: A microeconomic analysis', in Alberto Chong and Florencio López-de-Silanes, *Privatization in Latin America: Myths and reality*, World Bank and Stanford University Press, 2005, Chapter 2.
48. Chong and López-de-Silanes, *Privatization in Latin America*, p. 5.
49. Interview with the author, Mexico City, October 1997.
50. Chong and López-de-Silanes, *Privatization in Latin America*, Chapter 1.
51. Ibid.
52. Date from Vale.com website and *Veja*, 1 November 2006.
53. Edwards, *Crisis and Reform*, p. 199.
54. A study of 504 workers laid off by YPF in 1991 reckoned that over the following decade their earnings declined by around a half. In 2001, 26.4 per cent of this group were jobless, when the unemployment rate in Greater Buenos Aires stood at 13.9 per cent. See Galiani et al., 'Benefits and costs of privatization in Argentina', pp. 97–98.
55. Chong and López-de-Silanes, *Privatization in Latin America*, p. 27.
56. In addition to its telecoms interests, Slim's family controlled industrial, retailing and infrastructure businesses and a bank. See Michael Reid, 'Time to wake up: A survey of Mexico', *The Economist*, 18 November 2006.

57. Inter-American Development Bank, 'Competitiveness: The business of growth', Inter-American Development Bank, Washington, DC, 2001, p. 179.

58. Lourdes Casanova, 'What is the future of telecommunications in Latin America', World Economic Forum, 13 June 2016, www.weforum.org/agenda/2016/06/has-telecom-privatization-in-latin-america-been-a-success.

59. www.internetworldstats.com, accessed 12 January 2017.

60. Nellis et al., 'Privatization in Latin America'.

61. Quoted in Chong and López-de-Silanes, *Privatization in Latin America*, p. 51.

62. John Nellis and Nancy Birdsall (eds), *Reality Check: The distributional impact of privatization in developing countries*, Center for Global Development, Washington, DC, 2005, p. 26.

63. Ocampo, *Reconstruir el futuro*, p. 24.

64. Eduardo Lora and Ugo Panizza, 'Structural reforms in Latin America under scrutiny', Inter-American Development Bank Research Department paper, March 2002, Section 3.

65. This was an unweighted cross-country average rate. See ECLAC/CEPAL, *Economic Survey of Latin America and the Caribbean* (various years); Thorp, *Progress, Poverty and Exclusion*, p. 332.

66. Lora and Panizza, 'Structural reforms'; ECLAC/CEPAL, *Preliminary Overview of the Economies of Latin America and the Caribbean*, Santiago de Chile, 2005. Average weighted by size of economies.

67. *Financial Times*, 22 June 2005.

68. See Barry Eichengreen and Ricardo Hausmann, 'Original sin: The road to redemption', 2003, paper available at http://eml.berkeley.edu/~eichengr/research/osroadaug21-03.pdf.

69. Williamson, 'A short history of the Washington Consensus', p. 5.

70. Eduardo Cavallo and Tomás Serebrisky (eds), *Saving for Development*, Inter-American Development Bank, Washington, DC, 2016, Chapter 2.

71. Joseph E. Stiglitz, *Globalization and Its Discontents*, W.W. Norton, New York and London, 2002, Chapter 3.

72. Moisés Naím, *Paper Tigers and Minotaurs: The politics of Venezuela's economic reforms*, Carnegie Endowment for International Peace, Washington, DC, 1993, p. 141.

73. See, for example, Santiso, *Latin America's Political Economy of the Possible*.

74. It enacted a modest reform of labour law in 2012.

75. Stiglitz, *Globalization and Its Discontents*, p. 53.

76. In fact, these concerns had been enshrined in the presidential declarations at the Summits of the Americas from 1994 onwards. On the 'Post-Washington' consensus, see Nancy Birdsall and Augusto de la Torre, with Rachel Menezes, 'Washington contentious: Economic policies for social equity in Latin America', Carnegie Endowment for International Peace and Inter-American Dialogue, 2001; and Nancy Birdsall and Francis Fukuyama, 'The post-Washington Consensus', *Foreign Affairs*, March/April 2011.

77. *O Globo*, 26 March 2009.

78. Inter-American Development Bank, 'All that glitters is not gold', Inter-American Development Bank, Washington, DC, 2008, p. 15.

79. The term was coined by *The Economist* in 1977 to describe the impact of a North Sea gas bonanza on the economy of the Netherlands.

Chapter 7: The Venezuelan Disaster

1. Cristina Marcano and Alberto Barrera Tyszka, *Hugo Chávez Sin Uniforme: Una historia personal*, Debate, Caracas, 2005.

2. In a speech to several hundred officials and political cadres in November 2004, Chávez said: 'I want you to know that in this new stage, he who is with me is with me, he who is not with me is against me. I don't accept half-tones.' 'El nuevo mapa estratégico:

Intervenciones de Hugo Chávez Frias', 12–13 November 2004, available at www.urru. org/papers/El_nuevo_mapa_estrategico.pdf.

3. Gabriel García Márquez, 'El enigma de los dos Chávez', *Revista Cambio*, February 1999, available at www.voltairenet.org.

4. Teodoro Petkoff, 'Prólogo', in Marcano and Barrera, *Hugo Chávez Sin Uniforme*, p. 10.

5. See, for example, Richard Gott, *Hugo Chávez and the Bolivarian Revolution*, Verso, New York, 2005.

6. Interview with the author, Caracas, April 2005.

7. Carlos Fuentes, 'Nueva Izquierda?', *Reforma* (Mexico), 1 February 2006.

8. Enrique Krauze, *El Poder y El Delirio*, Tusquets Editores, Barcelona, 2008, p. 19.

9. Jennifer L. McCoy and David J. Myers (eds), *The Unraveling of Representative Democracy in Venezuela*, Johns Hopkins University Press, Baltimore, MD, 2004, p. 3.

10. Norman Gall, 'Desordem venezuelana afeta petróleo', *O Estado de São Paulo*, 5 February 2006.

11. Maddison, *The World Economy*; Naím, *Paper Tigers and Minotaurs*, p. 19.

12. Thorp, *Progress, Poverty and Exclusion*, p. 317.

13. Margarita López Maya, 'La crisis del chavismo en la Venezuela actual', *Estudios Latinoamericanos*, Nueva Época, 38 (July–December 2016), pp. 159–85.

14. See above, pp. 162–63.

15. In the two decades after 1982, Venezuela recorded an aggregate current account surplus of more than $50 billion. In normal circumstances, that should have strengthened the currency. In fact, by 2002 the bolívar was worth just 1 per cent of its value of January 1983. See Nelson Ortíz, 'Entrepreneurs: Profits without power?', in McCoy and Myers, *The Unraveling of Representative Democracy*, p. 79.

16. Walter Little and Antonio Herrera, 'Political corruption in Venezuela', in Walter Little and Eduardo Posada-Carbó (eds), *Political Corruption in Europe and Latin America*, Macmillan, Basingstoke, 1996.

17. For the strengths and weaknesses of the Punto Fijo system, see McCoy and Myers, *The Unraveling of Representative Democracy*; and George Philip, *Democracy in Latin America*, Polity, Cambridge, 2003, Chapter 8.

18. Gerver Torres, *Un Sueño para Venezuela*, Banco Venezolano de Crédito, 2001, p. 37; Naím, *Paper Tigers and Minotaurs*, p. 37. The fall in government oil revenues per head was partly the consequence of a growing population, as migrants flooded in, especially from Colombia and Peru; but it was also because of the government policy of pursuing a higher oil price rather than increased production.

19. Naím, *Paper Tigers and Minotaurs*, Chapter 2.

20. Inauguration covered by the author.

21. Philip, *Democracy in Latin America*, p. 142.

22. Michael Reid, 'Ex-President Perez set to return in Caracas poll', *Guardian*, 3 December 1988.

23. Naím, *Paper Tigers and Minotaurs*, p. 28.

24. Ibid., p. 39.

25. See Margarita López Maya, 'The Venezuelan Caracazo of 1989: Popular protest and institutional weakness', *Journal of Latin American Studies*, 35:1 (2003).

26. Ibid., p. 130. Others have cited figures of over a thousand dead, but without any hard evidence.

27. Quoted in García Márquez, 'El enigma de los dos Chávez'.

28. For Chávez's early life, see Marcano and Barrera, *Hugo Chávez Sin Uniforme*; and Bart Jones, *Hugo! The Hugo Chavez story from mud hut to perpetual revolution*, Bodley Head, London, 2008.

29. Zamora died after being shot in the back by one of his own men – a fate which Chávez seemed to fear. He was said to have confided to friends that he thought himself to be the reincarnation of Zamora. See Marcano and Barrera, *Hugo Chávez Sin Uniforme*, p. 153. Chávez later added a fourth root to the tree: Pedro Pérez Delgado (whose nom de guerre was *Maisanta*), the son of a lieutenant of Zamora's and sometime social bandit whom Chávez claimed as his great-grandfather.

30. Ibid., p. 118.
31. Ibid., pp. 125–26.
32. Naím, *Paper Tigers and Minotaurs*, p. 118.
33. Marcano and Barrera, *Hugo Chávez Sin Uniforme*, p. 151.
34. Pedro A. Palma, 'La economía Venezolana en el quinquenio 1994–1998: de una crisis a otra', *Nueva Economía*, VIII:12 (April 1999), pp. 99–104.
35. Venezuela had had three short-lived republics during the independence struggle. The fourth dated from 1830. Richard Gott suggests that the notion of a 'Fifth Republic' may have echoed the millenarian idea of a 'Fifth Monarchy' led by saints after those of Babylon, Persia, Greece and Rome. Gott, *Hugo Chávez and the Bolivarian Revolution*, p. 136.
36. López Maya, 'La crisis del chavismo'.
37. Gott, *Hugo Chávez and the Bolivarian Revolution*, p. 13.
38. 'Venezuela: On troubled waters', *The Economist*, 7 March 2002.
39. 'Venezuela's crisis: Towards the endgame', *The Economist*, 11 April 2002.
40. Marcano and Barrera, *Hugo Chávez Sin Uniforme*, pp. 245–46. The opposition blamed the attack on the demonstration on members of the Bolivarian Circles. The government claimed that the killings were the work of opposition agents provocateurs, but it used its majority in the National Assembly to block the appointment of a truth commission on the events of 11 April 2002.
41. Ibid., p. 248; Gott, *Hugo Chávez and the Bolivarian Revolution*, p. 227.
42. Marcano and Barrera, *Hugo Chávez Sin Uniforme*, p. 259.
43. Interview with Hugo Chávez, *Newsweek*, 10 October 2005.
44. 'El Nuevo Mapa Estratégico'. Chávez went on: 'So that's when we decided to work on the missions, we designed the first one here and I began to ask for help from Fidel.'
45. 'Venezuela: Mission impossible', *The Economist*, 16 February 2006.
46. Ibid.
47. Jennifer McCoy, 'By invitation: What really happened in Venezuela?', *The Economist*, 2 September 2004.
48. 'Venezuela: The revolution at bay', *The Economist*, 14 February 2015.
49. López Maya, 'La crisis del chavismo'.
50. 'El chavismo nunca pierde en el Supremo venezolano', *El País*, 12 December 2014.
51. Interviews with Teodoro Petkoff, Caracas, April 2005, and with Miguel Henrique Otero, Caracas, January 2015.
52. Visit by the author, April 2005.
53. 'Venezuela: Now for the reckoning', *The Economist*, 9 March 2013.
54. Interview with José Manuel Puente, IESA, Caracas, January 2016.
55. 'Oil shakes Venezuelan debt to its foundations', *Wall Street Journal*, 22 December 2014.
56. Quoted in Raúl Gallegos, *Crude Nation: How oil riches ruined Venezuela*, Potomac Books, Lincoln, NE, 2016, p. 165.
57. Visits by the author, November 2007.
58. 'Brazil scandal leaves dreams undone in Venezuela', *Wall Street Journal*, 4 January 2017.
59. 'Venezuela: Feeling the heat', *The Economist*, 15 May 2010.
60. In December 2016, the priority exchange rate was 10 bolívares to the dollar; the black-market rate began 2016 at 833 to the dollar, and ended it at 3,165 to the dollar, according to DolarToday, a website.
61. Author interview with Asdrúbal Oliveros, Ecoanalítica, Caracas, January 2016.
62. 'Venezuela politics: The billion-dollar fraud', *The Economist*, 10 August 2013; www.aporrea.org/contraloria/n257348.html.
63. 'Venezuela's wealthy build their own oasis', *Financial Times*, 17 October 2016.
64. See, for example, www.insightcrime.org.
65. 'Venezuelan first lady's nephews convicted in US drug trial', Reuters, 19 November 2016.
66. Author's visit to the Cuartel de la Montaña and the National Pantheon, Caracas, January 2016.
67. See www.youtube.com/watch?v=qv5dAqSS0XU.

68. Ricardo Hausmann and Miguel Ángel Santos, 'Should Venezuela default?', Project Syndicate, 5 September 2014.
69. 'Venezuela 2016 imports down more than half to $18 billion: president', Reuters, 10 January 2017.
70. 'Venezuela 2016 inflation hits 800 percent, GDP shrinks 19 percent: document', Reuters, 20 January 2017.
71. Credit Suisse, *Global Wealth Report 2016*, Credit Suisse AG Research Institute, Zurich, p. 10.
72. Gallegos, *Crude Nation*, Chapter 2.
73. 'Infant mortality soars in Venezuela', *Wall Street Journal*, 17 October 2016.
74. Interview with the author, Quito, July 2015.
75. See, for example, 'Venezuela: Tough talking', International Crisis Group, 16 December 2016.
76. 'Tareck El Aissami encabezará Comando Nacional Antigolpe', *Globovisión*, 8 January 2017.
77. 'Venezuela's military needs to get out of business', Bloomberg, 6 May 2016.
78. 'Antonini Wilson volvió a hablar de la valija', *La Nación*, 10 October 2013.
79. This survey was published at www.usb.ve, the website of Simón Bolívar University in Caracas.
80. Thais Maingon, 'Política social y régimen de bienestar en Venezuela 1999–2014', *Estudios Latinoamericanos*, Nueva Época, 38 (July–December 2016), pp. 115–43.

Chapter 8: The Stumbles of Reformers

1. Author visit and interview with Michelle Bachelet, August 2009.
2. Interview with Nicolás Eyzaguirre, finance minister, Santiago de Chile, January 2005.
3. Data at http://observatorio.ministeriodesarrollosocial.gob.cl.
4. Barry P. Bosworth, Rudiger Dornbusch and Raúl Labán (eds), *The Chilean Economy: Policy lessons and challenges*, The Brookings Institution, Washington, DC, 1994, p. 23.
5. Rudiger Dornbusch and Sebastian Edwards, 'Exchange rate policy and trade strategy', in ibid., p. 81.
6. Andrés Solimano, 'The Chilean economy in the 1990s: On a "Golden Age" and beyond', in Lance Taylor (ed.), *After Neoliberalism: What next for Latin America?*, University of Michigan Press, Ann Arbor, MI, 1999, p. 115.
7. Interview with the author, Santiago de Chile, January 2005.
8. Ricardo Lagos, *Conversaciones en el Camino*, Ediciones B, Santiago de Chile, 2003, pp. 48–49.
9. Alan Angell, 'Democratic governance in Chile', in Scott Mainwaring and Timothy Scully, *Democratic Governance in Latin America*, Stanford University Press, 2009.
10. Solimano, 'The Chilean economy in the 1990s', p. 123; SalmonChile, *La Acuicultura en Chile*, TechnoPress SA, Santiago de Chile, undated, Chapter 1.
11. According to Ricardo Lagos, interview with the author, Santiago de Chile, January 2005.
12. 'Chile: Testing times for Michelle Bachelet', *The Economist*, 24 June 2006.
13. 'Education in Chile: The fraught politics of the classroom', *The Economist*, 29 October 2011.
14. 'Chile: Progress and its discontents', *The Economist*, 14 April 2012.
15. Sergio Urzúa, 'La rentabilidad de la educación superior en Chile', Centro de Estudios Públicos, Santiago de Chile, 2012.
16. Interview with the author, Santiago de Chile, July 2014.
17. Author visit and interviews, Itaboraí, April 2015.
18. 'Pedro Parente anuncia que vai retomar obras no Comperj', *O Globo*, 16 June 2016.
19. See Lourdes Sola and Laurence Whitehead, *Statecrafting Monetary Authority: Democracy and financial order in Brazil*, Centre for Brazilian Studies, University of Oxford, 2006, Introduction, pp. 1–11.
20. Fernando Henrique Cardoso, *A Arte da Política: A História que Vivi*, Civilização Brasileira, Rio de Janeiro, 2006, p. 140.

21. For more on the constitution, see Michael Reid, *Brazil: The troubled rise of a global power*, Yale University Press, New Haven, CT, and London, 2014, pp. 119–21.
22. Much of the political science literature on Brazil published in the second half of the 1990s, especially in the United States, was deeply pessimistic, even as the country's prospects were being transformed. That was because it was based on fieldwork conducted during the 1980s or early 1990s.
23. Cardoso, *The Accidental President of Brazil*, p. 180.
24. Cardoso, *A Arte da Política*, p. 141.
25. Thomas, *From Inside Brazil*, p. 113.
26. Cardoso, *A Arte da Política*, p. 208.
27. Cardoso, *The Accidental President*, p. 167; Cardoso, *A Arte da Política*, pp. 130–35.
28. Interview with the author, Brasília, March 1999.
29. Cardoso, *A Arte da Política*, pp. 388 and 415.
30. Ibid., pp. 363–66.
31. 'Brazil 2015: A reform agenda', presentation by Armando Castelar Pinheiro, IDB, Washington, DC, 4 October 2005.
32. Cardoso, *A Arte da Política*, pp. 12–13.
33. Ibid., p. 524.
34. ECLAC/CEPAL, *Social Panorama of Latin America*, Santiago de Chile, p. 130.
35. 'Brazil's presidential election: The meaning of Lula', *The Economist*, 3 October 2002.
36. This anecdote was told to me by Julio María Sanguinetti, a former president of Uruguay.
37. Barry Bearak, 'Poor man's burden', *New York Times Magazine*, 27 June 2004.
38. Having governed the city for the best part of two decades, in 2004 the PT lost an election for mayor of Porto Alegre to José Fogaça, a PMDB member and supporter of Cardoso.
39. Meeting attended by the author, London, September 2003.
40. Interview with Lula, 'Brazil: Lula's Leap', *The Economist*, 2 March 2006.
41. Ibid.
42. Dirceu was among 25 politicians and officials eventually convicted of crimes including embezzlement, corruption and misuse of public funds by the Supreme Court in 2012. Dirceu and some of the others were jailed a year later.
43. Palocci resigned after an aide admitted leaking details of the bank account of the caretaker at a house in Brasília rented by several of the minister's former associates from Ribeirão Preto. The leak was an attempt to smear the caretaker, who had contradicted the minister's testimony to a congressional committee that he had not visited the house. See 'Corruption in Brazil: House calls', *The Economist*, 23 March 2006.
44. André Singer, *Os Sentidos do Lulismo: Reforma gradual e pacto conservador*, Companhia das Letras, São Paulo, 2012, Chapter 8.
45. Ricardo Batista Amaral, *A vida quer é coragem: A trajetória de Dilma Rousseff, a primeira presidenta do Brasil*, Sextante, Rio de Janeiro, 2011.
46. Remarks at press breakfast, Brazilian embassy, London, May 2011.
47. *Época*, 6 March 2015.
48. On Odebrecht's and Tavares's arrests, see Malu Gaspar, 'A organizaçao', *Revista Piauí*, 121, October 2016.
49. When I interviewed Moro at an *Economist* conference in São Paulo in October 2015 and put it to him that his critics thought he had simply mounted a fishing expedition in search of evidence that he didn't have, he shot back: 'If so, I've caught some pretty big fish.'
50. 'Brazil's Odebrecht to pay up to $4.5 billion to settle bribery case', *Wall Street Journal*, 21 December 2016; 'Odebrecht and Braskem plead guilty', US Department of Justice news release, 21 December 2016.
51. Press release from CADE, Brazil's competition authority, 24 January 2017.
52. Data from the Office of the Public Prosecutor, accessed at http://lavajato.mpf.mp.br on 15 February 2017. See also Brian Winter, 'Brazil's "Car Wash" probe: Tell me how this ends', *Americas Quarterly*, 28 September 2016.

53. Luiz Inácio Lula da Silva, 'Por que querem me condenar', *Folha de São Paulo*, 18 October 2016.

54. André Singer, 'O Lulismo Nas Cordas', *Revista Piauí*, 111, December 2015.

55. World Bank, 'Safeguarding against a reversal in social gains during the economic crisis in Brazil', World Bank Policy Note, World Bank, Washington, DC, December 2016; Otaviano Canuto, 'What's ailing the Brazilian economy?', available at www.interfima.org.

56. 'Petrobras probe turns to bribes in US refinery purchase', Bloomberg, 16 November 2015.

57. 'O mal-estar da esquerda', *Valor Econômico*, 19 August 2016; see also José de Souza Martins, *Do PT das Lutas Sociais ao PT do Poder*, Editora Contexto, São Paulo, 2016.

58. Some of these points are made in Leonardo Avritzer, *Impasses de Democracia no Brasil*, Editora Civilização Brasileira, Rio de Janeiro, 2016.

59. Reid, *Brazil*, Chapter 13; Matias Spektor and Eduardo Mello, 'How to fix Brazil', *Foreign Affairs*, September/October 2016.

60. World Bank, *Brazil – Systematic country diagnostic: Retaking the path to inclusion, growth and sustainability*, World Bank Group, Washington, DC, 2016.

61. 'Brazil's Rio de Janeiro state misses debt payment', *Wall Street Journal*, 25 May 2016.

62. Hugh Thomas, *The Conquest of Mexico*, Pimlico, London, 1993, pp. 296–98.

63. Elena Poniatowska, *La noche de Tlatelolco*, Ediciones Era, Mexico City, 1992, p. 170.

64. Author's translation. The poem was written especially for a book of interviews with survivors prepared by Elena Poniatowska, a young journalist who would later become one of Mexico's best-known writers, and which, when it was published in 1971, made the first dent in the regime's wall of silence concerning the massacre. Poniatowska, *La noche de Tlatelolco*, p. 163.

65. Krauze, *Mexico*, pp. 736–37.

66. Ibid., p. 681.

67. Ibid., p. 743.

68. Julia Preston and Samuel Dillon, *Opening Mexico: The making of a democracy*, Farrar, Straus and Giroux, New York, 2005, Chapter 4; Héctor Aguilar Camín, *Después del milagro*, 16th edition, Ediciones Cal y Arena, Mexico City, 2004, Chapter 1.

69. Preston and Dillon, *Opening Mexico*, Chapter 6. In 1994, Arturo Nuñez, the head of the IFE, admitted that the computer system had been forced to fail. See Jorge I. Domínguez and James A. McCann, *Democratizing Mexico: Public Opinion and Electoral Choices*, Johns Hopkins University Press, Baltimore, MD, 1996, pp. 151–52.

70. Interview with the author, Mexico City, July 1992.

71. Preston and Dillon *Opening Mexico*, p. 481.

72. 'Mexico: Ring in the old', *The Economist*, 14 March 1993.

73. Preston and Dillon, *Opening Mexico*, p. 219.

74. Silvia Gómez Tagle, 'Public institutions and electoral transparency', in Kevin J. Middlebrook, *Dilemmas of Political Change in Mexico*, Institute of Latin American Studies, London/Center for US–Mexican Studies, San Diego, 2004, p 89.

75. Interview with the author, Mexico City, July 1991.

76. 'Mexico: Salt of the earth', *The Economist*, 19 October 1991.

77. 'The clash in Mexico' and 'Mexico: The revolution continues', *The Economist*, 22 January 1994.

78. Stephen Haber, 'Why institutions matter: Banking and economic growth in Mexico', Stanford Center for International Development, Working Paper No. 234, November 2004.

79. Luis Rubio and Susan Kaufman Purcell, *Mexico Under Zedillo*, Lynne Rienner, Boulder, CO, 1998, p. 14.

80. The following paragraphs draw on Reid, 'Time to wake up'.

81. Press conference attended by the author, Mexico City, May 2005; 'Mexico: Will the real Andrés Manuel López Obrador please stand up?', *The Economist*, 28 May 2006.

82. The tribunal criticised Fox and the businessmen for their campaign interventions, though it is hard to imagine these would have provoked comment in many other countries.

83. Interview with the author, Mexico City, September 2006.
84. 'Dealing with drugs: On the trail of the traffickers', *The Economist*, 5 March 2009.
85. Interview with the author, Mexico City, January 2009.
86. 'Energy in North America: A new Mexican revolution', *The Economist*, 15 November 2014.
87. 'Murder in Mexico: The great mystery', *The Economist*, 30 April 2016.
88. 'A tale of two Mexicos: Growth and prosperity in a two-speed economy', McKinsey Global Institute, March 2014; 'Schumpeter: Open for business', *The Economist*, 12 March 2016.
89. Héctor Aguilar Camín, 'Nocturno de la democracia Mexicana', *Nexos*, May 2016.
90. Enrique Krauze, 'Desaliento de México', *Letras Libres*, May 2016.
91. Alfredo Corchado, *Midnight in Mexico: A reporter's journey through a country's descent into darkness*, Penguin, London, 2013, p. 51.
92. Luis Rubio, *The Problem of Power: Mexico requires a new system of government*, Wilson Center, Washington, DC, 2016.

Chapter 9: Changing Societies

1. 'Peru: The problems of staying alive', *The Sunday Times Magazine*, 12 November 1972.
2. Emma Raffo, *Vivir en Huáscar: Mujer y estrategias de sobrevivencia*, Fundación Friedrich Ebert, Lima, 1985.
3. Marcelo Giugale, Vicente Fretes Cibils and John L. Newman, *Perú: La oportunidad de un país diferente*, World Bank, Washington, DC, 2006, p. 51.
4. Income per head in Ekaterina Vostroknutova, Alberto Rodriguez, Pablo Saavedra and John Panzer, *Peru: Building on Success*, World Bank, Washington, DC, 2015. Poverty figures from Instituto Nacional de Estadística e Informática (INEI), *Evolución de la Pobreza Monetaria, 2009–15*, Informe Técnico, Lima, 2016. The official poverty line in 2015 was income per person of 315 soles (then worth around $97) per month.
5. José Matos Mar, *Desborde Popular y Crisis del Estado: Veinte años después*, Fondo Editorial del Congreso del Perú, Lima, 2004, p. 78.
6. de Soto, *El Otro Sendero*.
7. 'Peru: Go north, Limeño', *The Economist*, 13 May 2004.
8. Interview with Carlos Neuhaus, director of Megaplaza, November 2006.
9. Emma Raffo, *Huáscar 25 años después: De la estera al barrio consolidado*, Universidad de San Martín de Porres, Lima, 2011.
10. Ibid.
11. They thus negated the hypothesis of Hernando de Soto that property titling would of itself turn the 'dead capital' of the poor into productive assets leveraged by credit. See de Soto, *The Mystery of Capital*.
12. ECLAC/CEPAL, *Social Panorama of Latin America, 2015*.
13. Data from household surveys may understate the Gini coefficient, because it captures labour income, while high earners and income from capital are likely to be under-represented in the results. Some fragmentary studies of tax data suggest that the true income of the top 1 per cent would push up the Gini coefficient, but would not alter its declining trend in the region. See Augusto de la Torre, Eduardo Levy Yeyati, Guillermo Beylis et al., *Inequality in a Lower Growth Latin America*, World Bank, Washington, DC, 2014, pp. 27–39.
14. ECLAC/CEPAL, *Social Panorama of Latin America, 2015*, p. 23.
15. Fukuyama, 'The politics of Latin America's new middle class'.
16. Francisco H.G. Ferreira, Jamele Rigolini, Julián Messina et al., *Economic Mobility and the Rise of the Latin American Middle Class*, World Bank, Washington, DC, 2012; and Louise Cord, María Eugenia Genoni and Carlos Rodríguez-Castelán, *Shared Prosperity and Poverty Eradication in Latin America and the Caribbean*, World Bank, Washington, DC, 2015.
17. Author visit and interviews, September 2006.

18. Simone Cecchini and Aldo Madariaga, *Conditional Cash Transfer Programmes: The Recent Experience in Latin America and the Caribbean*, ECLAC and SIDA, Santiago de Chile, 2011.
19. Ibid., Chapters 5 and 7.
20. Interview, Santiago de Chile, January 2005.
21. Santiago Levy, 'Is social policy in Latin America heading in the right direction? Beyond conditional cash transfer programs', Brookings Institution, 21 May 2015.
22. Inter-American Dialogue/Fundación Santillana, *Construyendo una educación de calidad: Un pacto con el futuro de América Latina*, Buenos Aires, 2016.
23. Luis F. López-Calva and Nora Lustig, *Declining Inequality in Latin America: A decade of progress?*, Brookings Institution Press/UNDP, Washington, DC, 2010, Chapter 1.
24. Augusto de la Torre, Alain Ize, Guillermo Raul Beylis and Daniel Lederman, *Jobs, Wages and the Latin American Slowdown*, World Bank, Washington, DC, 2015.
25. Ferreira et al., *Economic Mobility*, Overview.
26. See OECD, *Pisa Results in Focus*, OECS, Paris, 2016; Inter-American Development Bank, 'Latin America and the Caribbean in PISA Briefs', 2016, available at www.iadb.org.
27. 'Bello: Viva la ignorancia!', *The Economist*, 17 December 2016.
28. Alejandro Foxley, 'Inclusive development: Escaping the middle-income trap', in Alejandro Foxley and Barbara Stallings (eds), *Innovation and Inclusion in Latin America: Strategies to avoid the middle-income trap*, Palgrave Macmillan, New York, 2016.
29. OECD, 'Avanzando hacia una mejor educación para Perú', 2016, available at www.oecd. org.
30. Barbara Bruns and Javier Luque, *Great Teachers: How to Raise Student Learning in Latin America and the Caribbean*, World Bank, Washington, DC, 2014.
31. Samuel Berlinski and Norbert Schady (eds), *The Early Years: Child well-being and the role of public policy*, Inter-American Development Bank, Washington, DC, 2015.
32. ECLAC/CEPAL, *Statistical Yearbook, 2015*, Santiago de Chile.
33. Pan American Health Organization, 'Health situation in the Americas: Health Indicators 2014'.
34. 'Health-system reform and universal health coverage in Latin America', *The Lancet*, 28 March 2015.
35. OECD Health Statistics 2016.
36. Author interview, Bogotá, August 2015.
37. Author telephone interview, January 2016.
38. Interview, San Juan de Lurigancho, March 2006.
39. 'Demography in Latin America: Autumn of the patriarchs', *The Economist*, 1 June 2013.
40. ECLAC/CEPAL, *Demographic Observatory*, Santiago de Chile, 2016.
41. Ruchir Sharma, *The Rise and Fall of Nations: Forces of change in the post-crisis world*, Norton, New York, 2016, p. 19.
42. Helen Joyce, 'Grounded: A special report on Brazil', *The Economist*, 28 September 2013.
43. Berlinski and Schady, *The Early Years*, pp. 150–52.
44. Cavallo and Serebrisky, *Saving for Development*. Author interview with Santiago Levy, Madrid, June 2016.
45. Interview conducted on the author's behalf by Nathália Sardelli, São Paulo, March 2016.
46. UNDP, *Multidimensional Progress*.
47. Reno Vakis, Jamele Rigolini and Leonardo Luchetti, *Left Behind: Chronic poverty in Latin America and the Caribbean*, World Bank, Washington, DC, 2015.
48. Author visit to Cotacachi and interview with Auki Tituaña, Quito, January 2004.
49. Germán Freire, Steven Daniel Schwartz Orellana, Melissa Zumaeta Aurazo et al., *Indigenous Latin America in the Twenty-First Century*, World Bank, Washington, DC, 2015, p. 25.

50. Berlinski and Schady, *The Early Years*, p. 39.
51. Fieldwork by Emma Raffo.
52. Interview, El Alto, January 2004.
53. Rachel Sieder (ed.), *Multiculturalism in Latin America: Indigenous rights, diversity and democracy*, Palgrave Macmillan, Basingstoke and New York, 2002, Introduction.
54. Deborah J. Yashar, *Contesting Citizenship: The rise of indigenous movements and the postliberal challenge*, Cambridge University Press, 2005, Chapters 2 and 3.
55. ECLAC/CEPAL, 'Current situation of indigenous and Afro-American peoples in Latin America', press release, July 2000.
56. Instituto de Pesquisa Econômica Aplicada (IPEA), *Boletim de Políticas Sociais*, No. 16, 2008, pp. 247–55.
57. Anthony W. Marx, *Making Race and Nation: A comparison of the United States, South Africa and Brazil*, Cambridge University Press, 1998, pp. 164–77.
58. *Gazeta Mercantil*, 28 April 1998.
59. *Newsweek*, 9 March 1998.
60. Marx, *Making Race and Nation*, Chapter 10.
61. Cardoso, *The Accidental President of Brazil*, pp. 252–53.
62. Reid, *Brazil*, pp. 182–83.
63. UN Economic Commission for Latin America and the Caribbean, ECLAC Notes, No. 47, August 2006, Santiago de Chile.
64. Observatorio de Igualdad de Género, 'Nota para la igualdad No. 18', ECLAC/CEPAL, 2016.
65. ECLAC/CEPAL, *Statistical Yearbook, 2016*.
66. Washington Office on Latin America, 'Violence against women in Ciudad Juárez', available at www.wola.org (updated 22 December 2006).
67. Interview, Ciudad Juárez, May 2005.
68. Author interview, Buenos Aires, March 2017; 'Violence against women: murder and machismo', *The Economist*, 5 November 2016.
69. Author interview with Esteban Caballero, UN Population Fund, May 2015.
70. See Chapter 4.
71. David Lehmann, *The Struggle for the Spirit: Religious transformation and popular culture in Brazil and Latin America*, Polity Press, Cambridge, 1996, Introduction.
72. 'Pentecostals: Christianity reborn', *The Economist*, 23 December 2006.
73. Véliz, *New World*, p. 53.
74. ECLAC/CEPAL, *Statistical Yearbook, 2016*. This defines anyone living in a settlement of more than 2,000 people as 'urban'. The World Bank applied a different definition, counting as 'rural' all those who live in places that have fewer than 150 inhabitants per square kilometre and are more than an hour's travel from a city of more than 100,000 people. On this definition, it found that 42 per cent of Latin Americans lived in the countryside. See David de Ferranti, Guillermo E. Perry, Daniel Lederman, William Foster and Alberto Valdés, *Beyond the City: The rural contribution to development*, World Bank, Washington, DC, 2005.
75. ECLAC/CEPAL, *Statistical Yearbook, 2016*.
76. Richard Webb, *Conexión y Despegue Rural*, Instituto del Perú, Universidad San Martín de Porres, Lima, 2013.
77. Andres Cadena et al., *Building Globally Competitive Cities: The Key to Latin American Growth*, McKinsey Global Institute, 2011.
78. UN Fund for Population Activities, Latin America and Caribbean division, statement on 12 August 2016.
79. www.internetworldstats.com.
80. GSMA, 'The mobile economy: Latin America and the Caribbean 2016', 20 September 2016, available at www.gsma.com.
81. Cardoso, *A Arte da Política*, p. 510.
82. Fukuyama, 'The politics of Latin America's new middle class'.

Chapter 10: The Defective State

1. Author visits to Ciudad Juárez, 2005 and 2016.
2. Author interviews, October 2016; *La Jornada*, 2 April 2016.
3. Speech to the Permanent Council of the Organization of American States, 14 June 2000.
4. See Hillel David Soifer, *State Building in Latin America*, Cambridge University Press, 2015.
5. Whitehead, 'State organization', p. 77.
6. The concept of 'patrimonialism' was used by Max Weber to refer to a form of traditional authority in which an administration and a military force are 'purely personal instruments' of a ruler, or by extension, of powerful individuals. See Weber, *Economy and Society*, Vol. 1, p. 231.
7. Whitehead, 'State organization', p. 36.
8. Eduardo Lora, 'State reform in Latin America: A silent revolution', in Eduardo Lora (ed.), *The State of State Reform in Latin America*, Inter-American Development Bank/ Stanford University Press, 2006, p. 5.
9. de Ferranti et al., *Inequality in Latin America*, pp. 251–55; Ana Corbacho, Vicente Fretes Cibils and Eduardo Lora (eds), *More than Revenue: Taxation as a development tool*, Inter-American Development Bank, Washington, DC, 2013.
10. Corbacho et al, *More than Revenue*, Chapter 1.
11. Ibid.; Organisation for Economic Co-operation and Development/IDB, *Government at a Glance: Latin America and the Caribbean*, OECD Publishing, Paris, 2017, p. 54.
12. ECLAC/CEPAL, *Social Panorama of Latin America, 2015*, p. 21.
13. Author interview, Lima, January 2016.
14. OECD/IDB, *Government at a Glance*, p. 10. The impact was greater, however, if the value of in-kind benefits such as hospital care and schooling was taken into account.
15. Juan Carlos Cortázar Velarde, Mariano Lafuente and Mario Sanginés (eds), *A Decade of Civil Service Reforms in Latin America, 2004–13*, Inter-American Development Bank, Washington, DC, 2014.
16. Mancur Olson, *Power and Prosperity: Outgrowing communist and capitalist dictatorships*, Basic Books, New York, 2000, Chapter 1.
17. Author interviews, Mexico City, October 2016.
18. Corporación Andina de Fomento – Banco de Desarrollo de América Latina (CAF), *Un Estado más efectivo*, CAF, Caracas, 2015.
19. Miguel Ángel Centeno, 'El Estado en América Latina', *Revista CIDOB d'Afers Internacionals*, 85–86, (2009), p. 17.
20. The Ceará reforms are the subject of Judith Tendler, *Good Government in the Tropics*, Johns Hopkins University Press, Baltimore, MD, and London, 1997.
21. Author interview, Guayaquil, July 2015.
22. Data from Chioda, *Stop the Violence in Latin America*; and UNDP, *Citizen Security with a Human Face*, Human Development Report for Latin America, UNDP, New York, 2013.
23. Laura Jaitman (ed.), *The Costs of Crime and Violence: New evidence and insights in Latin America and the Caribbean*, Inter-American Development Bank, Washington, DC, 2017.
24. Rafael de Hoyos, Halsey Rogers and Miguel Székely, *Out of School and out of Work: Risk and opportunities for Latin America's Ninis*, World Bank, Washington, DC, 2016.
25. 'Crime in Latin America: A broken system', *The Economist*, 10 July 2014.
26. See Hugo Fruhling, 'Police reform and the process of democratization', in Hugo Fruhling and Joseph S. Tulchin (eds), *Crime and Violence in Latin America: Citizen security, democracy and the state*, Johns Hopkins University Press, Baltimore, MD, and London, 2003, pp. 15–21.
27. Paulo Sérgio Pinheiro, 'O passado não está morto: nem passado é ainda', in Gilberto Dimenstein, *Democracia em pedaços*, Companhia das Letras, São Paulo, 1996, pp. 27–30.
28. See www.latinobarometro.org.

29. 'Brazil: Protecting citizens from themselves', *The Economist*, 20 October 2005.
30. Interview in Mexico City, October 2016.
31. United Nations Office on Drugs and Crime (UNODC), *Global Study on Homicide, 2013*, Vienna, 2014, p. 97.
32. 'Prisons in Latin America: A journey into hell', *The Economist*, 22 September 2012; 'Crime in Latin America: A broken system', *The Economist*.
33. Interview with the author, Bogotá, March 1988.
34. The term 'Medellín cartel' was coined by officials at the US Drug Enforcement Administration. But it is a misnomer. A cartel is a coalition of producers acting together to restrict supply and thus drive up the price of a product (such as OPEC with oil). But the 'Medellín cartel' presided over a massive increase in the supply of cocaine to the US and a steep fall in its price.
35. María Jimena Duzán, *Death Beat: A Colombian journalist's life inside the cocaine wars*, HarperCollins, New York, 1994, p. 91.
36. Simon Strong, *Whitewash: Pablo Escobar and the cocaine wars*, Macmillan, Basingstoke, 1995, Chapter 3.
37. Mark Bowden, *Killing Pablo*, Atlantic Monthly Press, New York, 2001, pp. 232–65.
38. Organization of American States, *The Drug Problem in the Americas: Studies – The economics of drug trafficking*, OAS, Washington, DC, 2012.
39. Michael Reid, 'Legacy of defeat in the fight against a deadly trade', *Guardian*, 14 August 1993; 'Colombia's Drugs Business: The wages of prohibition', *The Economist*, 24 December 1994.
40. Coletta A. Youngers and Eileen Rosin (eds), *Drugs and Democracy in Latin America: The impact of US policy*, Lynne Rienner, Boulder, CO, 2005, Chapter 1.
41. 'Youth gangs in Central America', Washington Office on Latin America, November 2006.
42. Author interview, Guatemala City, March 2011.
43. Author visit to Rosario and interviews, November 2015.
44. Visit by the author, February 2001.
45. Interview with the author, San Vicente del Caguán, February 2001.
46. Alfredo Rangel Suárez, 'Las FARC-EP: una mirada actual', in Malcolm Deas and María Victoria Llorente (eds), *Reconocer la Guerra para Construir La Paz*, Grupo Editorial Norma, Bogotá, 1999, pp. 23–51; see also Daniel Pécaut, *Guerra Contra La Sociedad*, Espasa Hoy, Bogotá, 2001, pp. 39–42; and Stephen Dudley, *Walking Ghosts: Murder and guerrilla politics in Colombia*, Routledge, New York and London, 2004.
47. Michael Reid, 'Drugs, war and democracy: A survey of Colombia', *The Economist*, 19 April 2001.
48. Interview, February 2001.
49. Quoted in Reid, 'Drugs, War and Democracy'.
50. Pécaut, *Guerra Contra la Sociedad*, p. 37.
51. Interview with the author near San Vicente del Caguán, February 2001.
52. Interview, Bogotá, February 2001.
53. Interview, Bogotá, May 2003.
54. Interview with Juan Carlos Pinzón, defence minister, Bogotá, May 2013.
55. 'Colombia and Venezuela: The FARC files', *The Economist*, 24 May 2008.
56. Interview with the author, London, August 2005.
57. Interview with the author, Bogotá, August 2015.
58. Details of the agreements are at www.altocomisionadoparalapaz.gov.co.
59. Interview with the author, Bogotá, August 2015.
60. Interview with the author, Bogotá, September 2016.
61. Interview with the author, Bogotá, September 2015.
62. Author visit to Tumaco and El Playón, September 2016.
63. 'US says Colombia coca production surges to record levels', Associated Press, 14 March 2017.
64. Author interview with Simón Gaviria, director of the National Planning Department, Bogotá, August 2015.

65. Author interview with General Óscar Naranjo, former police chief and government peace negotiator.

66. See Guy Edwards and J. Timmons Roberts, *A Fragmented Continent: Latin America and the global politics of climate change*, MIT Press, Cambridge, MA, 2015; Augusto de la Torre, Pablo Fajnzylber and John Nash, *Low Carbon, High Growth: Latin American Responses to Climate Change*, World Bank, Washington, DC, 2009.

67. *CBC News*, 2 April 2016.

68. Pew Research Center, 'What the world thinks about climate change', 18 April 2016, available at www.pewresearch.org.

69. Edwards and Roberts, *A Fragmented Continent*, Chapter 1.

70. Reid, *Brazil*, pp. 204–13; 'Green activism: Dying to defend the planet', *The Economist*, 11 February 2017.

71. 'Bello: The power of the Andean sun', *The Economist*, 10 December 2016.

72. *Andina*, 20 April 2017.

73. Author visit and interviews, December 2014.

74. Author visit, January 2016.

75. *Semana Económica* (Lima), 20 September 2015, p. 84.

76. Data from www.ocmal.org.

77. Interview with Miguel Inchaustegui, manager at Gold Fields, Lima, January 2016.

Chapter 11: The Stubborn Resilience of Flawed Democracies

1. 'El deshielo de los glaciares de Bolivia podría provocar graves inundaciones', *El País*, 3 November 2016.

2. Visit by the author.

3. See Jeffrey Sachs, *The End of Poverty*, Penguin, London, 2005, Chapter 5.

4. Interview with the author, presidential residence, La Paz, July 1997.

5. 'The Andean Coca Wars: A crop that refuses to die', *The Economist*, 4 March 2000.

6. Conversation with *Economist* editors, London, January 2004.

7. This observation was made by Olivia Harris in a talk at Canning House, London, in February 2006.

8. Interview with the author, Cochabamba, January 2004.

9. Lecture at the LSE, London, November 2010.

10. Quoted in Samuel P. Huntington, *The Third Wave: Democratization in the late twentieth century*, University of Oklahoma Press, Norman, OK, 1991, p. 6.

11. Robert A. Dahl, *On Democracy*, Yale University Press, New Haven, CT, 1998, Chapter 8.

12. BBC *Hardtalk*, 21 June 2010.

13. Dahl, *On Democracy*, Chapter 14.

14. See Juan J. Linz and Alfred Stepan, *Problems of Democratic Transition and Consolidation: Southern Europe, South America and post-communist Europe*, Johns Hopkins University Press, Baltimore, MD, 1996, Chapter 1; Philip, *Democracy in Latin America*, Chapter 1. On the importance of the state in supplying public goods, Linz and Stepan (p. 12) cite Adam Smith, who wrote of 'the [state's] duty of erecting and maintaining certain public works and certain public institutions which it can never be for the interest of any individual, or small number of individuals, to erect and maintain; because the profit could never repay the expense to any individual or small number of individuals, though it may frequently do much more than repay it to a great society'.

15. Roberto Stefan Foa and Yascha Mounk, 'The signs of deconsolidation', *Journal of Democracy*, 28:1 (2017).

16. 'Freedom in the world 2017', www.freedomhouse.org.

17. 'The Latinobarómetro poll: Democracy's low-level equilibrium', *The Economist*, 12 August 2004.

18. Data at www.latinobarometro.org.

19. Hartlyn and Valenzuela, 'Democracy in Latin América since 1930', p. 104.

20. Fernando Henrique Cardoso, 'Una Visión del Desarrollo de América Latina y el Caribe: Avances, Retos e Instituciones', lecture at the Inter-American Development Bank, 27 February 2003, p. 4.

21. In Guatemala, the following year, Jorge Serrano tried the same tactic, but failed and was dismissed from office by Congress.

22. Jorge Domínguez, 'Early 21st-century democratic governance', in Domínguez and Shifter, Constructing Democratic Governance in Latin America.

23. Interview with the author, São Paulo, October 2015.

24. See 'The United States and Venezuela: Tales from a failed coup', The Economist, 25 April 2002. A State Department spokesman denied the allegations of American involvement in the coup in a letter ('Events in Venezuela') published in The Economist, 16 May 2002. Otto Reich, the assistant secretary of state for western hemisphere affairs, was reported by the New York Times to have summoned several Latin American ambassadors to his office to urge them to support the change of government. William Finnegan, 'Castro's Shadow: America's man in Latin America and his obsession', The New Yorker, 14 and 21 October 2002.

25. International Institute for Strategic Studies, The Military Balance 2015, London, 2015, pp. 368–69.

26. 'Blaming the victims: Dictatorship denial is on the rise in Argentina', Guardian, 29 August 2016.

27. Foweraker et al., Governing Latin America, p. 127.

28. Christopher Sabatini, 'Latin America's lost illusions: Decentralization and political parties', Journal of Democracy, 14:2 (2003), p. 139.

29. Javier Corrales and Michael Penfold, 'Manipulating term limits in Latin America', Journal of Democracy, 25:4 (2014), p. 157.

30. Scott Mainwaring and Matthew Soberg Shugart (eds), Presidentialism and Democracy in Latin America, Cambridge University Press, 1997, p. 2.

31. Timothy J. Power, 'Political institutions in democratic Brazil', in Peter R. Kingstone and Timothy J. Power (eds), Democratic Brazil: Actors, institutions and processes, University of Pittsburgh Press, 2000, p. 12.

32. Hartlyn and Valenzuela, 'Democracy in Latin America since 1930', p. 114.

33. Inter-American Development Bank, 'The politics of policies, 2006', Inter-American Development Bank, Washington, DC, 2006, p. 37.

34. O'Donnell, Contrapuntos, p. 293.

35. Interview with the author, Lima, July 1995. See 'Peru: the dark side of the boom', The Economist, 5 August 1995.

36. Flavia Freidenberg and Tomás Dosek, 'Las reformas electorales en América Latina (1978–2015)' in Reformas Políticas en América Latina: Tendencias y Casos, Organización de los Estados Americanos, Washington, DC, 2016.

37. Javier Corrales, 'Constitutional rewrites in Latin America', in Domínguez and Shifter, Constructing Democratic Governance in Latin America.

38. Corrales and Penfold, 'Manipulating term limits in Latin America'.

39. Peter M. Siavelis, 'Executive–legislative relations and democracy in Latin America', in Richard L. Millet, Jennifer S. Holmes and Orlando J. Pérez, Latin American Democracy: Emerging reality or endangered species?, 2nd edition, Routledge, Abingdon, 2015.

40. IBD, 'Politics of policies', pp. 45–56.

41. Ibid., p. 51.

42. Scott Mainwaring and Timothy R. Scully (eds), Building Democractic Institutions: Party systems in Latin America, Stanford University Press, 1995, pp. 3–5.

43. Scott Mainwaring, Rethinking Party Systems in the Third Wave of Democratization, Stanford University Press, 1999, p. 5.

44. Steven Levitksy, 'Peru: The challenges of a democracy without parties', in Domínguez and Shifter, Constructing Democratic Governance in Latin America.

45. Tyler C. Boas, 'Mass media and politics in Latin America', in Domínguez and Shifter, *Constructing Democratic Governance in Latin America*.

46. Data at www.cpj.org.

47. *Excelsior*, 7 February 2017.

48. Peter Hakim, 'La permanencia de la corrupción en Latinamérica', Infolatam, 30 June 2014.

49. Telephone interview with the author, January 2017.

50. Telephone interview with the author, January 2017.

51. Kevin Casas-Zamora and Daniel Zovatto, *The Cost of Democracy: Essays on political finance in Latin America*, International IDEA/Organization of American States/The Dialogue, 2016.

52. Daniel Matamala, *Poderoso caballero: El peso del dinero en la política chilena*, Editorial Catalonia, Santiago de Chile, 2015.

53. 'Bello: He who pays democracy's piper', *The Economist*, 4 March 2017.

54. Telephone interview with the author, September 2016.

55. Rebecca Weitz-Shapiro, *Curbing Clientelism in Argentina: Politics, poverty and social policy*, Cambridge University Press, 2014, p. 5.

56. Ibid., Chapter 1.

57. Alberto Vergara and Juan Pablo Luna, 'Delegative democracy revisited: Latin America's problem of success', *Journal of Democracy*, 27:3 (2016), pp. 158–65.

Chapter 12: The Loneliness of Latin America

1. 'The loneliness of Latin America' was the title of Gabriel García Márquez's acceptance speech on being awarded the Nobel Prize for literature in 1982.

2. Michael Reid, 'Nervous Mexico prepares to wed a superpower', *Guardian*, 3 July 1992.

3. Trump's comment came in the campaign debate on 26 September 2016. See www.youtube.com/watch?v—AhCC6mE0zI.

4. *El País*; *New York Times*; *Washington Post*, 5 November 2005.

5. Quoted in Bushnell and Macaulay, *Emergence*, p. 25.

6. See Jeffrey Davidow, *The US and Mexico: The bear and the porcupine*, Markus Wiener, Princeton, NJ, 2004, Chapter 2. Davidow was the American ambassador to Mexico from 1998 to 2001, and prior to that the assistant secretary of state for western hemisphere affairs.

7. Interview with the author, Washington, DC, September 2006.

8. Michael Reid, 'Obama and Latin America: A promising day in the neighbourhood', *Foreign Affairs*, September/October 2015.

9. Inter-American Dialogue, China-Latin America Finance Database.

10. Jorge Guajardo, Manuel Molano and Dante Sica, 'Industrial development in Latin America: What is China's role?' Atlantic Council, Washington, DC, 2016.

11. 'Latin American geopolitics: The dragon in the backyard', *The Economist*, 13 August 2009.

12. Augusto de la Torre, Tatiana Didier, Alain Ize, Daniel Lederman and Sergio L. Schmukler, *Latin America and the Rising South: Changed world, changed priorities*, World Bank, Washington, DC, 2015, p. 27.

13. Interview with the author, Buenos Aires, March 2017.

14. See Lynch, *Bolívar*, pp. 212–15.

15. Alfredo Valladão, talk at Canning House, London, 2005.

16. Michael Reid, 'Remapping South America: A survey of Mercosur', *The Economist*, 12 October 1996.

17. Data from Argentina's foreign ministry, available at www.cei.gov.ar.

18. See, for example, Rubens Barbosa, 'A politização do Mercosul', *O Estado de São Paulo*, 25 July 2006; Felix Peña, an Argentine former diplomat and a leading promoter of

Mercosur, noted in 2006 that the group had come to be 'viewed with scepticism' by outsiders. 'Mercosur is in a very bad state . . . We can't continue like this' (Felix Peña, Newsletter, December 2006).

19. 'Argentina's energy shortages: The laws of economics bite back', *The Economist*, 22 April 2004.
20. Carlos Malamud, 'The obstacles to regional integration in Latin America', Newsletter of Real Instituto Elcano, Madrid, December 2005.
21. Reuters, 12 April 2006.
22. Interview with the author, Quito, July 2015.
23. See, for example, Roberto Abusada, 'Los designios coloniales de Brasil', *El Comercio* (Lima), 7 February 2017.
24. Boston Consulting Group, *Global Leaders, Challengers and Champions*, Boston, MA, 2016.
25. Dilek Aykut and Andrea Goldstein, 'Developing country multinationals: South–south investment comes of age', OECD Development Centre Working Paper No. 257, December 2006.
26. Javier Santiso, *The Decade of the Multilatinas*, Cambridge University Press, 2013, p. 43.

Chapter 13: So Near and Yet So Far

1. Author visit and interview with Pedro Olaechea, president of the board of CITE-Vid, Ica, March 2015.
2. 'La ampliación del aeropuerto Jorge Chávez se iniciará el 2017', *El Comercio*, 9 August 2016.
3. United Nations, *World Economic Situation and Prospects 2014*, Appendix, Country Classification, United Nations.
4. Alejandro Foxley, *La Trampa del Ingreso Medio: el desafío de esta década para América Latina*, Cieplan, Santiago de Chile, 2012.
5. Foxley, 'Inclusive development'.
6. Whitehead, 'State organization', p. 77.
7. Levy, 'Is social policy in Latin America heading in the right direction?'.
8. The growth in output not accounted for by increases in labour or capital and which can be taken as a measure of an economy's technological dynamism.
9. Augusto de la Torre, Tatiana Didier and Samuel Pienknagura, 'Crecimiento de largo plazo en América Latina: Hecho en China?', in Alejandro Foxley (ed.), *Desafíos post crisis de América Latina: Vínculos con Asia y rol de los recursos naturales*, Cieplan, Santiago de Chile, 2012.
10. International Labour Organization, *Panorama Laboral 2016, América Latina y el Caribe*, Geneva, 2016.
11. William Maloney, 'Informality revisited', *World Development*, 32:7 (2004).
12. OECD/ECLAC, *Latin American Outlook 2013: SME policies for structural change*, OECD, Paris, 2012.
13. Daniel Lederman, Julián Messina, Samuel Pienknagura and Jamele Rigolini, *Latin American Entrepreneurs: Many firms but little innovation*, World Bank, Washington, DC, 2014.
14. Ibid.
15. CAF, *Infrastructure for Integral Latin American Development*, Caracas, 2013.
16. Barbara Stallings, 'Innovation, inclusion and institutions: East Asian lessons for Latin America?', in Foxley and Stallings, *Innovation and Inclusion in Latin America*.
17. Gustavo Crespi, Eduardo Fernández Arias and Ernesto Stein, *Rethinking Productive Development: Sound policies and institutions for economic transformation*, Inter-American Development Bank, Washington, DC, 2014.
18. 'Schumpeter: The entrepreneurial state', *The Economist*, 31 August 2013.
19. Schlesinger and Kinzer, *Bitter Fruit*, p. 34.

Bibliography

Acemoglu, Daron and Robinson, James A., *Why Nations Fail: The origins of power, prosperity and poverty*, Profile Books, London, 2012

Aguilar Camín, Héctor, *Después del milagro*, 16th edition, Ediciones Cal y Arena, Mexico City, 2004

Amaral, Ricardo Batista, *A vida quer é coragem: A trajetória de Dilma Rousseff, a primeira presidenta do Brasil*, Sextante, Rio de Janeiro, 2011

Andrew, Christopher and Mitrokhin, Vasili, *The Mitrokhin Archive II: The KGB and the world*, Penguin Books, 2006

Aspe Armilla, Pedro, *El camino mexicano de la transformación económica*, Fondo de Cultura Económica, Mexico City, 1993

Avritzer, Leonardo, *Impasses de Democracia no Brasil*, Editora Civilização Brasileira, Rio de Janeiro, 2016

Aykut, Dilek and Goldstein, Andrea, 'Developing country multinationals: South–south investment comes of age', OECD Development Centre Working Paper No. 257, December 2006

Basadre, Jorge, *Perú: Problema y posibilidad*, 5th edition, Librería Studium, Lima, 1987

Berlinski, Samuel and Schady, Norbert (eds), *The Early Years: Child well-being and the role of public policy*, Inter-American Development Bank, Washington, DC, 2015

Bethell, Leslie (ed.), *Argentina since Independence*, Cambridge University Press, 1993
—— *Chile Since Independence*, Cambridge University Press, 1993

Bethell, Leslie and Roxborough, Ian (eds), *Latin America Between the Second World War and the Cold War 1944–48*, Cambridge University Press, 1992

Biden, Joseph R. Jnr, 'Building on success: Opportunities for the next administration', *Foreign Affairs*, September/October 2016

Biglaiser, Glen, *Guardians of the Nation? Economists, generals and economic reform in Latin America*, University of Notre Dame Press, Notre Dame, IN, 2002

Birdsall, Nancy and de la Torre, Augusto, with Menezes, Rachel, 'Washington contentious: Economic policies for social equity in Latin America', Carnegie Endowment for International Peace and Inter-American Dialogue, 2001

Blustein, Paul, *And the Money Kept Rolling In (and Out): Wall Street, the IMF and the bankrupting of Argentina*, PublicAffairs, New York, 2005

Bolívar, Simón, *El Libertador: Writings of Simón Bolívar*, Oxford University Press, 2003

Bonner, Raymond, *Weakness and Deceit: US policy and El Salvador*, Hamish Hamilton, London, 1985

Boston Consulting Group, *Global Leaders, Challengers and Champions*, Boston, MA, 2016

Bosworth, Barry P., Dornbusch, Rudiger and Labán, Raúl (eds), *The Chilean Economy: Policy lessons and challenges*, The Brookings Institution, Washington, DC, 1994

Bowden, Mark, *Killing Pablo*, Atlantic Monthly Press, New York, 2001

BP, *BP Statistical Review of World Energy 2016*, Centre for Energy Economics Research and Policy, Heriot-Watt University, Edinburgh, 2016

Bruns, Barbara and Luque, Javier, *Great Teachers: How to Raise Student Learning in Latin America and the Caribbean*, World Bank, Washington, DC, 2014

Buarque de Holanda, Sergio, *Raízes do Brasil*, 26th edition, Companhia das Letras, São Paulo, 1996

Bucheli, Marcelo, *Bananas and Business: The United Fruit Company in Colombia, 1899–2000*, New York University Press, 2005

Bulmer-Thomas, Victor, *The Economic History of Latin America Since Independence*, Cambridge University Press, 1994

Bushnell, David, *Colombia: Una nación a pesar de sí misma*, 5th edition, Planeta, Bogotá, 2000

Bushnell, David and Macaulay, Neill, *The Emergence of Latin America in the Nineteenth Century*, 2nd edition, Oxford University Press, 1994

Carbajo, José and Estache, Antonio, 'Public policy for the private sector', World Bank Note No. 88, September 1996

Carbonetto, Daniel et al., *El Perú Heterodoxo: un modelo económico*, Instituto Nacional de Planificación, Lima, 1987

Cárdenas, Enrique, Ocampo, José Antonio and Thorp, Rosemary (eds), *An Economic History of Twentieth-Century Latin America*, Vol. 1: *The Export Age*, Palgrave Macmillan, Basingstoke, 2000

Cardoso, Fernando Henrique, *A Arte da Política: A História que Vivi, Civilização Brasileira*, Rio de Janeiro, 2006

Cardoso, Fernando Henrique and Faletto, Enzo, *Dependencia y Desarrollo en América Latina*, Siglo XXI, Argentina, 2003

Cardoso, Fernando Henrique, with Winter, Brian, *The Accidental President of Brazil: A memoir*, PublicAffairs, New York, 2006

Carr, Raymond (ed.), *Spain: A history*, Oxford University Press, 2000

Casas-Zamora, Kevin and Zovatto, Daniel, *The Cost of Democracy: Essays on political finance in Latin America*, International IDEA/Organization of American States/The Dialogue, 2016

Castañeda, Jorge, *Utopia Unarmed: The Latin American left after the Cold War*, Vintage Books, New York, 1994

—— *Compañero: The life and death of Che Guevara*, Bloomsbury, London, 1997

—— 'Latin America's left turn', *Foreign Affairs*, May/June 2006

Cavallo, Eduardo and Serebrisky, Tomás (eds), *Saving for Development*, Inter-American Development Bank, Washington, DC, 2016

Cecchini, Simone and Madariaga, Aldo, *Conditional Cash Transfer Programmes: The Recent Experience in Latin America and the Caribbean*, ECLAC and SIDA, Santiago de Chile, 2011

Centeno, Miguel Ángel, 'El Estado en América Latina', *Revista CIDOB d'Afers Internacionals*, 85–86 (2009)

Chioda, Laura, *Stop the Violence in Latin America: A look at prevention from cradle to adulthood*, World Bank, Washington, DC, 2017

Chong, Alberto and López-de-Silanes, Florencio, *Privatization in Latin America: Myths and reality*, World Bank and Stanford University Press, 2005

Coatsworth, John H., 'Structures, endowments, and institutions in the economic history of Latin America', *Latin American Research Review*, 40:3 (2005)

Coatsworth, John H. and Williamson, Jeffrey G., 'Always protectionist? Latin American tariffs from independence to Great Depression', *Journal of Latin American Studies*, 36:2 (2004)

Conniff, Michael L. (ed.), *Latin American Populism in Comparative Perspective*, University of New Mexico Press, Albuquerque, NM, 1982

—— *Populism in Latin America*, University of Alabama Press, Tuscaloosa, AL, and London, 1999

Corbacho, Ana, Cibils, Vicente Fretes and Lora, Eduardo (eds), *More than Revenue: Taxation as a development tool*, Inter-American Development Bank, Washington, DC, 2013

Corchado, Alfredo, *Midnight in Mexico: A reporter's journey through a country's descent into darkness*, Penguin, London, 2013

Cord, Louise, Genoni, María Eugenia and Rodríguez-Castelán, Carlos, *Shared Prosperity and Poverty Eradication in Latin America and the Caribbean*, World Bank, Washington, DC, 2015

Corporación Andina de Fomento – Banco de Desarrollo de América Latina (CAF), *Infrastructure for Latin American Development*, Caracas, 2013
—— *Un Estado más efectivo*, Caracas, 2015
Corrales, Javier and Penfold, Michael, 'Manipulating term limits in Latin America', *Journal of Democracy*, 25:4 (2014)
Cortázar Velarde, Juan Carlos, Lafuente, Mariano and Sanginés, Mario (eds), *A Decade of Civil Service Reforms in Latin America, 2004–13*, Inter-American Development Bank, Washington, DC, 2014
Cotler, Julio, 'Political parties and the problems of democratic consolidation in Peru', in Scott Mainwaring and Timothy R. Scully, *Building Democratic Institutions: Party systems in Latin America*, Stanford University Press, 1995
Credit Suisse, *Global Wealth Report 2016*, Credit Suisse AG Research Institute, Zurich
Crespi, Gustavo, Fernández Arias, Eduardo and Stein, Ernesto, *Rethinking Productive Development: Sound policies and institutions for economic transformation*, Inter-American Development Bank, Washington, DC, 2014
da Cunha, Euclides, *Os Sertoes*, translated as *Rebellion in the Backlands*, Picador, London, 1995
Dahl, Robert A., *On Democracy*, Yale University Press, New Haven, CT, 1998
Davidow, Jeffrey, *The US and Mexico: The bear and the porcupine*, Markus Wiener, Princeton, NJ, 2004
Devlin, Robert and Giordano, Paolo, 'The old and new regionalism: Benefits, costs and implications for the FTAA', in Antoni Estevadeordal, Dani Rodrik, Alan M. Taylor and Andrés Velasco, *Integrating the Americas: The FTAA and beyond*, Harvard University Press, 2004
Dinges, John, *Our Man in Panama*, Random House, New York, 1990
Dinges, John and Landau, Saul, *Assassination on Embassy Row*, McGraw-Hill, London, 1980
Domínguez, Jorge I., 'US–Latin American relations during the Cold War and its aftermath', in Victor Bulmer-Thomas and James Dunkerley (eds), *The United States and Latin America: The new agenda*, Institute of Latin American Studies, University of London and David Rockefeller Center for Latin American Studies, Harvard University, 1999
Domínguez, Jorge I. and McCann, James A., *Democratizing Mexico: Public Opinion and Electoral Choices*, Johns Hopkins University Press, Baltimore, MD, 1996
Domínguez, Jorge I. and Shifter, Michael (eds), *Constructing Democratic Governance in Latin America*, 4th edition, Johns Hopkins University Press, Baltimore, MD, 2013
Dornbusch, Rudiger and Edwards, Sebastian (eds), *The Macroeconomics of Populism in Latin America*, University of Chicago Press, 1991
Dudley, Stephen, *Walking Ghosts: Murder and guerrilla politics in Colombia*, Routledge, New York and London, 2004
Dunkerley, James, *Rebellion in the Veins*, Verso, New York, 1984
—— *Power in the Isthmus: A political history of modern Central America*, Verso, New York, 1988
—— *Dreaming of Freedom in the Americas: Four minds and a name*, Institute for the Study of the Americas, London, 2004
Duzán, María Jimena, *Death Beat: A Colombian journalist's life inside the cocaine wars*, HarperCollins, New York, 1994
Edwards, Guy and Roberts, J. Timmons, *A Fragmented Continent: Latin America and the global politics of climate change*, MIT Press, Cambridge, MA, 2015
Edwards, Jorge, *Persona Non Grata*, Nation Books, New York, 1993
Edwards, Sebastian, *Crisis and Reform in Latin America: From despair to hope*, World Bank and Oxford University Press, 1995
Elliott, J.H., *Empires of the Atlantic World: Britain and Spain in America 1492–1830*, Yale University Press, New Haven, CT, and London, 2006
Engerman, Stanley L. and Sokoloff, Kenneth L., 'Factor endowments, institutions and differential paths of growth among New World economies', in Stephen Haber (ed.), *How Latin America Fell Behind: Essays on the economic histories of Brazil and Mexico, 1800–1914*, Stanford University Press, 1997
Fausto, Boris, *Getúlio Vargas*, Companhia das Letras, São Paulo, 2006

Fernández-Armesto, Felipe, *The Americas: A hemispheric history*, Random House, New York, 2003

de Ferranti, David, Perry, Guillermo E., Lederman, Daniel and Maloney, William F., *From Natural Resources to the Knowledge Economy: Trade and job quality*, World Bank, Washington, DC, 2002

de Ferranti, David, Perry, Guillermo E., Ferreira, Francisco H.G. and Walton, Michael, *Inequality in Latin America: Breaking with history?*, World Bank, Washington, DC, 2004

de Ferranti, David, Perry, Guillermo E., Lederman, Daniel, Foster, William and Valdés, Alberto, *Beyond the City: The rural contribution to development*, World Bank, Washington, DC, 2005

de Ferranti, David, Perry, Guillermo E. et al., *Closing the Gap in Education and Technology*, World Bank, Washington, DC, 2003

Ferreira, Francisco H.G., Rigolini, Jamele, Messina, Julián et al., *Economic Mobility and the Rise of the Latin American Middle Class*, World Bank, Washington, DC, 2012

Flores Galindo, Alberto, *La Agonía de Mariátegui*, Editorial Revolución, Madrid, 1991

Foa, Roberto Stefan and Mounk, Yascha, 'The signs of deconsolidation', *Journal of Democracy*, 28:1 (2017)

Foweraker, Joe, Landman, Todd and Harvey, Neil, *Governing Latin America*, Polity Press, Cambridge, 2003

Foxley, Alejandro, *La Trampa del Ingreso Medio: el desafío de esta década para América Latina*, Cieplan, Santiago de Chile, 2012

—— (ed.), *Desafíos post crisis de América Latina: Vínculos con Asia y rol de los recursos naturales*, Cieplan, Santiago de Chile, 2012

—— 'Inclusive development: Escaping the middle-income trap', in Alejandro Foxley and Barbara Stallings (eds), *Innovation and Inclusion in Latin America: Strategies to avoid the middle-income trap*, Palgrave Macmillan, New York, 2016

Foxley, Alejandro and Stallings, Barbara (eds), *Innovation and Inclusion in Latin America: Strategies to avoid the middle-income trap*, Palgrave Macmillan, New York, 2016

Frank, Andre Gunder, *Capitalism and Underdevelopment in Latin America*, Penguin, Harmondsworth, 1969

Freidenberg, Flavia and Dosek, Tomás, 'Las reformas electorales en América Latina (1978–2015)' in *Reformas Políticas en América Latina: Tendencias y Casos*, Organización de los Estados Americanos, Washington, DC, 2016

Freire, Germán, Schwartz Orcllana, Steven Daniel, Zumaeta Aurazo, Melissa et al., *Indigenous Latin America in the Twenty-First Century*, World Bank, Washington, DC, 2015

Fruhling, Hugo, 'Police reform and the process of democratization', in Hugo Fruhling and Joseph S. Tulchin (eds), *Crime and Violence in Latin America: Citizen security, democracy and the state*, Johns Hopkins University Press, Baltimore, MD, and London, 2003

Fukuyama, Francis (ed.), *Falling Behind: Explaining the development gap between Latin America and the United States*, Oxford University Press, New York, 2008

—— *The Origins of Political Order*, Profile Books, London, 2011

—— 'The politics of Latin America's new middle class', Inter-American Dialogue, Washington, DC, 2013

—— *Political Order and Political Decay*, Farrar, Straus and Giroux, New York, 2014

Galeano, Eduardo, *Open Veins of Latin America: Five centuries of the pillage of a continent*, Monthly Review Press, New York, 1997

Galiani, Sebastián et al., 'The benefits and costs of privatization in Argentina: A microeconomic analysis', in Alberto Chong and Florencio López-de-Silanes, *Privatization in Latin America: Myths and reality*, World Bank and Stanford University Press, 2005

Gallegos, Raúl, *Crude Nation: How oil riches ruined Venezuela*, Potomac Books, Lincoln, NE, 2016

García Márquez, Gabriel, *Vivir para contarla*, Knopf, New York, 2002

Gaspari, Elio, *A Ditadura Envergonhada*, Companhia das Letras, São Paulo, 2002

Gerrasi, John (ed.), *Venceremos: The speeches and writings of Ernesto Che Guevara*, Weidenfeld and Nicolson, London, 1968

Gillespie, Richard, *Soldiers of Perón: Argentina's Montoneros*, Oxford University Press, 1982

Giugale, Marcelo, Fretes Cibils, Vicente and Newman, John L., *Perú: La oportunidad de un país diferente*, World Bank, Washington, DC, 2006

Gootenberg, Paul, *Between Silver and Guano: Commercial Policy and the State in Postindependence Peru*, Princeton University Press, 1989

Gordon, Lincoln, *Brazil's Second Chance: En route toward the First World*, Brookings Institution Press, Washington, DC, 2001

Gott, Richard, *Cuba: A new history*, Yale University Press, New Haven, CT, and London, 2004

—— *Hugo Chávez and the Bolivarian Revolution*, Verso, New York, 2005

Green, Duncan, *Silent Revolution: The rise and crisis of market economics in Latin America*, Monthly Review Press, New York/Latin American Bureau, London, 2003

Guajardo, Jorge, Molano, Manuel and Sica, Dante, 'Industrial development in Latin America: What is China's role?' Atlantic Council, Washington, DC, 2016

Guevara, Che, *Guerrilla Warfare*, Penguin Books, Harmondsworth, 1969

Haber, Stephen, 'Introduction: Economic growth and Latin American economic historiography', in Stephen Haber (ed.), *How Latin America Fell Behind: Essays on the economic histories of Brazil and Mexico, 1800–1914*, Stanford University Press, 1997

Harrison, Lawrence E., *The Pan-American Dream: Do Latin America's cultural values discourage true partnership with the United States and Canada?*, Basic Books, New York, 1997

—— *Underdevelopment is a State of Mind: The Latin American case*, Madison Books, Lanham, MD, 2000

Hartlyn, Jonathan and Valenzuela, Arturo, 'Democracy in Latin America since 1930', in Leslie Bethell (ed.), *The Cambridge History of Latin America*, Vol. VI, Part 2, Cambridge University Press, 1994

Harvey, Robert, *Liberators: Latin America's struggle for independence 1810–1930*, Overlook Press, New York, 2000

Haya de la Torre, V.R., *El Antiimperialismo y el APRA*, 6th edition, APRA, Lima, 1985

Hoyos, Rafael de, Rogers, Halsey and Székely, Miguel, *Out of School and out of Work: Risk and opportunities for Latin America's Ninis*, World Bank, Washington, DC, 2016

Huntington, Samuel P., *The Third Wave: Democratization in the late twentieth century*, University of Oklahoma Press, Norman, OK, 1991

—— *The Clash of Civilizations and the Remaking of World Order*, Touchstone Books, New York, 1998

Instituto Cervantes, 'El Español en el Mundo: Informe 2016'

Instituto Nacional de Estadística e Informática (INEI), *Evolución de la Pobreza Monetaria, 2009–15*, Informe Técnico, Lima, 2016

Inter-American Development Bank (IDB), 'Competitiveness: The business of growth', IDB, Washington, DC, 2001

—— 'The politics of policies, 2006', IDB, Washington, DC, 2006

—— 'Remittances as a development tool', IDB, Washington, DC, 2006

—— 'All that glitters is not gold', IDB, Washington, DC, 2008

Inter-American Dialogue/Fundación Santillana, *Construyendo una educación de calidad: Un pacto con el futuro de América Latina*, Buenos Aires, 2016

International Institute for Strategic Studies, *The Military Balance 2015*, London, 2015

International Labour Organization, *Panorama Laboral 2016, América Latina y el Caribe*, Geneva, 2016

International Monetary Fund, *World Economic Outlook*, Washington, DC, October 2016

Jaitman, Laura (ed.), *The Costs of Crime and Violence: New evidence and insights in Latin America and the Caribbean*, Inter-American Development Bank, Washington, DC, 2017

Jaksić, Iván, *Andrés Bello: Scholarship and nation-building in nineteenth-century Latin America*, Cambridge University Press, 2001

Jonas, Susanne, *Of Centaurs and Doves: Guatemala's peace process*, Westview Press, Boulder, CO, 2000

Jones, Bart, *Hugo! The Hugo Chavez story from mud hut to perpetual revolution*, Bodley Head, London, 2008

Joyce, Helen, 'Grounded: A special report on Brazil', *The Economist*, 28 September 2013

Kempe, Frederick, *Divorcing the Dictator: America's bungled affair with Noriega*, G.P. Putnam's Sons, New York, 1990

Kingstone, Peter R. and Power, Timothy J. (eds), *Democratic Brazil: Actors, institutions and processes*, University of Pittsburgh Press, 2000

Klein, Herbert S., 'Migração Internacional na História das Americas', in Boris Fausto (ed.), *Fazer a América: A Imigração em Massa para a América Latina*, Editora da Universidade de São Paulo, 1999

Knight, Alan, *The Mexican Revolution*, Vol. 1: *Porfirians, Liberals and Peasants*, University of Nebraska Press, Lincoln, NE, 1990

Krauze, Enrique, *Mexico: Biography of power – a history of modern Mexico, 1810–1996*, HarperCollins, New York, 1997

Krauze, Enrique, *El Poder y El Delirio*, Tusquets Editores, Barcelona, 2008

Kryzanek, Michael J., *US–Latin American Relations*, Praeger, Westport, CT, 1996

Kuczynski, Pedro-Pablo, *Latin American Debt*, Johns Hopkins University Press, Baltimore, MD, 1988

Kuczynski, Pedro-Pablo and Williamson, John (eds), *After the Washington Consensus: Restarting growth and reform in Latin America*, Institute for International Economics, Washington, DC, 2003

Lagos, Ricardo, *Conversaciones en el Camino*, Ediciones B, Santiago de Chile, 2003

—— *The 21st Century: A view from the south*, FIRST, London, 2005

Lamounier, Bolívar, *Da Independência a Lula: dois séculos de política brasileira*, Augurium Editora, São Paulo, 2005

Landes, David, *The Wealth and Poverty of Nations*, Little, Brown and Co., New York, 1998

La Porta, Rafael, López de Silanes, Florencio, Schleifer, Andrei and Vishny, Robert W., 'Law and finance', National Bureau of Economic Research Working Paper 5661, 1996

—— 'Legal determinants of external finance', National Bureau of Economic Research Working Paper 5879, 1997

Larraín, Felipe and Meller, Patricio, 'The Socialist-Populist Chilean experience', in Rudiger Dornbusch and Sebastian Edwards (eds), *The Macroeconomics of Populism in Latin America*, University of Chicago Press, 1991

Lederman, Daniel, Maloney, William F. and Servén, Luis, *Lessons from NAFTA for Latin America and the Caribbean*, World Bank, Washington, DC, 2005

Lederman, Daniel, Messina, Julián, Pienknagura, Samuel and Rigolini, Jamele, *Latin American Entrepreneurs: Many firms but little innovation*, World Bank, Washington, DC, 2014

Lehmann, David, *The Struggle for the Spirit: Religious transformation and popular culture in Brazil and Latin America*, Polity Press, Cambridge, 1996

Levitsky, Steven and Roberts, Kenneth M. (eds), *The Resurgence of the Latin American Left*, Johns Hopkins University Press, Baltimore, MD, 2011

Levy, Santiago, 'Is social policy in Latin America heading in the right direction? Beyond conditional cash transfer programs', Brookings Institution, 21 May 2015

Lewis, Colin M., 'Public policy and private initiative: Railway building in São Paulo 1860–89', University of London, Institute of Latin American Studies Research Papers No. 26, 1991

Linz, Juan J. and Stepan, Alfred, *Problems of Democratic Transition and Consolidation: Southern Europe, South America and post-communist Europe*, Johns Hopkins University Press, Baltimore, MD, 1996

Little, Walter and Herrera, Antonio, 'Political corruption in Venezuela', in Walter Little and Eduardo Posada-Carbó (eds), *Political Corruption in Europe and Latin America*, Macmillan, Basingstoke, 1996

López Maya, Margarita, 'The Venezuelan Caracazo of 1989: Popular protest and institutional weakness', *Journal of Latin American Studies*, 35:1 (2003)

López Maya, Margarita, 'La crisis del chavismo en la Venezuela actual', *Estudios Latinoamericanos*, Nueva Época, 38 (July–December 2016)

López-Calva, Luis F. and Lustig, Nora, *Declining Inequality in Latin America: A decade of progress?*, Brookings Institution Press/UNDP, Washington, DC, 2010

Lora, Eduardo (ed.), *The State of State Reform in Latin America*, Inter-American Development Bank/Stanford University Press, 2006

Lora, Eduardo and Panizza, Ugo, 'Structural reforms in Latin America under scrutiny', Inter-American Development Bank Research Department paper, March 2002

Lowenthal, Abraham F. (ed.), *The Peruvian Experiment: Continuity and change under military rule*, Princeton University Press, 1975

Lustig, Nora (ed.), *Coping with Austerity: Poverty and inequality in Latin America*, Brookings Institution Press, Washington, DC, 1995

Lynch, John, *The Spanish American Revolutions 1808–1826*, 2nd edition, W.W. Norton & Company, New York, 1986

—— *Argentine Caudillo: Juan Manuel de Rosas*, Rowman and Littlefield, Wilmington, DE, 2001

—— *Simón Bolívar: A life*, Yale University Press, New Haven, CT, and London, 2006

McCoy, Jennifer L. and Myers, David J. (eds), *The Unraveling of Representative Democracy in Venezuela*, Johns Hopkins University Press, Baltimore, MD, 2004

McCullough, David, *The Path Between the Seas: The creation of the Panama Canal, 1870–1914*, Simon & Schuster, New York, 1977

McGuire, James W., *Peronism without Perón: Unions, parties and democracy in Argentina*, Stanford University Press, 1997

Maddison, Angus, *The World Economy: A millennial perspective*, OECD, Paris, 1998

Maddison, Angus et al., *The Political Economy of Poverty, Equity and Growth: Brazil and Mexico*, World Bank/Oxford University Press, New York, 1992

Maingon, Thais, 'Política social y regimen de bienestar en Venezuela 1999–2014', *Estudios Latinoamericanos*, Nueva Época, 38 (July–December 2016)

Mainwaring, Scott, *Rethinking Party Systems in the Third Wave of Democratization*, Stanford University Press, 1999

Mainwaring, Scott and Scully, Timothy (eds), *Building Democratic Institutions: Party systems in Latin America*, Stanford University Press, 1995

Mainwaring, Scott and Scully, Timothy, *Democratic Governance in Latin America*, Stanford University Press, 2009

Mainwaring, Scott and Shugart, Matthew Soberg (eds), *Presidentialism and Democracy in Latin America*, Cambridge University Press, 1997

Maloney, William, 'Informality revisited', *World Development*, 32:7 (2004)

Marcano, Cristina and Barrera Tyszka, Alberto, *Hugo Chávez Sin Uniforme: Una historia personal*, Debate, Caracas, 2005

Mariátegui, José Carlos, *Siete Ensayos de Interpretación de la Realidad Peruana*, 13th edition, Amauta, Lima, 1968

Marichal, Carlos (coordinador), *Las inversiones extranjeras en América Latina, 1850–1930*, Fondo de Cultura Económica, Mexico City, 1995

Martí, José, *Selected Writings*, Penguin Books, London, 2002

Martins, José de Souza, *Do PT das Lutas Sociais ao PT do Poder*, Editora Contexto, São Paulo, 2016

Marx, Anthony W., *Making Race and Nation: A comparison of the United States, South Africa and Brazil*, Cambridge University Press, 1998

Matamala, Daniel, *Poderoso caballero: El peso del dinero en la política chilena*, Editorial Catalonia, Santiago de Chile, 2015

Matos Mar, José, *Desborde Popular y Crisis del Estado: Veinte años después*, Fondo Editorial del Congreso del Perú, Lima, 2004

Matos Mar, José and Mejía, José Manuel, *La Reforma Agraria en el Perú*, Instituto de Estudios Peruanos, Lima, 1980

Mesa-Lago, Carmelo, *Market, Socialist and Mixed Economies: Comparative policy and performance – Chile, Cuba and Costa Rica*, Johns Hopkins University Press, Baltimore, MD, 2000

—— *Cuba en la era de Raúl Castro: Reformas económico-sociales y sus efectos*, Editorial Colibrí, Madrid, 2012

Mesa-Lago, Carmelo and Vidal-Alejandro, Pavel, 'The impact of the global crisis on Cuba's economy and social welfare', *Journal of Latin American Studies*, 42:4 (2010)

Middlebrook, Kevin J., *Dilemmas of Political Change in Mexico*, Institute of Latin American Studies, London/Center for US–Mexican Studies, San Diego, 2004

Millet, Richard L., Holmes, Jennifer S. and Pérez, Orlando J., *Latin American Democracy: Emerging reality or endangered species?*, 2nd Edition, Routledge, Abingdon, 2015

Morrison, Andrew, Buvinic, Mayra and Shifter, Michael, 'The violent Americas: Risk factors, consequences, and policy implications of social and domestic violence', in Hugo Fruhling and Joseph S. Tulchin, *Crime and Violence in Latin America: Citizen security, democracy and the state*, Johns Hopkins University Press, Baltimore, MD, and London, 2003

Moseley, Michael E., *The Incas and Their Ancestors*, Thames and Hudson, London, 2001

Mussa, Michael, *Argentina and the Fund: From triumph to tragedy*, Institute for International Economics, Washington, DC, 2002

Naím, Moisés, *Paper Tigers and Minotaurs: The politics of Venezuela's economic reforms*, Carnegie Endowment for International Peace, Washington, DC, 1993

National Research Council, *Cities Transformed: Demographic change and its implications in the developing world*, National Academies Press, Washington, DC, 2003

Nellis, John and Birdsall, Nancy (eds), *Reality Check: The distributional impact of privatization in developing countries*, Center for Global Development, Washington, DC, 2005

Nellis, John, Menezes, Rachel and Lucas, Sarah, 'Privatization in Latin America', Center for Global Development and Inter-American Dialogue Policy Brief, Washington, DC, January 2004, Vol. 3, Issue 1

Ocampo, José Antonio, *Reconstruir el futuro: Globalización, desarrollo y democracia en América Latina*, Editorial Norma, Bogotá, 2004

O'Donnell, Guillermo, *Contrapuntos: Ensayos escogidos sobre autoritarismo y democratización*, Paidós, Buenos Aires, 1997

Olson, Mancur, *Power and Prosperity: Outgrowing communist and capitalist dictatorships*, Basic Books, New York, 2000

Oppenheimer, Andres, *Castro's Final Hour: The secret story behind the coming downfall of communist Cuba*, Simon & Schuster, New York, 1992

Organisation for Economic Co-operation and Development (OECD), *PISA Results in Focus*, OECD, Paris, 2016

—— Health Statistics 2016

Organisation for Economic Co-operation and Development (OECD)/IDB, *Government at a Glance: Latin America and the Caribbean*, OECD Publishing, Paris, 2017

Organization of American States, *The Drug Problem in the Americas: Studies – The economics of drug trafficking*, OAS, Washington, DC, 2012

Palma, Pedro A., 'La economía Venezolana en el quinquenio 1994–1998: de una crisis a otra', *Nueva Economía*, VIII:12 (April 1999)

della Paolera, Gerardo and Taylor, Alan M., *Straining at the Anchor: The Argentine currency board and the search for macroeconomic stability, 1880–1935*, University of Chicago Press, 2001

—— *A New Economic History of Argentina*, Cambridge University Press, 2003

Parry, J.H., Sherlock, Philip and Maingot, Anthony, *A Short History of the West Indies*, 4th edition, Macmillan, Basingstoke, 1987

Partnership for Educational Revitalization in Latin America (PREAL), *Quantity without Quality: A report card on education in Latin America*, PREAL, Washington, DC, 2005

Paz, Octavio, *The Labyrinth of Solitude and Other Writings*, Grove Press, New York, 1985

Pécaut, Daniel, *Guerra Contra La Sociedad*, Espasa Hoy, Bogotá, 2001

Peet, John, 'Priceless: A survey of water', *The Economist*, 19 July 2003

Pérez, Louis A., *Cuba Between Reform and Revolution*, Oxford University Press, 1988

Pérez-Stabile, Marifeli, *The Cuban Revolution: Origins, course and legacy*, Oxford University Press, 1993

Philip, George, *Democracy in Latin America*, Polity, Cambridge, 2003

Pike, Frederick B., *The Modern History of Peru*, Praeger, Westport, CT, 1969

Pinheiro, Paulo Sérgio, 'O passado não está morto: nem passado é ainda', in Gilberto Dimenstein, *Democracia em pedaços*, Companhia das Letras, São Paulo, 1996

Platt, D.C.M., *Latin America and British Trade 1806–1914*, A & C Black, London, 1972

Poniatowska, Elena, *La noche de Tlatelolco*, Ediciones Era, Mexico City, 1992

Portocarrero, Gonzalo, *La Urgencia por Decir 'Nosotros': Los intelectuales y la idea de nación en el Perú republicano*, Fondo Editorial de la Pontificia Universidad Católica del Perú, Lima, 2015

Posada-Carbó, Eduardo, 'La historia y los falsos recuerdos', *Revista de Occidente* (Madrid), December 2003

Prats González, Carlos, *Memorias: Testimonio de un soldado*, Pehuén Editores, Santiago de Chile, 1985

Preston, Julia and Dillon, Samuel, *Opening Mexico: The making of a democracy*, Farrar, Straus and Giroux, New York, 2005

Przeworski, Adam with Curvale, Carolina, 'Does politics explain the economic gap between the United States and Latin America?', in Francis Fukuyama (ed.), *Falling Behind: Explaining the development gap between Latin America and the United States*, Oxford University Press, New York, 2008

Psacharopoulos, George and Patrinos, Harry (eds), *Indigenous People in Latin America*, World Bank, Washington, DC, 1994

Quijano, Aníbal, 'Coloniality of power, Eurocentrism and Latin America', *Nepantla: Views from South*, 1:3 (2000)

Raffo, Emma, *Vivir en Huáscar: Mujer y estrategias de sobrevivencia*, Fundación Friedrich Ebert, Lima, 1985

—— *Huáscar 25 años después: De la estera al barrio consolidado*, Universidad de San Martín de Porres, Lima, 2011

Rajapatirana, Sarath, *Trade Policies in Latin America and the Caribbean: Priorities, progress and prospects*, International Center for Economic Growth, Santiago de Chile and San Francisco, 1997

Ramírez, Sergio, *Adiós Muchachos: A memoir of the Sandinista revolution*, Duke University Press, Durham and London, 2012

Rangel Suárez, Alfredo, 'Las FARC-EP: una mirada actual', in Malcolm Deas and María Victoria Llorente (eds), *Reconocer la Guerra para Construrir La Paz*, Grupo Editorial Norma, Bogotá, 1999

Reid, Michael, 'Remapping South America: A survey of Mercosur', *The Economist*, 12 October 1996

—— 'Back on the pitch: A survey of business in Latin America', *The Economist*, 6 December 1997

—— 'The disorders of progress: A survey of Brazil', *The Economist*, 27 March 1999

—— 'Drugs, war and democracy: A survey of Colombia', *The Economist*, 19 April 2001

—— 'The long road back: A survey of Argentina', *The Economist*, 5 June 2004

—— 'Time to wake up: A survey of Mexico', *The Economist*, 18 November 2006

—— 'Cuba: Revolution in retreat', *The Economist*, 24 March 2012

—— *Brazil: The troubled rise of a global power*, Yale University Press, New Haven, CT, and London, 2014

Riding, Alan, *Distant Neighbors: A portrait of the Mexicans*, Knopf, New York, 1985

Rock, David, *Argentina 1516–1987: From Spanish colonization to Alfonsín*, University of California Press, Berkeley, CA, 1987

—— 'Argentina in 1914', in Leslie Bethell (ed.), *Argentina since Independence*, Cambridge University Press, 1993

Rodó, José Enrique, *Ariel*, Kapelusz Editora, Buenos Aires, 1994

Rodrik, Dani, Subramanian, Arvind and Trebbi, Francesco, 'Institutions rule: The primacy of institutions over geography and integration in economic development', NBER Working Paper No. 9305, November 2002

Rouquié, Alain, *The Military and the State in Latin America*, University of California Press, Berkeley, CA, 1987

—— *América Latina: Introducción al Extreme Occidente*, 4th edition (in Spanish), Siglo XXI Editores, Mexico City, 1997

Rubio, Luis, *The Problem of Power: Mexico requires a new system of government*, Wilson Center, Washington, DC, 2016

Rubio, Luis and Kaufman Purcell, Susan, *Mexico Under Zedillo*, Lynne Rienner, Boulder, CO, 1998

Saad, Paulo M., 'Demographic trends in Latin America and the Caribbean', ECLAC/CEPAL, Santiago de Chile, 2009

Sabatini, Christopher, 'Latin America's lost illusions: Decentralization and political parties', *Journal of Democracy*, 14:2 (2003)

Sachs, Jeffrey, *The End of Poverty*, Penguin, London, 2005

Sachs, Jeffrey D., Mellinger, Andrew D. and Gallup, John L., 'The geography of poverty and wealth', *Scientific American*, March 2001

SalmonChile, *La Acuicultura en Chile*, TechnoPress SA, Santiago de Chile, undated

Santiso, Javier, *Latin America's Political Economy of the Possible: Beyond good revolutionaries and free marketeers*, MIT Press, Cambridge, MA, 2006

—— *The Decade of the Multilatinas*, Cambridge University Press, 2013

São Paulo Justice and Peace Commission, *São Paulo: Growth and poverty*, The Bowerdean Press in association with the Catholic Institute for International Relations, London, 1978

Sarmiento, Domingo F., *Facundo: Or, civilization and barbarism*, Penguin, London, 1998

Schlesinger, Stephen and Kinzer, Stephen, *Bitter Fruit: The untold story of the American coup in Guatemala*, Sinclair Browne, London, 1982

Sharma, Ruchir, *The Rise and Fall of Nations: Forces of change in the post-crisis world*, Norton, New York, 2016

Shifter, Michael, *Hugo Chávez: A test for US policy*, Inter-American Dialogue, Washington, DC, 2007

Shumway, Nicolas, *The Invention of Argentina*, University of California Press, Berkeley, CA, 1993

Sieder, Rachel (ed.), *Multiculturalism in Latin America: Indigenous rights, diversity and democracy*, Palgrave Macmillan, Basingstoke and New York, 2002

Singer, André, *Os Sentidos do Lulismo: Reforma gradual e pacto conservador*, Companhia das Letras, São Paulo, 2012

Skidmore, Thomas E., *Politics in Brazil 1930–1964*, Oxford University Press, 1967

—— *Brazil: Five Centuries of Change*, Oxford University Press, 1999

Skidmore, Thomas and Smith, Peter H., *Modern Latin America*, 4th edition, Oxford University Press, 1997

Smith, Peter H., *Talons of the Eagle: Dynamics of US–Latin American relations*, Oxford University Press, 1996

Smith, Robert Freeman, 'Latin America, the United States and the European powers 1830–1930', in Leslie Bethell (ed.), *Cambridge History of Latin America*, Vol. IV, Cambridge University Press, 1986

Soifer, Hillel David, *State Building in Latin America*, Cambridge University Press, 2015

Sola, Lourdes and Whitehead, Laurence, *Statecrafting Monetary Authority: Democracy and financial order in Brazil*, Centre for Brazilian Studies, University of Oxford, 2006

Solimano, Andrés, 'The Chilean economy in the 1990s: On a "Golden Age" and beyond', in Lance Taylor (ed.), *After Neoliberalism: What next for Latin America?*, University of Michigan Press, Ann Arbor, MI, 1999

de Soto, Hernando, *El Otro Sendero*, Editorial El Barranco, Lima, 1986

—— *The Mystery of Capital*, Black Swan Books, London, 2001

Spektor, Matias and Mello, Eduardo, 'How to fix Brazil', *Foreign Affairs*, September/October 2016

Stiglitz, Joseph E., *Globalization and Its Discontents*, W.W. Norton, New York and London, 2002

Streeter, Stephen M., 'Interpreting the 1954 US intervention in Guatemala: Realist, revisionist and postrevisionist perspectives', *The History Teacher*, 34:1 (2000)

Strong, Simon, *Whitewash: Pablo Escobar and the cocaine wars*, Macmillan, Basingstoke, 1995

Sweig, Julia E., *Inside the Cuban Revolution: Fidel Castro and the urban underground*, Harvard University Press, 2002

—— *Cuba: What everyone needs to know*, Oxford University Press, 2009

Szulc, Tad, *Fidel: A critical portrait*, Avon Books, New York, 1986

Taylor, Lance (ed.), *After Neoliberalism: What next for Latin America?*, University of Michigan Press, Ann Arbor, MI, 1999

Tendler, Judith, *Good Government in the Tropics*, Johns Hopkins University Press, Baltimore, MD, and London, 1997

Thomas, Hugh, *Cuba or the Pursuit of Freedom*, Eyre & Spotiswoode, London, 1971

—— *The Conquest of Mexico*, Pimlico, London, 1993

Thomas, Vinod, *From Inside Brazil: Development in a land of contrasts*, Conference Edition, World Bank, Washington, DC, 2006

Thorp, Rosemary, *Progress, Poverty and Exclusion: An economic history of Latin America in the 20th century*, Inter-American Development Bank, Washington, DC, 1998

Thorp, Rosemary and Bertram, Geoffrey, *Peru 1890–1977: Growth and policy in an open economy*, Macmillan, Basingstoke, 1978

de la Torre, Augusto, Fajnzylber, Pablo and Nash, John, *Low Carbon, High Growth: Latin American Responses to Climate Change*, World Bank, Washington, DC, 2009

de la Torre, Augusto, Ize, Alain, Beylis, Guillermo Raul and Lederman, Daniel, *Jobs, Wages and the Latin American Slowdown*, World Bank, Washington, DC, 2015

de la Torre, Augusto, Didier, Tatiana, Ize, Alain, Lederman, Daniel and Schmukler, Sergio L., *Latin America and the Rising South: Changed world, changed priorities*, World Bank, Washington, DC, 2015

de la Torre, Augusto, Levy Yeyati, Eduardo, Beylis, Guillermo et al., *Inequality in a Lower Growth Latin America*, World Bank, Washington, DC, 2014

de la Torre, Carlos and Arnson, Cynthia (eds), *Latin American Populism in the Twenty-First Century*, Johns Hopkins University Press, Baltimore, MD, 2013

Torre, Juan Carlos and de Riz, Liliana, 'Argentina since 1946', in Leslie Bethell (ed.), *Argentina since Independence*, Cambridge University Press, 1993

Torres, Gerver, *Un Sueño para Venezuela*, Banco Venezolano de Crédito, 2001

Tountoundjian, Beatriz, 'La Lucha por la Sobrevivencia en la Hiperinflación Argentina', Mimeo, Fernand Braudel Institute of World Economics, São Paulo, 1990

United Nations Development Programme (UNDP), *Citizen Security with a Human Face*, Human Development Report for Latin America, UNDP, New York, 2013

—— *Multidimensional Progress: Well-being beyond income*, Regional Human Development Report for Latin America and the Caribbean, UNDP, New York, 2016

United Nations Economic Commission for Latin America (ECLAC/CEPAL), *Economic Survey of Latin America and the Caribbean*, Santiago de Chile (various years)

—— *Social Panorama of Latin America*, Santiago de Chile (various years)

—— *Preliminary Overview of the Economies of Latin America and the Caribbean*, Santiago de Chile (various years)

—— *Statistical Yearbook*, Santiago de Chile (various years)

—— *Demographic Observatory*, Santiago de Chile, 2016

United Nations Educational, Scientific and Cultural Organization (UNESCO), 'Regional overview: Latin America and the Caribbean', Education for All Global Monitoring Report, 2006

United Nations Office on Drugs and Crime (UNODC), *Global Study on Homicide, 2013*, Vienna, 2014

Urzúa, Sergio, 'La rentabilidad de la educación superior en Chile', Centro de Estudios Públicos, Santiago de Chile, 2012

Vakis, Reno, Rigolini, Jamele and Luchetti, Leonardo, *Left Behind: Chronic poverty in Latin America and the Caribbean*, World Bank, Washington, DC, 2015

Vargas Llosa, Álvaro, *Liberty for Latin America*, Farrar, Straus and Giroux, New York, 2005

Vargas Llosa, Mario, *La Utopía Arcaica: José María Arguedas y las ficciones del indigenismo*, Fondo de Cultura Económica, Mexico City, 1996

Véganzones, Marie-Ange, with Winograd, Carlos, *Argentina in the 20th Century: An account of long-awaited growth*, OECD Publishing, Paris, 1997

Véliz, Claudio, *The New World of the Gothic Fox: Culture and economy in English and Spanish America*, University of California Press, Berkeley, CA, 1994

Vergara, Alberto and Luna, Juan Pablo, 'Delegative democracy revisited: Latin America's problem of success', *Journal of Democracy*, 27:3 (2016)

Vostroknutova, Ekaterina, Rodriguez, Alberto, Saavedra, Pablo and Panzer, John, *Peru: Building on Success*, World Bank, Washington, DC, 2015

Walker, Charles F., *The Tupac Amaru Rebellion*, Belknap Press/Harvard University Press, 2014

Washington Office on Latin America (WOLA), 'Youth gangs in Central America', November 2006

Webb, Richard, *Conexión y Despegue Rural*, Instituto del Perú, Universidad San Martín de Porres, Lima, 2013

Weber, Max, *Economy and Society*, Vol. 1, University of California Press, Berkeley, CA, 1978

Weitz-Shapiro, Rebecca, *Curbing Clientelism in Argentina: Politics, poverty and social policy*, Cambridge University Press, 2014

White, Alastair, *El Salvador: Nation of the modern world*, Ernest Benn Ltd, London, 1973

Whitehead, Laurence, 'State organization in Latin America since 1930', in Leslie Bethell (ed.), *The Cambridge History of Latin America*, Vol. VI, Part 2, Cambridge University Press, 1994

—— 'The viability of democracy', in John Crabtree and Laurence Whitehead (eds), *Towards Democratic Viability: The Bolivian experience*, Palgrave Macmillan, New York, 2001

—— *Latin America: A new interpretation*, Palgrave Macmillan, New York, 2006

Wiarda, Howard, *The Soul of Latin America: The cultural and political tradition*, Yale University Press, New Haven, CT, and London, 2001

Wilcken, Patrick, *Empire Adrift: The Portuguese Court in Rio 1808–1821*, Bloomsbury, London, 2004

Williamson, John, 'Latin American adjustment: How much has happened', Institute for International Economics, Washington, DC, 1990

—— 'A short history of the Washington Consensus', 2004, https://piie.com/publications/papers/williamson0904-2.pdf

Wise, Carol and Roett, Riordan (eds), *Exchange Rate Politics in Latin America*, Brookings Institution Press, Washington, DC, 2000

Wolff, Laurence and de Mora Castro, Claudio, 'Education and training: The task ahead', in Pedro-Pablo Kuczynski and John Williamson, *After the Washington Consensus*, Institute for International Economics, Washington, DC, 2003

World Bank, 'Safeguarding against a reversal in social gains during the economic crisis in Brazil', World Bank Policy Note, World Bank, Washington, DC, December 2016

World Bank, *Brazil – Systematic country diagnostic: Retaking the path to inclusion, growth and sustainability*, World Bank Group, Washington, DC, 2016

Yarrington, Doug, 'The Vestey cattle enterprise and the regime of Juan Vicente Gómez 1908–1935', *Journal of Latin American Studies*, 35:1 (2003)

Yashar, Deborah J., *Contesting Citizenship: The rise of indigenous movements and the postliberal challenge*, Cambridge University Press, 2005

Youngers, Coletta A. and Rosin, Eileen (eds), *Drugs and Democracy in Latin America: The impact of US policy*, Lynne Rienner, Boulder, CO, 2005

Index